D0466522

Advances in the Theory of Computational Mathematics
Volume 5

PARALLEL PROGRAM DEVELOPMENT FOR CLUSTER COMPUTING

Methodology, Tools and Integrated Environments

Advances in the Theory of Computational Mathematics
Marcin Paprzycki (Editor)

Parallel Program Development for Cluster Computing: Methodology, Tools and Integrated Environments
José C. Cunha, Peter Kacsuk and Stephen C. Winter
ISBN 1-56072-865-5

Structured Matrices: Recent Advances and Applications
Dario Andrea Bini, Eugene Tyrtyshnikov and Plamen Yalamov
ISBN 1-56072-890-6

Recent Trends in Numerical Analysis
Donato Trigiante
ISBN 1-56072-885-X

High Performance Algorithms for Structured Matrix Problems
Peter Arbenz, Marcin Paprzycki, Ahmed Sameh and Vivek Sarin
ISBN 1-56072-594-X

We intend to publish books from any area of mathematics or computer science involved with computation broadly understood.
We plan to publish four types of high quality manuscripts:
- monographs
- topic-oriented volumes consisting of contributed papers devoted to the current research
- topic-oriented volumes consisting of invited overview papers, summarizing the state of the art
- proceedings from selected Workshops/Conferences/Minisymposia

To discuss a possible contribution, please contact the Managing Editor:

Lee Keener, Editor-in-chief
College of Science and Management
University of Northern British Columbia
Prince George, BC V2N 4Z9, CANADA
keener@unbc.edu

Marcin Paprzycki, Editor and Managing Editor
Department of Computer Science and Statistics
University of Southern Mississippi
Hattiesburg, MS 39406-5106, USA
m.paprzycki@usm.edu

Ilan Bar-On,
baron@cs.technion.ac.il
Graeme Fairweather,
gfairwea@mines.edu
Daniele Funaro,
funaro@giove.unimo.it
Dan Grigoras,
grigd@cs.tuiasi.ro
Andreas Karageorghis,
andreask@trikomo.mas.ucy.ac.cy
Michal Karonski,
karonski@math.amu.edu.pl
Erricos John Kontoghiorghes,
erricos.kontoghiorghes@info.unine.ch
Anna Lawniczak,
alawnicz@opal.mathstat.uoguelph.ca
alawnicz@fields.utoronto.ca

Michael Mascagni,
mascagni@cs.fsu.edu
Nikos E. Mastorakis,
mastor@softlab.ece.ntua.gr
Lawrence F. Shampine,
lshampin@post.cis.smu.edu
Jurij Silc,
jurij.silc@ijs.si
Wojciech Szpankowski,
spa@cs.purdue.edu
Gyorgy Turan,
gyt@uic.edu
Jerzy Wasniewski,
jerzy.wasniewski@uni-c.dk
Plamen Yalamov,
yalamov@ami.ru.acad.bg

Advances in the Theory of Computational Mathematics
Volume 5

Parallel Program Development for Cluster Computing

Methodology, Tools and Integrated Environments

EDITED BY
JOSÉ C. CUNHA, PETER KACSUK
AND STEPHEN C. WINTER

Nova Science Publishers, Inc.
Huntington, New York

Senior Editors:	Susan Boriotti and Donna Dennis
Office Manager:	Annette Hellinger
Graphics:	Wanda Serrano and Dorothy Marczak
Information Editor:	Tatiana Shohov
Book Production:	Cathy DeGregory, and Lynette Van Helden
Circulation:	Ave Maria Gonzalez, Ron Hedges, Andre Tillman

Library of Congress Cataloging-in-Publication Data
available upon request

ISBN 1-56072-865-5

Copyright @ 2001 by Nova Science Publishers, Inc.
    227 Main Street, Suite 100
    Huntington, New York 11743
    Tele. 631-424-6682   Fax 631-424-4666
    e-mail: Novascience@earthlink.net
    Web Site: http://www.nexusworld.com/nova

Printed in the United States of America

Contents

Preface

This book describes the results of a collaborative effort towards the development of tools and environments for parallel applications. There are still so many open issues in parallel and distributed software that we felt a strong motivation to share the results of our experience with a larger community of interested readers.

All the authors that have contributed to this book worked together in several European projects of the COPERNICUS Programme from 1994 to 1999, and have exploited a diversity of ideas, experiments, and sound approaches for tool development.

We have divided the book into two parts, the first one covering the concepts and methodologies, and the second describing the tools and integrated environments that were developed in those projects. In this way, we hope that the reader will find the book useful not only concerning an identification of current trends in parallel program development, but also concerning their practical illustration through concrete tools and environments.

We are confident that the reader will enjoy reading this book as much as we did enjoy working together and writing it.

Acknowledgments

On behalf of all the authors, we want to thank the European Union COPERNICUS Programme that has sponsored this research, in the context of the SEPP - Software Engineering for Parallel Processing (CIPA-CT93-0251) and HPCTI - High Performance Computing Tools for Industry (CP-93-5383) projects, and the SEIHPC - Stimulation of European Industry Thorugh High Performance Computing concerted action. In particular, we acknowledge the Keep-In-Touch INCO Parallel Processing Tools: Integration and Results Dissemination (Project 977100), for having made possible the writing of this book. We also thank Dr Marcin Paprzycki of Nova Science for all his help in the book preparation and for having supported this initiative. Last but not least, we want to express our thanks to Vítor Duarte and João Lourenço for their help in the book preparation and formatting.

José C. Cunha and Peter Kacsuk
Europe, January 2000

List of Authors

Ján Astaloš
astalos.ui@savba.sk
Institute of Informatics,
Slovak Academy of Sciences
Dúbravská cesta 9
842 37 Bratislava
SLOVAKIA

Olivier Audo
Cavendish School of Computer Science,
University of Westminster
115 New Cavendish Street
London W1M 8JS
UK

Jacques Chassin de Kergommeaux
Jacques.Chassin@imag.fr
ID-IMAG,
B.P.53,
F-38041 Grenoble Cedex 9
FRANCE

Ana Cortés
a.cortes@cc.uab.es
http://www.caos.uab.es/
Universitat Autònoma de Barcelona,
Computer Science Department,
08193, Bellaterra
SPAIN

José C. Cunha
jcc@di.fct.unl.pt
http://www.di.fct.unl.pt/
Departamento de Informática,
FCT/Universidade Nova de Lisboa
P-2825-114 Monte Caparica
PORTUGAL

Thierry Delaitre
delaitt@cpc.wmin.ac.uk
Cavendish School of Computer Science,
University of Westminster
115 New Cavendish Street
London W1M 8JS
UK

Miroslav Dobrucký
dobrucky.ui@savba.sk
Institute of Informatics,
Slovak Academy of Sciences
Dúbravská cesta 9
842 37 Bratislava
SLOVAKIA

Gábor Dózsa
dozsa@sztaki.hu
MTA SZTAKI Computer and Automation
Research Institute of the Hungarian
Academy of Sciences
H-1111 Budapest, Kende u. 13-17
HUNGARY

Dániel Drótos
drdani@mazsola.iit.uni-miskolc.hu
University of Miskolc,
Department of Automation
H-3515 Miskolc, Egyetemváros
HUNGARY

Vítor Duarte
vad@di.fct.unl.pt
http://www.di.fct.unl.pt/
Departamento de Informática,
FCT/Universidade Nova de Lisboa
P-2825-114 Monte Caparica
PORTUGAL

Porfidio Hernández
P.Hernandez@cc.uab.es
http://www.caos.uab.es/
Universitat Autònoma de Barcelona,
Computer Science Department,
08193, Bellaterra
SPAIN

Ladislav Hluchý
hluchy.ui@savba.sk
Institute of Informatics,
Slovak Academy of Sciences
Dúbravská cesta 9
842 37 Bratislava
SLOVAKIA

Peter Kacsuk
kacsuk@sztaki.hu
MTA SZTAKI Computer and Automation
Research Institute of the Hungarian
Academy of Sciences
H-1111 Budapest, Kende u. 13-17
HUNGARY

Henryk Krawczyk
hkrawk@pg.gda.pl
Faculty of Electronics, Telecommunications and Informatics, Technical
University of Gdansk
ul. Narutowicza 11/12
80-952 Gdansk
POLAND

Piotr Kuzora
Faculty of Electronics, Telecommunications and Informatics, Technical
University of Gdansk
ul. Narutowicza 11/12
80-952 Gdansk
POLAND

João Lourenço
Joao.Lourenco@di.fct.unl.pt
http://www.di.fct.unl.pt/
Departamento de Informática,
FCT/Universidade Nova de Lisboa
P-2825-114 Monte Caparica
PORTUGAL

Róbert Lovas
rlovas@sztaki.hu
MTA SZTAKI Computer and Automation
Research Institute of the Hungarian
Academy of Sciences
H-1111 Budapest, Kende u. 13-17
HUNGARY

Emilio Luque
E.Luque@cc.uab.es
http://www.caos.uab.es/
Universitat Autònoma de Barcelona,
Computer Science Department,
08193, Bellaterra
SPAIN

Éric Maillet
Eric_Maillet@ses-astra.com
SES,
L-6815 Château de Betzdorf,
LUXEMBOURG

Tomàs Margalef
Tomas.Margalef@uab.es
http://www.caos.uab.es/
Universitat Autònoma de Barcelona,
Computer Science Department,
08193, Bellaterra
SPAIN

Marcin Neyman
Faculty of Electronics, Telecommunications and Informatics, Technical
University of Gdansk
ul. Narutowicza 11/12
80-952 Gdansk
POLAND

Norbert Podhorski
pnorbert@sztaki.hu
MTA SZTAKI Computer and Automation
Research Institute of the Hungarian
Academy of Sciences
H-1111 Budapest, Kende u. 13-17
HUNGARY

Jerzy Proficz
Faculty of Electronics, Telecommunications and Informatics, Technical University of Gdansk
ul. Narutowicza 11/12
80-952 Gdansk
POLAND

Ana Ripoll
a.ripoll@cc.uab.es
http://www.caos.uab.es/
Universitat Autònoma de Barcelona,
Computer Science Department,
08193, Bellaterra
SPAIN

George R. Ribeiro-Justo
justog@westminster.ac.uk
Cavendish School of Computer Science,
University of Westminster
115 New Cavendish Street
London W1M 8JS
UK

Miquel A. Senar
m.a.senar@cc.uab.es
http://www.caos.uab.es/
Universitat Autònoma de Barcelona,
Computer Science Department
08193, Bellaterra
SPAIN

Joan Sorribes
Joan.Sorribes@uab.es
http://www.caos.uab.es/
Universitat Autònoma de Barcelona,
Computer Science Department,
08193, Bellaterra
SPAIN

Remo Suppi
Remo.Suppi@uab.es
http://www.caos.uab.es/
Universitat Autònoma de Barcelona,
Computer Science Department,
08193, Bellaterra
SPAIN

Ferenc Szalai
szferi@sztaki.hu
MTA SZTAKI Computer and Automation
Research Institute of the Hungarian Academy of Sciences
H-1111 Budapest, Kende u. 13-17
HUNGARY

Viet Dinh Tran
viet.ui@savba.sk
Institute of Informatics,
Slovak Academy of Sciences
Dúbravská cesta 9
842 37 Bratislava
SLOVAKIA

Jean-Marc Vincent
Jean-Marc.Vincent@imag.fr
ID-IMAG,
B.P.53,
F-38041 Grenoble Cedex 9,
FRANCE

Stephen C. Winter
S.C.Winter@westminster.ac.uk
Cavendish School of Computer Science,
University of Westminster
115 New Cavendish Street
London W1M 8JS
UK

Bogdan Wiszniewski
bowisz@pg.gda.pl
Faculty of Electronics, Telecommunications and Informatics, Technical University of Gdansk
ul. Narutowicza 11/12
80-952 Gdansk
POLAND

Mohamed-Jamal Zemerly
jamal@cpc.wmin.ac.uk
Cavendish School of Computer Science,
University of Westminster
115 New Cavendish Street
London W1M 8JS
UK

Part I

Concepts and Methodologies

Chapter 1

Tools and Environments for Parallel Program Development

José C. Cunha and Peter Kacsuk

Abstract

This chapter presents the main objectives of the book, that is to show how the task of the end user can be significantly facilitated through the use of suitable tools which are integrated into a unified parallel programming environment. The chapter briefly reviews the evolution of parallel and distributed computer architectures. Then it discusses the main issues of parallel software engineering and how they were addressed by the SEPP/HPCTI projects.

1.1 Introduction

We would like to start this book with a surprising statement:

Parallel programming based on message passing *can be made easy*.

It is a surprising statement due to several reasons:

(i) Usually parallel programming based on the shared memory concept is considered easier than the usage of the message passing paradigm.

(ii) The parallel program developer has to face several stages that do not appear in the sequential program development (mapping, load balancing, debugging in a non-deterministic environment, performance monitoring and visualization).

The objective of the book is to show that using suitable tools and by integrating them into a unified parallel programming environment, the task of the end user will be significantly facilitated. By means of convenient, graphical environments parallel programming becomes an enjoyable and fast procedure that can be offered even for non-professional programmers like biologists, physicists, etc. Obviously, the applied tools should hide the low level details of communication libraries, should provide automatic mapping and load balancing mechanisms without user involvement, should support replay and high-level graphical debugging techniques, low intrusion and accurate performance monitors, convenient and adequate visualization tools, etc.

The book reviews all these techniques and tools in the first part and then shows two particular graphical development environments as case studies to illustrate the integration of these tools as well as their usage in such integrated environments. The two environments provide proof for the claim of the first statement. It will be shown that the complexity of developing message passing parallel programs is really dramatically reduced by such integrated graphical environments.

1.2   Progress of Parallel and Distributed Computer Architectures

1.2.1   From Supercomputers to Metacomputing systems

Supercomputing has its roots in the 60s when the first vector computers appeared on the market with the aim of significantly speeding up vector and matrix based number-crunching scientific computations. Vector machines were soon followed by other types of supercomputers like array processors, shared memory symmetric multiprocessors (SMP), distributed memory parallel computers (or massively parallel processors) (MPP), distributed shared memory systems (DSM), etc. [11]. The real breakthrough of using supercomputers took place in the late 80s when they became generally accepted and more widely used both in the academic world and in companies. Their breakthrough was initiated by two major technological advances:

1. The new hardware technology resulted in powerful and cheap microprocessors with the necessary interconnection technology and hence the supercomputers built from these commodity microprocessors became affordable for a large user community.

2. The progress in software technology led to portable interprocess communication layers like PVM [7] and MPI [8], and to optimizing compilers for high level scientific languages like High-Performance Fortran [6].

However, in the early 90s a big competitor of supercomputers has arisen, called clusters. Though supercomputers were already affordable, their cost was still high for the academic world and hence scientists were searching for a cheaper alternative solution to achieve supercomputer performance. These efforts led to the introduction of clusters of PCs and workstations which became a very successful and competitive alternative to supercomputers [1, 2, 9, 13]. Interestingly, the software support systems for supercomputers and clusters are similar and hence, most of the results achieved in one platform can almost immediately be applied to the other one, provided due consideration is given to portability concerns.

Another motivation for replacing supercomputers with aggregation of PCs and workstations was the low-level utilization of a large number of PCs and workstations in companies and universities. Software tools like Codine [12] have been developed for better utilization of workstations and PCs through the intranet. This NOW (Network Of Workstations) systems typically include heterogeneous workstations and/or PCs. Some of the software techniques introduced in the NOWs are similar to the ones applied in metacomputing systems, although limited to a smaller scale, and hence they represent a major step towards distributed parallel systems.

The need for metacomputing had a different motivation and technically it required some other technological innovations mainly in the field of Internet, distributed computing and web computing. In the mid-90s application areas were pointed out for which the single supercomputers or clusters were not able to deliver the necessary performance. In parallel, the speed of Internet reached the threshold which made it possible to use the Internet-connected supercomputers and clusters as a single supercomputer from the point of view of the user. Multiple tasks of a program can be distributed via the Internet to several supercomputers and clusters that can work together in solving a single problem. Such technique is called metacomputing and it practically means parallel and distributed processing over the Internet. In a metacomputing environment supercomputers and/or clusters play a similar role as microprocessors within supercomputers as shown in Table 1.1.

Table 1.1 also illustrates how clusters and NOWs represent a transition from supercomputers to metacomputing systems. Clusters are closer to supercomputers and NOWs resemble to metacomputing systems in many respects. NOWs are usually also considered as a special type of clusters, namely as nondedicated clusters. However, the software technology used in these systems is much closer to the metacomputing systems than to the dedicated clusters and hence, in the current section we distinguish them. In later chapters (and also in the title of the book) we do not distinguish them, the term cluster covers both dedicated clusters and NOWs.

	Supercomputer	Cluster	NOW	Metacomputing system
Processing units (nodes)	Microprocessors	PCs, workstations	PCs, workstations	Supercomputers, clusters, PCs, workstations
Number of nodes	100 – 1000	10 – 1000	10 – 1000	100 – 10000
Communication network	Buses, switches	High performance LAN, switches	LAN	Internet
Node OS	Homogeneous	Typically homogeneous	Typically heterogeneous	Heterogeneous
Inter-node security	Nonexistent	Rarely required	Necessary	Necessary

Table 1.1: Comparison of supercomputers, clusters and metacomputing systems

1.2.2 Comparison of Parallel Supercomputers and Clusters

While supercomputers have specialized architectures containing usually a large number of processors, clusters combine ordinary computers, typically workstations or PCs. There are two characteristic features of clusters that distinguish them from parallel supercomputers:

1. A cluster connects complete computers (including processor, memory, I/O units).

2. The component computers of a cluster are loosely connected typically by a high performance LAN.

The first property distinguishes clusters from supercomputers since a supercomputer does not connect whole computers rather a replicated computer part which is typically the processor but in several kinds of supercomputers it could be even memory and cache units. Another important distinguishing feature is that the components of a cluster, i.e., the workstations or PCs are able to work independently of the cluster while replicated parts of a supercomputer cannot be used independently of the supercomputer, they work only inside the supercomputer as a structural component of the machine architecture. Supercomputers can be classified according to the replicated parts [11]. For example:

(i) SIMD (Single Instruction Multiple Data) supercomputers replicate only an arithmetic and logic unit along with some registers and memory.

(ii) MPP (Massively Parallel Processors) replicate processor-memory pairs. These can be either message passing, distributed memory systems or NUMA (Non-Uniform Memory Access) machines.

(iii) SMP (Symmetric Multiprocessors) supercomputers replicate the processors.

(iv) CC-NUMA (Cache-Coherent Non-Uniform Memory Access) architectures replicate processor-memory-cache units.

(v) COMA (Cache-Only Memory Access) machines replicate processor-cache pairs.

In fact, if we do not take into consideration the second property of clusters, they can be viewed as a special case of MPP supercomputers where even the I/O units attached to the processor-memory pairs are replicated. In order to distinguish clusters from this form of MPP supercomputers we need the second feature to define clusters.

Finally, to make complete the definition of clusters we give here their third main feature: a cluster is utilized as a single, unified computing resource.

This feature does not distinguish clusters from supercomputers on the contrary it expresses that, like supercomputers, clusters are also used to solve a single program by parallel techniques and both have a Single System Image (SSI). It means that the collection of resources appears to the user as a single but more powerful resource. The SSI infrastructure glues together all the resources (processors, memory, disk, operating systems, etc.) on all nodes in order to form a unified access mechanism to system resources. The SSI illusion can be created at hardware, operating system and middleware level. The SSI is provided typically by hardware in supercomputers. In clusters all the three levels can be found but the most typical one is the middleware layer.

Cluster programming has two main aspects:

1. Resource management and administration

2. Application programming

The aim of resource management and administration is to utilize cluster resources (processors, memories, disk units, etc.) at the highest possible degree. This aspect includes mechanisms and techniques like scheduling, load balancing, checkpointing, process migration, fault tolerance, etc. The development of these techniques is typically the task of system programmers. Application programming requires the use of tools and programming environments for supporting end users in their activity of developing parallel programs. Such tools include mapping tools, debuggers, performance monitors, simulators, performance prediction tools, visualization tools, etc. The current book covers mainly the second aspect of cluster programming though load balancing is also reviewed since it has a strong influence on the efficiency of message passing parallel application programs as well.

1.3   Parallel Software Engineering

The software engineering world is entering the second major crisis in twenty years. In the 60s, advances in computer architecture enabled the development of larger and more complex programs which inevitably began to fall over with increased frequency. The introduction and rapid acceptance of parallel computer platforms, ranging from high-performance supercomputers to clusters of PCs workstations has again signalled another degree of increased computer architecture complexity. Programs targeted for these platforms are no less complex than before, but whereas programmers could hitherto rely on a simple and stable programming model, based on Von Neumann machine principles, this is no longer the case. The possibility of infinitely variable parallel hardware topologies introduces the new dimension of program mapping. Parallel programmers are expected to navigate through this more complex design space having barely mastered the complexities of one-dimensional software design for serial computers! The response to the original software crisis was the stimulus for modern software engineering. Amongst the developed techniques were structured programming, formal specification, etc. It is expected that many existing techniques can be extended to encompass the new parallel paradigms. However, many assumptions made by serial software engineers no longer hold. For example, according to the traditional life-cycle models, performance engineering is a relatively low-priority activity. If it appears at all, it is at the end of the life-cycle, and then occupies a tiny part of the designer's attention. Yet in high-performance computing, an area in which parallel processing is being applied, clearly performance is a dominant issue. It follows that life-cycle models for conventional serial programming are insufficient to the task of parallel software engineering.

In response to this new problem, many researchers have begun to develop novel approaches to the development of suitable tools and methodologies for parallel programming. Typical first generation tools, developed largely by hardware vendors, and based on proprietary hardware, are suitable for raw programming, but are insufficiently sophisticated for large-scale project use. One aspect of the problem is that the community of programmers will not readily accept unfamiliar programming paradigms: practical tools will need to take account of sociological inertia and resistance to change. Furthermore, the existence of 'dusty decks' and 'legacy systems' creates specific challenges to relate the new technology to its forebears. Thus, there is a need for tools which will make the hardware usable, to a community of programmers with varying degrees of knowledge and skill.

In 1994, a consortium has been established to develop a state-of-the-art graphical parallel programming environment that covers the whole life-cycle of program development for parallel, message-passing systems, based on clusters of PCs and workstations. The consortium participated in two COPERNICUS research projects (SEPP — Software Engineering for Parallel Processing, and HPCTI — High Performance Computing Tools for Industry) [3, 4], and also formulated a large concerted action (SEIHPC — Stimulation of European Industry through High Performance Computing) for exploiting the industrial relevance of results of the research projects. The SEPP and HPCTI consortium consisted of 9 academic and industrial members while in the concerted action 24 universities, research institutes and industrial companies have been involved. During these projects a substantial knowledge of parallel software engineering has been accumulated both concerning parallel program development methodologies, supporting tools and applications.

The objective of this book is to transfer this knowledge to a wider community including both system designers and developers as well as application users. The book is useful as a textbook too, to teach parallel software engineering and parallel programming at universities. The authors of the book are all involved in teaching at various universities and many of them participated in European Tempus projects that aimed at developing teaching materials in the field of parallel systems. The graphical parallel programming environments developed in the SEPP and HPCTI projects will serve as case studies to demonstrate how complex graphical parallel programming environments can be built and used. Tutorial versions of these environments can be downloaded from the Web thus interested readers can do practical studies based on the material of the book.

1.4 Tools and Environments for Parallel Program Development

As a result of the improvements on hardware technology in the last decade, there is now a large diversity of parallel processing platforms that can potentially be used to obtain great speedups in many applications. The emerging field of cluster computing illustrates the increased importance of parallel and distributed hardware platforms for application development.

It also puts strong demands upon the parallel programming models and their supporting tools and environments. As a matter of fact, in general, such performance improvements are showing to be very difficult to achieve on many cases, due to recognized lack of adequate software development methodologies and tools.

1.4.1 Need of Parallel Program Development Environments

There are two related problems. One problem concerns correctness, that is the assurance that the produced parallel and distributed computations are faithful to the problem specification. The other issue concerns how to achieve an acceptable performance of the executable program on a given hardware architecture.

As in conventional program development, one would like to have a series of well-defined and clearly separated stages, ranging from problem analysis and specification, program design and implementation, to real execution. The main difficulty is that there are unavoidable interactions between those stages in the development life-cycle. Concerning correctness, there are complex interactions among parallel and distributed processes. They are due to concurrent accesses to both shared and distributed resources, and to the non-determinism of parallel and distributed computations. Concerning performance it is necessary to establish a relationship between problem specification and decomposition, and its mapping onto the hardware parallel architecture. It is necessary to have a detailed understanding about the characteristics and limitations of the parallel architecture in order to guide the problem decomposition activity. For instance, differences in shared memory or distributed memory models, or the latency of interprocessor communications, can have a great impact upon final performance.

In order to help the parallel programmer, there appeared a strong motivation to provide adequate tools and integrated development environments supporting the iterative process of problem specification and decomposition, followed by the stages of code generation and execution. All along those stages there must be adequate tools assisting the user to increase the understanding of program behavior, concerning both its correctness and performance. Such tools will contribute to produce software of higher quality.

1.4.2 Tool Integration Issues

A large diversity of tools have been developed in the past 10 years. However, the community of users has traditionally shown a very high resistance to use such tools to support the tasks of parallel program development. Several reasons to this situation have been recognized by the high performance community (PTOOLS Parallel Tools Consortium [10] and the EuroTools ESPRIT Working Group [5]), namely many of those tools are difficult to learn and install, and most often they do not contribute to ease the most common user tasks. This is not to say that there are no cases of highly successful commercial and academic tools.

Such issues are important regarding individual stand alone tools supporting specific functionalities such as debugging or performance analysis. Individual tools are insufficient to help the user in following the diversity of tasks in the distinct stages of the parallel software life-cycle, thus there is a requirement to integrate such distinct tools into complete and unified environments. This need poses additional requirements to the task of providing successful parallel development software, because tool integration requires uniform and coherent views among the multiple tools in an environment.

In the presence of multiple tools with differences concerning their user interfaces, the tool behavior, and the supported levels of abstraction, an integrated environment should offer an uniform view of all activities in the software life-cycle, centered on high levels of abstraction corresponding to application level concepts. Whenever possible, access to all the functionalities of an environment should be based on a common and uniform user interface.

The environment should guide the user in the navigation through such distinct contexts of operations, depending on each current stage in the life-cycle. Whenever there is a need to consider intermediate or lower levels, at a middleware layer, or at the operating system, and hardware architecture levels, the environment should help the user to establish the relationships between the corresponding concepts.

The above tool integration requirements are not further discussed in this chapter, as the reader will have plenty of opportunities to find (and evaluate) illustrations of those issues, in the remaining chapters of the book.

1.5 The SEPP/HPCTI Approach

This book describes the results of the research and development of high level tools for parallel program design in the scope of the SEPP/HPCTI projects.

In this section the main unifying issues and ideas behind the SEPP/HPCTI approach are discussed.

On one hand we aimed at developing and improving tools that could assist the user at each individual stage of the parallel application development life-cycle, including the following aspects:

- Construction of parallel applications from its graphical design down to automatic code generation

- Testing and debugging to ensure program correctness

- Simulation to predict program behavior and evaluate its performance on distinct hardware/system configurations

- Mapping and load balancing strategies, to improve execution efficiency

- Monitoring to observe dynamic program behavior

- Analysis of simulated or real execution with animation and visualization of program behavior

At the user interface level, the project exploited high level graphical concepts for visual parallel program development, as a way to help the user understanding the structural aspects of a message passing based program.

On the other hand, the project aimed at providing support to allow the user to understand relationships between distinct concepts:

- Between high level and low level abstractions

- Between structural or graphical concepts and textual or code blocks

- Between the application program and its observed program behavior under distinct working conditions and system configurations, in order to predict, assess or measure the quality of various program components

At the implementation level, the project addressed several difficult issues that one typically finds in current distributed memory platforms, namely clusters and NOWs platforms: mapping, and load balancing, software monitoring with no globally synchronized clock and with intrusion compensation, testing and debugging in a non deterministic environment, behavior simulation under complex layered hardware and software architectures, and high level graphical application design.

For portability reasons, a decision was taken to assume a minimal constraint on the common underlying platform for the tools and environment. The PVM system was adopted as the common target working platform for all of the mentioned classes of tools (note that the project begun in 1994). Thus, the resulting tools and environments are now able to run on a diversity of NOWs, cluster based platforms, as well as MPPs. Furthermore, several of the developed tools have intermediate system independent layers that allow them to be mapped onto distinct platforms such as the MPI, without requiring a major effort.

Besides intensive experimentation with several kinds of tools, this project involved several significant efforts into developing several types of pairwise tool integrations. Overall, the individual work on each tool and the experiments on tool integration have contributed to several innovative approaches towards achieving the desired functionalities of a parallel development environment.

1.6   The SEPP/HPCTI Components

In this section a brief overview is given of the dimensions addressed in the SEPP/HPCTI projects, which are illustrated in Figure 1.1.

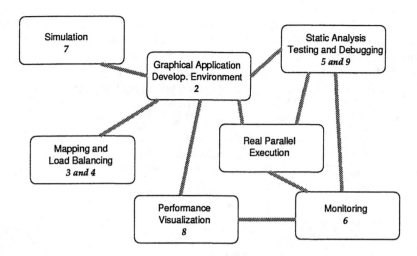

Figure 1.1: The SEPP/HPCTI Concepts

1.6.1 Visual Parallel Program Development

The collaborative effort involving all of the above mentioned partners could be integrated by one partner in the **GRADE** environment. This environment allows the user to develop applications based on the **GRAPNEL** high level visual parallel programming language for message-passing. Namely, the following activities are all performed within the same graphical environment, and they all relate to application level graphical concepts:

- Use a graphical editor to construct the parallel program

- Build the executable for real execution under PVM

- Simulate the execution by interacting with a simulation tool

- Submit to real execution under debugging or trace mode

- Monitor the real program execution

- Improve the efficiency by experimenting with alternative mapping and load-balancing strategies

- Visualize the execution/simulation trace for performance

The implementation of such facilities relied upon the interfacing of distinct types of tools which were developed by the project partners.

1.6.2 Simulation

The topic of simulation is addressed in the book from two complementary perspectives:

- Performance studies of parallel systems and architectures

- Performance-oriented design of parallel software for PVM

The first perspective is supported by a complete simulation toolset (the UAB Simulator) that allows the user to follow a cycle covering the description of a parallel program, including its simulation, visualization and animation of the simulated behavior. The Simulator can be used autonomously in general to investigate the impact of alternative hardware parallel architectures and alternative mapping strategies, upon the performance of a parallel program. As an experiment in tool integration, the Simulator was interfaced to the GRADE environment, for simulation of GRAPNEL programs.

The second perspective is supported by the EDPEPPS environment for rapid prototyping in performance-oriented design of parallel software. EDPEPPS supports a graphical design — simulation — visualization life-cycle, in an integrated development environment for PVM based applications. The user can:

- Design a parallel algorithm, graphically and textually

- Build and execute/simulate the prototype

- Animate/visualize the predicted behavior

- Debug the intermediate and final code

- All with a common GUI and graphical environment

1.6.3   Integrated Testing and Debugging

The book describes the theoretical framework and the most common approaches for testing and debugging of parallel and distributed programs.

The search for correctness in parallel program development is a very complex issue. The best solutions to this problem try to integrate both static analysis and dynamic analysis methods. The main goal is to be able to identify as many undesired program behaviors as possible during a static analysis stage so that less bugs would remain unidentified during run-time execution. Of course, as both static analysis and dynamic analysis are complex tasks, they are best handled by individual tools. In this project, a static analysis and testing tool, STEPS, is able to generate testing scripts that describe the structural and communication aspects of C/PVM programs. Such testing scripts are used to inspect the dynamic behavior of the regions of the program that may be considered suspect by STEPS. This is an interactive tool that relies upon user directions to help identifying the mentioned suspected regions. Otherwise, the complexity of the static program analysis would probably preclude the feasibility of a completed automated approach, even for very simple programs. The detailed dynamic behavior of a program is investigated with the help of a distributed debugging tool, DDBG, allowing the user to inspect possible bugs, by following the computation paths that are specified in the testing script.

The main novelty of this work is that it illustrates a composition of two separate tools, STEPS and DDBG, such that a new functionality was obtained through their integration, without requiring the modification of any of these tools. The focus is put into an integrated testing and debugging methodology which is used to perform the systematic state exploration of parallel C/PVM programs. This is illustrated in detail by explaining the workings of each individual tool (STEPS and DDBG), and their integration.

1.6.4   Monitoring

This book reports on the theoretical and practical results concerning the development and use of monitoring tools for parallel and distributed programs.

The collection of monitoring data is a critical issue for performance evaluation of parallel programs. Among existing monitoring techniques, software tracing is one of the important approaches, because it eases the portability of the software, a critical aspect when one considers the diversity of target platforms. One of the characteristics of cluster computing platforms is the absence of a globally synchronized physical clock, so the monitoring tool must ensure a precise timing of events that allows a coherent analysis of the traces by performance visualization or measurement tools. The book reports on innovative solutions to handle the global clock problem and to compensate the probe effect due to the software monitoring approach. Such solutions were proposed for Tape/PVM, a software tracing tool for PVM programs, which was developed in a previous project. This tool was extensively used by all the partners and it was successfully integrated with several tools in the SEPP project, thus enabling the development of several performance visualization tools.

1.6.5   Performance visualization

A significant effort of this project concerns the use of visualization tools to help the user identifying the performance behavior of a parallel program. The book presents an overview of several dimensions of performance visualization, and it describes several tools that were developed in this project. Visualization tools for the GRADE and EDPEPPS environment are described, and it is shown how they contribute to identify performance problems, and to relate them to the application level abstractions. Such relationship between visualization tools and other user interface tools is described in detail, and shown to greatly contribute to ease the user's task of performance evaluation and tuning. The interaction of such performance visualization tools and an off-line monitoring tool is also described as an example of a successful tool integration.

1.6.6   Mapping, Scheduling and Load Balancing

In order to ensure an efficient execution of parallel and distributed programs on cluster computing platforms, there is a requirement for adequate techniques for distributing the application processes among the processors. Efficiency goals correspond to minimizing the execution times and the communication delays, and improving the resource utilization by balancing the processors' workload. Static mapping, scheduling, dynamic load balancing or a mixture of such methods have been deeply studied in the SEPP/HPCTI projects, both from the theoretical and the practical points of view. Several mapping and load balancing tools were developed and integrated into the SEPP environment. The forms of transparent resource management that such kinds of tools perform can greatly contribute to ease the use of cluster computing platforms. They enable practical experimentation of different strategies that can be assessed with real parallel applications.

1.7   The Main Results of the SEPP/HPCTI Projects

The above sections briefly introduced some of the results of these projects that are further detailed in the chapters of Part II. Besides pairwise tool integrations, complete environments and toolsets were produced under the above mentioned topics.

Contributions were made to the following aspects:

- The development of high level graphical parallel program development tools and their use to support unifying abstractions to offer an integrated view to the end-user of a development environment. The prototype of the GRADE environment, as initially developed in these projects, was later redesigned and is currently being marketed by one of the partners.

- The development of simulation tools.

- The development of testing and debugging tools.

- The extensive use and assessment of an off-line tracing and monitoring tool for PVM.

- The development of several mapping, scheduling, and load balancing packages.

- The development of several performance visualization tools

Figure 1.2 shows all the component tools and their interactions.

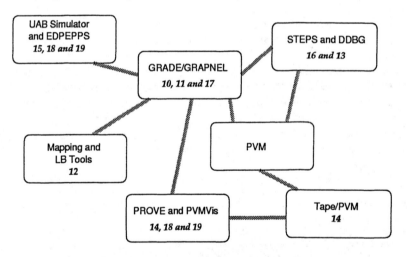

Figure 1.2: The SEPP/HPCTI Tools

Currently, the above mentioned components are being used and assessed by researchers in several institutes, as well as by students in some of the universities of the project partners. Some of the tools and environments can be downloaded through the Web.

Further work on the above tools and environments has continued in order to make improvements, extensions and portings to other platforms, namely MPI.

1.8   Organization of the book

The book is divided into two parts.

Part I gives a comprehensive state-of-the-art survey of the relevant techniques, methodologies, and tools that are used in the life-cycle of parallel program development. Its chapters cover the topics of program design by visual programming, mapping and load balancing of parallel programs, monitoring and debugging, simulation and performance prediction of parallel programs, visualization for performance analysis, and quality issues including usability, testability and safety. Part I can be used as teaching material for courses at universities, and may give valuable insights to designers and developers of programming tools, as it also presents a survey of recently available parallel programming tools (see Figure 1.1 with the numbers of the book chapters that discuss the corresponding theoretical concepts).

Part II provides several case studies of the tools and environments that were developed in the SEPP and HPCTI projects. These tools and environments demonstrate the actual implementations of those principles that are summarized and explained in Part I (see Figure 1.2 with the numbers of the book chapters that discuss the corresponding tools). The two parts can be considered as two sides of the coin. The first one gives a general view of all the techniques while the second one demonstrates the practical realization of those techniques.

1.9   How to read the book

For those who are interested only in the general overviews of parallel programming tools and environments Part I is sufficient to read. Those who would like to get some more detailed explanations and extensions of the topics of Part I, can read on two integrated parallel programming environments described in detail in Part II. The first one is GRADE (further developed as a professional version) which is covered by the following chapters: Chapter 10, 11, 12, 13, 14, 15 and 17. The second environment is EDPEPPS which is explained in Chapter 18 and 19 but also the DDBG debugger of Chapter 13 and the Tape/PVM monitoring tool of Chapter 14 are integrated into both environments. For those who have no time to read on both environments there are several suggestions on how to choose only one of these environments to read:

(i) Those who are specifically interested in PVM will enjoy EDPEPPS since it is an environment specialized for supporting the design and development of PVM programs.

(ii) Those who are specifically interested in MPI programming or both in PVM and MPI GRADE is advised to learn since parallel programs developed in GRADE can run on top of both PVM and MPI.

Other distinguishing features between GRADE and EDPEPPS are that GRADE is more graphical design and debugging oriented while EDPEPPS is more simulation and performance prediction oriented.

If the book is used as a textbook for teaching parallel program development both environments are worth teaching and comparing them during the course. Both environments have downloadable version, detailed tutorials, user's manuals and developed examples on their web page providing excellent teaching materials for students interested in practical experiments with such environments and tools. The two web pages are:

GRADE: http://www.lpds.sztaki.hu/projects/grade/

EDPEPPS: http://www.cpc.wmin.ac.uk/ edpepps/

Readers of the book are kindly invited to visit these web pages and use the materials provided there.

For those who would like to read on specific aspects of parallel program development and tools there are groups of chapters to recommend:

(i) Visual/graphical programming: Chapter 2, 10, 11, 17, 18, 19.

(ii) Mapping and load balancing: Chapter 3, 4, 12.

(iii) Testing and debugging: Chapter 5, 9, 13, 16, 17, 19.

(iv) Performance monitoring and visualization: Chapter 6, 8, 14, 17, 18, 19.

(v) Simulation and performance prediction: Chapter 7, 15, 18, 19

References

[1] M. Bertozzi and et al. Disco report on the state-of-the-art of pc cluster computing. Technical report, DISI-TR-98-09, 1998.

[2] R. Buyya, editor. *High Performance Cluster Computing*. Prentice Hall, 1999.

[3] HPCTI Consortium. High performance computing tools for industry. Technical report, University of Westminter, 1996.

[4] SEPP Consortium. Software engineering for parallel processing. Technical report, University of Westminster, 1997.

[5] EuroTools. Eurotools esprit working group. http://www.eurotools.org.

[6] High Performance Fortran Forum. High performance fortran language specification. *Scientific Programming*, 2(1-2):1–179, 1993.

[7] A. Geist, A. Beguelin, J. Dongarra, W. Jiang, R. Manchek, and V. S. Sunderam. *PVM: Parallel Virtual Machine – A Users' Guide and Tutorial for Networked Parallel Computing*. MIT Press, 1994.

[8] W. Gropp, E. Lusk, and A. Skjellum. *Using MPI : Portable Parallel Programming with the Message-Passing Interface*. MIT Press, 1994.

[9] G. F. Pfister. *In Search of Clusters*. Prentice-Hall, 1995.

[10] PTOOLS. Ptools parallel tools consortium. http://www.ptools.org.

[11] D. Sima, T. Fountain, and P. Kacsuk. *Advanced Parallel Computer Architectures - A Design Space Approach*. Addison-Wesley, 1997.

[12] Genias Software. Codine technical description. http://www.geniasoft.com/products/ codine/tech_desc.html.

[13] L. H. Turcotte. *Parallel and Distributed Computing Handbook (ed. A. Y. H. Zomaya)*, chapter Cluster Computing. McGraw-Hill, 1996.

Chapter 2

Visual Programming to Support Parallel Program Design

Gábor Dózsa

Abstract

Graphical support for program development has become more and more popular and important since high resolution color graphical displays and powerful microprocessors are available at reduced cost. In this chapter, a classification of visual programming languages supporting parallel program development is presented. We identify some basic criteria upon which various graphical notations having been developed so far for message-passing applications can be compared in general. We also outline the most important issues affecting the potential usability of those languages. Finally, some representatives of existing visual programming environments are discussed.

2.1 Introduction

Graphical support for program development has become more and more popular and important since high resolution color graphical displays and powerful microprocessors are available at reduced cost. Advanced graphical user interfaces played an ultimate role in having made desktop computers as popular and widely used as it is the case today. Just to mention one of the most well known examples, the success of Microsoft was based on its graphical windows system that was provided as an alternative to the textual DOS prompt.

Today, it would be impossible to imagine (or what is much more important, to sell) a program development tool without advanced graphical components that are highly involved into the development process. These graphical components may include file browsers, GUI generators, etc.

It is a quite natural idea to try to avoid the tedious work of hand writing thousands of lines of program code by defining programs visually rather than in text from. Intensive research work has been carried out in this field during the last decade. However, only very few systems are available up to now which are accepted by professional (i.e., industrial) users. A bulk of software is still being developed by applying traditional languages like

Fortran, C or Basic usually extended by some kind of GUI generators (like in case of MS Visual Basic) or other auxiliary visual aid.

The low success of visual languages can be explained by the fact that a textual form is better suited to express the traditional imperative procedural programming paradigm found in the most widely used ordinary languages. Real successful visual programming environments are all specialized in some sense. For instance, the LabVIEW [12] development environment, which is commercially available, puts the focus on specific applications like control or measurement software systems. It provides high-level visual symbols emulating complex hardware equipments like oscilloscope, AD/DA converters, etc. that the user can arrange and connect with the help of a graphical editor in order to build up specific test, measurement and control applications. A similar example is the Simulink [11] system that provides a visual interface to access the high-level mathematical functions of the Matlab environment. On the other hand, Prograph CPX [5, 14], another successful graphical programming environment, supports the development of general user applications but is based on a declarative programming model which differs quite radically from the well known procedural languages. For example, there are no program variables in Prograph applications, all the constants are defined by graphical symbols and the user must draw fine grain dataflow graphs to define the application though the environment supports OOP concepts as well.

Based on these practical facts, distributed and parallel programs are really promising candidates to be defined (at least partially) by visual means as they exhibit complex and specialized features which are absent in ordinary sequential applications. However, it is important to emphasize that in the following we concentrate on the development of applications where interaction between parallel execution units can take place only by message-passing (MP) and sequential computations are expressed by means of ordinary imperative textual languages.

Visual representations of such applications have a number of advantages. They allow the programmers to easily view and directly modify the structure of a program. Thus, programmers understand their program's structure, and this is important since high performance depends upon careful structural design. Factors that programmers must keep in mind include what processes are created by their program, what computations are performed by the processes, what are the process interactions, the size of the messages, the conditions for sending the messages, and the granularity of the processes.

Graphs are a natural mechanism for organizing such information statically. Furthermore, they lend themselves to dynamic display via animation of runtime performance and structural data. Animation can be performed directly on the program representation thus, programmers are not forced to manually relate animated displays to separate textual program representations.

The major goal of the research in the field of visual parallel languages is to reduce the user's involvement in parallel programming issues. Difficulties mainly come from having to consider a large number of components and their interactions. Some kind of user involvement is necessary in any case since current compiler technology is not able to cope with the problem of automatic generation of coarse-grain parallel programs from sequential applications. However, appropriate visual programming languages can contribute to enrich the power of program development environments in a significant way. They achieve this by hiding low level details of message-passing and process management to allow the user to concentrate on really relevant design issues like parallel problem decomposition and granularity of computation units. Furthermore, visual programming environments can provide high-level support for rapid prototype design and test which is crucial for efficient development of parallel and distributed applications.

The rest of the chapter is organised as follows. It consists of two main parts. The first one describes a classification of visual parallel programming models and identifies some general criteria to compare them. The second part is a survey of existing visual parallel programming environments. The chapter ends with some conclusions and some words about future trends.

2.2   Classification of Visual Parallel Languages

In this section we identify some basic issues that can be used to compare MP based visual parallel languages. Such issues include the underlying programming and process model, the supported process interactions, the handling of regular parallel structures, the possibility of hierarchical program design and the support for code reuse.

Before discussing these questions in detail in separate subsections, we define some criteria upon which particular answers of different languages to these issues can be evaluated. They are defined as follows.

Applicability   The applicability of a language refers to the range of potential applications that can be implemented in that particular language. The wider is the range of applications that are supported by a language the better is its applicability.

Expressiveness   Expressiveness describes all design concepts provided by the language to help the user expressing an algorithm as conveniently and easily as possible. It may happen that the applicability of a language is quite good but the expressiveness is rather poor since the language requires complicated and awkward code to implement some types of programs, e.g., possibility of collective communication reduces the complexity of the code of algorithms using broadcast messages thus, the existence of support for broadcast improves the expressiveness.

Friendliness   Friendliness measures how much user's involvement is required by a particular language to construct the parallel structure of the application. Reducing user's involvement in parallel programming issues is the main goal of visual languages studied through this chapter. As it is already mentioned in the introduction, some kind of user's involvement is always necessary since fully automatic conversion of sequential applications into coarse-grain parallel programs is an open problem up to know. However, the less involvement is required the better is the friendliness of the language since it allows the user to focus on the more abstract problem specification of parallel activities instead of dealing with low level technical details of the required code constructs. It is important to emphasize that we consider user's involvement here only with respect to the definition of parallelism related activities in the code.

Portability   One of the most important obstacle against a wider dissemination of parallel programming is the poor portability of the application software. A very promising attempt to overcome this problem in the field of message-passing is the definition of the MPI standard [9]. However, there are still situations where support only for MPI is not enough (e.g., because of performance reasons) so programming environment support for multiple potential MP platforms is of great interest to the users.

In the rest of the section, existing visual languages are classified based on the existence or lack of some general properties. Several classification trees are given in different figures. Notations in these figures *a+*, *e+*, *f+* and *p+* mean that existence of the particular property improves the *a*pplicability, *e*xpressiveness, *f*riendliness or *p*ortability of a language, respectively.

Performance issues of existing programming environments are not addressed here. This is because they depend rather on the implementation details of the code generators than on the graphical notations provided by the language. They also highly depend on the particular user. There may be a good chance that a professionally optimized code generator produces more efficient parallel code from a high-level description of a program than an ordinary programmer can provide by using MP primitives in text form. The situation is similar to the relation of sequential high-level and assembly languages.

2.2.1   General Programming Model

We have identified three different general programming models to which existing MP based visual languages can be associated. They are shown in Figure 2.1 and explained in detail as follows.

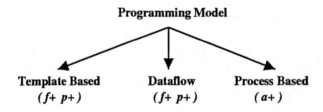

Figure 2.1: General Programming Models of MP based Visual Languages

Template-based Tools

Tools falling into this class provide some pre-defined process interaction structures called templates for the programmer to construct his/her parallel application. Templates implement various types of interactions found in parallel systems, but with the key components — the application specific procedures — unspecified. A user provides the application specific procedures and the tool provides the glue to bind it all together.

Essentially, most parallel and distributed programs take advantage of several frequently occuring communication structures, such as process farm, pipe-line, etc. The idea is the following. Provided that all of these structures could be built into the tools as some sort of skeleton code (i.e., template) the user should only select the proper ones and fill out the empty slots in them (i.e., the sequential code fragments performing the actual computations).

The fundamental advantage of this approach is the — ideally complete — separation of specification. It means that parallelization aspects of the application (i.e., templates) can be specified separately from the application code of each individual component. The user does not have to worry about communication and synchronization issues as they are defined by the tool itself. It also implies that one of the most difficult and time consuming development steps required for distributed applications could be eliminated, namely, fixing program bugs related to the interactions among components (i.e., deadlocks, unintended communications, etc.).

Although templates encourage code reuse, templates do not eliminate the need to rewrite existing sequential code to adapt it to a parallel environment. Like any other parallel tool, some code rewriting or restructuring may be necessary to expose the parallelism, satisfy the programming constraints of the tool, or achieve improved performance.

In order to illustrate the visual appearance of a template-based model, we have selected an example application that performs graphic animation. Let the name of the program be *Animation*. The application takes a sequence of graphical images, called frames, as input data and animates them. It consists of three main computation units called *Generate()*, *Geometry()* and *Display()*. For each frame, *Generate()* computes the location and motion of objects. Then *Geometry()* is called to perform various actions like viewing transformations, projection and clipping. Finally, the frame is passed to *Display()* that performs hidden-surface removal and anti-aliasing and stores the frame on the disk. After this, computation continues by having *Generate()* to take the next frame and the whole process is repeated.

In the parallel version of this application, the three units work in a pipeline fashion. Furthermore, several instances of *Display()* must work in parallel since hidden-surface removal and anti-aliasing require much more time in reality than the other tasks. So, the structure of the parallel application can be nicely expressed by a combination of a "pipeline" and a "process farm" topology templates. For instance, the Enterprise graphical programming environment provides such templates. The visual code of the program is shown in Figure 2.2. Double border surrounds the whole application or *enterprise* in the Enterprise tool terminology. It contains a (pipe)line template denoted by the dash rectangle. In the pipeline three workers are defined according to the three computation units of the application. The last worker (i.e., *Display*) represents a farm of processes since it is replicated up to eight times. More details about the Enterprise programming model are given later on in Section 2.3.2.

entire application
(enterprise)

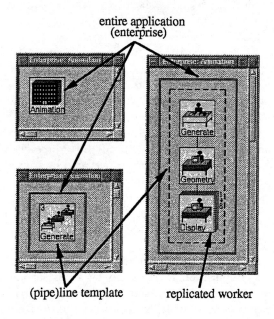

(pipe)line template   replicated worker

Figure 2.2: Hierarchical Views of the *Animation* Example in the Enterprise Environment

The main limitation of the template based tools stems from the fact that real world applications often need irregular communication connections to be defined among processing units. For such applications the user must be able to define individual interaction steps which cannot be expressed by any regular communication schemes. Even if the required parallel structure of an application could be described by regular patterns it is not sure that these patterns are included in a particular template based tool. Extensibility of the pre-defined set of templates is not solved in existing tools thus, the users might be forced to use a possibly inappropriate parallel structure, or to abandon the tool altogether.

On the other hand, if a particular application or some of its subtasks fit to a regular parallel structure, it makes no sense to force the programmer to design and implement it every time from scratch, so templates, in general, can add significant benefits to any parallel programming environment.

Coarse-grain Dataflow Approach

A program represented by coarse-grain dataflow graph consists of nodes and links. Nodes correspond to sequential computations and links indicate the flow of data. Thus, programs can be thought of as directed graphs (as indeed are visualised as such on the screen) representing the data flow relations plus a collection of ordinary sequential code fragments attached to the nodes to indicate the computations.

The programming paradigm supported by languages belonging to this class is based on the dataflow approach. However, unlike classical dataflow, nodes of programs carry out significant computations. This so-called coarse-grain dataflow model is motivated by the relatively high cost of communication in distributed systems due to the high-latency, low-bandwidth of the usual networks in such systems. Only by keeping the communication-to-computation ratio to reasonable levels can we expect reasonable performance from parallel applications in such computing environments. Unfortunately, it is up to the user to adopt an appropriate definition for "large grain" in decomposing an application to its parallel components for a particular system.

While extremely simple, the above programming paradigm has several desirable properties. First, application parallelism is explicit in its notation — all nodes that have no data dependencies can execute in parallel. Second, the few abstractions that the programmer has to deal with are familiar from sequential programming. In particular, there are no new linguistic constructs for communication and synchronization.

Programmers also benefit from a separation of concerns. They first specify a set of sequential computations and then, separately, specify how these are to be composed into a parallel program. Furthermore, the debugging activity can be partitioned into the tasks of debugging a set of sequential routines and debugging the parallel interactions among the routines (which are then viewed as being atomic).

In Figure 2.3, the visual code of the *Animation* example application (see Section 2.2.1) programmed in a coarse-grain dataflow language, called HeNCE is depicted. Opposite to the template-based approach, each node and arcs are created and arranged by the programmer explicitly. The circle nodes (i.e., nodes 1,2,4) denote the worker processes performing sequential computations. Replication is expressed by a pair of fan-out and fan-in nodes (i.e., nodes 3,5). The replication factor is attached to the fan-out node as a text property much like as sequential text code is attached to worker nodes. Description of the HeNCE programming environment is given in Section 2.3.4.

However, the coarse-grain dataflow approach also has some limitations. First, the se-

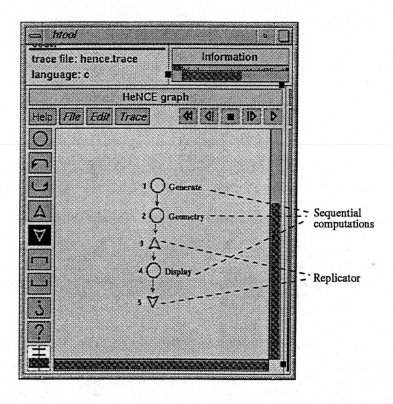

Figure 2.3: HeNCE graph of the *Animation* Example Application

quential computations attached to the nodes cannot use shared variables, i.e., all global information needed by some computation units must be transferred explicitly to them even if those computations must be executed sequentially because of data dependencies among them.

Another common problem with the coarse-grain dataflow approach is that it forces computations to be split into separate nodes when communications occurs or when branching decisions control communications. This can result in complicated, awkward, and large graphs. Let us consider a simple imaginary computation in which F and G are sequential functions.

```
array A, B, C; scalar x=0, y, z;
1: receive A from some process.
2: B = F(A);
3: Send parts of B to the processes: S1, S2 and S3;
4: Receive z from each process S1, S2 and S3; x += z;
5: if (x < 0) then
6:   receive y from process Q1;
7: else
8:   receive y from process Q2;
9: C = G(A, y, x);
```

Since communications cannot be embedded within node computations, this program must be split into multiple nodes. Namely, a separate computation node is needed for lines 1, 4, 6 and 8. They are labeled as P1, P2, P3 and P4, respectively, in Figure 2.4 that depicts the resulted graph using an abstract visual coarse-grain dataflow notation. Lines executed by each of them are listed next to the node icons. Names of the variables to be passed are written along the particular arcs in the figure. By using a dataflow notation, each data dependency must be expressed explicitly as a communication arcs between nodes. It yields an artificially complex graph in spite of the quite simple computation to be accomplished.

Process-based Methods

The central idea of process-based languages is that the programmer defines the process structure and message-passing operations explicitly by himself. The process structure of a parallel program is defined by a process graph where nodes and arcs represent the processes themselves and (usually) the possible communication paths, respectively. In the code of each process, operations to interact with other processes are defined either as a call to an MP library function (i.e., text form) or by some sort of visual representation. In both cases, location of such operations are not restricted to the start and end point of a computation as it happens in case of the coarse-grain dataflow paradigm. Comparing to the template based languages, the set of potential target applications are not restricted as well because both regular and irregular parallel structures can be expressed.

The process-based model is less abstract than the coarse-grain dataflow but provides greater expressive range. It is illustrated by the example code fragment in Section 2.2.1 which can be described in a straight-forward natural way as a single process replacing nodes (P1, P2, P3, P4) of Figure 2.4. The model is also closer to the current programming practice thus, its learning curve is less steep. Furthermore, it does not impose any limitation on the set of potential target applications thus, the range of its applicability is wider than that of the template based models.

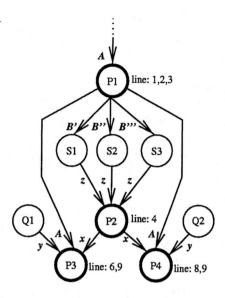

Figure 2.4: Abstract Coarse-grain Data-flow Graph

On the other hand, the process-based paradigm usually requires more programmers' involvements during program construction than the other two approaches since it provides a less abstract representation of the parallel applications under development. Nevertheless, targets and sources of messages are specified graphically in all programming environments of this type which simplifies the programmer's task comparing to the use of MP libraries without any additional support.

2.2.2 Process Model

The process model of a visual language specifies how the parallel structure of an application can be defined. Basically, it can be defined either *implicitly* or *explicitly*. In the former case, the programmer only specifies the logical computation units of the program and some dependencies among them but it is up to the code generator to arrange these units into physical processes running in parallel. In the latter case, the user defines the physical processes explicitly. An explicit model may provide support for grouping of processes and dynamic process creation.

As it is indicated in Figure 2.5, the implicit process model improves friendliness (i.e., the user does not have to define the parallel structure of the program by himself) and the portability of the language (all MP primitives are generated automatically). It also gives the freedom to the code generator to analyse the computational units and select an optimized process granularity for a particular target machine.

On the other hand, explicit dynamic process creation enhances the applicability of a language by making it possible, for instance, to implement an efficient parallel program for multiplication of matrices in arbitrary size (i.e., the number of processes is proportional to the size of the input matrices). It also improves the expressiveness, as well as process group support does, since there are a great number of algorithms that can be expressed more elegantly by using dynamic creation of processes and/or collective communication

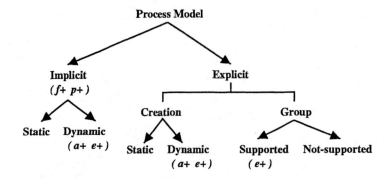

Figure 2.5: Classification Based on Process Model

techniques.

2.2.3 Process Interactions

Process interactions play a central role in case of message-passing programs since complexity and run-time behaviour of such applications are mainly determined by the synchronization and communication connections among the parallel units of the program.

Supported Process Interactions

Basic types of process interactions are shown in Figure 2.6. Two main branches can be identified which correspond to *point-to-point* and *collective* interactions. In each group, both synchronization and communication (i.e., data movement) operations can be present. Additionally, collective interactions may include computation routines like, for instance, reduce operations.

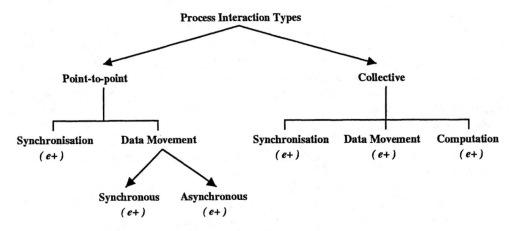

Figure 2.6: Basic Process Interaction Types

In general, the more types of process interactions are available in a programming environment, the better is the expressiveness. This is reflected as plus signs at each leaf of the tree in Figure 2.6.

Specification of Process Interactions

Similarly to the process structure, process interactions can be defined either *implicitly* or *explicitly* (see Figure 2.7). In case of implicit definition, the programmer only specifies data or execution dependencies among logical computation units of the program which are defined as pure sequential computations. This means that communication or synchronization can occur only at the beginning or at end of a procedure (or function). In the explicit case, the programmer defines statements in the code of execution units to perform interactions among parallel processes. Definition can be done either by textual or by visual means. Furthermore, textual definition of process interaction operations may happen either by use of direct calls to existing MP libraries (like PVM [7] or MPI [9]) or by using a tool-specific text interface which hides the underlying MP primitives. The last two cases are referred to as *direct* and *indirect* specification, respectively.

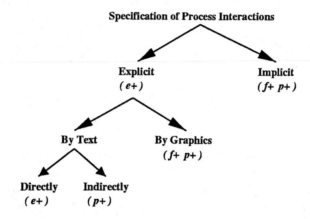

Figure 2.7: Specification Methods of Process Interactions

Advantages of the different approaches are shown in Figure 2.7, too. The user benefits from implicit definition with respect to the portability and friendliness properties due to the same reasons as in case of the implicit process model (see Section 2.2.2).

On the other hand, explicit definition improves the expressiveness as it is demonstrated in Section 2.2.1.

Furthermore, providing graphical support for the explicit definition improves portability and friendliness since the low-level MP primitives can be automatically generated based on the visual code.

2.2.4   Regular Parallel Structures

In practice, regular parallel structures such as pipelines, process farms, rings, 2D-mesh, etc. often occur as parts of applications. It is quite tedious for the user to design such structures from scratch every time thus, some sort of support is needed evidently.

As it is depicted in Figure 2.8, two fundamental techniques can be applied for providing support for such regular patterns: *replicators* and *templates*. Replicators are used to replicate various visual elements of the code (e.g., computational units, processes or communication channels) while templates define complete parallel structures belonging to particular regular patterns. Both approaches can be either static or dynamic depending on whether the number of components in the regular structures is determined at either compile or runtime, respectively.

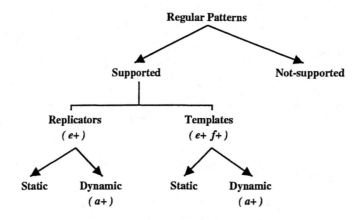

Figure 2.8: Support of Regular Parallel Patterns

Naturally, both replicators and templates improve the expressiveness of a visual language. Templates also enhance the friendliness property by encapsulating the complete parallel structure of particular regular patterns. Thus, the programmer can get rid of having to define the components and the connections among the components separately which is required if replicators are applied. Furthermore, dynamic creation of components improves the applicability of the language in all cases.

2.2.5   Hierarchical Design

Programs that consists of more than dozen of components running in parallel are rather difficult to be handled (i.e., perceived, modified) without some sort of support for hierarchical design. Such support basically means the capability to define compound nodes (i.e., subgraphs) in the visual code which may contain — possible complex — parts of the parallel application but which are presented by a simple visual symbol. In this way, the programmer can always control the level of visual detail shown. Subgraph abstraction can be used either to hide parts of the graph that are not currently of interest to the user or to give the user an uncluttered display of a particular subgraph alone. In either case, the subgraph abstraction is used to focus the user's attention on the relevant portions of the visual code. Such structuring of the visual code is inevitable in case of realistic size programs.

Existence of hierarchical design support improves the applicability of a language because it makes possible the design and implementation of parallel applications which cannot be handled in a completely flat model due to the large number of their components.

2.2.6 Code Reuse

Possibility of code reuse is another important issue since it can ease and speed up the work of the programmer significantly. It holds equally for development of both sequential and parallel programs. In our case, reuse of sequential code is ensured by the ordinary textual language which is applied to define the pure sequential computations in the message-passing program. Thus, we are interested in code reuse only at a higher-level, i.e., reuse of visual code.

Different alternatives to provide support for reusing visual code are depicted in Figure 2.9. Basically, we can distinguish between the reuse of a single component in the program graph (e.g., a process) and a complete subgraph (e.g., a group of processes). In both cases, the reuse can take place either in the same or in a separate application which are referred to as intra- and inter-application reuse, respectively. Inter-application reuse means that parts of the visual code can be saved individually and can be retrieved later on during a separate development session. On the other hand, intra-application reuse requires the possibility of using several instances of the same visual component (or subgraph) in one application (like procedures in sequential languages).

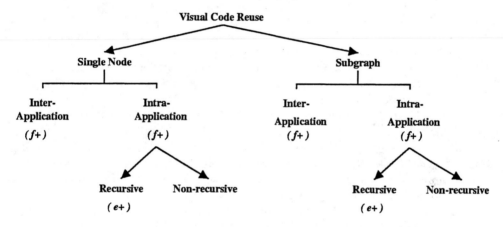

Figure 2.9: Visual Code Reuse Support

Friendliness of the language is improved by each case since the programmer can get rid of the unnecessary re-implementation of existing visual code segments. Moreover, using different logical instances of a physical code segment to perform the same tasks in the program may ease the debugging phase since an error occuring in the computation of that particular task needs to be fixed only once (i.e., in the common code segment).

Furthermore, the expressiveness of the language can be enhanced by allowing recursion in intra-application reuse because several algorithms can be expressed in more concise and natural way in a recursive form (e.g., parallelized divide-and-conquer computations).

2.3 Example Visual Environments

In this section, we present some representative examples of visual parallel programming environments that have been developed so far. We use terms visual languages and visual environments in an interchangeable way since practically there is always a one-to-one relationship between the language and its graphical editor or programming environment. Moreover, in most cases there is no individual name for the language itself.

All the environments surveyed here support development of parallel and distributed applications based on ordinary imperative textual languages (e.g. C, Fortran) extended with some sort of message-passing support. We put the focus on the programming methodology and on the advantages/drawbacks of each particular solution.

2.3.1   The FrameWorks system

The FrameWorks system is a template based programming environment [18]. Processes running in parallel are called *modules* in Frameworks terminology and they can communicate to each other via remote procedure calls. Each module can have at most one *entry* procedure that can be called from other modules. A remote procedure call is expressed by an explicit `call` statement in the code of a module and it is realized by message-passing. If output parameters are defined for an entry procedure, the calling module is suspended (i.e., synchronised communication) until the called routine executes an explicit `reply` statement to pass back the output values.

The `call` statement always defines the name of the target module but graphical templates are provided to specify the number of available runtime instances of a module and the way how the corresponding messages are distributed among those instances. A module needs up to three different templates to be completely defined: input and output templates dealing with incoming and outgoing messages, respectively, and an optional body template.

Three input templates are provided by FrameWorks (see Figure 2.10, left side, top row). The *initial* template allows no input at all, the *in-pipeline* serves input requests in an first-called-first-served manner and the *assimilator* requires one input data from each input process before processing starts. Similarly, three output templates are available (see Figure 2.10, left side, middle row) to disallow output (*terminal*), to send output requests in a pipe-line fashion (*out-pipeline*) and to distribute the output calls among multiple instances of the same modules (*manager*). Additionally, two types of body template can be attached to a module (see Figure 2.10, left side, bottom row). The *executive* template redirects the standard error, input and output streams of the module to the user's terminal while the *contractor* template creates multiple instances of the module (process) at runtime to serve simultaneous requests in parallel if there are free processors available.

The graphical code of our *Animation* example (see Section 2.2.1) is also depicted in Figure 2.10. The three main computation units are defined as three modules: *Generate*, *Geometry* and *Display*. *Generate* has an *initial* input and an *out-pipeline* output template. Both the input and output templates of *Geometry* are of pipeline types. Finally, *Display* has an *in-pipeline* input and a *terminal* output template. To define replicated execution of the last module, a *contractor* body template is attached to it.

The FrameWorks system suffers from some severe limitations listed as follows. The parallelism is expressed in the code (`call` statements) *and* in the graphical user interface which violates the ultimate goal of separation of specification. The consequence is that changes in the template specification have to be mirrored in the code, increasing the chance of user error. Furthermore, FrameWorks requires three different templates for each process to describe the parallel structure of the application. In practice, it is more comfortable to select one well-defined communication/synchronization structure for a process or even for a whole group of processes to specify its run-time behaviour completely concerning parallel interactions. Finally, templates cannot be nested, i.e., the communication structure of the

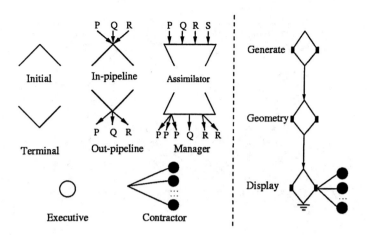

Figure 2.10: FrameWorks Templates (on the left) and the *Animation* Application (on the right)

application is completely flat.

General characteristics of FrameWorks are summarized in Table 2.1.

Programming Model	*Template based*
Process Model	*Explicit, dynamic creation is supported*
Interaction Types	*Point-to-point synch/asynch data movement*
Interaction Specification	*Explicit, indirectly by text*
Regular Patterns	*Supported by (dynamic) templates*
Hierarchical Design	*Not supported*
Visual Code Reuse	*Not supported*

Table 2.1: General Characteristics of the FrameWorks System

2.3.2 Enterprise Parallel Programming System

Enterprise [15, 19] is the successor of the FrameWorks system. It applies the template based model but it eliminates most of the limitations that occurred in FrameWorks.

Templates are called *assets* in the Enterprise's terminology and a few basic operations are provided to combine them. Their names are based on an analogy of a human organization and they are depicted in Figure 2.11. The most important ones are listed as follows.

An *enterprise* represents a program and is analogous to an entire business organization. By default, every *enterprise* asset contains a single *individual*. A developer can transform this into a *line, department* or *division* thus, facilitating hierarchical structuring and refinement.

An *Individual* represents a procedure that executes sequentially and is analogous to a person in an organization. If all the code of a program were entered into a single *individual*, the program would execute sequentially.

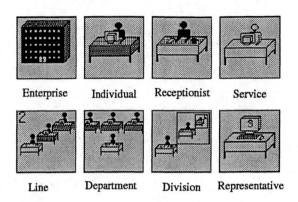

Figure 2.11: Enterprise Assets

A *line* represents a pipeline and is analogous to an assembly or processing line. It contains a fixed number of heterogeneous assets in a specified order.

A *department* represents a master/slave relationship and is analogous to a department in an organization. It contains fixed number of heterogeneous assets and a *receptionist* that directs each incoming communication to the appropriate asset. All assets execute in parallel.

A *division* asset represents a parallel recursive divide-and-conquer computation and contains a hierarchical collection of *individual* assets among which the work is distributed. It is the only recursive template in Enterprise.

Construction of a parallel program begins by representing it as a single *enterprise* asset containing a single *individual*. This "one person business" represents a sequential program. Four basic operations are used to transform this sequential program into a parallel one: asset expansion, asset transformation, asset addition and asset replication. Using the analogy, the simple business grows into a (possibly complex) organization.

The visual code of the *Animation* example program is depicted and explained in Figure 2.2 and in Section 2.2.1, respectively.

Enterprise represents an advancement over FrameWorks in several ways. It combines the three-part templates of FrameWorks into a single unit, called *assets* which can be combined hierarchically to form a parallel program. In addition, Frameworks `call` and `reply` keywords are eliminated. Furthermore, recursion is supported as well through *division* assets.

General characteristics of the language are summarized in Table 2.2.

Programming Model	*Template based*
Process Model	*Explicit*
Interaction Types	*Point-to-point synch/asynch data movement*
Interaction Specification	*Explicit, indirectly by text*
Regular Patterns	*Static templates and replicators*
Hierarchical Design	*Subgraph abstraction*
Visual Code Reuse	*Limited subgraph intra-application with recursion*

Table 2.2: General Characteristics of the Enterprise System

2.3.3 The CODE 2.0 Language

The CODE [4, 13] series of programming environments are based on the coarse-grain dataflow approach.

CODE 2.0 programs consist of a set of graph instances that interact by means of Call nodes. Graph instances in CODE 2.0 play the role of subroutines in conventional programming languages. The number and type of instances is determined at runtime, but each graph is instantiated from one of a fixed set of graph templates. When the user draws a graph in the programming model, a template is created, not an instance. Instances are created at runtime when they are referenced from a Call node.

Graphs consist of nodes and arcs. Arcs represent channels for the flow of data from one node to another. They serve as FIFO buffers. There are several types of nodes. As alluded to before, Call nodes specify arc connections to other graph instances (much like subroutine calls in procedural languages). Interface nodes specify points at which a called graph can connect to another graph. Unit of computation nodes (UCs) represent basic sequential computations. They consume data from incoming arcs, perform a computation, and place data onto outgoing arcs for other nodes to consume.

UC nodes have a large number of text attributes. For example, the node's computation is expressed as a call to a subroutine in a conventional sequential language, and input rules specify conditions under which this computation is allowed to execute. UC nodes also have input and output ports for the communication of data to and from the node. Arcs are bound to specific ports. Hence, multiple arcs may enter or leave a node without ambiguity.

The CODE 2.0 language is able to cope with the problem of describing applications with dynamic program structure (e.g., the program structure may depend on some input variable). Such dynamic structures are specified by complex input and output rules. In those rules, ports are referred to by abstract indices whose ranges are defined by replicator expressions.

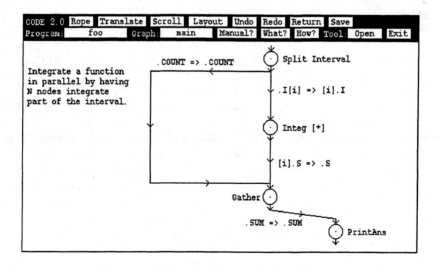

Figure 2.12: Integration program in CODE 2.0

To illustrate the visual appearance of CODE applications, the graph of a simple integration example is depicted in Figure 2.12.

Comparing with other coarse-grain dataflow approaches, one of the most advanced features of CODE 2.0 is the capability of defining dynamic application graphs. However, the solution provided does not fit completely to the basic concept that claims to define the model structure of the application by graphics. Dynamic structures are completely hidden in the graphics, they are defined only by text attributes of CU nodes (i.e., input/output rules and arc topology specifications). This can be a source of confusion and causes the CODE 2.0 graphs to reflect the real structure of parallel programs rather poorly when dynamic nodes/arc creations are applied.

General characteristics of CODE 2.0 are summarized in Table 2.3.

Programming Model	*Coarse-grain dataflow based*
Process Model	*Implicit, dynamic*
Interaction Types	*Point-to-point asynch data movement*
Interaction Specification	*Implicit*
Regular Patterns	*Supported by dynamic replicators*
Hierarchical Design	*Subgraph abstraction*
Visual Code Reuse	*Subgraph intra-application with recursion*

Table 2.3: General Characteristics of CODE 2.0

2.3.4   The HeNCE Programming Environment

In HeNCE [2–4], the programmer specifies parallelism by drawing graphs that express the dependencies and control flow of the program. Although these graphs are not of type coarse-grain dataflow in strict sense, we classify HeNCE as that type of tool because the global semantics of the approach is the same. Nodes can start sequential computations whenever the necessary incoming data is available and data can enter or leave nodes only at the beginning and at the end of their computations, respectively.

Each node in a HeNCE graph represents a sequential subroutine written in either Fortran or C. An arc from one node to another represents the fact that the tail node of the arc must run before the node at the head of the arc. During the execution of a HeNCE graph, procedures are automatically executed when their predecessors, as defined by dependency arcs, have completed.

Communication between subroutine nodes takes place by means of a parameter passing interface. Programmers need only specify which parameters are to be used to invoke each subroutine node. Names of the parameters constitute a global name space for the whole application. If a parameter with a given name is needed by a subroutine node as input data, HeNCE needs to find that parameter as output of one of the predecessor subroutine nodes.

In addition to simple dependency arcs, HeNCE provides constructs which denote four different types of control flow: conditionals, loops, fans and pipes. They add subgraphs to the current program graph dynamically based upon expressions which are attached to those nodes as text attributes and evaluated at runtime. Thus, arcs represent the possible flow of data as well as control dependencies. Each of these constructs is represented by two nodes that wrap around the subgraph to be added dynamically to the program graph. They are explained as follows.

The *Conditional construct* executes the subgraph conditionally. The *Loop construct* adds the loop body repeatedly to the program graph based upon the boolean expression evaluated each time through the loop. The *fan construct* creates a dynamic number of subgraphs to execute the same task in parallel based upon the integer expression attached to the begin fan node. Finally, the *pipe construct* can add the subgraph to the program graph every time a new data item arrives in order to execute the additional data item in a pipelined fashion.

The HeNCE code of the *Animation* example application is depicted in Figure 2.3 in Section 2.2.1.

The most interesting features of the HeNCE environment is its parameter passing interface and the capability to handle dynamic graphs. The parameter passing scheme allows the user to access all parameters to be passed among components in a global name space which may reduce the graphical complexity since no direct connections are needed between nodes to communicate. However, it also means that it might be difficult to find out which node produced a particular input data based only on the program graph especially, if large graphs are concerned. Other limitations also relate to how the model deals with large applications: lack of hierarchical design, visual code-reuse and collective communication support.

General characteristics of HeNCE are summarized in Table 2.4.

Programming Model	*Semantically: coarse-grain dataflow based*
Process Model	*Implicit, dynamic*
Interaction Types	*Point-to-point asynch data movement*
Interaction Specification	*Implicit*
Regular Patterns	*Supported by dynamic replicators*
Hierarchical Design	*Not supported*
Visual Code Reuse	*Not supported*

Table 2.4: General Characteristics of the HeNCE System

2.3.5   The TRAPPER programming environment

TRAPPER [16, 17] is definitely the most well-known member of the process-based graphical programming environments. TRAPPER is the successor of the GRACIA system which itself originated from the SPECTRAL project. The programming model remained the same in all of these consecutive systems, only the target platforms have changed and the tool-set in the programming environment has been enhanced significantly. TRAPPER has been commercialized and its most recent version runs on Windows NT as well as on UNIX machines and supports development of PVM and MPI based message passing applications [1].

In TRAPPER, the parallel structure of the application is described by a graphical representation (process graph) whereas the sequential components are described by textual representations (process code). The process graph consists of nodes and edges, where nodes represent processes and edges represent communication channels. Each process consists of a unique process identifier, a process type denoted by the process name and dedicated communication interfaces called ports. A port has a name and a direction. Possible port directions are "bidirectional", "input" or "output".

Large process graphs can be designed hierarchically as a composition of *subsystems*. A subsystem is a graphical building block and can be viewed as a black box, which contains a subgraph of the process graph.

The behaviour of a process is described textually by the process code. The programmer selects a process in the process graph and activates a text editor. TRAPPER checks whether the associated code file exists and generates a process frame if no process code exists. The frame contains automatically generated statements including a parameter list which contains names of the ports defined for that particular process in the process graphs. However, the remaining of the process code, including all necessary communication or synchronization primitives, must be written explicitly by the user as text code.

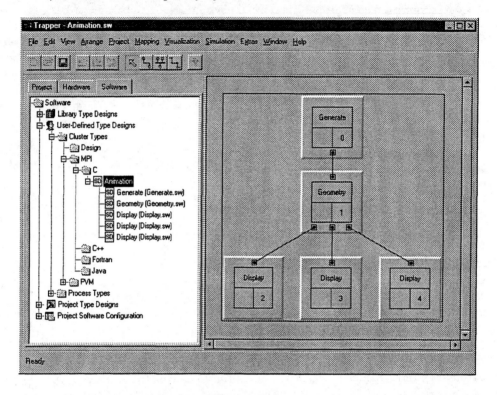

Figure 2.13: TRAPPER Graph of the *Animation* Example Program

The TRAPPER process graph of the *Animation* example application is depicted in Figure 2.13. Since TRAPPER provides no particular support for defining regular communication patterns, the number of *Display* processes must be fixed at design time. In the figure, three of such processes are defined.

Despite of the fact that it has been commercialized, TRAPPER suffers from certain limitations. The most important ones include the lack of support for dynamic process creation and regular process topologies.

Another problem could be the explicit use of PVM or MPI primitives in the code of processes. This requires the programmer to know the exact syntax and semantics of all low level MP primitives provided by those MP libraries. Moreover, the programmer is responsible for maintaining the consistency between the process graph and the text code by using the proper low level MP primitives in a proper way in the code of processes.

On the other hand, use of explicit MP primitives in the code provides a chance to exploit the full available performance possibilities of the underlying low level communication interface.

General characteristics of TRAPPER are summarized in Table 2.5.

Programming Model	*Process based*
Process Model	*Explicit, static process creation*
Interaction Types	*Point-to-point synch/asynch data movement*
Interaction Specification	*Explicit, directly by text*
Regular Patterns	*Not supported*
Hierarchical Design	*Subgraph abstraction*
Visual Code Reuse	*Subgraph intra-application*

Table 2.5: General Characteristics of the TRAPPER System

2.3.6   The Meander Environment

Meander [8, 20] is another process-based development environment but its graphical notation differs relevantly from previously presented examples. In Meander, the programmer builds up the complete message-passing application as one specification graph which describes the parallel (coarse-grain) control flow of the whole program.

Meander is a hybrid language built up from a fixed set of graphical nodes. The graphical constructs are quite similar to the building blocks of the CSP language. All parallel aspects of an application are formulated by a so-called specification graph.

Control flow is specified by connecting nodes of the specification graph by directed causal edges. Additional edges are used to create processes and to define communication connections between send and receive nodes. The following types of nodes are provided by the system.

Seq nodes represent the sequential computations in the application. Actual computations are defined as C code through annotation of **seq** nodes.

Create-child/wait-child nodes (cc/wc) are used to introduce parallelism. Each outgoing arc of a **cc** node defines a new process consisting of all nodes of the subgraph originating from that arc and closed by a corresponding **wc** node. Parallel processes created at a specific **cc** are synchronised at the corresponding **wc** node.

Send/receive nodes (snd/rcv) represent message-passing operations. Communication takes place between send and receive nodes connected by communication edges. Each communication node is annotated by a pointer either to the data which are to be sent or to the memory location where they are to be received and the size of the message. Communication edges may be either of type **sync** or **async**. Only point-to-point type of communication is supported.

Do, Alt and Guard nodes are used to define conditional (**alt**) and loop (**do**) constructs. Each alternative of an **alt** or **do** contains a special **guard** as its first node controlling the execution of the next sequential graph fragment.

The graphical code of a parallel sort application is depicted in Figure 2.14. Nodes are labeled according to their types and are identified by integer numbers automatically generated by the system.

Meander supports hierarchical design by allowing folding structured subgraphs of the specification graph into a single node. Structured means that the subgraph must have

seq node (SEQ)   create-child node (CC)   do node (DO)   guard node (..G)

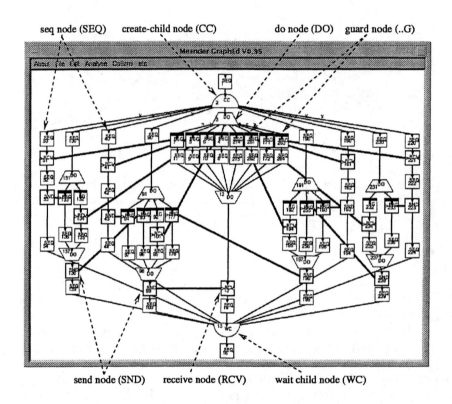

send node (SND)   receive node (RCV)   wait child node (WC)

Figure 2.14: A Parallel Sort Program in Meander

exactly one incoming and one outgoing control line. These kind of subgraphs can also be put into modules and saved separately to support code reuse.

Furthermore, process replication is used for a built-in set of standard topologies (independent processes, grid and torus in 1 up to 3 dimensions, regular n-trees).

The Meander approach to define process creation and communication operations at the same graphical level in one graph is unique among the existing process-based environments. We note that this approach can result in large and chaotic graphs that are very difficult to understand and maintain.

Some limitations of the system might stem from the fact that Meander has been developed originally for transputer based machines although, it has been extended later on to produce C+PVM code. This explains the introduction of CSP like loop and conditional constructs which differ semantically from their counterparts in ordinary procedural languages. Another problem is the lack of support for collective process interactions (i.e., broadcast, etc.).

General characteristics of Meander are summarized in Table 2.6.

Programming Model	*Process based*
Process Model	*Explicit with dynamic creation*
Interaction Types	*Point-to-point synch/asynch data movement*
Interaction Specification	*Explicit, by graphics*
Regular Patterns	*Supported by templates with dynamic replicators*
Hierarchical Design	*Subgraph abstraction*
Visual Code Reuse	*Subgraph intra- and inter-application (modules)*

Table 2.6: General Characteristics of the Meander System

2.3.7   The **EDPEPPS** Programming Environment

The EDPEPPS project aimed at the development of an integrated programming environment for PVM applications [6, 10]. It includes the PVMGraph editor that provides a graphical interface for constructing the code of PVM programs. PVMGraph falls into the class of process-based languages but it uses a unique way to define process interaction graphically.

In PVMGraph, processes (or better to say *tasks* due the strong relationship with PVM) are represented by rectangles on the screen as it is usual in case of a process-based visual language. However, there are no means of defining channels or ports. Instead, (almost) every PVM routine appearing in the code of a process is represented as a separate visual symbol — basically as a small triangle — attached to the task icon. In PVMGraph terminology, they define various *actions* like communication (i.e., sending or receiving message(s)) or creation/destruction of other tasks.

The user can build up a PVM application by creating task icons in the graphical editor and defining various actions for these tasks by visual symbols. From such a graphical description, PVMGraph generates the skeleton PVM/C code of each task. Every action defined graphically in the graph causes a particular PVM routine call to be inserted into the skeleton code. Note, however, that most of the actual parameters of these calls must be defined by the user. Skeleton codes for tasks can be edited by the user with the help of a special text editor that tries to ensure the consistency between the graphical and the text code as much as possible.

A sample master-slave application is depicted in Figure 2.15 together with the skeleton of the master task. Although icons of appropriate send and receive actions can be connected by the user (as it can be seen in Figure 2.15), such connections in the graph are only comments since no extra C code is generated for them, i.e., they are independent from the actual parameters of the corresponding PVM routines.

PVMGraph also supports definition of process groups but without the notion of encapsulation (i.e., without providing sub-graph abstraction). Groups can be defined by (possible overlapped) ellipses in the task graph.

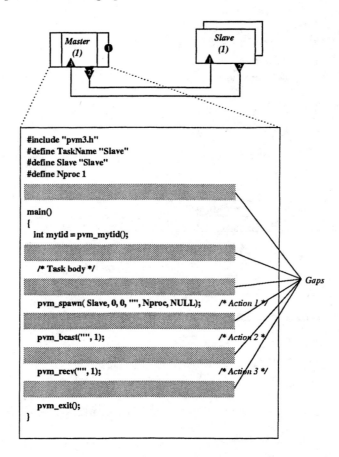

Figure 2.15: Sample Task Graph and Code Skeleton in PVMGraph

A detailed description of PVMGraph can be found in Chapter 18. General characteristics of the system are summarized in Table 2.7.

2.3.8   The **GRADE** Environment

The GRADE programming environment has been developed in the framework of the SEPP and HPCTI Copernicus projects so its graphical language called GRAPNEL is explained in Chapter 10 in detail.

Programming Model	*Process based*
Process Model	*Explicit with dynamic creation*
Interaction Types	*Point-to-point & collective data movement*
Interaction Specification	*Explicit, by text*
Regular Patterns	*Not supported*
Hierarchical Design	*Not supported*
Visual Code Reuse	*Node intra- and inter-application*

Table 2.7: General Characteristics of EDPEPPS/PVMGraph

The GRAPNEL belongs to the class of process based languages. It provides two hierarchical levels of graphical code. The top level is used to construct the communication graph of the processes while the lower one provides the possibility for the user to define every communication action (i.e., send and receive operations) graphically for each process. In fact, the code of each process is defined as a very coarse-grain control flow graph in which all send and receive actions are represented by icons. Coarse-grain means in this context that arbitrary large and complex parts of the process code containing no send or receive operations are defined as text code attached to a single node of the graph. Graphical symbols for conditional and loop constructs are provided since communication operations (that are always defined by icons in GRAPNEL) may occur in a particular branch of control or in a loop body.

In this way, no explicit calls to the underlying MP system's routines appear in the user's code, all of them are generated automatically based on the graphical code of the processes. It ensures independence from the actual underlying MP systems to a high extend thus, GRADE provides the opportunity to run users' application on different MP platforms without modifying their GRAPNEL code provided that the code generator supports those platforms. In practice, the GRP2C code generator is able to produce PVM+(C/C++) code from GRAPNEL programs.

The GRAPNEL code of our *Animation* example application (see Section 2.2.1) is depicted in Figure 2.16. Different windows illustrate the different hierarchical levels of the language. The *Application Window* contains the top level communication graph. Since GRADE provides no support for regular patterns, fix number of *Display* processes must be defined. In the figure, three such processes can be seen (*Display1*, *Display2* and *Display3*) and graphical code of the last one is shown in the *Process Window*.

A more detailed description of the system can be found in Chapter 10. General characteristics are summarized in Table 2.8.

Programming Model	*Process based*
Process Model	*Explicit, static, no support for groups*
Interaction Types	*Point-to-point synch/asynch data movement,*
Interaction Specification	*Explicit, by graphics*
Regular Patterns	*Not supported*
Hierarchical Design	*Partially supported (process level only)*
Visual Code Reuse	*Subgraph intra- and node inter-application*

Table 2.8: General Characteristics of GRADE/GRAPNEL

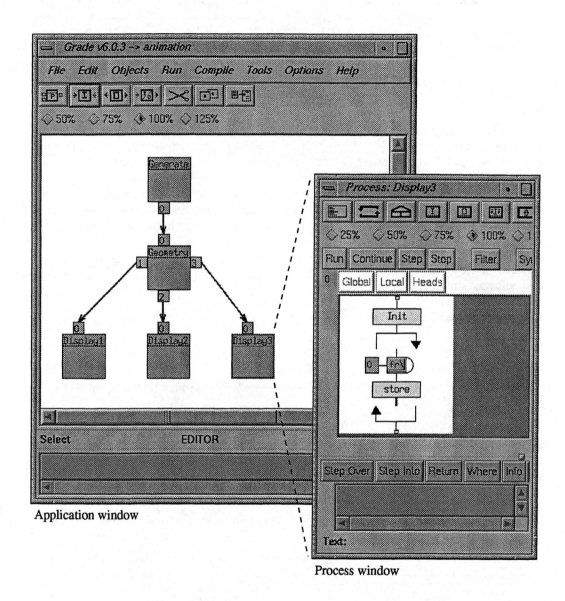

Figure 2.16: The Animation Application in GRAPNEL

2.4   Conclusions and Future trends

In this chapter, a classification and survey of existing message-passing based visual parallel programming languages are presented. Although implementation issues are not addressed here, it is important to emphasize that practical usefulness of any graphical language highly depends on the program development environment into which the model is embedded.

A comfortable and user-friendly integrated program development environment with an adequate abstract visual design methodology can make easier of the parallel application development by orders of magnitude. It can shorten tremendously the development time of prototype applications by hiding details of low-level MP primitives thus, allowing the user to manipulate an application at a more abstract level. Fast prototype creation and easy modification of task decomposition are the key issues for efficient development of distributed and parallel programs. A visual design methodology is a promising candidate to provide adequate solutions to these questions.

Concerning the general visual programming models described in this chapter, the most promising alternative is definitely the process based approach. The TRAPPER environment has already been commercialized and there are some initiatives to do the same with GRADE as well. However, it is still an open question whether they can satisfy the expectations of real application developers.

Since no visual message-passing language could have achieved ultimate success yet, the research in this field is still active. Ongoing high speed evolution of graphical displays and software support (e.g. 3D animation, virtual reality) gives the chance to design and implement more and more complex visual representations of application programs to capture their sophisticated features and runtime behaviour in a more and more complete way.

In general, the future of visual message-passing languages depends on the future of the message-passing paradigm completely. At the time of writing this survey, the MPI standard is spreading at high speed and exhibits spectacular performance results due to optimized implementations made by most of the hardware vendors. On the other hand, virtual shared memory distributed systems present an alternative to message-passing programming. The initiative of the OpenMP standard, which defines text pragmas to be used in ordinary textual programs to make them run in parallel on a virtual shared memory platform, represent a competitive alternative for the MP programming paradigm. Visual support for that type of applications requires rather different techniques than that of distributed memory applications.

References

[1] D. Ahr, A. Bäcker, O. Krämer-Fuhrmann, R. Lovas, H. Mierendorff, H. Schwamborn, J. G. Silva, and K. Wolf. WINPAR - windows based parallel computing. In E. H. D'Hollander, G.R. Joubert, F. J. Peters, and U. Trottenberg, editors, *PARALLEL COMPUTING: Fundamentals, Applications and New Directions*, pages 495–502. Elsevier, Amsterdam, The Netherlands, 1998.

[2] A. Beguelin, J. Dongarra, G. A. Geist, R. Manchek, and V. S. Sunderam. Graphical development tools for network-based concurrent supercomputing. In *Proceedings of Supercomputing 91*, pages 435–444, Alburquerque, 1991.

[3] A. Beguelin, J. Dongarra, G. A. Geist, and V. S. Sunderam. Visualization and debugging in a heterogeneous environment. *IEEE Computer*, 26(6), June 1993.

[4] J. C. Browne, S. I. Hyder, J. Dongarra, K. Moore, and P. Newton. Visual programming and debugging for parallel computing. *IEEE Parallel and Distributed Technology*, 3(1), 1995.

[5] P. T. Cox and T. J. Smedley. Visual languages for the design and development of structured objects. *Journal of visual Languages and Computing*, 8:57–84, 1997.

[6] T. Delaitre, G. R. Ribeiro-Justo, F. Spies, and S Winter. A graphical toolset for simulation modelling of parallel systems. *Parallel Computing*, 22(13):1823–1836, 1997.

[7] A. Geist, A. Beguelin, J. Dongarra, W. Jiang, R. Manchek, and V. S. Sunderam. *PVM: Parallel Virtual Machine – A Users' Guide and Tutorial for Networked Parallel Computing*. MIT Press, 1994.

[8] H. Giese and G. Wirtz. Modular development of correct Meander programs. In *Proceedings of Int. Conf. on Parallel and Distributed Processing Techniques and Applications (PDPTA'97)*, Las Vegas, Nevada, USA, July 1997.

[9] W. Gropp, E. Lusk, and A. Skjellum. *Using MPI : Portable Parallel Programming with the Message-Passing Interface*. MIT Press, 1994.

[10] G. R. Justo, P. Vekariya, T. Delaitre, M. J. Zemerly, and S. C. Winter. Prototype-oriented development of high-performance systems. In *Proceedings of 2nd International Workshop on Software Engineering for Parallel and Distributed Systems*, pages 74–84, Boston, USA, May 1997.

[11] The MathWorks Inc. *Simulink User's Guide*, 1993.

[12] National Instruments Corporation. *LabVIEW for Windows - Tutorial*, 1994.

[13] P. Newton and J. C. Browne. The CODE 2.0 graphical parallel programming language. In *Proceedings of ACM Intl. Conf. on Supercomputing*, 1992.

[14] Pictorius Inc. *Prograph Reference Manual*, 1996.

[15] J. Schaeffer, D. Szafron, G. Lobe, and I. Parsons. The Enterprise model for developing distributed applications. *IEEE Parallel and Distributed Technology*, 1(3):85–96, 1993.

[16] L. Schäfers, C. Scheidler, and O. Krämer-Fuhrmann. Trapper: A graphical programming environment for parallel systems. *Future Generations Computer Systems*, 11:351–361, 1995.

[17] S. Scheidler and L. Schafers. TRAPPER: A graphical programming environment for industrial high-performance applications. In *Proceedings of PARLE'93: Parallel Architectures and Languages Europe*, Munich, Germany, 1993.

[18] A. Singh, J. Schaeffer, and M. Green. A template-based approach to the generation of distributed applications using a network of workstations. *IEEE Transactions of Parallel and Distributed Systems*, 2(1):52–67, 1991.

[19] D. Szafron and J. Schaeffer. An experiment to measure the usability of parallel programming systems. *Concurrency: Practice and Experience*, 8(2):146–166, 1996.

[20] Guido Wirtz. Modularization and process replication in a visual parallel programming language. In *Proc. of IEEE Visual Languages*, St. Louis, USA, September 1994.

Chapter 3

Mapping and Scheduling of Parallel Programs

Ladislav Hluchý, Miquel A. Senar, Miroslav Dobrucký, Tran Dinh Viet,
Ana Ripoll and Ana Cortés

Abstract

A concrete application in distributed computing systems is represented as a set of interacting sequential sub-problems (tasks). In order to achieve a fast response time in such systems, an efficient assignment of tasks to the processors is imperative. In this chapter we describe the models adopted to solve the static mapping problem, a taxonomy of the mapping methods according to the algorithmic strategy used and the review of some mapping tools.

3.1 Introduction

The fast progress of network technologies and sequential processors has made parallel and distributed computing systems, such as massively parallel machines or networks of homogeneous/heterogeneous workstations or PCs, an attractive choice for high-performance computing. Distributed computing, especially on a cluster of loosely-coupled workstations, has become widely used for scientific computing.

A concrete application is a set of interacting sequential sub-problems (tasks). In order to achieve a fast response time in such systems, an efficient assignment of tasks to the processors is imperative. The task assignment problem, also known as the allocation problem or the mapping problem, arises as parallel programs are developed for distributed-memory, message-passing parallel computers. In such systems each processor can only access its local memory. Synchronization and coordination among processors are achieved through explicit message passing. However, the design of efficient applications for parallel systems is not straightforward. An efficient parallel program should exploit the full potential power of the architecture of these systems. Processor idle time and the interprocessor communication overhead may lead to poor utilization of the architecture, hence to poor overall system performance.

Parallel program design for parallel systems can be divided into two steps. The first one is the decomposition of the problem into a set of tasks which can be executed in parallel. The second step is the assignment of these tasks to individual processors of the parallel architecture, also known as mapping, in such a way that the program exploits as much as possible the available system performance. If the tasks of the parallel program have explicit precedence relationship we not only assign tasks to processors, but also have to define the order of execution of the tasks. In this case the mapping problem is referred more specifically as the scheduling problem.

The aim of mapping is to achieve the shortest execution time of parallel programs. However, the execution time cannot be determined from the assignment of tasks. So the primary optimization objectives of mapping are to balance the workload of processors and to minimize the interprocessor communication cost. The first objective means to place tasks that are able to execute concurrently on different processors so as to enhance concurrency. The second objective means to place tasks that communicate frequently on the same processor so as to increase locality. Sometimes the above objectives are in conflict so this will involve tradeoffs. In addition resource limitation may restrict the number of tasks that can be placed on a single processor.

Unfortunately, the mapping problem is known to be NP-complete, meaning that no computationally treatable (polynomial time) algorithm can exist for evaluating these tradeoffs in the general case [12]. Because of this complexity, it is difficult to compute an optimal mapping and numerous heuristic solutions have been proposed representing different tradeoffs between computation cost and quality of mapping.

Mapping can be specified statically or dynamically depending upon the time at which the assignment decisions are made. If the structure of inter-task interactions of the parallel program is statically characterizable at compile time, then a static mapping scheme is very attractive since the mapping analysis only needs to be done once and run-time overheads are minimized. On the other hand, dynamic mapping is the best solution when the behavior of the program is not predictable a priori, that is, shows a great variation depending on the program input values.

When a static solution is adopted, the mapping problem is solved in two phases:

1. A modeling phase analyzes the code of the program and builds at compile time a model of the program characterizing the structure and the interactions of tasks. The information obtained is represented by a weighted program graph including a node for each task of the program.

2. The mapping phase establishes the allocation of tasks using the information in the program graph to minimize a suitable cost function. Depending on the task graph model, this phase could be followed by a scheduling operation. Task graphs with precedence require a scheduling phase to assign an execution order to each task.

In data parallel SPMD (Single Program Multiple Data) applications, every processor executes the same program but on different data. Here mapping is often reduced to the problem of balancing the data properly. This chapter deals with applications consisting of different tasks that are able to run in parallel, i.e., MPMD (Multiple Program Multiple Data) model.

Depending on the characteristics of programs and architectures, different cost functions have been proposed. Almost all the models proposed require an estimation of the average amount of communication (communication cost) and of the average amount of internal computation of each task (computational cost). Both of these costs depend upon an estimation of the number of times each statement is executed during a generic execution of the program.

This chapter is organized as follows. Section 3.2 describes the models adopted to solve the static mapping problem. Section 3.3 presents a taxonomy of the mapping methods according to the algorithmic strategy used and its corresponding complexity. Section 3.4 reviews some mapping tools. Finally, Section 3.5 discusses the main conclusions.

3.2   Models in the Mapping Problem

In broad terms, three aspects of the mapping problem are required to be included in a model [34]: the computation tasks and their communication patterns (program models), the processors and their communications facilities (architecture models), and the function which is used to determine the cost of a mapping (cost function models).

3.2.1   Program models

The mapping problem has been investigated for two different models used for representing the program graph, the *Directed Acyclic Graph* (DAG) with task precedence relations [22] and the *Task Interaction Graph* (TIG) [36] (see Figure 3.1).

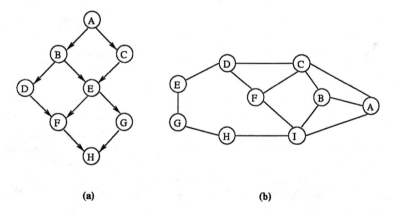

(a)   (b)

Figure 3.1: Examples of DAG (a) and TIG (b) models.

The choice of the program model depends on the abstraction level we are interested in and on the structure of the computations. The DAG model is well suitable for computations where interactions take place only in the beginning and at the end of each task (e.g., when we are dealing with parallelism at the instruction level extracted from a sequential program). On the other hand, programs in which communications among tasks can take place at any time, in general according to iterative and non-deterministic patterns, are best modeled by a TIG. In the following definitions of DAG and TIG the differences between them are highlighted.

The DAG model

In the DAG model, a parallel program is represented by a *Directed Acyclic Graph* (DAG). A graph $GT(V, E)$, where $V = \{V_1, V_2, \dots V_v\}$ is the set of nodes and $E \subset V \times V$ is the set of **directed** edges, is a DAG if and only if E represents a partial ordering among the nodes in V. The nodes represent the program tasks and the directed edges represent both the precedence relationship and the communication among the tasks. A function $ET : V \to \mathcal{R}^+$, briefly $ET(V_i) = e_i$, gives the computation cost of tasks and $CT : E \to \mathcal{R}^+$, briefly $CT(V_i, V_j) = c_{ij}$, gives the communication cost of message passing on edges, where $\mathcal{R}^+$ is the set of non-negative real numbers. We define $c_{ij} = 0$ for not-connected nodes. Therefore, weights are associated with both nodes and edges representing, respectively, the computational cost (e_i) of task V_i and the communication (c_{ij}) cost between tasks V_i and V_j.

A task V_i is a **parent** of a task V_j and V_j is a child of V_i if $(V_i, V_j) \in E$. Each task receives data from its parent, processes it and sends the results to its children for further processing. A task V_i is ready to execute on processor P_k only if all its parents have finished and the data from them have arrived on P_k. If tasks V_i, V_j, where $(V_i, V_j) \in E$, are assigned to the same processor, the communication delay between them is zero, otherwise it is c_{ij}.

The DAG model is widely used in static scheduling because it can represent both the precedence relationship and the communication delay. The precedence relationship is especially important for scheduling; therefore almost all static scheduling algorithms are based on the model.

The TIG model

In the TIG model, a parallel program is represented by a *Task Interaction Graph* (TIG) $GT(V, E)$, where $V = \{V_1, V_2, \dots V_v\}$ is the set of nodes and $E \subset V \times V$ is the set of edges. The nodes represent the program tasks and the edges represent the **mutual** communication among the tasks. A function $ET : V \to \mathcal{R}^+$ gives the computation cost of tasks and $CT : E \to \mathcal{R}^+$ gives the communication cost for message passing on edges. As for the DAG model we define $ET(V_i) = e_i$, $CT(V_i, V_j) = c_{ij}$ and for not-connected nodes $c_{ij} = 0$.

A task V_i is a **neighbor** of a task V_j if $(V_i, V_j) \in E$. The relationship is **commutative**, it means that if $(V_i, V_j) \in E$ then $(V_j, V_i) \in E$. Tasks in TIG exchange information during their execution. There is no precedence relationship among tasks; each task cooperates with its neighbors. If tasks V_i, V_j, where $(V_i, V_j) \in E$, are assigned to the same processor, the communication cost between them is zero, otherwise it is c_{ij}.

The TIG model is used to represent programs, where their tasks are considered to be executed simultaneously. In this model, temporal dependencies in the execution of tasks are not explicitly addressed: all the tasks are considered simultaneously executable and communications can take place at any time during the computation. Also in this case, nodes and edges are usually labeled with weights describing computational and communication costs.

3.2.2 Architecture models

In order to solve the mapping problem, the parallel architecture must also be modeled in a way that represents its architectural features. Parallel architectures can easily be represented by a *Processor Organization Graph* (POG) $GA(P, L)$ where nodes $P = \{P_1, P_2, \dots P_p\}$ represent the processors and undirected edges L represent bidirectional physical communication channels or links. In fact, POG is a graphical representation of the interconnection topology used for the organization of the processors of the parallel architecture. In such graph, nodes and edges are not associated with weights if the parallel system is homogeneous with identical processors and communication links. On the other hand, in systems with unrelated processors, weights are associated with each processor indicating its processing speed.

In a parallel architecture, two adjacent processors communicate with each other over the communication link connecting them. However, each nonadjacent pair of processors can also communicate with each other by means of software or hardware routing. These communications are usually routed in a static manner over the shortest paths in terms of the number of links between the communicating pairs of processors. The communication cost between nonadjacent pairs of processors depends on message size, on the distance d_{ij} between source i and destination j processors and on the contention for paths in the processor graph between the communication and other communications. Approaches to modeling contention in parallel systems are complicated and are usually presented as modeling methodologies rather than being proposed as objective functions in mapping problems [34].

Information in a processing system can be transferred from source to destination either directly or indirectly, with indirect transfer in general requiring a more complex communication structure (see Figure 3.2). For internal communications $(i = j)$ $d_{ii} = 0$; for direct and indirect POG with centralized routing $d_{ij} = 1$, $i \neq j$, for indirect POG with decentralized routing $d_{ij} \geq 1$.

If the parallel machine is **heterogeneous**, each task $V_i \in V$ in graph S has more than one load value (for each processor's node it has one load value), i.e., it is represented by **extended** function $ET : V \times P \to \mathcal{R}^+$. Similarly, communication cost is represented by **extended** function $CT : E \times L \to \mathcal{R}^+$.

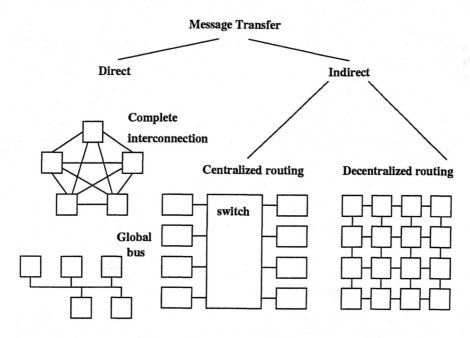

Figure 3.2: Architecture models.

3.2.3   Cost function models

The objective in mapping a program graph to an architecture graph is the minimization of the expected execution time of the parallel program on the target architecture. The quality of a certain mapping will depend on the execution time of the parallel program. A mapping has better quality if the obtained assignment reduces the execution time of the application in comparison to its execution time with a different assignment. Thus the mapping problem can be seen as an optimization problem by defining a cost function that is directly related to the execution time and must be minimized. For **heterogeneous** architectures the **extended** *ET* and *CT* functions should be used (see Section 3.2.2). Other names for such a cost function are also fitness function, energy, aspiration criterion etc. (see Section 3.3.3).

Cost function for the DAG model

The only objective function for the DAG model is the overall execution time of the scheduled program, also called **makespan**. It is the time interval from the start of the first task to the end of the last task. Tasks are executed in non-preemptive mode with the precedence constraint.

A **schedule** of the task graph $GT(V, E)$ on a system of p processors is a function S that maps each task to a processor by using a cost function. Formally, $S : V \rightarrow P \times [0, \infty]$. If $S(V_i) = (P_k, t)$ for some $V_i \in V$, we say that task V_i is mapped to processor $P_k \in P$ at time t.

Assume that a DAG $GT(V, E)$ is scheduled on p processors. The function $PR(V_i)$ gives the processor on which the task V_i is executed, $PA(V_i)$ is the set of parents of V_i, $RT(V_i)$ gives the time when task V_i is ready to execute, $ST(V_i)$ is the time when task V_i starts and $FT(V_i)$ is the time when task V_i finishes, $LT(V_i)$ is the time when the task before V_i on $PR(V_i)$ finishes. If V_i is the first task on $PR(V_i)$, $LT(V_i) = 0$.

A task V_i is ready when all its parents have been executed and data from them have arrived on $PR(V_i)$. It means:

$$RT(V_i) = \max_{V_k \in PA(V_i)} (FT(V_k) + CT(V_k, V_i) * d_{PR(V_k), PR(V_i)}, 0) \tag{3.1}$$

If $PA(V_i)$ is empty, value 0 will take place in the max function. Task V_i can start when it is ready and its processor is idle. It means that the last task on $PR(V_i)$ has finished:

$$ST(V_i) = max(RT(V_i), LT(V_i))$$

$$FT(V_i) = ST(V_i) + ET(V_i) \tag{3.2}$$

The cost function of a DAG $GT(V, E)$ is the time when its last task finishes:

$$CF = max(FT(V_i) | V_i \in V) \tag{3.3}$$

An example of DAG scheduling

An example of DAG is shown on Figure 3.3a. The number above each node and edge is the execution time of the node and the communication time of the edge, respectively. An example of the schedule of this DAG on two processors is shown in Figure 3.3b. When two tasks are assigned to the same processor, the communication between them is neglected. The value of the cost function is the time when the last task finishes, i.e., 17.

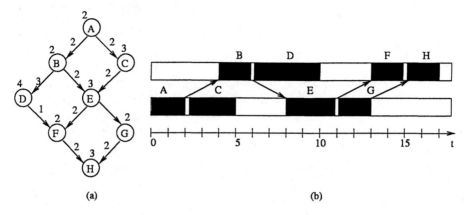

Figure 3.3: Example of scheduling the DAG.

Cost function for the TIG model

In practice, the execution time of a program modeled as a TIG, is difficult to evaluate due to the appearance of run-time dependencies; therefore, a set of cost functions have been proposed in the literature. On one hand, these cost functions try to approximate the execution time expected for the application and, on the other hand, they simplify the real situation in order to become easy to use in a certain heuristic. Thus, the mapping problem can be seen as an optimization problem by defining a cost function, CF, that is directly related to the execution time and must be minimized.

In general, cost functions consider both computation and communication costs incurred by each task in the TIG, but they may be handled in different ways. Basically, cost functions that have been used with the task-mapping problem may be broadly categorized as belonging to one of two models: a *minimax* model [30, 49] or a *summed total cost* model [20, 36].

In the model of the **minimax cost function**, the cost incurred by each processor (computation cost + communication cost) for a certain mapping M, known as *processor work load*, is estimated and the maximum cost between all processors is to be minimized. The cost of each processor q is the total cost due to computation and communication of all tasks mapped onto it.

A **mapping** of the task graph $GT(V, E)$ on a system of p processors is a function M that maps each task to a processor by using cost function. Formally, $M : V \rightarrow P$. If $M(V_i) = P_k$ for some $V_i \in V$, we say that task V_i is mapped to processor $P_k \in P$.

$$cost(q) = \alpha * \sum_{i|M(V_i)=q} e_i + \beta * \sum_{\substack{i|M(V_i) = q, \\ j|M(V_j) = r \neq q}} c_{ij} * d_{qr} \ , \quad P_q \in P \qquad (3.4)$$

e_i being the computational weight of task V_i; c_{ij} denotes the communication weight for the edge that joins task V_i and task V_j; and $M(V_i)$ denotes the processor to which task V_i is mapped to. The proportionality constants α and β represent the relative cost of a computation unit and a communication unit, respectively. The minimax cost function used to evaluate the quality of a mapping instance M is defined by the cost of the most loaded processor:

$$cost\_minimax(M) = \max_{\forall q \mid P_q \in P} (cost(q)). \tag{3.5}$$

Therefore, the objective of a mapping heuristic using the minimax cost model consists of finding assignments that minimize the cost of the most loaded processor.

The **summed cost function** model tries to balance the computation cost between all the processors, i.e., by minimizing the *load imbalance cost* $Imb(q)$, while keeping the amount of interprocessor communication to a minimum, i.e., by minimizing the *global communication cost*. The summed cost function can be formulated as:

$$cost\_summed(M) = \delta * \sum_{\forall q \mid P_q \in P} Imb(q) + \varphi * \sum_{\forall q \mid P_q \in P} \sum_{\substack{i \mid M(V_i) = q, \\ j \mid M(V_j) = r \neq q}} c_{ij} * d_{qr}$$

$$Imb(q) = \left| \sum_{i \mid M(V_i) = q} e_i - \overline{W} \right| \tag{3.6}$$

$\overline{W}$ being the average computational weight for all the processors. The first term in the addition stands for the load imbalance of all the processors, while the second term indicates the total communication cost incurred between pairs of tasks assigned to different processors. The proportionality constants δ and φ reflect the relative penalties for computation load imbalance and communication, respectively. As pointed out in [11], whereas α and β used in the minimax cost model capture the physical system parameters of instruction cycle time and interprocessor communication latency per word, respectively, a physical interpretation for δ and φ under the summed cost model is not as readily given.

An example of TIG mapping

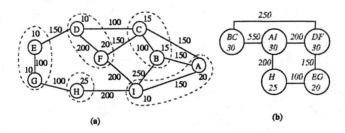

(a)   (b)

Figure 3.4: Example of mapping the TIG: (a)task graph (b)processor graph. Mapping is depicted on both pictures by dashed ellipses (a) or italic font (b). Imbalancing value is 8.33%, $\overline{W} = 27$, external communication 1450 and internal communication 550.

An example of how to map a parallel program consisting of 9 communicating tasks represented by a TIG graph into a 5-processor heterogeneous type parallel computer is shown in Figure 3.4. All processors have equal power and all communication links are equally fast, but some processors do not have direct connection and thus a communication mechanism is necessary for the transfer of data through intermediaries. Therefore, for communication cost function part $d_{xy} * c_{ij}$ was chosen, where d_{xy} is the distance between processors, i.e., the number of communication lines through which the transferred data have to pass, and c_{ij} is the value of the original function for the case of a full-connected architecture.

The conditions of architecture can be also given such that when there is no direct link between processors, the communicating tasks cannot be placed on such processors. In our example, we have succeeded to do so. Then, it is good to choose for d_{xy} a function with three values (0 for zero distance, 1 for distance 1 and a large enough number, e.g. 9999, for larger distances) rather than the distance function.

The formula for computing the imbalance was chosen so that $Imb() = 100\%$ would correspond to the state when all tasks are located on the same processor, and $Imb() = 0$ corresponds to the state of total uniform balancing, which often cannot be achieved.

3.3   A Taxonomy of Mapping Strategies

As we have pointed out in Section 3.1, the mapping problem is known to be NP-complete except in a few special situations with very unrealistic constraints that do not hold in practice. According to the algorithmic method followed by mapping strategies proposed in the literature, task-mapping algorithms for DAGs and TIGs can be classified according to the taxonomy shown in Figure 3.5.

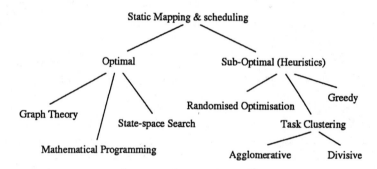

Figure 3.5: Taxonomy of mapping and scheduling strategies.

Optimal algorithms for TIGs yield solutions in a polynomial time by restricting the structure of the programs and/or the parallel system using mathematical programming [52] or graph theory [28, 46]. Non-restricted optimal algorithms consider the problem in a more general context using a state-space search approach and they give optimal solutions but not necessarily in a polynomial time [21, 43]. Optimal solutions for DAGs exist for scheduling tree-structured task graphs with identical computation costs on an arbitrary number of processors and scheduling arbitrary task graphs with identical computation costs on two processors [17, 42]. As a consequence, non-restricted optimal solutions can only be used when the space of configurations is small enough; for instance few tasks have to be allocated to a machine with a small number of processors. These algorithms give the optimal solutions but in practical cases they can not be used because of the combinatorial explosion of the number of solutions.

Hence, several **heuristic** algorithms capable of producing **sub-optimal** solutions in a reasonable amount of computation time are proposed. According to their computational complexity, heuristic methods fall into three main categories: Greedy algorithms, Randomized optimization (or iterative) algorithms and Task Clustering algorithms.

Greedy algorithms assign one task at each step until a complete assignment is obtained. In general, mapping is done without backtracking: the assignment of one task on one processor is based on a criterion that depends on the assignment of previously scanned tasks. In these algorithms the tasks are first sorted usually on a given criterion and then are mapped in that order on the processors.

Randomized optimization (or iterative) algorithms start from a complete initial solution (or a population of complete solutions) and search for an improvement in the assignment. Usually, this initial solution is found at random or, better, using some greedy mapping. These algorithms improve that solution by exchanging or moving tasks between processors (e.g. Simulated Annealing or Tabu Search) or by merging previous solutions (Genetic Algorithms). The algorithms try these improvements actions iteratively (for that reason they are also known as iterative algorithms) and, moreover, they also use some kind of random perturbation mechanism to skip local minima and to obtain better solutions.

Task clustering heuristics look for a trade-off between the computational efficiency of greedy methods and the solution quality of the pure iterative methods by merging some tasks into clusters before mapping, thus increasing grain size (also decreasing problem size). Clustering algorithms can be distinguished between two classes of clustering:

1. Agglomerative Algorithms. The graph is initially considered to have N clusters of 1 element each. $N - p$ steps are made through the graph where each step merges the two most suitable clusters (p being the number of processors).

2. Divisive Algorithms. Initially, the graph is considered to be a single cluster, and then is successively split until the number of final clusters is equal to the number of processors.

According to the underlying architecture adopted (heterogeneous/homogeneous processors), the program model adopted (DAG/TIG) and the algorithmic method used (Greedy, Randomized, Clustering), mapping and scheduling strategies can be classified as Table 3.1 shows. The table is not an exhaustive classification but reflects some representative strategies for the corresponding category.

Mapping					
Program model		DAG		TIG	
Architecture		Homogen.	Heterogen.	Homogen.	Heterogen.
Clustering	Divisive	————	————	[35] [11] [28]	[30] [3] [18]
	Agglomerat.	[19] [48] [51] [25]	[44]	[49] [39]	[8]
Randomized		[26]	[45] [47]	[5] [7]	[1] [15] [38]
Greedy		[14]	———	[7]	———

Table 3.1: Classification of representative heuristic mapping strategies.

3.3.1   Optimal algorithms

Several strategies can be developed for obtaining exact algorithms. These algorithms used for solving the mapping problem have an exponential complexity. A lot of them are issued from artificial intelligence or operations research like the explorations of a search tree: Branch and Bound, Breadth first search, Best first search, A^*, etc. [43, 46]. When designing exact algorithms, the main difficulty is to reduce the space of the solutions trying to eliminate "silly" solutions. We will now describe a method based on this last idea.

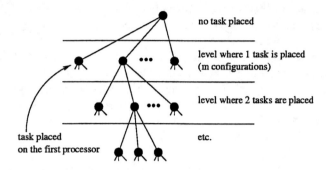

Figure 3.6: An A^* search.

The idea behind the A^* algorithm is to explore all the possible solutions organized as a tree (the search tree) but not in an exhaustive way. It consists of a best first search guided by an appropriated heuristics whose goal is to limit the number of configurations to explore. Each node n of the search tree represents a partial configuration. The tree includes p^v nodes. The algorithm computes the cost of each partial mapping done $g(n)$ to which a sub-estimation $h(n)$ of the cost of all realizable mappings based on this partial solution is added. Then, the node n whose cost function $f(n) = g(n) + h(n)$ is the lowest is developed. The sub-estimation of the cost is based on a heuristic, which must be as close as possible to the cost function. This restricts the search only to the most interesting branches of the tree. For instance, any sub-optimal algorithm for which a lower bound of $h(n)$ is known can be used as the heuristic.

Many other strategies can be used. For instance, classical graph theory methods like maximum flow or cutting [30, 37], or some techniques originated from mathematical programming (combinatorial optimization, dynamic programming, etc.). Note that such methods can also be used for finding good heuristic functions for the A^*.

The quality of a mapping is estimated using a global cost function. A possible heuristic part of the A^* could be the following algorithm [43]: after the placement of the ith task, a sub-estimation of the placement cost of the $(i+1)^{th}$ task is computed, corresponding to 3.4, 3.5 and so choosing for $(i+1)^{th}$ task the same processor as for i or another. If i is on the most loaded processor (the processor determining the value of the objective function), then $h(n)$ is taken equal to this sub-estimation, otherwise it is taken as zero.

3.3.2   Greedy algorithms

In a greedy algorithm, the mapping or scheduling is done without backtracking (a choice already made can never be reconsidered). The mapping or scheduling of the ith task is based on a criterion depending on the mapping or scheduling of the $(i-1)^{th}$ first tasks. Two kinds of greedy algorithms can be envisaged for the mapping or scheduling problem: the first ones are based on empirical methods and the second ones come from the relaxation of classical graph theory algorithms which are optimal for some restricted cases [28, 30, 46]. Greedy algorithms are easy to implement and have a polynomial complexity, often less than $\mathcal{O}(p^3)$.

The greedy algorithms for scheduling (DAG) are in literature known rather as **priority list scheduling** or **heuristic scheduling**. Tasks in DAG model have precedence constraints, so it is natural to consider the tasks to be scheduled according to the partial order of them. Since several tasks may be ready for scheduling at the same time, some heuristics have to be used to choose which task should be scheduled sooner.

The basic idea of priority list scheduling is choosing tasks according to their priorities. The tasks which are ready to execute are arranged to a waiting queue in descending order of priorities. As soon as a processor is idle, we remove the task with the highest priority from the waiting queue and assign it to the processor. If there is no task in the waiting queue, the processor remains idle.

There are many different heuristics, which can be used to calculate priorities of tasks. In general we can distinguish two classes of priorities: static and dynamic. Static priorities can be determined before the scheduling process and do not change, while dynamic priorities are calculated during the scheduling process and their values can be changed in relation to processors. Typical examples of dynamic priorities are Earliest Enable, Least Scheduled Flexibility [10]. Typical examples of static priorities are Largest Processing Time (also called Heaviest Task First), Highest Level First, Longest Path First [10].

Examples of greedy scheduling algorithms (for DAG):

(i) **HLF** (Highest Level First): In HLF, the priority of tasks depends on the location of tasks in DAG. Tasks located at the higher level have higher priority and are executed sooner.

(ii) **LPF** (Longest Path First): In LPF, the priority of a task depends on the length of its exit path. Tasks with longer exit path have higher priority.

(iii) **ETF** (Earliest Task First): In ETF, the priority of a task depends on the length of its entry path. Tasks with shorter entry path have higher priority.

Examples of greedy mapping algorithms (for TIG):

(i) The **modulo** algorithm - is one of the simplest. It is a greedy algorithm that consists of placing the ith task onto the (i^{th} modulo m) processor. So this algorithm has the same behavior as a random mapping algorithm with a great number of tasks.

(ii) **LPTF** (Largest Processing Time First) is a heuristic whose criterion is restricted to load balancing. The tasks are first sorted by decreasing computation costs. Next the first task is placed on the first processor. The ith task is placed on the less loaded processor.

(iii) **LGCF** (Largest Global Cost First) algorithm tries to load balance the total cost of the different tasks among the processors. The tasks are first sorted by decreasing global computation and communication costs. Next the first task is placed on the first processor. The ith task is placed on the less globally loaded (communication and computation costs taken into account) processor.

3.3.3 Iterative (randomized) algorithms

Iterative algorithms start from an initial solution and try to improve it. Note that the initial solution can be found using a greedy algorithm. Usual iterative algorithms try to exchange tasks between processors to locally improve the solution. Most such algorithms use random perturbations to leave local minima and to jump to better solutions.

A well-known iterative algorithm is the Bokhari algorithm [5]. Its cost function (called *cardinality*) takes into account the number of tasks correctly mapped on the processor network and uses pair-wise exchanges of tasks to improve it. The basic hypothesis is that the number of tasks must be equal to the number of processors. Grouping methods (clustering) must be used to take into account a greater number of tasks.

The basic iterative algorithm, called *hill climbing*, consists of starting from a given solution and to improve it iteratively using a neighborhood relation. This solution leads directly to a local optimum.

Simulated annealing

One well known iterative method is the simulated annealing [6]. This method is based on an analogy with statistical physics. The annealing technique is used to obtain a metal with the most possible regular structure. It consists of heating the metal and reducing slowly the heat so that it keeps its equilibrium. When the heat is low enough, the metal is in an equilibrium state corresponding to its minimal energy. At high temperature, there is a lot of thermic agitation, which can locally increase the energy of the system. This phenomenon occurs with a given probability decreasing with the heat. It corresponds mathematically to give a chance to leave a local minimum of the function to optimize.

The corresponding algorithm consists of improving a mapping by task exchanges. The percentage of bad exchanges (leading to a worse solution) is high at the beginning and will decrease to zero during the execution of the algorithm. However, this algorithm is very hard to tune: to choose the starting heat, to find the heat decreasing steps, etc.

In our context a lattice defect (analogy to physics) corresponds to a mapping M with the value of cost function $CF(M)$ higher than its optimal value. The current value $CF(M)$ is formally interpreted as the energy of a physical system with a structure described by the mapping M. An ensemble of such a system in thermal equilibrium is simulated. As the parameter T (a formal analogy of temperature) is decreasing, the system is frozen out to a state with the current value $CF(M)$ low. If the mapping M is transformed onto another mapping M_{new}, then the resulting mapping is accepted if it gives the lower value of CF; otherwise, the new mapping is accepted with probability $exp(CF(M) - CF(M_{new})/T)$.

In each temperature step a pool N of mappings can be examined. The annealing schedule required some experimentation. The procedure is initialized by random generation of N mappings. The starting temperature T_{max} must be chosen, so that initial percentage of successful applications with respect to all applications should be roughly 50%. We proceed downwards in multiplicative steps amounting to a 20% decrease in T. The whole optimization process is stopped, if a current value of T becomes smaller than the value T_{min}.

Tabu search

Tabu search is an iterative meta-heuristic [13]. It tries to find the best neighbor of a given solution. To avoid cycling and local optima, a tabu list is established. This tabu list contains information concerning the last moves. A tabu move is not allowed excepted if an aspiration criterion (cost function) is satisfied (if the proposed neighbor gives a better value of the objective function). A lot of parameters have to be tuned or defined: the neighborhood relation, the tabu list attributes, the tabu list length, the aspiration criterion, etc. A lot of improvements can also be taken into account, such as some diversification functions, intensification functions, a tabu list with dynamic length, etc.

Genetic algorithms

Genetic algorithms (GA) were developed to study the adaptive processes of natural systems and to develop artificial systems that mimic the adaptive mechanism of natural systems. Recently, genetic algorithms have been successfully applied to various optimization problems [15, 45, 47].

Genetic algorithms consist of a string representation ("genes") of the nodes in the solution search space, a set of genetic operators for generating new search nodes and a fitness function to evaluate the search nodes. The fitness (cost) function is opposite of the cost function, the node with smaller value of the cost function has larger fitness. The genetic operators are *crossover* and *mutation*. The crossover function exchanges parts of genes of two nodes (parents) in order to create a new node (child) and the mutation function makes a small modification in the gene of the new node. At the beginning, GA creates a set of initial solution nodes, also called population. At each iteration step, GA chooses two genes with larger fitness from population, performs genetic operation on them to create a new node (reproduction process). The best fit nodes have higher chance to be chosen for the reproduction process, so their good properties can be inherited by their children and expanded, when the unfit nodes will be removed from the population.

The diffusion method for static mapping

The diffusion method looks for the most loaded (in terms of computation and communication costs) processor and tries to decrease its load. First it tries to transfer tasks from this processor to other ones; if that is impossible, it tries to exchange a task from this processor with a task of another processor. This leads to a local minimum. The principle of the diffusion method can be represented by the following procedures [4, 15]. In the starting condition all tasks are located at the root node of the multicomputer network. The tasks are transferred by centrifugal force $f1$ (following from the requirement of uniform processor load), against which centripetal force $f2$ is acting, trying to keep the processes with mutual communication as close to each other as possible. This way, uniform load is obtained and this method can be considered as an improvement of the "pure" load balancing method. The resulting sum of forces is a vector with components for each task placed in a node and directed to each communication link (to all its neighbors). A task and a direction with maximum (positive) value are chosen. The following relation is the definition of changes in the cost function, where $\alpha(t) = const.$ and function $g(t)$ hides the weight coefficient:

$$\Delta CF(M) = \alpha(t).f1(t) + g(t).f2(t) \tag{3.7}$$

where t is the iteration step. Individual forces $f1_{ijk}$ and $f2_{ij}$ are calculated in each iteration for each node i from set of nodes P and for each possible transfer direction (into node j) of each task k from set of tasks V located on it.

The HME method

The heuristic move-exchange method was proposed in [38]. The optimization method is described as follows: the tasks are randomly assigned to the processors. This configuration is recorded as the `best_configuration` and its cost as the `best_cost`. While there are moves which decrease the cost function value, that move which decreases the cost function the most is done. Next, if there are any exchanges which decrease the cost function value, then that exchange which decreases the cost function the most is done and the algorithm starts with moves again. If there are no such moves and exchanges, the value of the current configuration is appended to a queue of cost function values of length L. If the current cost function value is less than that of the `best_cost` achieved, we record the current configuration as the `best_configuration` and the current cost as the `best_cost`.

If the elements in the queue are in strictly descending order of the cost function, then R random moves are performed which change the configuration, and then the moves and exchanges are performed again. If that is not so and the queue is full, the algorithm exits. If that is not so and the queue is not full yet, all but the last element in the queue are deleted, and R random moves are performed, thus changing the configuration and returning to the moves and exchanges.

3.3.4 Clustering strategies

As stated before, clustering strategies can be classified as *Agglomerative* or *Divisive*. It can be seen from Table 3.1 that, in general, clustering algorithms for DAGs belong to the Agglomerative class because the existence of vertex dependencies constitutes an additional criterion for traversing the graph that guides the cluster merging. Clustering algorithms for TIGs belong either to the Agglomerative class or the Divisive class.

Clustering strategies for DAGs

Clustering strategies for DAGs have been proposed with large variations in the models adopted for both programs and architectures. On one hand, there is a set of strategies that assume the availability of an unlimited number of processors. On the other hand, another set of strategies assume that the number of processors is limited, and the processors are either fully connected or arbitrarily connected. Moreover, when the number of processors is considered to be limited, the scheduling could be solved by means of either a one-step approach or a two-step approach. DAG strategies that solve the mapping problem in one step take into account the underlying architecture from the beginning of the assignment process. In contrast, DAG strategies based in the two-step approach solve the scheduling problem using the following procedure:

1. Map the task graphs on an unbounded number of completely connected processors. That will create clusters of tasks, with the constraint that all tasks in a cluster have to execute on the same processor. We can deal with all tasks in a cluster as a single large task. This step is called *grain packing* or *task clustering*. It helps to reduce the number of tasks and increase the granularity.

2. If the number of cluster is larger than the number of physical processors, then merge the clusters to the number of physical processor. Usually, a heuristic strategy for TIGs is applied at this step (the cluster graph is TIG). Afterwards, the final schedule of tasks

is computed taking into account the delay incurred by communications due to processor distances.

Heuristics based in this two-step approach usually exhibit a complexity lower than heuristics based on a single step. Moreover they have proved to be well suited when the task graph is at fine grain level. In this case, both iterative and greedy iterative algorithms become ineffective because of the large number of tasks and the large communication weights.

Moreover, there exists also a separate group of approaches that solve the scheduling problem using task duplication, i.e., tasks can appear in several processors [2, 24, 32, 33]. When communication cost is large, sometimes it is worth creating duplicates of tasks on processors, where their results are needed, in order to minimize the communication cost. In fine-grain task graphs, communication is more critical than computation, so using task duplication can reduce the overall execution time. However, it increases the processors load, so it should only be used when the number of computation resources available is enough.

A complete overview of the different strategies is out of the scope of this section. However, below we will briefly review three of the most efficient strategies that do not use task duplication and have been proposed to machines with either an unbounded number of processors or machines with a fixed number of fully connected processors. A more extensive taxonomy on the general scheduling problem can be found in [9] and a recent taxonomy is also presented in [27]. The three strategies reviewed below are based on the Critical Path (CP) of the program graph. That means that they determine scheduling order or give a higher priority to a node that belongs to the critical path.

(i) **Dominant Sequence Clustering (DSC).** The DSC algorithm [51] is based on the *dominant sequence*, which is the critical path of the partially scheduled task graph at each step. At each step, the DSC algorithm checks whether the highest CP node is ready. If it is ready, the node is scheduled to a processor that allows the minimum start time. It may require rescheduling some of parent nodes of the node to the same processor. If the highest CP node is not ready, the DSC algorithm chooses the highest node that lies on the path leading to the CP for scheduling. The node will be assigned to a processor that does not increase the length of CP. This strategy allows an incremental detection of the next highest CP node and minimizes the length of CP, as well as the overall execution time.

(ii) **Dynamic Critical Path (DCP).** The DCP algorithm [25] uses the *dynamic critical path*, which is the critical path of the partially scheduled task graph at each step, to define a dynamic priority for each node. Nodes on the dynamic critical path have the highest priority. The start time of scheduled nodes is not fixed and can change until all nodes have been scheduled. At each step, DCP chooses the node with the highest priority and looks for the most suitable processor for it in order to minimize the start time of the node's critical child.

(iii) **Modified Critical Path (MCP).** The MCP algorithm [49] is based on the concept called the latest possible start time of a node. This time is determined by traversing the task graph upward from the exit nodes to the entry nodes and pulling the nodes downwards as much as possible constrained by the length of the CP. The latest possible start time is computed for all nodes and each node is associated also with a list of possible start times. The algorithm creates also a sorted list of all nodes according to the latest start time. At each step, the first node in the list is removed from it and scheduled to the processor giving the earliest start time.

(iv) **On the performance of clustering strategies for DAGs.** From the performance point of view, one of the most recent and extensive studies can be found in [27]. Although the authors consider that further research is required in this area, their work provides several important findings: for instance, they state that strategies that emphasize the scheduling of nodes that belong to the critical path are in general better than algorithms that do not do it. Moreover, the use of a dynamic critical path (like in DSC and DCP algorithms) proves to be better than the use of a static critical path.

Task clustering for TIGs

Task Clustering strategies proposed in the literature for TIGs belong both to the agglomerative and the divisive classes. Many solutions include a pure clustering phase followed by a second phase that consists of an iterative algorithm. This iterative algorithm uses a basic mechanism of task movements and/or task exchanges between cluster that is similar to the mechanism used by several randomized strategies. However, in contrast to randomized strategies, this iterative phase does not include any mechanism of random perturbations to skip local minima. In that sense, the clustering phase obtains a good solution that needs only to be slightly improved by a simple iterative phase that does not incur in the time complexity of pure randomized methods.

Strategies for TIGs can be further classified into single-step and two-step algorithms according to their considerations of the underlying architecture. Single-step algorithms take into account the interconnection network from the beginning. In contrast, two-step clustering algorithms perform a first allocation considering an architecture with fully connected processors and then they perform a second allocation of the clustered graph taken into account the interconnection network.

Moreover, strategies in the agglomerative class can also be divided into edge-directed or vertex-directed methods, depending on whether the algorithm selects an edge or a vertex at each step in order to merge two clusters.

Like in the DAG case, a complete overview of the different strategies is out of the scope of this section. Below we will briefly review some significant strategies that have been proposed to either heterogeneous or homogeneous systems and exhibit a high degree of generality, without imposing severe restrictions in the problem formulation.

Mincut-maxflow methods. This kind of strategies is based in the mincut-maxflow algorithm that was used originally by Stone to obtain optimal solutions in heterogeneous systems with two processors [46]. Basically, all the methods transform the original task graph into an extended task graph. This transformation usually consists of the inclusion of two new nodes in the task graph: a source node and a terminal node. These nodes are connected to the rest of the graph with additional arcs. The weight of the additional arcs depends on a formula that reflects, for instance, the different computation cost of each task in each processor and some characteristics of the interconnection system. Once the extended task graph is constructed, a mincut-maxflow algorithm is applied that splits the graph in two and a partial allocation is found. After applying the graph transformation and the mincut-maxflow algorithm several times the complete allocation is found. In this group of methods, V.M.Lo [30] presents a generalization of Stone's method that can be applied to any number of processors; Lee and Shin [28] apply a similar strategy for homogeneous systems with the additional concept of *attached tasks*; and Hui and Chanson [18] reduce the graph by applying a sequence of merging steps and use the mincut algorithm to merge several nodes at each step.

Allocation by Recursive Mincut (ARM). This is a divisive algorithm proposed in [11] to map TIGs onto hypercube architectures. It is based on the mincut heuristic for graph bisection proposed by Kernighan and Lin [23]. The ARM strategy partitions the TIG into as many clusters as the number of processors. The original TIG is considered to be a single cluster and is recursively divided into two partitions with a vertex-weight as equal as possible. Moreover, the algorithm tries to obtain partitions with minimal total weight of inter-partition edges by using a sequence of maximally improving node transfers from the partition with currently greater load to the partition with lower load. Once the two partitions at one step are found, they are partially assigned to a sub-cube of the architecture. This means that at level k of the bisection process, for each task, the kth bit of the address of its processor assignment is determined. This bisection process is repeated recursively $log_2 K$ times for an hypercube with K processors. After that, the complete allocation is found.

Clustering and REassignment-based Mapping Algorithm (CREMA). This is a multi-step strategy that was initially proposed for fully connected architectures [39] and extended later to direct connected architectures [41]. This strategy uses a two-stage method. The first stage contracts the graph to a smaller graph with a number of clusters equal to or less than the number of processors. The second stage performs a physical mapping of the contracted graph to K physical processors, taking into account the distances between processors in the interconnection network. Contraction reduces the original task graph by means of an agglomerative step followed by a reassignment step. The agglomerative step performs a sequence of edge zeroing operations taking into account the gain obtained by merging the nodes connected by each edge. These gains are computed dynamically along the agglomerative step. The reassignment step refines the allocation already found by moving individual tasks between clusters. Physical mapping assigns each cluster on one processor in three steps: first the cluster graph is embedded on the processor graph; then, a cluster reassignment step follows in order to map intensively communicating clusters closely to each other, i.e., trying to match intensive communications with architecture links; finally, individual tasks in each cluster are also reassigned to additionally improve the cost of the final mapping.

On the performance of clustering strategies for TIGs. In contrast to the DAG case, no extensive studies can be found to assess and compare the effectiveness of mapping strategies for TIGs. In general, proposed strategies have been compared only with a reduced set of other strategies. For instance, a comparison between two clustering strategies and a Simulated Annealing algorithm applied to hypercubes can be found in [36] and [11]. These methods used a summed cost function to evaluate the quality of a solution. In [40] two clustering approaches, two greedy methods and two randomized methods are compared in terms of their relative performance when applied to map TIGs onto fully connected architectures, and using a minimax cost function. As a general result from all these works, clustering methods provide always the best trade-off between computational complexity and solution quality, randomized methods obtain slightly better results at the expense of a considerably larger computational time, and greedy methods always obtain the worst results, being their temporal complexity the lowest.

3.3.5 Distributed methods (DSM, distributed static mapping)

As we have an available parallel or distributed computing facility, why not using it? Therefore we can distribute the mapping algorithm itself as well [15] (see Chapter 12).

The data parallelism paradigm may be one possibility to do this. If we can divide the search space, each processing unit can solve the mapping problem separately and then we can choose the best result. This way we improve the quality of solution, not the consumed time or speed-up.

A second possibility may be used if the mapping algorithm allow some kind of cooperation, e.g., use genetic action in some stage in simulated annealing algorithm to improve partial results.

A third possibility is used in the diffusion method as each parallel process can manage its own load by moving a task mapped on it to its neighbors [15, 16].

3.4 Mapping and scheduling in parallel development environments

Mapping and scheduling tools help the users within parallel development environments (PDE) to optimize parallel application programs to run faster in the parallel/distributed environment. Mapping and scheduling tools are integrated in PDE software like: PYRROS, OREGAMI, Parallax, DSM&S, etc.

3.4.1 Scheduling in PYRROS

PYRROS [50] uses the two-step method for scheduling, particularly for coarse grain parallelism:

(i) Clustering on an unbounded number of processors of a completely connected architecture.

(ii) Scheduling the clusters on a fixed number of p processors of the physical architecture.

PYRROS uses the Dominant Sequence Algorithm (DSC, see Section 3.3.4) to automatically determine the clustering for task graphs. It performs a sequence of clustering refinement steps and at each refinement step, it tries to zero an edge to reduce the parallel time. The parallel time is determined by the longest path in the scheduled graph.

3.4.2 Mapping in OREGAMI

In OREGAMI [31], mapping is usually achieved in three steps: contraction of the task graph to a smaller graph (in case where the number of tasks exceeds the number of processors), embedding, i.e., assignment of the contracted clusters of task to processors, and routing of the messages trough the interconnection network in order to minimize contention. The mapping algorithms fall into three groups: precomputed results (developed a priori using human ingenuity) taken from a library for well-known graph families such as binary tree, tailored algorithm for the specific regular Cayley graphs, and clustering greedy heuristic algorithm. As target architecture only the mesh and the hypercube are supported.

3.4.3 Scheduling in Parallax

Scheduling tool incorporates seven traditional and non-traditional scheduling heuristics [29] and allows developers compare their performance for real application on real parallel machines. Although Parallax's heuristics all schedule the highest priority task first (see Section 3.3.2), they use different techniques to assign priorities to tasks and tasks to processors. The heuristics range from simple to polynomial complexity. Simple schedulers ignore communication delays, the most complicated scheduler considers also network interconnection topology and link contention. One of the schedulers uses duplication of calculation on all processors that need the result.

3.4.4 Mapping and scheduling in **GRADE**

DSM&S (Distributed Static Mapping and Scheduling) - the task allocation tool [16] - is optimization environment contains a scheduling and mapping tools for parallel programs represented by DAG and TIG models, respectively.

(i) **Scheduling.** The user can try several scheduling algorithms and choose the best one or the scheduling tool proposes the best algorithm on the basis of the characteristics of the DAG. The scheduling tool contains two *iterative* algorithms: simulated annealing (SA) and genetic algorithm (GA); and three *heuristic* algorithms: Highest Level First (HLF), Longest Path First (LPF) and Earliest Task First (ETF).

Both iterative algorithms are time-consuming processes suitable for smaller DAG. However, the user can choose them if he has enough time and wants to have a good schedule for his parallel program. Heuristic algorithms are much faster than iterative algorithms and are recommended by the scheduling tool for large DAG. However, they may become ineffective in comparison to SA and GA when the granularity of the DAG is small.

(ii) **Mapping.** The distributed static mapping tool (DSM) [15] contains several implemented methods: *greedy* mapping algorithms - they are easy to implement and have a polynomial complexity: modulo, Large Processing Time First (LPTF), Large Global Cost First (LGCF) and *Iterative* (randomized) algorithms: augmented simulated annealing, diffusion method, HME. DSM tool manages homogeneous and heterogeneous parallel architectures as well.

3.5   Conclusion and Future Trends

Mapping and scheduling of parallel processes have significant influence on the performance and can improve the utilization of parallel resources - clusters of workstations. As the problem is NP-hard, using some heuristics is needed to obtain the result in a reasonable time for larger problems, i.e., many communicating parallel tasks to be allocated on a few processors. Such size as 10 processes to be mapped on 5 processors can be hard to solve, because the optimal result is to be found among $5^{10} \doteq 10^7$ all possible mappings.

As we usually do not know the values of mapping and scheduling input data such as the execution time for the parallel processes or communication delays in the real heavy-loaded network, prior to the running final mapping and scheduling we have to estimate these values by some heuristics. Alternatively, we can use some simple mapping and scheduling algorithms (e.g., greedy) to generate near-optimal solution and run the application in a monitoring environment to measure these values. Then the final mapping and scheduling can take place to obtain an optimal result.

Some of the currently active areas as well as future research and development directions in static mapping and scheduling include:

(i) Development of a **DAG/TIG generator** tool: The input to a DAG/TIG generator will be a parallel program, written in the user's choice of language, and its output will be the DAG/TIG equivalent of the program.

(ii) Development of an **execution time estimation** tool: One of the most important characteristics of static mapping and scheduling is the assumption that the task execution times are known before the actual execution of the tasks. This assumption is often unrealistic since the execution times of the tasks may vary, due to conditional and loop constructs and variations in input values. Several directions can be investigated in this regard:

(i) user estimates

(ii) simulation-based estimates

(iii) profile-based estimations

(iv) Development of **data distribution** tool: The existing mapping and scheduling methods are based simply on function distribution, ignoring the data distribution issue. This omission causes performance degradations, due to the runtime communication delays for accessing data at remote sites.

Acknowledgements

This work has been supported by the CICYT under contracts TIC 95-0868 and TIC 98-0433 and by the Slovak Scientific Grant Agency within Research Projects No.2/4102/97-99.

References

[1] I. Ahmad and M. K. Dhodhi. Task assignment using problem-space genetic algorithm. *Concurrency: Practice and Experience*, 7(5):411–428, August 1995.

[2] I. Ahmad and Y. K. Kwok. A new approach to scheduling parallel programs using task duplication. In *Proc. of Int'l Conf. Parallel Processing*, volume II, pages 47–51, 1994.

[3] H. Ali and H. El-Rewini. Task allocation in distributed systems: a split-graph model. *J. of Combinatorial Mathematics. and Combin. Computing*, 14:15–32, 1993.

[4] J. Boillat, N. Iselin, and P. Kropf. Marc: A tool for automatic configuration of parallel programs. In *Transputing 91*, pages 311–329, 1991.

[5] S. H. Bokhari. On the mapping problem. *IEEE Trans. on Computers*, C-30(3):207–214, March 1981.

[6] S. W. Bollinger and S. F. Midkiff. Processor and link assignment in multicomputers using simulated annealing. In *International Conference on Parallel Processing*, pages 1–7, 1988.

[7] P. Bouvry, J. Chassin de Kergommeaux, and D. Trystram. Efficient solutions for mapping parallel programs. In *Proc. of EuroPar'95*, pages 379–390. Springer-Verlag, 1995.

[8] N. S. Bowen, C. N. Nikolaou, and A. Ghafoor. On the assignment problem of arbitrary process systems to heterogeneous distributed computer systems. *IEEE Trans. on Computers*, 41(3):197–203, March 1992.

[9] T.L. Casavant and J.G. Kuhl. A taxonomy of scheduling in general-purpose distributed computing systems. *IEEE Transaction on Software Engineering*, 14(2):141–154, February 1988.

[10] C. Coroyer and Z. Liu. Effectiveness of heuristics and simulated annealing for the scheduling of concurrent tasks - an empirical comparison. In *Proc. of PARLE'93*, volume LNCS 694 of *Lecture Notes on Computer Science*, pages 452–463, 1993.

[11] F. Ercal, J. Ramanujam, and P. Sadayappan. Task allocation onto a hypercube by recursive mincut bipartitioning. *J. Parall. and Distrib. Comput.*, 10:35–44, 1990.

[12] M. Garey and D. Johnson. *Computers and Intractability*. W. H. Freeman and Co., San Francisco, 1979.

[13] F. Glover and M. Laguna. *Tabu Search, a Chapter in Modern Heuristic Techniques for Combinatorial Problems*. W. H. Freeman, N.Y., 1992.

[14] R. Graham, E. Lawler, J. Lenstra, and A. Rinnoy Kan. Optimization and approximation in deterministic sequencing and scheduling, a survey. *Ann. Discr. Math.*, 5:236–287, 1979.

[15] L. Hluchý, M. Dobrucký, and J. Astaloš. Hybrid approach to task allocation in distributed systems. In *PACT'97*, volume LNCS 1277 of *Lecture Notes on Computer Science*, pages 210–216. Springer-Verlag, 1997.

[16] L. Hluchý, M. Dobrucký, and J. Astaloš. Hybrid solving method for task allocation in distributed systems. In I. Plander, editor, *Proceedings of the Seventh International Conference on Artificial Intelligence and Information - Control Systems of Robots*, pages 189–201. World Scientific, 1997.

[17] T. C. Hu. Parallel sequencing and assembly line problems. *Oper. Research*, 19(6):841–848, 1961.

[18] C. C. Hui and S. T. Chanson. Allocating task interaction graphs to processors in heterogeneous networks. *IEEE Trans. on Par. and Distr. Systems*, 8(8):908–925, 1997.

[19] J. J. Hwang, Y. Ch. Chow, F. D. Anger, and Ch. Y. Lee. Scheduling precedence graphs in systems with interprocessor communication times. *SIAM J. Comput.*, pages 244–257, 1989.

[20] B. Indurkhya, B. Stone, and L. Xi-Cheng. Optimal partitioning of randomly generated distributed programs. *IEEE Trans. Software Eng.*, 12(3):483–495, 1986.

[21] M. Kafil and I. Ahmad. Optimal task assignment in heterogeneous computing systems. In *Workshop on Heterogeneous Systems, IPPS'97*, 1997.

[22] H. Kasahara and S. Narita. Practical multiprocessor scheduling algorithms for efficient parallel processing. *IEEE Trans. Comp.*, C-33(11):1023–1029, 1984. November.

[23] B. W. Kernighan and S. Lin. An efficient heuristic procedure for partitioning graphs. *Bell Systems Tech. J.*, 49(2):291–308, 1970.

[24] B. Kruatrachue and T. G. Lewis. Duplication Scheduling Heuristics (dsh): a new precedence task scheduler for parallel processor systems. Technical report, Oregon State University, OR 97331, 1987.

[25] Y. Kwok and I. Ahmad. Dynamic critical-path scheduling: an effective technique for allocating task graphs to multiprocessors. *IEEE Trans. Parallel and Distrib. Systems*, 7(5):506–521, 1996.

[26] Y. Kwok and I. Ahmad. Efficient scheduling of arbitrary task graphs to multiprocessors using a parallel genetic algorithm. *J. Parallel and Distr. Comput.*, 47:58–77, 1997.

[27] Y. Kwok and I. Ahmad. Benchmarking the task graph scheduling algorithms. In *Proc. of Int. Par. Proc. Symp. & Symp on Par. and Dist. Proc. (IPPS/SPDP '98)*, pages 531–537, 1998.

[28] C. H. Lee and K. G. Shin. Optimal task assignment in homogeneous networks. *IEEE Trans. on Par. and Distrib. Systems*, 8(2):119–129, 1997.

[29] T. Lewis and H. El-Rewini. Parallax: A tool for parallel program scheduling. *IEEE Par. & Distrib. Technology*, 1(2):62–72, 1993.

[30] V. M. Lo. Heuristic algorithms for task assignment in distributed systems. *IEEE Trans. Comput.*, 37(11):1384–1397, 1988.

[31] V. M. et al. Lo. Oregami: Tools for mapping parallel computations to parallel architectures. *Int'l J. of Parallel Programing*, 20(3):237–270, 1991.

[32] E. Luque, A. Ripoll, P. Hernandez, and T. Margalef. Impact of task duplication on static scheduling performance in multiprocessor systems with variable execution-time tasks. In *Proc. of Int. Conf. on Supercomputing*, pages 439–446, June 1990.

[33] E. Luque, A. Ripoll, T. Margalef, and A. Cortés. Scheduling of parallel programs including dynamic loops. *Future Generation Computer Systems*, 10:301–304, 1994. Elsevier.

[34] M. G. Norman and P. Thanisch. Models of machines and computation for mapping in multicomputers. *ACM Comp. Surveys*, 25(3):263–302, 1993. Sep.

[35] P. Sadayappan and F. Ercal. Nearest-neighbor mapping of finite element graphs onto processor meshes. *IEEE Trans. Comput*, 36(12):1408–1424, December 1987.

[36] P. Sadayappan, F. Ercal, and J. Ramanujam. Cluster partitioning approaches to mapping parallel programs onto a hypercube. *Parallel Computing*, 13:1–16, 1990.

[37] N. W. Sauer and M. G. Stone. Preemptive scheduling of interval orders is polynomial. *Order*, 5:345–348, 1989.

[38] S. Selvakumar and C. S. R. Murthy. An efficient heuristic algorithm for mapping parallel programs onto multicomputers. *Microprocessing and Microprogramming*, 36:83–92, 1992/1993.

[39] M. A. Senar, A. Cortés, A. Ripoll, and E. Luque. A clustering-reassigning strategy for mapping parallel programs. In *Proc. of 8th IASTED Int. Conf. on Parallel and Distributed Computing and Systems*. ACTA Press, 1996.

[40] M. A. Senar, A. Ripoll, A. Cortés, and E. Luque. Performance comparison of strategies for static mapping of parallel programs. In *Proc. of HPCN'97*, volume LNCS 1225 of *Lecture Notes on Computer Science*, pages 575–587, 1997.

[41] M. A. Senar, A. Ripoll, A. Cortés, and E. Luque. Clustering and reassignment-based mapping strategy for message-passing architectures. In *Proc. IPPS/SPDP '98*, pages 415–421, 1998.

[42] R. Sethi. Scheduling graphs on two processors. *SIAM J. Computing*, 5(1):73–82, 1976.

[43] C. C. Shen and W. H. Tsai. A graph matching approach to optimal task assignment in distributed computing systems using a minimax criterion. *IEEE Trans. Computers*, C-34(3):197–203, March 1985.

[44] G. C. Sih and E. A. Lee. A compile-time scheduling heuristic for interconnection-constrained heterogeneous processor architectures. *IEEE Trans. Par. and Dist. Systems*, 4(2):75–87, 1993.

[45] H. Singh and A. Youssef. Mapping and scheduling heterogeneous task graphs using genetic algorithms. In *Proc. of year = 1997 Heterogeneous Computing Workshop (HCW '97)*, 1997.

[46] H. S. Stone. Multiprocessor scheduling with the aid of network flow algorithms. *IEEE Trans. Software Eng.*, SE-4:85–93, 1977.

[47] L. Wang, H. J. Siegel, V. P. Roychowdhury, and A. A. Maciejewski. Task matching and scheduling in heterogeneous computing environments using a genetic-algorithm-based approach. *J. Parallel and Distr. Comp.*, 47:8–22, 1997.

[48] M. Y. Wu and D. D. Gajski. Hypertool: a programming aid for message-passing systems. *IEEE Trans. Parallel and Distributed Systems*, 1(3):330–343, 1990.

[49] S. S. Wu and D. Sweeting. Heuristic algorithms for task assignment and scheduling in a processor network. *Parallel Computing*, 20:1–14, 1994.

[50] T. Yang and A. Gerasoulis. Pyrros: Static task scheduling and code generation for message passing multiprocessors. In *Proc. of 6th ACM Inter. Conf. on Supercomputing (ICS 92)*, pages 428–437, Washington D.C., July 1992.

[51] T. Yang and A. Gerasoulis. Dsc: Scheduling parallel tasks on an unbounded number of processors. *IEEE Trans. Parallel and Distrib. Comput.*, 5(9):951–967, 1994.

[52] P. Yio, R. Ma, and Y. S. Lee. A task allocation model for distributed computing systems. *IEEE Trans. on Computers*, 31(1):41–47, 1982.

Chapter 4

Dynamic Load Balancing

Miquel A. Senar, Ana Cortés, Ana Ripoll, Ladislav Hluchý and Jan Astalos

Abstract

Dynamic load balancing deals with the redistribution of work among processors during execution time. This chapter provides an overview of the existing solutions to this problem. First, the main issues involved in dynamic load balancing are reported. This section describes the different phases under which the problem may be decomposed and identifies the main decisions that must be taken in each one. Subsequent sections present a taxonomy of load-balancing algorithms, a general description of the main techniques and a brief description of some relevant methods. The final section describes the general architecture of software packages that support load migration and presents some representative examples.

4.1 Introduction

When a parallel application is divided into a fixed number of processes that are to be executed in parallel, each process performs a certain amount of work. However, it may be that some processors will complete their tasks before others and become idle because the work is unevenly divided, or some processors operate faster than others, or both situations. Achieving the minimum execution time by spreading the tasks evenly across the processors is called load-balancing. Load-balancing can be attempted statically before the execution of any process or dynamically during the execution of the processes. Static load-balancing is usually referred to as the mapping problem and it was studied in chapter three. Dynamic load-balancing techniques assume little or no compile-time knowledge about the runtime parameters of the problem, such as task execution times or communication delays. These techniques are particularly useful in efficiently solving applications that have unpredictable computational requirements or irregular communication patterns. Adaptive calculations, circuit simulations and VLSI design, N-body problems, parallel discrete event simulation, and data mining are just a few of those applications.

Dynamic load-balancing (DLB) is based on the redistribution of load among the processors during execution time, so that each processor would have the same or nearly the same amount of work to do. This redistribution is performed by transferring load units (*data*, *threads, processes*) from the heavily loaded processors to the lightly loaded processors with the aim of obtaining the highest possible execution speed. DLB and load sharing are used as interchangeable terms in the literature. While DLB views the redistribution as the assigning of the processes to the processors, load sharing defines the redistribution as the sharing of the system's processing power among the processes. The result of applying an ideal DLB algorithm to a 3x3 torus is shown in Figure 4.1. The numbers inside the circles denote the load value of each processor. Initially, at time (t_0) the load is unevenly distributed among the processors. The load becomes the same in all of the processors after executing an ideal DLB strategy (time t_f).

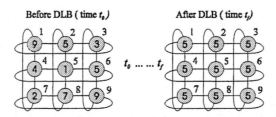

Figure 4.1: Dynamic load-balancing process.

Every DLB strategy has to resolve the issues of *when* to invoke a balancing operation, *who* takes the load-balancing decision according to *what* information, and *how* to manage load migrations between processors.

The advantage of dynamic load-balancing over static load-balancing is that the system needs not be aware of the run-time behavior of the applications before execution. Nevertheless, the major disadvantage of DLB schemes is the run-time overhead due to the load information transfer among processors, the execution of the load-balancing strategy, and the communication delays due to load relocation itself.

This chapter gives an overview of the dynamic load-balancing problem in parallel and distributed computing and is organized as follows: Section 2 describes the key issues that must be considered in the load-balancing problem. Section 3 presents a taxonomy of load-balancing algorithms that illustrates how load distribution can be carried out; a description of the most relevant dynamic load-balancing strategies is presented in Section 4; Section 5 describes environments and existing tools for supporting load-balancing and, finally, Section 6 summarizes the main conclusions.

4.2   Key issues in the Load Balancing process

Facing the design of a dynamic load-balancing algorithm requires resolving issues as: who specifies the amount of load information made available to the decision-maker; who determines the condition under which a unit of load should be transferred; and who identifies the destination processor of load to transfer, amongst others. Combining different answers to the above questions results in a large set of possible load-balancing algorithms with widely varying characteristics. On one hand, there are decisions which must be taken at processor level, and others that require a certain degree of co-ordination between different processors, so the latter become system-level decisions.

In order to be systematic in the description of all necessary decisions related to the load balancing process, we distinguish two different design points of view: the *processor level* point of view and the *system level* point of view. We refer to *processor level* when the load-balancing operations respond to decisions taken by a processor. Otherwise, we talk about *system level* when the decisions affect a group of processors.

In the following, we outline the description of each one of these levels.

4.2.1   Processor level

A processor which intervenes in the load-balancing process will execute both computational operations for the application, and balancing operations. This section describes the load-balancing operations carried out at processor level and their design alternatives. In order to perform the load-balancing operations, a processor must allocate three functional blocks to effectively implement the load-balancing process: the *Load Manager (LM)*, the *Load-Balancing Algorithm (LBA)* and the *Migration Manager (MM)*. The *Load Manager block* is the one related to all load-keeping issues. The *Load-Balancing Algorithm block* is related to the concrete specification of the load-balancing strategy. Finally, a *Migration Manager block* is needed in order to actually perform the load movements. The processors which incorporate each one of these three blocks will be referred to as *running processors*.

The next sections discuss the implementation issues for each one of these blocks, as well as their cooperation.

Load Manager block

One of the most important issues in the load-balancing process is to quantify the amount of load (*data*, *threads* or *processes*) of a given processor (*load index*). It is impossible to quantify exactly the execution time of the resident processes in a processor. Therefore, some measurable parameters should be used to determine the load index in a system such as the process sizes, the number of ready processes, the amount of data to be processed and so on. However, previous studies have shown that simple definitions such as the number of ready processes are particularly effective to quantify the load index of a processor [36].

The Load Manager block has the responsibility of updating the load information of the running processor, as well as gathering load information from a set of processors of the system (underlying domain). The time at which the load index of each processor is to be updated is known as the *load evaluation instant*. A non-negative variable (integer or real number), taking on a zero value if the processor is idle and taking on increasing positive values as the load increases, will be measured at this time according to the load unit definition [24]. There must be a trade-off between the load gathering frequency and the aging of the load information kept by the LM block, in order to avoid the use of obsolete values by the Load Balancing Algorithm block. This trade-off is captured in the following three load collection rules:

(i) On-demand: Processors collect the load information from each other whenever a load-balancing operation is about to begin or to be initiated [55, 69].

(ii) Periodical: Processors periodically report their load information to others, regardless of whether the information is useful to others or not [33, 67].

(iii) On-state-change: Processors disseminate their load information whenever their state changes by a certain degree [48, 65].

The on-demand load gathering method minimizes the number of communication messages, but postpones the collection of system wide load information till the time when a load-balancing operation is to be initiated. Its main disadvantage is that it results in an extra delay for load-balancing operations. Conversely, the periodic method allows processors in need of a balancing operation to initiate the operation based on maintained load information without delay. The problem with the periodical scheme is how to set the interval for information gathering. A short interval would incur heavy communication overheads, while a long interval would sacrifice the accuracy of the load information used in the load-balancing algorithm. The on-state-changing rule is a compromise of the on-demand and periodic schemes.

Nevertheless, how the LM block proceeds to collect and hold load information is not relevant to the Load Balancing Algorithm block. The information required by this block is limited to a set of non-negative numbers that represent the load index of each one of the processors belonging to the underlying domain. These values will be used to evaluate whether it is necessary to perform load movements or not and how these movements must be performed.

Load Balancing Algorithm block

The Load Balancing Algorithm block uses the load information provided by the previous LM block to decide if it is necessary or not to balance the load, source and destination processors of load movements, as well as the amount of load to be transferred. A LBA algorithm can be divided into two phases: *Load Balancing Activation* and *Work Transfer Calculation*.

1. The *Load Balancing Activation* phase uses the load information kept by the LM block to determine the presence of a load imbalance. The criterion used to evaluate whether a processor is balanced or not is known as the*trigger condition* and it is normally associated to a threshold value that can be defined as:

    (i) Fixed threshold: one or several fixed values are used as criteria to determine whether a processor is overloaded or not [42, 68].

    (ii) Adaptive threshold: the threshold values are evaluated during the execution of the load-balancing algorithm and their values are usually state dependent [16, 62, 66].

    All running processors in the system will evaluate the trigger condition at the start of the execution of the load-balancing algorithm. However, not all the running processors will overcome their trigger condition. The processors whose trigger condition evaluation does not fail will be called *active processors*. We refer to sender-initiated (SI) approaches when active processors are the ones with load excess and we refer to received-initiated (RI) schemes, [22, 62], when the underloaded processors will became the active processors by requesting load to their overloaded counterpart.

2. The *Work Transfer Calculation* phase is concerned with devising an appropriate transfer strategy to correct the imbalance previously detected and measured. After determining that load-balancing is required, *source* and *destination* processors pairs are determined, as well as *how much work* should be transferred from one processor to another. The function used to determine the destination of load can be implemented using one of the following choices:

(i) Randomly: no information about the domain state of the underlying processor is needed and destination processors are chosen at random [68].

(ii) Fixed: decisions produced by the active processors are not state dependent. The quantity of load to be transferred from one processor to another is set *a priori* as a fixed value [17, 64].

(iii) Evaluated: the amount of load to be moved between processors is evaluated at run time following some predetermined function [16, 62].

Migration Manager block

The Migration Manager (MM) block receives as input the information generated by the Load Balancing Algorithm block, i.e., the destination processors and the amount of load that should be transferred to them. This block can be divided into two phases: *load unit selection* and *load transfer*, in order to differentiate between the way of choosing the individuals load units to be transferred, and the physical transfer of those elements.

1. *Load unit selection.* Source processors *select* the most suitable *load units* (processes, threads, data,...) which properly match the load value to be moved. The quality of load units selection directly impacts the ultimate quality of load-balancing. Sometimes, it may prove to be impossible to choose a group of load units whose associated load index corresponds exactly to the value that needs to be moved. The problem of selection which load units to move is weakly NP-complete, since it is simply the subset sum problem. Fortunately, approximation algorithms exist which allow the subset sum problem to be solved to a specified nonzero accuracy in polynomial time [44]. Before considering such an algorithm, it is important to note that other concerns may constrain load transfer options. In general, we would like to associate a cost with the transfer of a given set of load units and then find the lowest cost set for a particular desired transfer.

2. *Load transfer.* This module should provide the appropriate mechanisms to correctly migrate several load units (which can be either processes, data or threads) to any destination processor. Data migration load-balancing systems support dynamic balancing through transparent data redistribution. Data migration mechanisms usually exhibit the lowest complexity among the three mechanisms as they only have to move data. Systems based on thread migration support dynamic load balancing through thread redistribution in multithreading environments. In such systems, a user application consists of a number of processes assigned to different processors and each process encapsulates a certain number of threads that can be created/destroyed dynamically. Transparent migration of threads implies the movement of the data and the computation state of a particular thread for one process located in a processor to another process located in a different processor. Process migration load-balancing systems support dynamic load balancing through transparent process redistribution in parallel and/or distributed computing environments. As in thread migration load-balancing systems, process migration implies the movement of the data and the computation state. However, process migration mechanisms exhibit the highest complexity as they must be aware of a huge amount of information. In the case of a process, the computation state is considerably more complex compared to the thread case and, moreover, the application binaries must also be moved.

After having described the behavior of each one of the blocks corresponding to the load-balancing operations, it is important to indicate that this decomposition in the load-balancing process in different modules allows us to experiment in a plug-and-play fashion with different implementations at each one of the above blocks, allowing the space of techniques to be more fully and readily explored.

4.2.2   System level

This level analyzes which processors intervene in the load-balancing process and how this cooperation is carried out. Hence, the first decision that must be considered is the election of the set of running processors, i.e., processors that will have allocated a copy of the Load-Balancing Algorithm code. Depending on the number of processors belonging to this set we can distinguish between: *centralized, totally distributed* and *semi-distributed* approaches [10]. In totally distributed and semi-distributed schemes the load-balancing goal is obtained because load-balancing operations are concurrently executed in more than one processor as the time goes on. In particular, when the load-balancing operations are executed simultaneously in all running processors of the system, we are considering a *synchronous* implementation of the load-balancing process. Otherwise, the system works in an *asynchronous* way. The influence of each one of above characteristics in the load-balancing process will be discussed in next subsections.

Centralized

Centralized load balancing strategies are characterized by the use of a dedicated processor for maintaining a global view of the system state and decision making. This processor is called *central scheduler* (or *central job dispatcher*). A central scheduler can improve resource utilization by having all the information about the nodes and it can achieve optimal performance by using sophisticated algorithms. It can impose less overhead on the communication network by avoiding transfers of duplicate or inaccurate host state information. A central scheduler can also avoid task thrashing caused by contradictory load balancing decisions. However, centralized models have low reliability. If the central processor fails, the operation of the whole system can be corrupted. In addition, in large systems with high load fluctuation, the messages with load information can overload the interconnection structure around the central processor.

Totally distributed

An alternative to centralized approaches is a *distributed* scheme, in which the load-balancing decisions are carried out by all the processors of the system. Load information exchanges are restricted to a local sphere of processors and load-balancing operations are also performed within this sphere or domain. Depending on the existing relationship between different domains, we can distinguish between *overlapped* domains or *non-overlapped* domains. The marked nodes in Figure 4.2 indicate the running processor of the drawn domains. We refer to *overlapped* domains (Figure 4.2.a) when there are some common processors between the inspected domains. Otherwise, we refer to *non-overlapped* domains (Figure 4.2.b).

When the domain includes a given processor and its immediate neighbors we refer to it as a *nearest-neighbor* approach. Nearest-neighbor load-balancing methods operate on the principle of reducing the load imbalance between each processor and its immediate

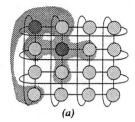 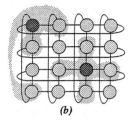

Figure 4.2: Overlapped domains (a) and non-overlapped domains (b).

neighbors with the aim of diffusing workload through the system converging toward a system-wide balance. Otherwise, load-balancing strategies are categorized as *non-nearest-neighbors* approaches. Non-nearest-neighbors methods work in a decentralized form by using local information, which is not restricted to immediate neighbors. Under this assumption the scope of the domain is extended to a large *radius* that may also include the neighbors' neighbors and so on.

Totally distributed approaches, in using local information, do not make such effective balance decisions as centralized approaches, but, in contrast, they incur smaller synchronization overheads.

Partially distributed

For large systems (in the order of thousands of nodes), neither centralized, nor distributed strategies proved to be appropriate. Although centralized strategies have the potential of yielding optimal performance, they also have disadvantages that make them suitable only for small or moderate systems [5]. On the other hand, the distributed strategies have good scalability, but for large systems it is difficult to achieve a global optimum because the processors have often a limited view of the global system state. Partially distributed (or semi-distributed) strategies were proposed as a trade-off between centralized and fully distributed mechanisms. They divide the system into regions and thus split the load-balancing problem into subtasks. These strategies can be viewed at two levels: (i) load-balancing within a region, (ii) and load-balancing among all the regions.

Different solutions can be devised for each level of the strategy. Each region is usually managed by a single master-processor using a centralized strategy and, at the level of the region, master-processors may (or may not) exchange aggregated information about their corresponding regions.

Synchronous versus asynchronous strategies

Taking into account the instant at which load-balancing operations are invoked, both totally and partially distributed strategies can be further subdivided into synchronous and asynchronous strategies. From this point of view, we talk about *synchronous* algorithms when all processors involved in load-balancing (running processors) carry out balancing operations at the same instant of time, so that each processor cannot proceed with normal computation until the load migrations demanded by the current operations have completed. Otherwise, if each running processor performs load-balancing operations discretely based on their own local load distribution and invocation policies, we refer to *asynchronous* approaches. Notice that the distinction between synchronous and asynchronous does not apply for centralized schemes due to the existence of only one running processor in the entire system.

4.3   Load-balancing algorithm taxonomy

Most of the load-balancing strategies proposed in the literature are focused basically on the development of approaches for solving the Load Balancing Algorithm block. In terms of the algorithmic method used by these strategies we can derive the taxonomy shown in Figure 4.3. The main criteria in classifying these algorithms concerns the way in which load distribution is carried out.

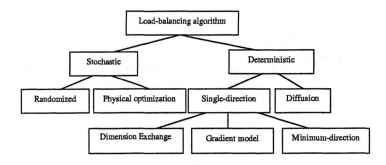

Figure 4.3: Load-Balancing taxonomy in terms of algorithmic aspects at the processor level.

In **Stochastic** methods, the load is redistributed in some randomized fashion, subject to the objective of load balancing. Stochastic load balancing methods attempt to drive the system into an equilibrium state with high probability. Two different approaches can be found: **Randomized** allocation and *Physical optimization*.

Randomized allocation methods are very simple methods that do not use information about potential destination processors. A neighbor processor is selected at random and the process is transferred to that processor. No exchange of state information among the processors is required in deciding where to transfer a load unit. Stochastic algorithms, where physical optimization is applied, are based on analogies with physical systems. They map the load-balancing problem onto some physical systems, and then solve the problem using simulation or techniques from theoretical or experimental physics. Physical optimization algorithms offer a little more variety in the control of the randomness in the redistribution of load units. This control mechanism makes the process of load balancing less susceptible to being trapped in local optima and therefore stochastic algorithms are superior to other randomized approaches which could produce locally but not globally optimal results.

Deterministic methods proceed according to certain predefined strategies. These solutions are usually performed in an iterative form when the execution of the load balancing process is repeated more than once in a given processor, before restarting the execution of the user application. Deterministic methods can be classified into two categories according to the load distribution within a domain: **Diffusion** and **Single-direction**.

Firstly, in diffusion methods the load excess of an overloaded processor could achieve simultaneous distribution amongst all processors of the underlying domain, following an iteration of the load-balancing algorithm. In contrast, in single-direction methods only one processor of the underlying domain can be chosen as destination processor after executing one iteration of the load-balancing algorithm. Single-direction methods are further classified according to how the destination processor is selected. When the direction of the closer lightly loaded processor is used as a selection criterion we refer to the **Gradient Model**, and when the chosen processor is the less loaded processor of the underlying domain we talk about **Minimum-direction** schemes. Techniques where all processors are considered one by one at each load-balancing iteration are called **Dimension Exchange** strategies.

4.4   Dynamic load-balancing strategies

This section will review some of the most relevant dynamic load-balancing strategies according to the global classification proposed in Figure 4.4. This figure illustrates the combination of the design characteristics at processor-level as well as at system level, mentioned in Section 4.2. Particularly, in the case of processor level, the algorithmic aspects seen in Section 4.3 are used. At each box, the mnemonic for the strategy and its reference are given. Strategies indicated with a continuous line are not feasible or have not been proposed as far as the authors know. We now describe some of the strategies indicated in the figure, starting with those classified in the randomized category.

Dynamic Load-Balancing			System Level View		
		Centralized	Totally Distributed		Semi-Distributed
			Non-Nearest Neighbors	Nearest Neighbors	
Randomized (Stochas.)		——	Reservation [22] RANDOM [68] THRDL [68] LOWEST [68] MYPE [67]	——	——
Physical Opt.		GTCA [5] CBLB [5]	——	SA [25]	CSAM [11] MFAM [11]
Diffusion (Determ.)		Multi-level-Diffusion [26]	NA [48] DDE [63] AN-n [13]	Diffusion [7, 17] SID, RID [62] ATD [61] DASUD [16] AN [13, 19, 28]	Member-ship-exc. [23] Join-member-ship [23]
(Single-Direct.)	Dimension Exchange	——	EDN [13]	DE [17] GDE [64] DN [13]	——
	Gradient Model	——	——	GM [37] B [4] X-GM [39] EG [42]	——
	Minimum-Direction	Central [68] LBC [38]	GLRM [66] GMLM [66]	CWN [33] ACWN [50] LLRM [66] LMLM [31, 32, 66]	Sphere-like [1] Hierch. Sched. [18]

Figure 4.4: Load-Balancing techniques classified by system level view and processor level view.

4.4.1   Randomized

In randomized load-balancing algorithms, the destination processors for load transfer are chosen in a random fashion. Therefore, this kind of algorithms use less system state information than deterministic algorithms. These algorithms use only local load information to make movement decisions. In those cases a threshold value is preset as a criterion to determine whether a processor must send out part of its load or not. Several randomized algorithms based on a threshold value (T_l) as a trigger condition are presented in [68]. In the **RANDOM** algorithm when a processor detects that its local load is bigger that T_l, a processor is randomly selected as a destination of load movements. Since all processors are able to make load movement decisions, according to the system level taxonomy, this algorithm is classified as a totally distributed and non-nearest-neighbors approach. **THRHLD** and **LOWEST** algorithms are similar to the **RANDOM** algorithm in the sense that they also select the destination processor in a random way. However, a number of randomly selected processors, up to a limit L_p, are inspected instead of selecting only one candidate. In the THRHLD algorithm, extra load is transferred to the first processor whose load is below the threshold value. In contrast, the LOWEST algorithm chooses the most lightly loaded processor as destination processor. A similar scheme is used in the **MYPE** algorithm [67], although it uses two threshold values to determine the state of the underlying processor.

4.4.2   Physical Optimization

The most common physical optimization algorithm for the load-balancing problem is simulated annealing. Simulated annealing is a general and powerful technique for combinatorial optimization problems as was explained in Chapter 3.

Since simulated annealing is very expensive and one of the requirements on dynamic load balancing is yielding the result in limited time, two hybrid methods, combining statistical and deterministic approaches, are proposed in [11]: the Clustering Simulated Annealing Model (CSAM) and the Mean Field Annealing Model (MFAM). They were proposed to allocate or reallocate tasks at run time, so that every processor in the system had a nearly equal execution load and the total interprocessor communications were minimized. In these methods, load balancing was activated on a specific processor called the local balancer. The local balancer repeatedly activates the task allocation algorithm among a subset of processors. Each local balancer makes task allocation decisions for a group of four to nine processors. Groups were overlapped with each other, allowing tasks to be transferred throughout the whole system.

The **CSAM** combines a heuristic clustering algorithm (HCA) and the simulated annealing technique. The HCA generates clusters, where each cluster contains tasks which involve high intertask communication. Various task assignments (called system configurations) are generated from the HCA to provide clusters in various sizes that are suitable for the annealing process. During the annealing process, system configurations are updated by reassigning a cluster of tasks from one processor to another. The procedure of simulated annealing is used to either accept or reject a new configuration.

The **MFAM** (Mean Field Annealing Model) was derived from modelling the distributed system as a large physical system in which the load imbalance and communication costs cause the system to be in a state of non equilibrium. The imbalance is compensated through a dynamic equation whose solution reduces the system imbalance. The dynamics of the MFAM are derived from the Gibbs distribution. Initially all tasks have the same probability of being allocated to each processor. Several iterations of an annealing algorithm bring the system to a situation where each process is assigned only to one processor.

A similar load-balancing algorithm that uses simulated annealing technique is reported in [25].

In addition to the simulated annealing technique, genetic algorithms constitute another optimization method that borrowed ideas from natural sciences and has also been adapted to dynamic load-balancing. Examples of genetic load-balancing algorithms can be found in [5]. The first algorithm presented in the paper is Genetic Central Task Assigner (**GCTA**). It uses a genetic algorithm to perform entire load-balancing action. The second one, Classifier-Based Load Balancer (**CBLB**), augments an existing load-balancing algorithm using a simple classifier system to tune the parameters of the algorithm.

4.4.3 Diffusion

One simple method for dynamic load-balancing is for each overloaded processor to transfer a portion of its load to its underloaded neighbors with the aim of achieving a local load balance. Such methods correspond closely to simple iterative methods for the solution of diffusion problems; indeed, the surplus load can be interpreted as diffusing through the processors towards a steady balanced state. Diffusion algorithms assume that a processor is able to send and receive messages to/from all its neighbors simultaneously.

Corradi *et al.* propose a more precise definition of diffusive load-balancing strategies in [13]. In particular, they define a LB strategy as diffusive when:

1. It is based on replicated load-balancing codes, each with the same behavior and capable of autonomous activity;

2. The LB goal is locally pursued: the scope of the action for each running processor is bound to a local area of the system (domain). Each running processor tries to balance the load of its domain as if it were the whole system, based only on the load information in its domain; and

3. Each running processor's domain overlaps with the domain controlled by at least one other running processor and the unification of these domains achieves full coverage of the whole system.

Cybenko describes in [17] a simple **diffusion** algorithm where a processor i compares its load with all its immediate neighbors in order to determine which neighbor processors have a load value smaller than the underlying processor's load. Such processors will be considered as underloaded neighbor processors. Once underloaded neighbors are determined, the underlying processor will evaluate the load difference between itself and each one of its neighbors. Then, a fixed portion of the corresponding load difference is sent to each one of the underloaded neighbors.

The convergence of a synchronous diffusion method was studied by Cybenko [17] and Boillat [7]. Cybenko showed that, under the assumption that no new load is generated or existing load completed during the execution of the load-balancing process, the diffusion method is convergent given any initial load distribution. Without this assumption, he showed that the diffusion method can control the growth in the variance of the processors' unbalanced load distribution and keep it bounded.

The convergence of an asynchronous diffusion method was studied by Bertsekas and Tsitsiklis in [6]. In an asynchronous environment, the information maintained in a processor concerning its neighbors' load could be outdated. Using linear systems theory, Bertsekas and Tsitsiklis showed that the asynchronous version of the diffusion method is convergent provided that the communication delays are bounded. They referred to this scheme as a *partially asynchronous* environment.

As we have mentioned, the above methods proceed in an iterative way to improve the balance degree of the system moving the load as the load-balancing iteration proceeds. Some authors denote this approach as a one-phase diffusion approach. Other works use the diffusion iteration as a preprocessing to determine a balancing flow. Thus, the real movements of load will be performed in a second phase [19, 28]. These approaches are referred to as two-phase approaches. By exploiting the fact that this two-phase diffusion method can be modeled analytically, a fundamental property, such as convergence has been also studied.

The strategies outlined above were originally conceived under the assumption that load can be divided into arbitrary fractions, i.e., the load was treated as a non-negative real quantity. To cover medium and large grain parallelism which are more realistic and more common in practical parallel computing environments, we must treat the loads of the processors as non-negative integers as was carried out in [13, 16, 27, 54, 61, 62]. A relevant strategy in this area is the **SID** (Sender Initiated Diffusion) algorithm [62]. In this algorithm, each processor i uses its local load average ($\overline{\omega_i}(t)$) as a trigger condition. If the load of processor i is bigger than the load average of its domain, then it is an overloaded processor. Otherwise, the processor was referred to as underloaded. An overloaded processor distributes its excess load (*i.e.*, $\overline{\omega_i}(t) - \omega_i(t)$) among its underloaded neighbors. A neighbor processor j of the underlying processor i, is a deficient neighbor if its load is smaller than the load average of the underlying domain ($\overline{\omega_i}(t) > \omega_j(t)$). Then, the surplus of a given processor i is distributed among its deficient neighbors in a proportional way. This strategy is classified as sender-initiated scheme because the overloaded processors are the active processors. The same authors described a similar strategy called **RID** (Receiver Initiated Diffusion) which is based on the same idea as the SID algorithm, but using a receiver-initiated scheme to determine the active processor.

However, the problem with the strategies that use a discrete load model is that they may fail to guarantee a global load balance when the algorithm terminates. These strategies may produce solutions which, although the load of each processor differs by only one unit at most from that of each of its neighbors, the global load balance is very poor [15, 58]. None of these load-balancing strategies based on the pairwise comparison of loads of neighboring processors recognizes such situation as unbalanced. The convergence property of diffusion load-balancing algorithms, which use a discrete load model, has not been widely explored. Corradi *et alter* in [13] introduce the constraint of having a serialization of the activity on overlapping domains to avoid situations in which balancing actions take place concurrently in overlapping domains. They ensure that under this assumption their load-balancing algorithms converge. The **DASUD** (Diffusion Algorithm Searching Unbalanced Domains) algorithm [15, 16] is a dynamic load-balancing algorithm which has been developed for the discrete load model and DASUD's convergence has been proved [14] under partially asynchronous assumption. DASUD searches unbalanced domains to achieve an even load distribution in all the domains of the system. Essentially, one iteration of DASUD consists of load exchanges between each processor and its neighbors followed by two load-balancing stages. In the first stage, load is distributed following a similar strategy to the SID method. In the second stage, firstly, each processor checks its own domain to determine whether it is unbalanced or not. A domain is considered to be unbalanced when the maximum load difference between any two processors through it is larger than one. In order to balance the underlying domain, each processor can proceed by completing its excess load distribution in a more refined way.

The reader can find more examples of deterministic diffusion load-balancing strategies in [13, 23, 26, 48, 61, 63].

4.4.4   Dimension Exchange

This load-balancing method was firstly studied for hypercube topologies where the processor neighbors are inspected by following each dimension of the hypercube. Thus, this is the origin of the dimension exchange (DE) name. Originally, in the **DE** methods, the processors of a k-dimensional hypercube pair up with their neighbors in each dimension and exchange half of the difference in their respective workloads [17]. The load value of the underlying processor is updated at each neighbor inspection and the new value is considered for the next revision. Going through all the neighbors once consists of carrying out a "sweep" of the load-balancing algorithm.

Xu and Lau present in [64] a generalization of this technique for arbitrary topologies, which they call the bf GDE (Generalized Dimension Exchange) strategy. For arbitrary topologies the technique of edge colouring of undirected graphs (where each node of the graph identifies one processor of the system and the edges are the links) is used to determine the number of dimensions and the dimension associated with each link. The links between neighboring processors are minimally coloured so that no processor has two links of the same colour [27]. Subsequently, a "dimension" is then defined to be the collection of all edges of the same color. At each iteration, one particular color/dimension is considered, and only processors on edges with this color execute the dimension exchange procedure. The portion of load exchanged is a fixed value and is called the exchange parameter. This process is repeated until a balanced state is reached. The DE algorithm uses the same value of the exchange parameter for all topologies, while the GDE algorithm uses different values depending on the underlying topology.

The above algorithms were originally proposed for loads treated as real numbers and their convergence has been theoretically analyzed by their authors.

The **DN** (Direct neighbor) algorithm is a strategy based on the dimension exchange philosophy, which uses a discrete load model [13]. This strategy allows load exchange only between two processors directly connected by a physical link. A balancing action within a domain strives to balance the load of the two involved nodes. In order to assure the convergence of this method, the running processors must synchronize among themselves in such a way that the running processors that are active at any given moment have non-overlapping domains. The same authors describe an extension to this algorithm, the **EDN** (Extended Direct neighbor) algorithm, which works as a non-nearest neighbors strategy. This strategy allows a dynamic domain definition by moving load between direct neighbors overcoming the neighborhood limit through underloaded processors. Load reallocation stops when there are no more useful movements, i.e., a processor is reached whose load is minimal in its neighborhood.

4.4.5   Gradient Model

With gradient-based methods, load is restricted to being transferred along the direction of the most lightly loaded processors in the system. That is, an overloaded processor will send its excess load only to one neighbor processor at the end of one iteration of the load-balancing algorithm. Therefore, the main difference between the gradient model and the dimension exchanged scheme is that at each iteration the load information of the entire underlying domain is considered to decide the destination processor, whilst in DE methods only one processor is considered at each iteration.

In the Gradient Model (**GM**) algorithm described in [37] two-tiered load-balancing steps are employed. The first step is to let each individual processor determine its own loading condition: light, moderate or heavy. The second step consists of establishing a system-wide gradient surface to facilitate load migration. The *gradient surface* is represented by the aggregate of all *proximities*, where a proximity of a processor i is the minimum distance between the processor and a lightly loaded processor in the system. The gradient surface is approximated by a distributed measurement called the *pressure surface*, then the excessive load from heavily loaded processors is routed to the neighbor with the least pressure (proximity). The resulting effect is a form of relaxation where load migrating through the system is guided by the proximity gradient and gravitates towards underloaded processors.

This basic gradient model has serious drawbacks. Firstly, when a large portion of moderately loaded processors suddenly turn lightly loaded, the result is considerable commotion. Secondly, since the system load changes dynamically, the proximities information kept by a processor may be considerably out-of-date. And finally, if there are only few lightly-loaded processors in the system, more than one overloaded processor may emit some load toward the same underloaded processor. This "overflow" effect has the potential to transform underloaded processors into overloaded ones. The authors of [39] and [42] propose two extensions to the GM scheme, the Extended Gradient Model (**X-GM**) and the **EG** (Extended Gradient) mechanism, respectively, to overcome the mentioned problems. Another algorithm based in the gradient model can be found in [4].

4.4.6 Minimum-direction

The minimum-direction scheme is an alternative to the dimension exchange methods and gradient model within the single-direction category of deterministic load-balancing algorithms. In the strategies based on this scheme, the running processor chooses the less loaded processor within its domain as the only destination of a load movement after executing the load-balancing algorithm once. Notice that, depending on the scope of the domain, the less loaded processor within the underlying domain may coincide with the less loaded processor in the whole system. Such a match is typically produced in centralized load-balancing systems where the running processors have access to the load of the entire system.

The **LBC** strategy reported in [38] makes load-balancing decisions based on global state information which is maintained by a central job dispatcher. Each processor sends a message to the central site whenever its state changes. Upon receiving a state-change message, the central dispatcher updates the load value kept in its memory accordingly. When a processor becomes underloaded, the state-change message is also used as a load request message. In response to this load request, the dispatcher consults the table where load values are kept, and the most loaded processor is chosen as load source. Then this processor is notified to transfer some load to the requesting processor.

The **CENTRAL** algorithm described in [68] is a centralized algorithm that works in a complementary form to the LBC strategy. When a processor detects that it is an overloaded processor, it notifies the *load information center* (LIC) about this fact by sending a message with its current load value. The LIC selects a processor with the lowest load value and informs the originating processor to send the extra load to the selected processor.

GLRM (Global Least Recently Migrated) and **GMLM** (Global Minimum Load Maintained) are two totally distributed non-nearest-neighbors strategies where the domain of each processor includes all processors in the system [66]. Both GLRM and GMLM strategies use the global load average in the system as a threshold to determine whether a processor is overloaded or not. This threshold is computed at each processor using the load values received from the information collector (IC) processor. The IC processor has the responsibility of collecting the load of the entire system and broadcasting it to all nodes. These actions will be performed on a time window basis. Once a processor is considered to be overloaded, a destination processor must be chosen. GLRM selects the destination processor by applying the last recently migrated discipline in a time window and the GMLM strategy determines the destination processor as the processor with minimum load value in the current time window. If the domain of each processor is restricted to the immediate neighbors, two nearest-neighbor strategies are easily derived from the two previous ones: **LLRM** (Local Least Recently Migrated) and **LMLM** (Local Minimum Load Maintained).

Another algorithm based on the minimum-direction scheme is the **CWN** (Contracting Within neighborhood) strategy [33]. CWN is a totally distributed strategy where each processor only uses load information about its immediate neighbors. A processor would migrate its excess load to the neighbor with the least load. A processor that receives some load keeps it for execution if it is most lightly loaded when compared with all its neighbors; otherwise, it forwards the load to its least loaded neighbor. This scheme has two parameters: the *radius*, i.e., the maximum distance a load unit is allowed to travel, and the *horizon*, i.e., the minimum distance a load unit is required to travel. If we allow these parameters to be tunable at run-time, the algorithms become **ACWN** (Adaptive Contracting Within a Neighborhood) [50].

In the semi-distributed strategy proposed by Ahmad [1], called **Sphere-like**, the system is divided into symmetric regions called 'spheres'. Considering the load-balancing method applied among these spheres, this strategy falls into the minimum-direction category. This strategy has a two-level load-balancing scheme. At the first level the load is balanced among different spheres using global system information. At the second level, load balancing is carried out within individual spheres. Each sphere has a processor that acts as a centralized controller for its own sphere. Since this strategy is primarily designed for massively parallel systems, it also addresses the problem of creating the spheres. The state information, maintained by each centralized controller is the accumulative load of its sphere. In addition, a linked list is maintained in non-decreasing order that sorts the processors of the sphere according to their loads. The scheduling algorithm first considers the load of the least loaded processor in the local sphere and if it is less than or equal to chosen *threshold1*, the task is scheduled on that processor. Otherwise the scheduler checks the cumulative load of other spheres. If the load of the least loaded sphere is less than *threshold2*, the task is sent to that sphere where it is executed without further migration to any other sphere. If there are more than one such spheres, one is selected randomly. In the case that there is no such sphere the task is scheduled in the least loaded processor of the local sphere. The parameters *threshold1* and *threshold2* are adjustable depending upon system load and network characteristics.

Other dynamic load-balancing algorithms that fall within the minimum-direction category are reported in [18, 31, 32].

4.5 Software facilities for supporting dynamic load-balancing

Software systems that support some kind of adaptive parallel application execution are basically classified into two main classes: system-level class and user-level class.

In the system-level class, load-balancing support is implemented at the operating system level [52]. In contrast, the user-level class includes all the systems where the load-balancing support is not integrated into the operating system level. They are built on top of existing operating systems and communication environments. In that sense, load-balancing systems supported at the system level provide more transparency and less interference (migration can be carried out more efficiently, for instance) compared to load-balancing systems supported at the user level. However, they are not as portable as the user-level implementations. In the remainder of the section we focus mainly on the second class of systems. Readers interested in load-balancing systems based on system-level support could refer to the description of systems such as Sprite [21], V System [60] and Mach [41].

Load-Balancing Systems (LBS) implemented at the user level can be further subdivided into data-based, thread-based or process-based systems, according to the item that is migrated, as was mentioned previously in Section 4.2.1. Therefore, we will refer to item migration as a general term that does not differentiate whether migration involves data, threads or processes.

Moreover, data-based and thread-based LBS are usually based on a distributed shared memory paradigm. As a consequence, some problems addressed in process-based LBS (process communication, for instance) do not always appear in data-based and thread-based LBS. Below we will focus mainly on the design issues related to process-based LBS, although the reader should bear in mind that many issues are also applicable to the other two classes of LBS.

4.5.1 Architecture of Process-based LBS

Despite the particular characteristics of different LBS, a similar system architecture is shared by most of them. This architecture is based on a set of layers where upper layer components interact with lower layer components through library functions (see Figure 4.5).

A parallel application is made of a set of processes that execute in a distributed environment and co-operate/synchronize by means of message passing. For that purpose the *Communication Environment* (CE) offers a set of services that serve to communicate information between tasks in a transparent way and conceal the particular OS network characteristics. Similarly, the *Load Balancing* (LB) layer will take advantage of the services offered by the Communication layer. PVM and MPI constitute common examples of such a communication layer that have been used in many existing LBS.

The LB layer is responsible for carrying out all the actions involved in process migration. In that sense, this layer includes all the mechanisms that implement the object migration. Moreover, this layer should also include the policies mentioned in Section 4.3 that manage the resources and are responsible for maintaining load balancing. Interaction between the user application and the LB layer could be done by invoking certain functions of the LB layer directly. Alternatively, the programming language of the application may be augmented with new constructs and a code pre-processor will transform those constructs to LB functions. In both cases, the LB functions will be linked to the user application at a later stage. In contrast to LBS where the interaction between the application and the LB layer is accomplished

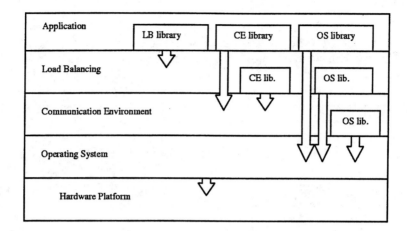

Figure 4.5: Layered structure of a Load Balancing System.

through a linked library, there are LBS where such interaction is carried out by means of messages using the services of the Communication layer. In this case, the user application treats the LB system as another application task within the communication domain of the message-passing environment.

4.5.2 Design issues of a process migration mechanism

A major requirement for LBS is that the migration should not affect the correctness of the application. Execution of the application should proceed as if the migration had never taken place, the migration being "transparent". Such transparency can be ensured if the state of a process on the source processor is reconstructed on the target processor. The process migration mechanism can be roughly divided into four main stages: *migration initiation, state capture, state transfer* and *process restart*. Below, we present the most important issues that a process migration environment must address in practice.

Migration Initiation

This stage triggers the decision of starting the migration of a given process, i.e., it decides *when* migration occurs. Moreover it should indicate which process should migrate and where to. In principle, this information depends on the decisions adopted by the load balancing strategy running in the system. The scope of the migration event causes the migration mechanism to be synchronous or asynchronous. *Asynchronous migration* allows a process to migrate independently of what the other processes in the application are doing. *Synchronous migration* implies that all the processes are first executing and agree to enter into a migration phase where the selected processes will be finally relocated.

State Capture

This stage implies capturing the process' state in the source processor. In this context, the process' state includes: (i) the processor state (contents of the machine registers, program counter, program status word, etc.), (ii) the state held by the process itself (its text, static and dynamic data, and stack segments), (iii) the state held by the OS for the process (blocked and pending signals, open files, socket connections, page table entries, controlling terminals, process relationship information, etc.), and (iv) the OS state held by the process (file descriptors, process identifiers, host name and time).

The previous information, known to the process, is only valid in the context of the local execution environment (local operating system and host). In addition, a process has a state from the point of view of the communication layer. In this regard, a process' state includes its communication identifiers and the messages sent to/from that process.

Capturing the process state can be non-restricted or restricted.

(i) *Non-restricted capture* of the process' state means that the state can be saved at any moment. The LBS must block the process (for instance, using the Unix signal mechanism) and capture its state.

(ii) *Restricted capture* means that the state will be saved only when the process executes a special code that has been inserted in the application. This implies that all points where a process may be suspended for migration must be known at the time of compilation. The special code usually consists of a call to an LB service that passes control to the LB layer. Then the LB layer decides whether the process should be suspended for migration or if the call is serviced and the control returned to the process. In the latter case, the service invocation also serves to capture and preserve the process state information.

The process state can be saved on disk, creating a *checkpoint* of the process. Readers interested in this area should refer to [59] for a detailed description of the *checkpointing* mechanism applied to a single user process in the Condor system. The checkpoint mechanism has the advantage of being minimally obtrusive and providing fault-tolerance. However, it requires a significant disk space consumption. Other migration mechanisms do not store the process state on disk. They create a *skeleton* process on the target processor to receive the migrating process and then the process state is sent by the migrating process directly to the skeleton process.

State Transfer

For LBS implemented at user-level, the entire virtual address of a process is usually transferred at this stage [9]. There are different mechanisms to transfer this information and they depend on the method that was used to capture the process state.

When the checkpoint of the process has been stored on disk (*indirect checkpointing*), the state transfer is carried out by accessing the checkpoint files from the target processor. The use of a certain global file system (NFS, for instance) is the simplest solution in this case. Otherwise, checkpoint files must be transferred from one host to another through the network.

When a skeleton process mechanism is used (*direct chekpointing*), this stage of the migration protocol implies that the skeleton process was successfully started at the target processor (using the same executable file automatically "migrates" the text of the process). Then the process must detach from the local processor and its state, which was previously preserved (data, stack and processor context), must be transferred to the target processor through a socket [9, 43].

Process Restart

The process restart implies that a new process is created in the target host and its data and stack information is assimilated according to the information obtained from the state of the process in the source host. The new process in the target host reads data and stack either from disk or a socket, depending on the mechanism used to capture the process state. Once the new process has assimilated all the information needed as its own process state, the process in the source host is removed from there.

Before the new process can re-participate as part of the application, it first has to re-enrol itself with the local server of the Communication layer. This action implies that some actions are carried out to ensure the correct delivery of messages. It must be ensured that all processes send all their future messages destined for the migrated process to the new destination and that no in-transit messages are dropped during migration. These actions must also solve problems related to the process identifiers within the communication environment and message sequencing. Different mechanisms have been proposed to ensure the correct delivery and sequencing of in-transit messages. They can be roughly classified into three main categories:

1. *Message forwarding*: a shadow process can be created in the processor where the process was originally created. This shadow process will be responsible for forwarding all the messages directed to the process in its new location. When a message arrives at a processor and finds that the destination process is not there the message is forwarded to the new location [9]).

2. *Message restriction*: this technique ensures that a process should not be communicating with another process at the moment of migration. That imposes the notion of critical sections where all interprocess communication are embedded in such sections. Migration can only take place outside a critical section [43].

3. *Message flushing*: in this technique, a protocol is used to ensure that all pending messages have been received. Therefore, the network will be drained when all the pending messages are received [46].

Prior to restarting a migrated process, it must be connected again to the Communication Environment in order to establish a new communication identifier. The new identifier must be broadcast to all the hosts so that a mapping of old identifiers to new identifiers for each process is maintained in a local table. All future communications will go through this mapping table before they are passed into and out of the Communication Environment.

4.5.3 Limitations of process migration mechanisms

In practice, there are additional problems that must also be addressed in the implementation of the LBS. These problems are related to the management of file I/O (which includes application binaries, application data files and checkpoint files), management of terminal I/O and GUIs, and management of cross-application communication and inter-application communication.

Access to the same set of files can be done via a networked file system (NFS, for example). When there is no common file system, the remote access is accomplished by maintaining a "shadow" process on the machine where the task was initially running. The "shadow" process acts as an agent for file access by the migrated process. Similar solutions can be devised for accessing terminal I/O.

However, some limitations are imposed by existing LBS. For instance, processes which execute *fork()* or *exec()*, or which communicate with other processes via signals, sockets or pipes are not suitable for migration because existing LBS cannot save and restore sufficient number of these processes' state. This limitation is reasonable according to the layering architecture of Figure 4.5. User applications are restricted to use the facilities provided by the Communication layer or the LB layer to establish communication between processes or to create/destroy processes.

Additionally, process migration is normally restricted between machines with homogeneous architectures, i.e., with the same instruction sets and data formats. However, there are some systems that allow migration of sequential processes between heterogeneous machines. For instance, **Tui** [53] is a migration system that is able to translate the memory image of a program (written in ANSI-C) between four common architectures (MC68000, SPARC, i486 and PowerPC). Another example is the **Porch** compiler [57] that enables machine-independent checkpoints by automatic generation of checkpointing and recovery code.

4.5.4 Examples of existing packages for supporting dynamic load balancing

In this subsection, we briefly review some of the most significant software packages that have been developed or are in an early stage of development in the framework of dynamic load balancing and item migration. These tools usually fall into two main classes [3]:

(i) *Job Management Software*: these software tools are designed to manage application jobs submitted to parallel systems or workstation clusters. Most of them might be regarded as direct descendants from traditional batch and queuing systems [3, 30]. Process-based LBS usually belong to this group.

(ii) *Distributed Computing Environments*: these software tools are used as an applications environment, similar in many ways to a distributed shared memory system. The application programmer is usually provided with a set of development libraries added to a standard language that allows the development of a distributed application to be run on the hardware platform (usually, a distributed cluster of workstations). The environment contains also a runtime system that extends or partially replaces the underlying operating system in order to provide support for item migration. Data-based and thread-based LBS mainly belong to this group of tools.

For each class of LBS, we briefly describe the main characteristics of one of the most relevant tools, which serves as a representative example of tools of that class. This description is completed with a list of references for other similar tools.

1. *Data-based LBS*. Most of the dynamic migration environments that distribute data are based on the SPMD model of computation, where the user program is replicated

in several processors and each copy of the program, executing in parallel, performs its computations on a subset of the data.

Dome [2] is a computing environment that supports heterogeneous checkpointing through the use of C++ class abstractions. When an object of one class is instantiated it is automatically partitioned and adapted within the distributed environment. The load balancing is performed by remapping data based on the time taken by each process during the last computational phase. Due to the SPMD computational nature of the applications, the synchronization between computational phases and load-balancing phases is straightforward.

Other systems similar to Dome that also provide data migration are described in [51] and [8]. An architecture independent package is presented in [51], where the user is responsible for inserting calls to specify the data to be saved and perform the checkpoints. A framework implemented in the context of the Charm++ system [34] is presented in [8]. This framework automatically creates load balanced Charm++ applications by means of object migration. Load balancing decisions are guided by the information provided by the run-time system, which can measure the work incurred by particular objects and can record also object-to-object communication patterns. In this framework migration can only occur between method invocations, so that migration is limited to data members of the object.

2. *Thread-based LBS.* These systems are usually object-based systems that provide a programming environment that exports a thread-based object oriented programming model to the user. The objects share a single address space per application that is distributed across the nodes in the network, and the objects are free (under certain constraints) to migrate from one node to another.

   Arachne [20] is a thread system that supports thread migration between heterogeneous platforms. It is based on C and C++ languages, which have been augmented in order to facilitate thread migration. Conventional C++ is generated by a pre-processor that inserts special code to enable the saving and subsequent restoration of a thread's state. Migrating threads must be previously suspended, and suspension takes place when a thread invokes an Arachne primitive. Therefore, threads may be suspended (and potentially migrated) only at particular points that must be known at the time of compilation. The Arachne environment includes also a runtime system that manages the threads during program execution. Generating executables beforehand for each machine supports the heterogeneity of the environment.

   Other examples of object-based environments that support migrating threads are **Ariadne** [40], **Emerald** [56] and **Ythreads** [49]. In contrast, **UPVM** [35] is a process-based environment that provides thread migration for PVM programs written in single program multiple data (SPMD) style.

3. *Process-based LBS.* **Condor/CARMI** [46] constitutes one of the most notable examples of process migration environments implemented at the user-level. It is based on Condor, a distributed batch processing system for Unix that was extended with additional services to support parallel PVM applications. Condor uses a checkpoint/rollback mechanism to support migration of sequential processes. The Condor system takes a snapshot of the state of the programs it is running. This is done by taking a core dump of the process and merging it with the executable file. At migration time, the currently running process is immediately terminated and it is resumed on another

host, based on the last checkpoint file. Condor was extended with CARMI (Condor Application Resource Management Interface) which provides an asynchronous Application Programming Interface (API) for PVM applications. CARMI provides services to allocate resources to an application and allows applications to make use and manage those resources by creating processes to run there. **CoCheck** (Consistent Checkpointing) is the third component of the system. It is built on top of Condor and implements a network consistency protocol to ensure that the entire state of the PVM network is saved during a checkpoint and that communication can be resumed following a checkpoint.

Process migration and checkpointing (with certain limitations in most cases) have also been developed or are under development in some research packages such as **MIST** [9], **DynamicPVM** [43], **PBeam** [45] and **Hector** [47], and in some commercial packages that were based also on Condor such us **Codine** [12] and **LoadLeveler** [29].

4.6   Concluding remarks and future trends

Dynamic load balancing on parallel and distributed systems is a challenge, due to the autonomy of the processors and the inter-processor communication overhead incurred in the collection of state information, communication delays, redistribution of loads, etc.. In this chapter we have presented an overview of the load balancing problem and a unified treatment of many of the results obtained in the literature has been provided. The focus has been on the load balancing methods designed by transferring processes from the heavily loaded processors to the lightly loaded processors with the aim of improving the performance of the application. Additionally, we have also reviewed the software packages that currently exist for supporting load balancing.

The study reported here opens up a range of interesting and challenging research opportunities. In particular, with the emerging software technologies that allow us to use networked workstations/supercomputers/parallel computers, dynamic load balancing appears to be a crucial issue in harnessing the computing capabilities offered by such systems.

The development of efficient policies for load information distribution and placement decision-making would be of interest in the development of emerging metacomputing environments. Such systems are based on wide-area heterogeneous computing resources that are presented to the user as a single computing environment. In such a system, computing power should be balanced between the workload of all parallel and sequential applications running in the environment. Many efforts should still be devoted to the development of software support needed to use aggregated distributed resources in a coordinated manner. Fundamental issues associated with load sharing, load balancing, process migration and remote access are still open to research.

Therefore, we feel that the emphasis in this area will be the incorporation of a set of tools at the distributed operating system level, used to implement different load balancing policies depending on the system architecture and application requirements.

Acknowledgements

This work has been supported by the CICYT under contracts TIC 95-0868 and TIC 98-0433 and by the Slovak Scientific Grant Agency within Research Projects No.2/4102/97-99.

References

[1] I. Ahmad and A. Ghafoor. Semi-distributed load balancing for massively parallel multi-computer systems. *IEEE Transactions on Software Engineering*, 10(17):987–998, 1991.

[2] J. Arabe, A. Beguelin, B. Lowekamp, E. Seligman, M. Starkey, and P. Stephan. Dome: parallel programming in a distributed computing environment. In *Procc. of the International Parallel Processing Symposium (IPPS-96)*, pages 218–224, 1996.

[3] M.A. Baker, G.C. Fox, and H.W. Yau. A review of commercial and research cluster management software. Technical report, Northeast Parallel Architectures Center, Syracuse University, 1996.

[4] C. Barmon, M.N. Faruqui, and G.P. Battacharjee. Dynamic load balancing algorithm in a distributed system. *Microprocessing and Microprogramming*, 29:273–285, 1990/91.

[5] J. Baumgartner, D. J. Cook, and B. Shirazi. Genetic solutions to the load balancing problem. In *Proc of the International Conference on Parallel Processing ICPP. Workshop on Challenges for Parallel Processing*, pages 72–81, 1995.

[6] D. P. Bertsekas and J. Tsitsiklis. *Parallel and Distributed Computation: Numerical Methods*. Prentice-Hall Englewoods-Cliffs, 1989.

[7] J. E. Boillat. Load balancing and Poisson equation in a graph. *Concurreny: Practice and Experience*, 2(2):289–313, December 1990.

[8] R. K. Brunner and L. V. Kalé. Handling application-induced load imbalance using parallel objects. Technical Report 99–03, Department of Computer Science, University of Illinois at Urbana-Champaign, 1999.

[9] J. Casas, D. Clark, P.S. Galbiati, R. Konuru, S. Otto, R. Prouty, and J. Walpole. MIST: PVM with transparent migration and checkpointing. In *Proc. of the Third annual PVM User's group Meeting*, 1995.

[10] T.L. Casavant and J.G. Kuhl. A taxonomy of scheduling in general-purpose distributed computing systems. *IEEE Transaction on Software Engineering*, 14(2):141–154, February 1988.

[11] H.W. Chang and W. J. Oldham. Dynamic task allocation models for large distributed computing systems. *IEEE Transactions on Parallel and Distributed Systems*, 6(12):1301–1315, December 1995.

[12] Codine. *Codine: Computing in Distributed Networked Environments*. GENIAS Software, URL: http://www.genias.de/genias/english/codine.html, 1997.

[13] A. Corradi, L. Leonardi, and F. Zambonelli. Diffusive load-balancing policies for dynamic applications. *IEEE Concurrency, Parallel, Distributed and Mobile Computing*, pages 22–31, January 1999.

[14] A. Cortés, A. Ripoll, M. A. Senar, F. Cedó, and E. Luque. On the stability of a distributed dynamic load balancing algorithm. In *Proc. of the IEEE Int'l Conf. on Parallel and Distributed Systems (ICPADS)*, pages 435–446, 1998.

[15] A. Cortés, A. Ripoll, M. A. Senar, and E. Luque. Dynamic load balancing strategy for scalable parallel systems. In *Proceedings in Parallel Computing: Fundamentals, Applications and New Directions (ParCo97)*, pages 735–738. Elsevier Science B.V., 1998.

[16] A. Cortés, A. Ripoll, M. A. Senar, and E. Luque. Performance comparison of dynamic load-balancing strategies for distributed computing. In *Proc. of the IEEE Hawaii Int'l Conference on Systems Sciences (HICSS-32)*, 1999.

[17] G. Cybenko. Dynamic load balancing for distributed memory multiprocessors. *Journal of Parallel and Distributed Computing*, pages 279–301, 1989.

[18] S. P. Dandamudi and M. Lo. A hierarchical load sharing policy for distributed systems. In *Proc. of the IEEE Int. Symp. on Modeling, Analysis and Simulation of Computer and Telecomm. Systems (MASCOTS)*, pages 3–10, 1997.

[19] R. Diekmann, A. Frommer, and B. Monien. Efficient schemes for nearest neighbors load balancing. *Parallel Computing*, 25:789–812, 1999.

[20] B. Dimitrov and V. Rego. Arachne: a portable threads system supporting migrant threads on heterogeneous network farms. *IEEE Trans. on Parallel and Distrib. Systems*, 9(5):459–469, 1998.

[21] F. Douglis and J. Ousterhout. Transparent process migration: design alternatives and the Sprite implementation. *Software - Practice and Experience*, 21(8):757–785, August 1991.

[22] D. L. Eager, E. D. Lazowska, and J. Zahorjan. Adaptive load sharing in homogeneous distributed systems. *IEEE Transactions on Software Engineering*, 12(5):662–675, May 1986.

[23] D. J. Evans and W. U. Butt. Load balancing with network partitioning using host groups. *Parallel Computing*, 20:325–345, 1994.

[24] D. Ferrari and S. Zhou. An empirical investigation of load indices for load balancing applications. In *Proc. of Performance' 87*, pages 515–528, 1987.

[25] G.C. Fox, W. Furmanski, J. Koller, and P. Simic. Physical optimization and load balancing algorithms. In *Proceedings of the Int. Conference on Hypercube Concurrent Computers and Applications*, pages 591–594, 1989.

[26] G. Horton. A multi-level diffusion method for dynamic load balancing. *Parallel Computing*, 19:209–218, 1993.

[27] S.H. Hosseini, B. Litow, M. Malkawi, J. McPherson, and K. Vairavan. Analysis of a graph coloring based distributed load balancing algorithm. *Journal of Parallel and Distributed Computing*, pages 160–166, 1990.

[28] Y.F. Hu and R.J. Blake. An improved diffusion algorithm for dynamic load balancing. *Parallel Computing*, 25:417–444, 1999.

[29] IBM. *IBM LoadLeveler: General information*. IBM, September 1993.

[30] J.P. Jones and C. Brickell. Second evaluation of job queieng/scheduling software: Phase 1 report. Technical Report NAS-97-013, Nasa Ames Research Center, June 1997.

[31] P. Kacsuk. Wavefront scheduling in LOGFLOW. In *Proceedings of the 2nd EUROMI-CRO Workshop on Parallel and Distributed Processing*, pages 503–510, 1994.

[32] P. Kacsuk, Zs. Németh, and Zs. Puskás. Tools for mapping, load balancing and monitoring in the LOGFLOW parallel prolog project. *Parallel Computing*, 22(13):1853–1881, 1996.

[33] L. V. Kalé. Comparing the perfomance of two dynamic load distribution methods. In *Proceeding of the 1988 International Conference on Parallel Processing*, volume 1, pages 8–12, 1988.

[34] L.V. Kalé and S. Krishnan. *Parallel Programming using C++*, chapter Charm++: Parallel programming with message-driven objects, pages 175–213. MIT Press, 1996.

[35] R.B. Konuru, S.W. Otto, and J. Walpole. A migratable user-level process package for PVM. *Journal of Parallel and Distributed Computing*, 40:81–102, 1997.

[36] T. Kunz. The influence of different workload descriptions on a heuristic load balancing scheme. *IEEE Trans. on Software Engineering*, 17(7):725–730, 1991.

[37] F. H. Lin and R. M. Keller. The Gradient Model load balancing method. *IEEE Transactions on Software Engineering*, 13(1):32–38, January 1987.

[38] F. H. Lin and C.S. Raghavendra. A dynamic load-balancing policy with a central job dispatcher (LBC). *IEEE Transactions on Software Engineering*, 18(2):148–158, February 1992.

[39] R. Lülinf, B. Monien, and F. Ramme. Load balancing in large networks: A comparative study. In *Proceedings of 3th. IEEE Symposium on Parallel and Distributed Processing*, pages 686–689, December 1991.

[40] V. Mascarenhas and V. Rego. Ariadne: Architecture of a portable threads system supporting thread migration. *Software - Practice and Experience*, 26(3):327–357, 1996.

[41] D.S. Milojicic, W. Zint, A. Dange, and P. Giese. Task migration on top of the Mach microkernel. In *Proc. of the Mach 3rd Symposium*, pages 273–289, April 1993.

[42] F. Muniz and E. Zaluska. Parallel load-balancing: An extension to the Gradient Model. *Parallel Computing*, 21:287–301, 1995.

[43] B.J. Overeinder, P.M.A. Sloot, R.N. Heederick, and L.O. Hertzberger. A dynamic load balancing system for parallel cluster computing. *Future Generation Computer Systems*, pages 101–115, May 1996.

[44] C. Papadimitriou. *Computational Complexity*. Addison-Wesley, 1994.

[45] S. Petri, M. Bolz, and H. Langendörfer. Migration and rollback transparency for arbitrary distributed applications in workstation clusters. In *Proc. of Workshop on Run-Time Systems for Parallel Programming, held in conjunction with IPPS/SPDP'98*, 1998.

[46] J. Pruyne and M. Livny. Providing resource management services to parallel applications. In *Proceedings of the 2nd Workshop on Environments and Tools for Parallel Scientific Computing*, pages 152–161, 1995.

[47] S.H. Russ, K. Reece, J. Robinson, B. Meyers, R. Rajan, L. Rajagopalan, and C-H. Tan. Hector: An agent-based architecture for dynamic resource management. *IEEE Concurrency*, pages 47–55, April 1999.

[48] V. A. Saletore. A distributed and adaptive dynamic load balancing scheme for parallel processing of medium-grain tasks. In *Proc. of the 5th Distributed Memory Comput. Conf.*, pages 995–999, 1990.

[49] J. Sang, G. Peters, and V. Rego. Thread migration on heterogeneous systems via compile-time transformations. In *Proc. Int'l Conf. Parallel and Distributed Systems (ICPADS)*, pages 634–639, 1994.

[50] W. Shu and L.V. Kalé. A dynamic scheduling strategy for the Chare-kernel system. In *Proceedings of Supercomputing 89*, November 1989.

[51] L. Silva, B. Veer, and J. Silva. Checkpointing SPMD applications on Transputer networks. In *Procc. of the Scalable High Performance Computing Conference*, pages 694–701, 1994.

[52] P. K. Sinha. *Distributed Operating Systems. Concepts and Design*. IEEE Press, 1997.

[53] V Smith and N. C. Hutchinson. Heterogeneous process migration: The Tui system. Technical report, Department of Computer Science, University of British Columbia, March 1997.

[54] J. Song. A partially asynchronous and iterative algorithm for distributed load balancing. *Parallel Computing*, 20:853–868, 1994.

[55] J.A. Stankovic and I.S. Sidhu. An adaptive bidding algorithm for processes, clusters and distributed groups. In *Proceedings of 4th. International Conference on Distributed Computer Systems*, pages 49–59, May 1984.

[56] B. Steensgaard and E. Jul. Object and native code thread mobility among heterogeneous computers. In *Proc. ACM Symp. Oper. Syst. Princ.*, pages 68–78, 1995.

[57] V. Strumpen and B. Ramkumar. *Fault-Tolerant Parallel and Distributed Systems*, chapter Portable Checkpointing for Heterogeneous Architectures, pages 73–92. Kluwer Academic Press, 1998.

[58] R. Subramain and I. D. Scherson. An analysis of diffusive load-balancing. In *Proceedings of 6th ACM Symposium on Parallel Algorithms and Architectures*, 1994.

[59] T. Tannenbaum and M. Litzkow. The Condor distributed processing system. *Dr. Dobb's Journal*, pages 40–48, 1995.

[60] M. M. Theimer, K. A. Lantz, and D. R. Cheriton. Preemptable remote execution facilities for the V system. In *Proceedings of the 10th ACM Symposium on Operating Systems Principles*, pages 2–12, 1985.

[61] J. Watts and S. Taylor. A practical approach to dynamic load balancing. *IEEE Trans. Parallel and Distributed Systems*, 9(3):235–248, March 1998.

[62] M. Willebeek-LeMair and A. Reeves. Strategies for dynamic load balancing on highly parallel computers. *IEEE Trans. Par. and Distrib. Systems*, 4:979–993, 1993.

[63] M. Y. Wu and W. Shu. The Direct Dimension Exchange method for load balancing in k-ary n-cubes. In *Proc. of the IEEE Symposium on Parallel and Distributed Processing*, pages 366–393, 1996.

[64] C. Xu and F. C. Lau. *Load Balancing in Parallel Computers. Theory and Practice*. Kluwe Academic Publishers, 1997.

[65] C. Xu, S. Tschoeke, and B. Monien. Performance evaluation of load distribution strategies in parallel branch-and-bound computations. In *Proceedings of 7th. Symposium of Parallel and Distributed Systems*, pages 402–405, October 1995.

[66] J. Xu and K. Hwang. Heuristic methods for dynamic load balancing in a message-passing multicomputer. *Journal of Par. and Distrib. Computing*, 18:1–13, 1993.

[67] S.M. Yuan. An efficient periodically exchanged dynamic load-balancing algorithm. *International Journal of Mini and Microcomputers*, 12(1):1–6, 1990.

[68] S. Zhou. A trace-driven simulation study of dynamic load balancing. *IEEE Trans. on Software Engineering*, 14(9):1327–1341, September 1988.

[69] T.F. Znati, R.G. Melhem, and K.R. Pruhs. Dilation-based bidding schemes for dynamic load balancing on distributing processing systems. In *Proceedings of 6th Distributed Memory Computing Conference*, pages 129–136, April 1991.

Chapter 5

Debugging of Parallel and Distributed Programs

José C. Cunha, João Lourenço and Vítor Duarte

Abstract

This chapter surveys the main issues involved in correctness debugging of parallel and distributed programs. Distributed debugging is an instance of the more general problem of observation of a distributed computation. This chapter briefly summarizes the theoretical foundations of the distributed debugging activity. Then a survey is presented of the main methodologies used for parallel and distributed debugging, including state and event based debugging, deterministic re-execution, systematic state exploration, and correctness predicate evaluation. Such approaches are complementary to one another, and the chapter discusses how they can be supported using distinct techniques for observation and control.

5.1 Introduction

The correctness debugging activity is first discussed within the general context of software development, and then the main characteristics of debugging of sequential programs are outlined. Finally, this section discusses the main dimensions involved in the debugging of parallel and distributed programs. Throughout this chapter, the term *distributed debugging* (DD) is used to refer to the debugging of parallel and distributed programs.

5.1.1 The debugging activity

Given an application, one typically reasons in relation to some specification of its intended behavior. Ideally, such specification would be expressed by a formal notation to ensure or assess the correctness of any implementation of the application in terms of a programming model. One would like to describe the application using a formal specification that would automatically generate correct (and efficient) program code. In such a case, bugs could only appear at the level of the application specification, in relation to its intended behavior (*specification bugs*). Given the general lack of automated code generation tools for high level formal specification languages, a programmer becomes responsible for the mapping from the formal specification to the program code. Even if the clarity and expressiveness of each programming model can greatly contribute to ease the mentioned mapping, such an activity gives the opportunity to introduce another kind of bugs, at the level of program design and implementation (*programming bugs*). These ideas are shown in Figure 5.1 below.

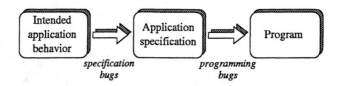

Figure 5.1: Specification and programming bugs

In common practice, however there is typically no complete application formal specification available so the correctness of the program can only be assessed in relation to the intended application behavior, which only exists in the mind of the developer (to be optimistic...). This makes the debugging activity extremely complex, as specification and programming bugs appear at the same level, embedded into the program code.

Below the program level one would also have to consider the mapping to the operating system and machine code levels as potentially contributing to the appearance of other kind of bugs. However, in general, such bugs are beyond the reach of the application developer and programmer.

Due to the above difficulties, debugging becomes a fundamental activity even if it is not a desired one.

In the past fifty years, there was a huge amount of work concerning the debugging of sequential applications. Several significant debugging techniques were developed, addressing both specification and programming bugs, depending on the abstractions and paradigms of the programming languages (e.g., imperative or declarative) [16]. A sequential application is executed by a sequential system so a state-based approach is adequate to analyze its behavior. Interactive debuggers allow the user to inspect the succession of states followed by a sequential computation. Due to the deterministic behavior of a sequential system, it is easy to re-execute the program under a given set of input conditions in order to examine its behavior in detail. Even if the programming language exhibits some form of internal nondeterminism in its computation strategy, e.g., like Prolog, it is possible to apply the cyclic state-based debugging technique in order to repeatedly examine the deterministic execution path followed by the sequential Prolog executor. Sequential debugging is also made simpler because one has only to think about one thread of control at each point during a debugging session. The large number of states that may be generated for a sequential computation is easily handled by placing breakpoints at desired conditions or regions of code and having the debugger stopping the execution. Such an external control by a debugger has no logical effect upon the sequential computation behavior.

The increased complexity of developing parallel and distributed applications makes it more difficult to use the above approach for debugging.

5.1.2 Distributed debugging

In this chapter, a *distributed program* (DP) consists of a collection of sequential processes which cooperate by using some distributed-memory communication model. The term *distributed* is emphasized because such distributed processes cannot rely on physically shared memory or global clock abstractions for synchronization purposes. Parallel applications are naturally included in this concept, when distributed-memory systems are considered, such as the ones based on cluster computing platforms. A distributed program is based upon the semantics of the specific programming language that is used to express the concurrency, distribution and parallelism, and communication between processes. A distributed program is executed in the context of a *distributed system* (DS). A distributed system provides the computational mechanisms to support the execution of a distributed program, in terms of a virtual architecture defined by the operating system and the hardware platform.

Given a distributed program, one would like to be able to specify its correctness properties in term of predicates on the expected program behavior and then having a distributed debugger automatically comparing them to the observed program behavior (see Figure 5.2).

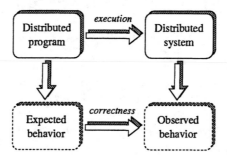

Figure 5.2: Expected and observed behaviors

Specification of desired properties would be possible, as well as detection of undesired or erroneous situations corresponding to programming bugs. This would require the distributed debugger to support three distinct aspects:

- A language to specify the correctness predicates.

- Algorithms to evaluate those predicates.

- Observation and control mechanisms to allow the user to observe the computation states corresponding to the detected erroneous situations.

Such an ideal picture is difficult to achieve in an asynchronous distributed system with no global clock, no global shared memory, and no bounds on message transmission times. The following dimensions make distributed debugging much more difficult than sequential debugging [36]:

1. The large number of parallel and distributed entities, with dynamic interactions in a distributed program.

2. The intrinsic non-deterministic behavior of a distributed program.

3. The difficulties of constructing accurate, up-to-date, and consistent observations of the global states of an asynchronous distributed system.

4. The intrusion effect due to the observation and control mechanisms.

The first dimension (*distributed dynamic interacting entities*) must consider a large number of computation states, and unforeseen dynamic interactions whose influence on the global program behavior is difficult to understand. To address this dimension, the distributed debugger must be able to observe computations both at a global level, to understand the interactions, and at the level of the individual processes. This has implications concerning the debugging functionalities and its software architecture.

The second dimension (*nondeterminism*) makes the actual execution behavior dependent on actual process speeds (due to distinct processor speeds and to distinct operating system scheduling effects) and unpredictable communication delays. On one hand, this characteristic is related to the expected benefit of speeding up the computations through parallel processing. On the other hand, it may originate erroneous situations, when two concurrent actions involving distinct distributed processes are in conflict and may occur in distinct orderings depending on the above timing effects. Examples of such *race conditions* occur for shared-memory communication models, and for message-passing models [35]. This dimension requires the distributed debugger to provide facilities to detect those situations, and in general to evaluate program correctness properties, in a way that must be valid for all possible execution orderings. It also requires techniques to allow reproducible coherent observation of such error situations, without precluding user interaction.

The third dimension (*observation of global states*) must be considered because the evaluation of erroneous situations depends on accurate observations. These can only be approximately achieved, in a distributed system, by remote observation, based on message passing, so they face the difficulty of absence of a global system state. The distributed debugger must provide strategies for the observation of consistent computation states.

The fourth dimension (*probe- or intrusion-effect*) recognizes the unavoidable fact that any observation affects the system under study, so the distributed debugger must rely on techniques that ensure the lowest possible intrusion, and still allow user interaction, even knowing that this is a highly intrusive activity.

In order to understand how the above dimensions are addressed by a distributed debugging system, some formal concepts are necessary from the distributed systems theory.

The concept of a *distributed computation* (DC) represents all possible behaviors which result from executing a distributed program in a distributed system (see Figure 5.3).

In order to understand and ensure the correctness of a distributed program, one must observe and control the distributed computations which are generated when running the program. So, the debugging activity becomes an instance of the more general problem of observation and control of distributed computations because the above mentioned correctness predicates must be evaluated in meaningful computation states.

This chapter has two main goals. One is to explain the reasons why it is so difficult to develop such an ideal distributed debugging framework addressing all the above dimensions. The other goal is to discuss the main methods and techniques that are actually being used by existing distributed debuggers, and their expected evolution.

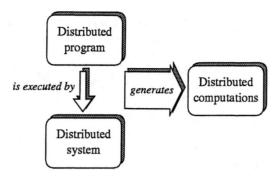

Figure 5.3: Distributed computations

5.1.3 Organization of the chapter

In the remaining of this chapter we discuss solutions to face the above difficulties in the context of the distributed debugging activity. The concept of distributed computation is presented in Section 5.2 and the observation problem is discussed in Section 5.3. The detection of global predicates is discussed in Section 5.4. Then, an overview of the main distributed debugging methodologies and techniques is presented respectively in Section 5.5 and Section 5.6. Finally, the main issues involved in the implementation of distributed debuggers are summarized in Section 5.7 and some conclusions are drawn in Section 5.8.

Significant references may be found in [1–3, 5, 43, 47].

5.2 Distributed Computations

The results of this section may apply to general distributed programming models based on processes and/or threads, and using communication models based on message-passing or shared-memory, with forms of synchronous and asynchronous interactions.

A distributed program is usually based on an abstract model of concurrency and communication. Its operational semantics can be defined in terms of events that correspond to process control and communication actions. Such high level entities (e.g., processes) and events are mapped into low level primitive events that are recognized and generated by the underlying distributed system. So, in this perspective a distributed system is defined as a collection of processes that communicate using a basic message-passing model with the classical *send* and *receive* primitives. A distributed system has the characteristics of an asynchronous system, so that one cannot reason in terms of an accurate global physical time reference in order to follow the chain of computation states that may lead to the cause of a bug in the distributed program.

Due to the arbitrary process speeds and message transmission delays that occur in a distributed system, distinct execution paths can be generated when repeatedly running a distributed program with a given set of input conditions, possibly leading to different results. Such nondeterminism makes it very difficult to evaluate correctness properties that should hold for all possible executions of a distributed program, and not only for a single observed execution.

The concept of distributed computation describes all possible execution runs of a program by a distributed system. See [5] for a detailed presentation of the fundamental issues concerning distributed computations and the observation of global states. It is defined in terms of two concepts. One is the concept of local history (LH) of each sequential process that is involved in the execution of a distributed program. The other concept is the cause-and-effect relationship due to local process ordering and to the event dependences originated by process interactions [29].

A *process* P_i is defined as a sequence of *events*, also called its local history LH_i. There are two types of events. *Internal* events represent local state transitions made by P_i alone, not involving any other processes in the distributed system. *Interaction* events represent process communications corresponding to message send and receive actions. The totally ordered events in P_i's local history represent the evolution of the values of all the P_i's variables and of the interactions involving P_i in a distributed program execution.

$$LH_i = e_i(0), e_i(1), \ldots, e_i(f)$$

In this sequence, $e_i(0)$ is the initialization event of P_i. It defines the process initial state, denoted by $LS_i(0)$. In general, the kth event in the process history, denoted by $e_i(k)$, produces the local state $LS_i(k)$, as the state immediately right after $e_i(k)$ occurrence. One can assume $e_i(f)$ is the termination event of P_i, and $LS_i(f)$ is P_i's final state. Discussion of perpetual processes is beyond the scope of this chapter, but similar conclusions may be drawn.

A prefix of LH_i, for example up to and including the kth event, is denoted by $LH_i(k)$ and it represents the partial history of P_i, up to a certain point in P_i's computation.

A *global history* (GH) is the set defined by the union of all local histories:

$$GH = LH_1 \cup LH_2 \cup \ldots \cup LH_N$$

A fixed number (N) of processes is usually assumed without loss of generality. Among all the event orderings represented by a global history, only some of them can possibly occur that are compatible with the causal precedence relationship ($\rightarrow$) as defined by Lamport [29]. One has relation $e \rightarrow e'$ iff e causally precedes e'. One has relation $e \parallel e'$ iff neither $e \rightarrow e'$ nor $e' \rightarrow e$. Although such relationship is only a potential causality dependence, it is generally used as the basis of distributed debugging to track causes of the errors.

A distributed computation is a partially ordered set (poset) defined by $(GH, \rightarrow)$. Intuitively, this reflects all physically feasible event combinations that must be obeyed by all possible executions of a distributed program in a distributed system. A distributed computation may be represented by a process-time diagram where the event causality chains replace the classical notion of instant physical time in a centralized system with a global clock (see Figure 5.4).

The observation problem in distributed debugging requires one to think about the global states of a distributed computation. A *global state* (GS) is a n-tuple of LS:

$$GS = (LS_1, LS_2, \ldots, LS_N)$$

where LS_i ($i \in \{1, \ldots, N\}$) is the local state of P_i corresponding to some prefix of P_i's local history. The initial global state (denoted by $GS(0)$) of a distributed computation is defined by the initial local states of all processes i.e., $LS_i(0) : \forall i \in \{1, \ldots, N\}$. The final global state of a distributed computation (denoted by $GS(f)$) is defined by the final local states of all processes i.e., $LS_i(f) : \forall i \in \{1, \ldots, N\}$. The difficulty with the "intermediate" global states

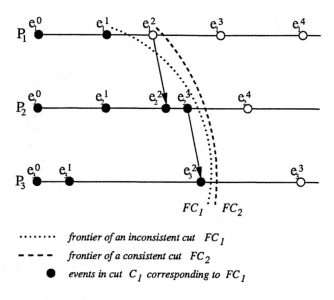

$$\cdots\cdots\quad \textit{frontier of an inconsistent cut } FC_1$$
$$- - - -\quad \textit{frontier of a consistent cut } FC_2$$
$$\bullet\quad \textit{events in cut } C_1 \textit{ corresponding to } FC_1$$

Figure 5.4: Process-time diagram

is that all combinations of local state tuples cannot occur in real executions of a distributed program ...

In relation to a process-time diagram, like the one shown in Figure 5.4, the concept of a *cut* (C) is defined as a subset of the global history. It represents a partial global history of a distributed computation because it is made of prefixes of all processes' local histories. The *frontier* (FC) of a cut C is the n-tuple of the last events in each prefix of LH_i for all $i \in \{1, \ldots, N\}$. The frontier FC seems to represent a view of the global progress of a distributed computation up to a certain point in the execution in terms of the last occurred events (see Figure 5.4). There is a well-defined unique global state corresponding to each frontier FC, that gives the last occurred local states for each process.

However, only *consistent cuts* (CC) are significant for the purpose of distributed debugging. A consistent cut CC is "left closed" under the $\rightarrow$ relationship, i.e.,

$$\forall e, e' \in GH : e \in CC \wedge e' \rightarrow e \Rightarrow e' \in CC$$

Intuitively, a consistent cut incorporates all the past of its own events. A cut that would include some event e and not all events causally preceding e, cannot correspond to a possible view of a distributed program execution.

A *consistent global state* (CGS) is the global state defined by the frontier FC of a consistent cut. A consistent global state represents a global state that can possibly occur during a distributed program execution because it represents a view of the global state that respects the causal precedence among events. In Figure 5.4 the global state corresponding to FC_2 is a consistent state, unlinke the state corresponding to FC_1.

The consistent cut and consistent global state concepts can be used as a basis to define observation models for distributed debugging purposes. An intuitive notion of the *current state* of a distributed computation can be visually caught by considering the events (and states) to the "left" of the frontier of a consistent cut, as equivalent to a past history, and the events to the "right", as the ones in the future. This suggests one could consider an incremental progression of the distributed computation, followed by the user under the control of a distributed debugger where "successive" consistent global states would be examined for evaluation of correctness predicates. Indeed this is an important research direction in distributed debugging, but it has several inherent difficulties that will be discussed in the following.

In order to understand the behavior of a distributed program one has to consider all intermediate consistent global states that can possibly occur starting by the initial state $GS(0)$ until the final state $GS(f)$. For each execution of a distributed program, a distinct set of consistent global states may be followed so each execution generates a distinct sequences of states, due to the nondeterminism of a distributed system. However, to ensure correctness, one needs to reason in terms of all such possible sequences of consistent global states.

The concept of *consistent run* (CR) represents a possible observation of a distributed computation where all the events appear in a total ordering that extends (i.e,. is compatible to) the partial ordering defined by Lamport's causal precedence relation. A consistent run can be obtained from the process-time diagram by building a sequence of events that respects the causality chains and additionally imposes an arbitrary ordering among the concurrent events. A consistent run defines a sequence of consistent global states such that

$$CR = GS_1, GS_2, \ldots, GS_k, GS_{k+1}, \ldots, GS_m$$

where $GS_1 = GS(0)$, $GS_m = GS(f)$, and GS_{k+1} only differs from GS_k in one local state in one of the processes. Intuitively, a consistent run defines a sequence of consistent global state where each new global state in the sequence is obtained by making a "single step" in a single process. One says GS_k *leads-to* GS_{k+1} in a consistent run CR if they are immediate neighbors in that consistent run. A GS is reachable from a GS' in a consistent run iff $GS' \mapsto GS$ in that CR, where $\mapsto$ is the transitive closure of the *leads-to* relation.

Although the consistent run concept artificially restricts the distributed computation to make progress one event at a time, its arbitrary event ordering represents the nondeterminism of a distributed program execution. In order to generate all possible sequences of consistent global states in a distributed computation, one has to consider the set of all possible consistent runs. The set of all consistent global states, ordered by the leads-to relation defines the *lattice* $\mathcal{L}$ of global states that characterizes all possible execution paths in a given distributed computation. $GS(0)$ and $GS(f)$ are respectively the *infimum* and *supremum* elements of $\mathcal{L}$, and the set of all consistent runs is the set of all paths from $GS(0)$ to $GS(f)$.

In summary, the operational semantics of a distributed program can be described in terms of the distributed computations that are generated when the program is run by a distributed system (see Figure 5.5 for a summary and [5] for a deeper presentation). The distributed computation describes all possible sequences of consistent global states that can occur, starting with the initial $GS(0)$ and leading to the final $GS(f)$ state. Such set of possible sequences is only constrained by the local process event ordering and by the Lamport causal precedence relation.

An exhaustive traversal of such paths would be necessary to verify or detect correctness properties of a distributed program. This approach is in general infeasible due to the large combinatory of consistent global states that would have to be examined. Moreover, the problem of constructing individual consistent global states poses itself additional difficulties.

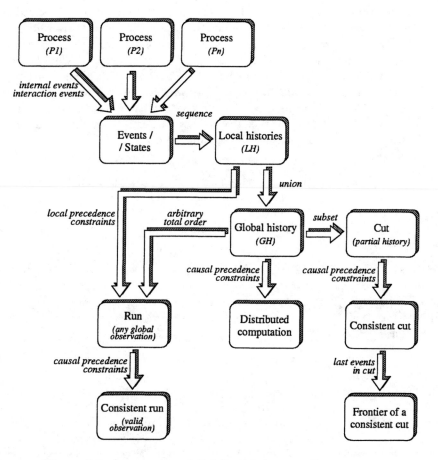

Figure 5.5: A summary of distributed computation concepts

5.3   Observation of Global States

The intuitive notion of global state of a distributed computation consists of a collection of
local states that could be viewed by some ideal external observer. Note that the notion of
global states, as presented above, implicitly includes the state of interprocess communication
channels. In a distributed system, the only possible way for an external observer to build
such a view is through message exchange with each remote individual process. There are
several aspects related to the observation problem:

- The global state can be *obsolete* at the time the global view is actually constructed by
  the external observer. This occurs in case the observation is performed online, during
  actual distributed program execution. This aspect is particularly relevant in distributed reactive applications [5, 9]. In distributed debugging using online observation of
  a distributed computation, if the goal is to track a particular global state in order to
  detect bugs, mechanisms will be required to halt the execution in all processes and
  restore the n-tuples of local states that one wants to examine in detail. Techniques to
  tackle this problem will be reviewed in a section ahead. If the observation is performed
  off-line, in a postmortem analysis of the distributed computation global histories, this
  problem does not arise.

- The observed global state is a cut of the distributed computation. In the online observation approach, the constructed global state corresponds to a cut of the distributed
  computation, so it only allows one to reason about what happened so far. In the off-
  line observation mode, both the past and the future are known and may be accessed
  by the observer.

- The observed global state must be a consistent cut of the distributed computation.
  Observation of inconsistent cuts may occur due to the unpredictable message delivery
  orderings in a distributed system. An inconsistent sequence of events may be built by
  the observer that does not preserve the causal precedence relationship. Approaches to
  build consistent cuts are discussed in this section.

- Multiple independent observers may build distinct views of the same distributed computation. Even if consistent cuts are ensured, several independent observers may
  build distinct consistent cuts. The presentation of uniform views of a distributed
  computation to multiple concurrent and independent observers requires an adequate
  coordination between them, and has been discussed in the scope of distributed system
  research [5]. This is an issue that has not been considered in most of existing distributed debugging tools. However, its relevance is increasing with the emergence of
  integrated development environments where several concurrent tools act as observers
  (and sometimes controllers) of an ongoing distributed computation. Tool coordination
  is briefly mentioned in Section 5.7 and illustrated in several chapters in Part II of this
  book.

The practical methods for observation of distributed computation depend on the distributed debugging approach:

Off-line In this approach, it is possible to analyze global histories of a distributed com-
    putation that were generated by a previous distributed program execution or by a
    simulation of the distributed program model. These methods always deal with com-
    plete histories.

Online In this approach, it is necessary to develop algorithms to construct a global state or a consistent run of a distributed computation during an actual distributed program execution. These methods deal with partial histories.

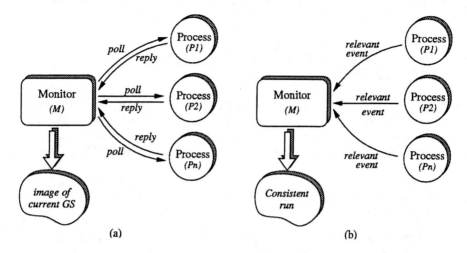

Figure 5.6: Two observation approaches: (a) Global snapshot (b) Active notification

The main approaches to construct online observations of a distributed computation rely on an external observer or monitor process (called $\mathcal{M}$ hereafter). In distributed debugging, they can be used to build snapshots of global states of the distributed computation in order to evaluate correctness properties at those points in a computation. They can also be used to build observations of consistent runs that could have been followed during execution of a distributed program. In all observation strategies it is necessary to consider the problem of the probe effect. Here an assumption is made that the probe effect has a negligible effect in the sense that the message exchanges between $\mathcal{M}$ and each process P_i, do not affect the event ordering of the distributed computation when compared to a unmonitored computation. A detailed discussion of the probe effect is presented in Chapter 6.

All existing approaches for online observation make specific assumptions on the message delivery rules that should be enforced by the distributed system, ranging from FIFO ordering between pairs of processes to causal delivery of messages. Such assumptions are important so that the external observer may be able to construct consistent global states. A discussion of such delivery rules, e.g., based on vector timestamps, is beyond the scope of this chapter. Here one should note the relevance of vector timestamps to support event relationships that exactly capture the causality. The reader may find complete surveys in [13, 34, 46].

The first strategy tries to build a *global snapshot* [7] that corresponds to a consistent global state of the distributed computation (see Figure 5.6 (a)). The observer $\mathcal{M}$ is responsible for polling all the processes and these must reply by sending their corresponding local states. The observer then constructs a consistent global state, so that the method ensures there is a path in $\mathcal{L}$ that contains the constructed consistent global state. Successive polling requests by $\mathcal{M}$ can be used to try to build an image of the evolution of the consistent global states followed by the distributed computation. Unfortunately, this method may miss important consistent global states, and it exhibits either too much overhead due to the polling or a great delay in the observation.

The second strategy allows $\mathcal{M}$ to build an entire observation or consistent run of the distributed computation (see Figure 5.6 (b)). Each distributed program process is responsible for notifying $\mathcal{M}$ when each relevant[1] event occurs. $\mathcal{M}$ collects all information from all the processes and ensures it builds a consistent run. Such a consistent run corresponds to one of the possible paths that the distributed computation could actually have followed.

Each observation method has its limitations and uses as discussed in the following.

5.4   Detection of Global Predicates

A general method underlies the work by several authors [9, 19, 25, 51] to support the distributed debugging activity, according to the three following steps: specification of global correctness conditions, their (off-line or online) evaluation, and corresponding reaction of the distributed debugger, depending on the result of the evaluation [4]. A complete approach should allow:

1. Specification of behavior. There are several approaches to specify global predicates in terms of local and global states.

2. Detection of global predicates. There are several proposals for off-line and online global predicate detectors for distinct kinds of global predicates [6, 17].

3. Reaction of the distributed debugger. The distributed debugger must perform the (off-line or online) reconstruction of the consistent global state that satisfies the detected global predicate.

These issues underly the theoretical framework to implement several distributed debugging techniques for observation and control (see Section 5.6).

5.4.1   Global Predicate Specification

This step starts by the identification of desired or undesired distributed program properties corresponding to the program correctness criteria.

These properties are then expressed as global predicates (GP) which are boolean expressions involving conditions on the local variables of multiple processes or on the states of communication channels. Multiple authors have proposed distinct specification languages for global predicates in terms of global states or events, as well as in terms of sequences of states or patterns of events [6, 17].

The main issues in the design of such specification languages are:

(i) Expressiveness of the language, to be adequate to specify the desired conditions corresponding to correctness or erroneous situations.

(ii) Computational complexity, to be amenable to an efficient implementation. A highly expressive notation is of reduced practical interest if it implies a NP-complete evaluation.

(iii) An adequate compromise between the abstraction level of the distributed program model and the observation level of the distributed debugger. This means allowing an easy mapping between the correctness conditions, the distributed program concepts (and the

---

[1]The specification of "relevant events" depends on the kind of state changes one wants to observe.

program code itself), and the actually observed entities by the distributed debugger, e.g., the low level events or global states.

The main obstacle to the full adoption of this predicate based approach in distributed debugging has been the complexity of the evaluation of the global conditions in a distributed system.

5.4.2   Evaluation of global predicates

This step is responsible for the detection of global predicates using off-line or online approaches. The problem of evaluating general forms of global predicates has been studied and found NP-hard [8], so several authors have focused on the evaluation of restricted forms of global predicates, such as conjunctive [18, 24] and disjunctive global predicates. Although restricted, such global predicates are still useful in distributed debugging. An important distinction is established among so-called stable and unstable properties of a distributed program. Once a stable property becomes true in a specific global state GS, it remains true in all the following ones that can be reached from GS. Deadlock and termination are examples of stable properties. On the other hand, an unstable property may dynamically change its truth value during the distributed execution. Both types of properties are important for analyzing the correctness of a distributed program. Unstable properties reflect many situations resulting from the dynamic behavior of a distributed program, e.g., distributed mutual exclusion.

The evaluation of stable and unstable properties poses different requirements. The former properties can be caught by online observations based upon the global snapshot approach, provided the polling requests are repeated until a consistent global state is found where the required stable property holds. Unfortunately, the detection of unstable properties is more difficult. It cannot be ensured by online observations based on the global snapshot approach, as the constructed global state may miss the point of the distributed computation where that property temporarily holds, due to the uncertainties arising in a distributed system. Concerning the online construction of consistent runs, based on the active notification approach (see Figure 5.6), even if the property holds for a certain consistent global state in that constructed run, this does not gives information about how the property behaves in other possible consistent runs.

Extended forms of global properties have been proposed by several authors that try to express the distributed program behavior in terms of the entire distributed computation, instead of a single consistent global state. These have the forms:

$Definitely(GP)$: for all consistent runs of a distributed computation, there exists a consistent global state that satisfies GP.

$Possibly(GP)$: there is a consistent run of a distributed computation such that it contains a consistent global state satisfying GP.

The second form is particularly useful for distributed debugging, for a property expressing an undesirable or erroneous condition, it would be sufficient to find a consistent global state where the corresponding GP holds. This may also require the search along the lattice of consistent global states but only until such a consistent global state is found.

For a correctness property expressing a condition that must hold in all possible executions of a distributed program, the corresponding GP must be true in all the paths in the lattice of consistent global states defined by a distributed computation.

Several authors have exploited approaches for building and traversal the entire lattice of consistent global states [9], which are adequate for evaluation of both stable and unstable predicates, of the possibly and definitely kinds. Other authors have tried to exploit specific and simplified forms of GP, e.g., conjunctive or disjunctive, in order to avoid an exhaustive search of $\mathcal{L}$. A summary of these approaches can be found in [17].

A distinct approach, albeit with the same objectives of evaluating correctness properties, concerns specific forms of race conditions and their detection. Such mechanisms are usually embedded as implicit functionalities of a distributed debugger [23, 41].

5.4.3   Reaction on detection of a global predicate

Depending on the user interpretation of the logical condition that was evaluated, a particular reaction may be necessary. For example, if the detected global predicate corresponds to a bug situation, a distributed debugger should be able to execute the following actions:

(i) Stop the distributed program execution.

(ii) Restore the local states of all processes in a meaningful consistent global state that satisfies the detected global predicate.

(iii) Allow the user to examine individual local states of that consistent global state as well as of its past.

The first action is obviously only required when the predicate detection is made online. Its implementation is open to multiple interpretations because of the asynchronous evolution of independent computation processes. The above actions are simpler for a post-mortem approach that accesses the complete computation histories. Such approach may even allow the user to traverse the execution paths into the past and the future of the reconstructed global state. In Section 5.6 a review of existing implementation techniques is presented.

5.5   Debugging Methodologies

In this section three main criteria are used to classify distributed debugging methodologies: (i) What steps of distributed debugging activities are supported in the development cycle? (ii) At what time in the application development cycle do such distributed debugging activities take place? (iii) What is the observation model used?

5.5.1   The steps in the cycle of distributed debugging activities

Distributed debugging methodologies can be classified according to the level of support they provide to the user concerning the activities of global predicate specification and detection, and the search for the causes of the distributed program bugs (see Figure 5.7).

In the following, these approaches are successively discussed, starting from the simpler approaches to the more complex ones. These approaches are complementary to one another, in the sense that each approach tries to overcome a limitation of the previous approach in the sequence.

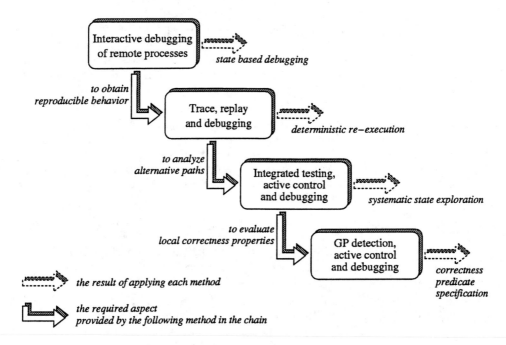

the result of applying each method

the required aspect
provided by the following method in the chain

Figure 5.7: Distributed debugging methodologies

Interactive debugging of remote sequential processes

This is based on an extension of conventional sequential debugging commands to allow individual online observation and control of the execution of remote sequential processes. This is a limited approach that only allows to examine local histories of individual processes of a distributed program. As each local history describes only the evolution of each process in terms of its internal and interaction events, it is the programmer's task to build the global picture of the corresponding distributed computation. However, as such basic remote debugging mechanisms are required to enable more sophisticated approaches, they are supported by almost all existing commercial or academic distributed debuggers. The main distinction between existing distributed debuggers of this kind is related to the functionalities and design of their architectures.

In particular, this approach does not handle the nondeterminism behavior that is exhibited by a distributed program on a distributed system.

Trace, replay and debugging

In order to address the non-reproducibility issue, this approach is based on collecting a trace of the relevant events generated by a distributed computation, during a first run of the distributed program. The trace describes a computation path (a consistent run) that can be analyzed at a post-mortem stage. If erroneous situations are found, the distributed program can be re-executed under the control of a supervisory mechanism. This mechanism uses the traced sequence of events to force the distributed computation to follow the same path as the one executed by the previous run. This allows the user to examine the behavior of that path within a cyclic interactive debugging session, in a reproducible way. In such a session, the user may use the observation and control functionalities provided by the previous approach. The trace and replay technique has been the focus of intensive research in the past decade, mostly concerning the reduction of the probe effect and of the volume of the traced information (see Section 5.6). However, not all commercial debuggers include such a facility. This approach is also used in monitoring systems, as discussed in Chapter 6.

From the view point of distributed debugging, there is a limitation in this approach if it gives no support to analyze other distributed computation paths besides the traced one. If the first run which is used to collect the trace is a "free" run i.e., under the control of no supervisory mechanism, the resulting trace describes only a randomly occurring path from the large set of possible paths. This gives no guarantee that such is an (the) interesting path to consider for analysis. Indeed, it is highly unlikely this will be the case.

Integrated testing, active control and debugging

This approach tries to overcome the above mentioned limitation of a simple passive trace and replay approach. Multiple authors have proposed approaches for the active control of distributed program execution for distributed debugging purposes. They all share a similar goal, namely to provide a facility to enforce the execution of specific runs of a distributed computation in order to ease the location of erroneous situations. They differ in the way they generate and specify the desired consistent run that a controlled execution should follow. In the following, one of these approaches is briefly described for illustrative purposes.

The approach considers two separate phases in the distributed debugging activity. It is based on the integration of a static analysis and testing phase (hereafter called the T phase) and a dynamic analysis and debugging stage (called the D phase). The goal of the T phase is to assist the user in the generation of interesting consistent runs that may exhibit violations of correctness properties. In general it is not feasible (or even possible) to provide a completely automated T phase. An interactive testing tool is useful to cooperate with the user to specify and refine the conditions and regions of distributed program code that should be considered for analysis. The T phase is then used to generate a sequence of commands that will be used to drive a distributed program run, in order to exercise the paths defined by the above testing scenarios. Such a distributed program run can then be the subject of a trace and replay approach, and integrated in a cyclic debugging session.

The main advantage of this methodology is that it allows the user to interactively "walk" through the T and D phases, until one is convinced about the satisfaction of the correctness properties that are being investigated. Another advantage of this approach is that it combines the benefits of static and dynamic analysis in order to help the user to understand distributed program behavior.

The main problem with this approach is that it basicly relies upon the user conviction that all relevant scenarios were specified and generated, tested and analyzed, so that one gets confidence on distributed program correctness. There is no full guarantee that no important situations went unnoticed (this is a classical characteristic of testing approaches: *How do you specify a complete test suite?* See Chapter 9).

Automated detection of global predicates, active control and debugging

This approach is an attempt to help the user increasing the confidence on the results of the previous approach, by allowing the specification of the correctness criteria in terms of global predicates. Such global predicates are then automatically evaluated by detection algorithms, working off-line or online. A summary of the main goals of this approach was given in a previous section.

As the efficient evaluation of global predicates is limited to restricted classes of predicates, this approach may be seen as complementary to the testing and debugging approach. Their integration seems a promising research direction to improve distributed debugging.

5.5.2 The times of the distributed debugging activities

Distributed debugging approaches can also be classified according to the phases of the development cycle (see Figure 5.8).

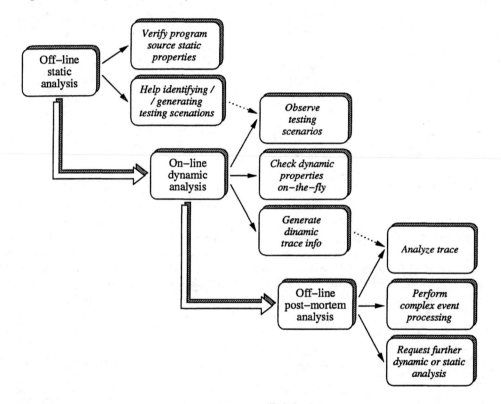

Figure 5.8: Program analysis and debugging at distinct phases of development

Off-line distributed debugging based on static analysis

This approach uses the program code as a basis and it does not require an actual program execution. It relies on formal models of program behavior that can be used to check certain kinds of properties, usually expressed as temporal logic formulas. However, model checking techniques can only be used to analyze certain properties and do not give information on dynamic properties that depend on actual runtime program behavior, e.g., termination. Also, they usually incur great computational costs in their search for all allowable state transitions in the modeled computation space.

Still, static analysis of the program code is one approach that can be of great importance for distributed debugging, when adequately combined with complementary approaches.

Online distributed debugging based on dynamic analysis

Due to the mentioned limitation of static analysis, one needs to use online approaches that help evaluating the actual program behavior on-the-fly. Such approaches rely upon online observation techniques so they must deal with the difficulties of accurate construction of consistent global states. Once a specific program behavior pattern was detected, these approaches also require adequate control mechanisms to help the user inspecting the individual computation states of interest. This approach must deal with the probe effect, in order to ensure that the observed computation path exhibits the same logical behavior as the original computation would, when running under no observation mechanisms ... (see Section 5.6 and Chapter 6).

Dynamic and static analysis approaches can be combined in order to provide the distributed debugging with functionalities as the ones illustrated by the mentioned integrated testing, active control and debugging approach.

Off-line distributed debugging based on post-mortem analysis

Post-mortem analysis approaches provide an effective way to analyze program behavior because they rely upon previously collected traces of the processes' local histories. On one hand, it becomes easier to construct a consistent global state, out of these local histories, by regenerating the causal precedence chains. This reduces the runtime overhead incurred by online approaches. It also enables facilities for analysis of complete computation histories, with the help of a diversity of event analysis and visualization tools. On the other hand, post-mortem techniques can be integrated with online techniques, in order to exploit tracing, replay and debugging methods, to address the non-reproducibility issue. Incremental methods consisting of online and postmortem stages also allow to handle the potentially large volume of traced information. A first run is used to collect only the minimum amount of information to ensure reproducible re-execution, and further post-mortem analysis can determine the need to collect further information on successive runs (see also Chapter 6, on the use of this approach for performance debugging purposes).

The summary of how such approaches are complementary to one another is illustrated in Figure 5.8.

Off-line: verify certain properties using static analysis and help identifying relevant scenarios for testing.

Online: check dynamic properties on-the-fly, and observe testing scenarios, under actively controlled execution.

Post-mortem: analyze traces of complete global histories, perform more complex event processing (e.g., high level event abstractions) and visualization. Use the results of such analysis to determine further runs and dynamic analysis.

5.5.3   The observation models

Finally, distributed debugging approaches can be classified according to the observation model of distributed computations (see Figure 5.9).

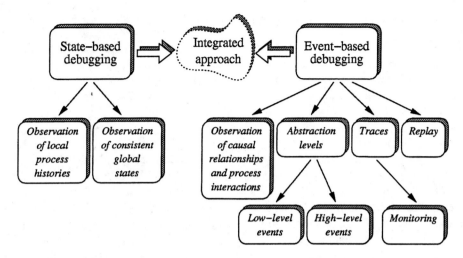

Figure 5.9: Debugging approaches according to the observation model

State-based views in distributed debugging

This approach aims to provide the equivalent functionalities to state-based sequential debugging but must address consistency issues. It considers state exploration at two distinct levels.

The "component level" considers processes and threads as individual computation units, whose sequential state transitions must be examined.

The "distributed program level" considers component interactions at a global level. Typically, in a distributed-memory model, global process interactions are of the message-passing or RPC types. In a computational model including distributed processes and multithreading within each process, shared-memory interactions are also considered among the threads in each process.

Formally, a state based view interprets process communication as a way of having one process affecting the state of the other. For example, some authors interpret a message receive operation as equivalent to an assignment of the value of a variable of the sender process (the send buffer, indeed) to a variable in the receiver buffer. This allows to directly express dependencies and correctness conditions in terms of state variables.

State-based approaches for distributed debugging try to explicitly handle the observation problem by describing distributed program evolution in terms of global states. While this view is necessary as an important way of identifying errors, it makes it difficult to relate logical correctness conditions, distributed program code locations, and actually observed computation states.

An explicit event based approach seems more adequate, both to describe the dynamic distributed program evolution, and to provide a transparent interpretation of correctness properties.

However, the state based view has also an important role in distributed debugging to allow to examine local states and global states.

Event-based views in distributed debugging

Event-based approaches for distributed debugging are important for a number of reasons.

Events are the natural concepts to track causality relationships as they underly the theoretical concepts proposed by Lamport's precedence relations. They are also at the root of a large diversity of work, both on the theory of distributed computations, and on the support of causality mechanisms like the vector timestamps.

Event-based models enable distinct levels of interpretation of a distributed computation, at distinct levels of abstraction. They ease the mapping from the high level abstractions of a distributed programming model into the low level abstractions of a distributed system. So, it becomes possible to use an event-based model to specify the desired program behavior, in terms of user-level abstractions, and check if it matches the observed program behavior. Concerning practical interactive distributed debugging tools, event abstractions allow to provide a high-level view to the user, in terms of the application level model, e.g., graphical notation or a high level semantics.

Events are the adequate concepts to handle the reproducibility issue through deterministic replay techniques as discussed in a section ahead.

Events allow to bridge the gap from theoretical concepts to the practical tools that support the distributed debugging activity. Namely, event-based models ease the combination of trace-based monitoring, distributed debugging, and visualization techniques.

In summary, event-based models provide the adequate concepts to capture the semantics of distributed programs, and they ease the development of practical distributed debugging tools:

- They relate to the theory: causal precedence and "poset" of a distributed computation.

- They specify behavior at distinct abstraction levels.

- They enable reproducibility using traces.

- They allow runtime detection of relevant conditions, related to breakpoints.

- They relate to analysis and visualization tools so they bridge the gap from theory to practice.

- They allow unification with monitoring tracing approaches.

5.5.4   Integrating event and state based distributed debugging

An event-based model can be used to specify program behavior and to detect the occurrence of a particular program behavior. This will then require the examination of the corresponding global computation states. So it becomes natural to associate event with state based distributed debugging techniques. Inspection of local histories of individual process can be based on a state-based debugging technique, as provided by typical sequential debuggers. Global state views should be triggered by the detection of significant events, so that state examination may enlight the reasons for the errors.

The main difficulty of this integration is due to the need of (re-)constructing a consistent global state of a distributed computation, whenever some particular event is detected. Only then will the user be able to inspect meaningful individual process histories, using a state-based debugging technique. This problem is discussed in the following section.

5.6   Debugging Techniques

The main techniques supporting distributed debugging can be classified according to the main goal: observation or control of the distributed computations. In the following sections, the main characteristics of existing techniques are surveyed.

5.6.1   Observation

Here, a wide interpretation of the observation concept is assumed. It encompasses the low level observation of actual running computations, up to the consistent observation of global computation states, and including the logical observation of distributed program behavior that is the realm of high level visualization tools. In distributed debugging, all those observation dimensions must be considered so that logical program properties can be studied.

The general goals of observation techniques are:

(i) To collect the required information [33] (see Chapter 6).

(ii) To evaluate (re-)construct consistent global states in order to evaluate correctness conditions.

(iii) To interpret, analyze, visualize and animate distributed program behavior, at multiple levels of abstraction (see Chapters 2 and 8).

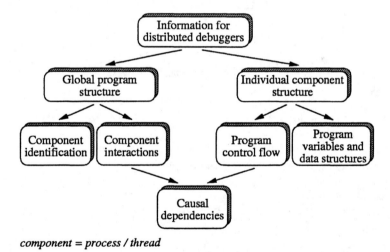

component = process / thread

Figure 5.10: Information for distributed debugging

In general a distributed debugger should provide information of distinct types, as illustrated in Figure 5.10. The component and global program level views were already explained. The Figure 5.10 puts the focus of the distributed debugging activity on the observation of significant information in order to understand the causal dependencies that explain program behavior.

This information can be examined at several phases during program development. Minimal information on process interactions and program control flow is usually obtained using a trace-based approach while the remaining information on the global computation states and individual process states is usually obtained dynamically, on user demand, using an interactive debugging cycle. This is not the case when debugging distributed real-time applications where interactive debugging is not used due to the real-time constraints. Real-time distributed debugging is not discussed here (see [10, 53]).

Due to its practical importance, trace based techniques are briefly discussed in the following, from the perspective of distributed debugging.

Using tracing techniques for correctness distributed debugging

Event based techniques rely on monitoring to collect the relevant information and generate the traces describing the distributed computation histories (see Chapter 6).

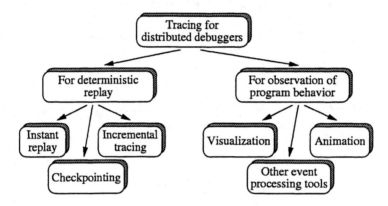

Figure 5.11: Tracing for distributed debugging

Tracing provides the following main functionalities for distributed debugging (see Figure 5.11):

(i) To enable deterministic re-execution [30, 54].

(ii) To gather sufficient information to allow further event analysis by other tools, aiming at the interpretation, visualization, and animation of distributed program behavior, at adequate levels of abstraction.

A critical aspect is how to determine the required information that should be traced.

Concerning deterministic re-execution, a conservative approach (called the event log approach) saves the contents of all the process state information, including values of variables and contents of exchanged messages. It also includes information related to the possible sources of internal nondeterminism in a process, such as consulting real clock values, communication with external I/O devices, and internal nondeterministic choices. This allows deterministic re-execution in the more general case and it has the advantage of allowing to repeat single (or groups of) processes in isolation, i.e., just by providing the traced input information from their external environment. However, such an approach often generates a

large volume of traced information. The main risks of such approach are the increased requirements in memory and disk space, and the increased perturbation due to the monitoring
activity.

So, in applications where each individual process exhibits a deterministic behavior, it
is sufficient to register the ordering of the relevant distributed computation events, namely
the interaction events, instead of all their associated state information. This is called the
Instant Replay approach [30] that is a landmark in the distributed debugging area. In its
simplest form, this requires all processes to be re-run, during a replay session, but allows
one to examine further detailed state information on each process and event of the observed
distributed computation path, using interactive debugging commands.

For long running applications, a checkpointing technique may be needed to allow the
replay to start from intermediate points in the computation, instead of from the beginning.
Such a facility requires a mechanism to perform consistent global checkpoints (corresponding
to consistent global states).

Concerning the use of tracing for high level observation and analysis of program behavior,
it seems one would need to collect much more information in order to enable the post-
processing tasks related to program behavior analysis and visualization. However, if there
is an adequate event modeling abstraction, the user may be able to specify the desired level
of abstraction that is required at each point during application development. This allows to
filter, cluster or ignore certain kinds of events or/and processes, thus contributing to reduce
the trace volume. If further analysis reveals the need for further details, it is possible to
(deterministically) re-run the distributed program with the trace facility enabled to gather
such additional information. This incremental tracing facility has been used in a diversity of
distributed debuggers [38]. A good compromise between the event logging and the instant
replay approaches can be reached by following incremental tracing techniques, driven by
user demands, during an interactive debugging cycle based on deterministic replay.

For off-line or post-mortem processing tools, clearly all needed information had to be
collected, in a single run or in a series of incrementally traced runs. For online processing,
e.g., visualization, such tools may actually consume the generated events during execution,
so there is less need to save large event traces.

Even for the instant replay technique, one cannot avoid the probe effect so there is the risk
of a logical distinction between the instrumented and non instrumented program behaviors.
For software monitoring approaches, some authors propose to keep the instrumentation
probes integrated into the application all the time, so that there is no such distinction. This
is only feasible if the corresponding intrusion is minimal and compatible to the required
application performance (see Chapter 6).

In the past decade there was intense research concerning the reduction of the tracing
time and memory space overheads [12, 39, 40, 45]. An example of an optimization is to
avoid tracing unnecessary event orderings corresponding to program regions that are known
to be deterministic.

State exploration in distributed debugging

One of the main requirements of a distributed debugger is a facility to allow the exploration
of computation states of a distributed program (Figure 5.12).

In classical sequential debugging an instant observation technique has been used since
the early days of the Von Neumann machine: the memory dump. In a sequential debugging context, the main criticism results from the low level abstraction and the amount of

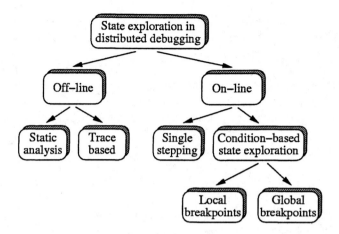

Figure 5.12: State exploration in distributed debugging

information that is provided by this technique. This kind of technique is, however, also the basis of state-based sequential debugging, although the information is shown at a higher level and is structured according to the program entities of interest at each point (e.g., stack frames, etc.). In a distributed debugging context, the corresponding technique of making such kind of complete global snapshots of the ongoing distributed computation is not easy to achieve as previously discussed. One can also argue that the technique is of limited use in distributed debugging, due to the existence of too many states.

A single-stepping facility, as found in sequential debugging, is not much useful in distributed debugging, although it is conceptually possible to achieve, in terms of a succession of consistent cuts (see Section 5.2), corresponding to a consistent run. The problem is that there is a large space of alternative consistent runs that would have to be searched, step-by-step, using this method. Even if such an approach is used in association with high level abstractions, that try to focus on interaction events, the approach is still generally infeasible for realistic programs, except for a few toy programs.

Off-line visualization tools, based on an interpretation of traces, can contribute to identify interesting patterns of program behavior. Interactive, user-driven visualization tools allow the user to select the abstraction levels and the areas of the program that should be considered.

Condition based state exploration is a technique that allows the user to specify logical conditions such that, once satisfied in a certain state, force the program execution to be suspended in that state. The goal is to allow the user to perform state exploration selectively, as a strategy to avoid an exhaustive, albeit systematic, search of the computation states. This is clearly an important approach that recognizes the impossibility of completely automating the distributed debugging task, so it opens a way for the user to direct the state search.

In sequential debugging those conditions usually involve the program variables, status, or instruction locations. Such breakpoints or watchpoints have a simple and well defined semantics in a sequential program but allow several possible interpretations in distributed programs. Furthermore breakpoints and interactive debugging techniques are highly intrusive and affect program behavior in an unpredictable way. So, the combination of breakpoints with deterministic replay-based techniques becomes of the utmost importance in distributed debugging.

The global conditions can be expressed in several forms. They can be expressed in terms of variables, code locations or local states of the individual processes of the distributed program. A local predicate is one which refers to a single process, so it corresponds to a local breakpoint that may be easily detected by the distributed debugger. A global predicate is a boolean expression involving conditions that are local to multiple processes. Common forms are conjunctions and disjunctions of local predicates, respectively called conjunctive and disjunctive global predicates. Other kinds of global conditions express temporal relations between abstract events, aiming at easing the task of relating the occurrence of errors to the logical abstractions in individual processes.

Most existing distributed debuggers only allow the specification of local breakpoints. This is due to the difficulty of evaluating general forms of global predicates, as previously discussed. Indeed, efficient detection algorithms exist only for very restricted forms of global predicates.

However, even for simple local breakpoints, one has to decide what to do when a local condition is detected during execution in a specific process. For an online approach, the question is how to stop the distributed program at a consistent global state that is meaningful for the examination of the detected condition. Typically, one finds two main approaches [21, 37]:

(i) To send stopping messages to all other processes.

(ii) Just wait until all other processes "naturally" block, waiting for input or for synchronization with the initial process.

In both cases there is a delay in the detection of the stop condition in other processes. As this will be an unpredictable delay, such approaches should only be used when there is a guarantee that the other processes cannot possibly affect the investigation of the detected conditions. This obviously depends on the types of conditions. For local predicates, the above approaches seem reasonable.

For global breakpoints, their associated conditions are global predicates, so in general there is a detection algorithm that forces the involved processes to stop while the remaining processes continue running as above. For example, consider a distributed computation consisting of 4 processes P_1, P_2, P_3, and P_4, and a global breakpoint involving variables in P_1 and P_2, but not in P_3 and P_4. Processes P_1 and P_2 are forced to stop on the global breakpoint, but P_3 and P_4 continue. In general, P_3 and P_4 may affect the global system state, e.g., by sending and receiving messages, in a way that may change the conditions that explain a bug situation.

Reconstruction of a meaningful global state may require the aid of rollback and checkpointing techniques. It may become a difficult problem if a non-replay based approach is followed.

In a replay based approach, breakpoints are only set during replay. In order to handle such situations, replay-based distributed debuggers have been proposed [32] that are able to reconstruct a consistent global state such that each process is at its last local state where it could cause the involved processes (P_1 and P_2, in the example) making the global predicate true. The reconstruction of this global state relies upon the trace to identify the desired halting local states. In some proposals a new annotated trace is generated so that one may replay the distributed program to the last consistent global state defined by such directives.

Besides reconstructing the "last" consistent global state for a given global breakpoint, one now needs to be able to inspect the local states of individual processes. This can be achieved by integrating an event-based distributed debugger that allows global breakpoints and halting in consistent global states, with individual state-based sequential debuggers that may be applied to each application process in isolation.

5.6.2   Control

Control of distributed computation is necessary for distributed debugging purposes in order to achieve the following objectives (Figure 5.13):

(i) Handle nondeterminism.

(ii) Enforce specific distributed computation paths.

(iii) Enforce specific global predicates.

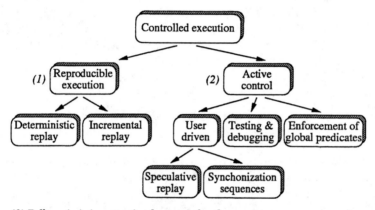

(1) *Follows / mimics a previously executed path*
(2) *Enforce a new generated path*

Figure 5.13: Controlled execution

Due to the nondeterminism of distributed programs, multi-execution testing cannot be achieved by simply trying to repeat "free" uncontrolled program runs. This requires a deterministic re-execution. This technique is based on a form of passive control because the re-execution just blindly mimics the behavior of a previous run.

Additionally, more active forms of control are required (called *controlled execution* or *active control* [50]) because specific alternative distributed computation paths need to be pursued in order to examine the dynamic program behavior. A supervisory process controls event ordering, for re-execution, e.g., by exercising distinct message delivery orderings, or alternative process schedules, in order to investigate the consequences of nondeterministic execution.

Desired event orderings may be specified as event expressions or as command scripts that are interpreted by the distributed debugger. The goal is to generate and test all/some possible permutations of events. Such forms of active control allow a distributed debugging to perform a complementary role to static analysis and testing tools, in order to ease the evaluation of correctness properties through the exploration of the space of distributed computation paths. The specification of such paths can be:

(i) Given by the user.

(ii) Generated by an automated testing tool.

(iii) Automatically enforced by a global predicate evaluator/controller.

An example of approach (i) is given by the *speculative replay* technique [48]. During speculative replay, the user can select any of the potential consistent global states and ask the distributed debugger to re-execute the program using a message log. So the user can detect how different event orderings may originate different observable behaviors. The user may then add additional interprocess dependencies, and re-run the program under new synchronization constraints.

Another example is given by the use of *synchronization sequences* in an approach called *deterministic execution testing* [49]. This forces the execution of a concurrent program, with a given input, according to a user-defined sequence of synchronization commands, corresponding to a different test of the program, for a given input. Another use of a similar technique was mentioned in a previous section, where an annotated trace is generated by a distributed debugger in order to force the computation to follow a specific path leading to a consistent global state associated with a global breakpoint.

An example of approach (ii) was discussed in a previous section, corresponding to the testing, active control and debugging methodology. This approach is the basis of the work done in the SEPP projects [31] on integration of testing and debugging tools which are further discussed in Chapters 9, 13 and 16. This approach also uses a partial specification from the user.

Approach (iii) is related to the automated evaluation of global predicates that was also discussed in the section on distributed debugging methodologies. Its integration into a distributed debugging cycle only(!) requires the user to specify the correct program behavior in terms of global predicates. Then it is up to the distributed debugger to monitor the execution in order to detect or enforce the satisfaction of those logical conditions. The user can then inspect consistent global states and get more information on the causes of errors. At this point in the debugging cycle, the user may have new information on program behavior that allows to assert certain global properties that should be enforced by the global predicate controller [50, 52]. Then an active control phase begins where the controller is responsible for enforcing those conditions, thus allowing the investigation of other potential error situations. The third approach is the more ambitious one. Conceptually, it would allow having a distributed debugger controller automatically imposing the required synchronization constraints so that some high level specification of a distributed application would be enforced. Only a few distributed debuggers are able to enforce specific global predicates or assertions, and for very restricted expressions [52].

5.7   The Architecture of Distributed Debugging Systems

The design of a distributed debugging system must meet the requirements for basic observation and control functionalities, as discussed in previous sections. The architectures of most existing parallel and distributed debuggers have followed the approach of the p2d2 architecture [22] which is based on a client — server model. Additionally, existing debuggers provide very sophisticated visual and graphical user interfaces, and cover a wide range of functionalities for interactive debugging of individual distributed processes and threads [11].

In the recent past, some distributed debuggers have been developed aiming at being integrated into complete parallel software development environments. However, there are still many open issues concerning a successful tool integration [44].

Instead of an architecture providing a fixed set of functionalities, the software architecture of a distributed debugger should be extensible and allow adequate integration with other parallel software development tools. This is necessary so that the multiple methodologies and approaches for distributed debugging may be supported within a common architectural framework. In the SEPP projects, such an approach has been followed for the design of the DDBG debugger (see Chapter 13) and its results are discussed in related chapters in this book.

5.8   Conclusions

The distributed debugging activity still faces enormous difficulties to increase its impact upon the users. As mentioned in [20] referring to a **PTOOLS** report, about 90% of the parallel and distributed application developers using PVM still relied on classical "`print`" based approaches to debug their programs. Furthermore one doesn't known if the remaining 10% are really happy with currently existing distributed debugging tools (both commercial and academic). In this chapter, the main dimensions of distributed debugging have been discussed. The foundations of the distributed debugging activity were related to the theory of distributed computations in order to show the difficulties of distributed debugging, and explain why naive "`print`" based approaches do not work for distributed debugging.

Several methodologies for distributed debugging were presented which illustrate the complementary roles played by static analysis, testing, and dynamic analysis approaches, towards the understanding of the behavior of distributed programs. The Figure 5.14 summarizes the main dimensions of this view of distributed debugging. The main observation and control techniques were described, with emphasis to the interactive replay-based distributed debugging and how it promotes a cycle where the user repeatedly investigates and incrementally collects information to improve the analysis on the distributed program behavior. An ideal approach was also outlined for distributed debugging, starting with a specification of program correctness properties, followed by attempts to match them to the observed program behavior. Such approach was related to the interactive cyclic replay based distributed debugging approach, in order to allow the user to examine the relevant global computation states.

The research and development efforts in distributed debugging in the past decade have increased our belief that the distributed debugging activity only makes sense when adequately integrated with other complementary tools, for analysis, visualization, and program observation and control. So, besides highly sophisticated stand alone and autonomous distributed debugging tools [11], the future generation of distributed debuggers will require more and more flexible and extensible distributed debugging architectures, to ease the integration of distributed debugging functionalities with other tools. This requirement is even more important due to the current developments in homogeneous and heterogeneous parallel and distributed computing platforms, including the cluster computing systems.

In the forthcoming years we will witness the appearance of standard definitions for distributed debugging application interfaces, along the line of the HPDF initiative [14]. We

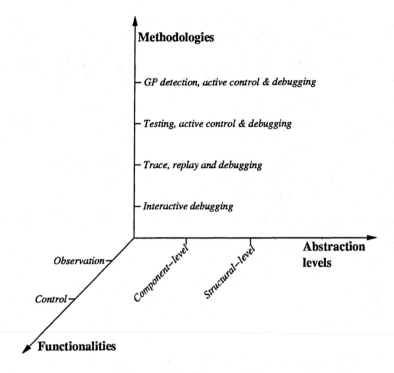

Figure 5.14: The user's view

will witness an increasing trend towards distributed debugger's designs and architectures that can be adapted to the emerging parallel and distributed programming models, with component based and mobile computation abstractions.

Even with such high expectations for the near future, the impact of such approaches critically depends on how successfully they are integrated into easy to learn and to use tools, with friendly user interfaces, that meet practical user demands. Such topics have been increasingly discussed among users, tool developers and software engineers. This trend is also confirmed by current awareness towards considering the importance of the human factors for the design of the user interfaces and the functionalities provided by parallel development tools [15, 42, 44].

Acknowledgements

This work was partially supported by the Centre for Informatics and Information Technologies (CITI) and the Department of Informatics (DI) of FCT/UNL, by the PRAXIS XXI SETNA-ParComp (Contract 2/2.1/TIT/1557/95), and by the French Ambassy — INRIA/ Portuguese ICTTI and the Hungarian/Portuguese Governments cooperation protocols.

References

[1] *Proceedings of the ACM Workshop on Parallel and Distributed Debugging*, volume 24 of *ACM SIGPLAN Notices*. ACM Press, January 1988.

[2] *Proceedings of the ACM Workshop on Parallel and Distributed Debugging*, volume 26 of *ACM SIGPLAN Notices*. ACM Press, 1991.

[3] *Proceedings of the ACM/ONR Workshop on Parallel and Distributed Debugging*, volume 28 of *ACM SIGPLAN Notices*. ACM Press, 1993.

[4] O. Babaoğlu, E. Fromentin, and M. Raynal. A unified framework for the specification and run-time detection of dynamic properties in distributed computations. Technical Report UBLCS-95-3, University of Bologna, Italy, June 1995.

[5] O. Babaoğlu and K. Marzullo. Consistent global states of distributed systems: Fundamental concepts and mechanisms. In S. J. Mullender, editor, *Distributed Systems*, chapter 4, pages 55–96. Addison-Wesley, second edition, 1993.

[6] P. Bates. Debugging heterogeneous distributed systems using event-based models of behavior. In *Proceedings of ACM Workshop on Parallel and Distributed Debugging* [1], pages 11–22.

[7] M. Chandy and L. Lamport. Distributed snapshots: Determining global states of distributed systems. *ACM Trans. Comput. Syst.*, 3(1):63–75, 1985.

[8] C. M. Chase and V. K. Garg. Detection of global predicates: Techniques and their limitations. *Distributed Computing*, 11(4):191–201, 1998.

[9] R. Cooper and K. Marzullo. Consistent detection of global predicates. In *Proceedings of the ACM/ONR Workshop on Parallel and Distributed Debugging* [3], pages 167–174.

[10] P. S. Dodd and C. V. Ravishankar. Monitoring and debugging distributed real-time programs. *Software—Practice and Experience*, 22(10), 1992.

[11] Etnus Inc., Framingham, MA. *TotalView User's Guide (v3.9.0)*, June 1999. http://www.etnus.com/.

[12] A. Fagot and J. Chassin-de Kergommeaux. Optimized execution replay mechanism for rpc-based parallel programming models. Technical report, LMC-IMAG, Grenoble, France, 1995.

[13] C. J. Fidge. Partial orders for parallel debugging. In *Proceedings of ACM Workshop on Parallel and Distributed Debugging* [1], pages 183–194.

[14] J. Francioni and C. M. Pancake. High performance debugging standards effort. http://www.ptools.org/hpdf/.

[15] J. M. Francioni. *Debugging and Performance Tuning for Parallel Computer Systems*, chapter Determining the Effectiveness of Interfaces for Debugging and Performance Analysis Tools, pages 127–142. IEEE Computer Society Press, 1996.

[16] P. Fritzson, editor. *Automated and Algorithmic Debugging*, volume 749 of *LNCS*. Springer-Verlag, May 1993.

[17] E. Fromentin, M. Raynal, V. K. Garg, and A. Tomlinson. On the fly testing of regular patterns in distributed computations. In K. C. Tai, editor, *Proceedings of the 23rd International Conference on Parallel Processing. Volume 2: Software*, pages 73–76, Boca Raton, FL, USA, August 1994. CRC Press.

[18] V. Garg and C. Chase. Distributed algorithms for detecting conjunctive predicates. In *Proceedings of the 15th International Conference on Distributed Computing Systems (ICDCS'95)*, pages 423–430, Los Alamitos, CA, USA, May 30–June 2 1995. IEEE Computer Society Press.

[19] V. Garg, C. Chase, J. R. Mitchell, and R. Kilgore. *Tools and Environments for Paralell and Distributed Systems*, chapter Efficient Detection of Unstable Global Conditions Based on Monotonic Channel Predicates, pages 195–226. Kluwer Academic Publishers, 1996.

[20] G. A. Geist. *Debugging and Performance Tuning for Parallel Computer Systems*, chapter Visualization, Debugging, and Performance in PVM, pages 65–77. IEEE Computer Society Press, 1996.

[21] D. Haban and W. Weigel. Global events and global breakpoints in distributed systems. In Bruce D. Schriver, editor, *Proceedings of the Twenty-First Annual Hawaii International Conference on System Sciences*, volume II (Software Track), pages 166–175. IEEE Computer Society Press, January 1988.

[22] R. Hood and D. Cheng. *Tools and Environments for Parallel and Distributed Systems*, chapter Accomodating Heterogeneity in a Debugger – a Client– Server Approach, pages 175–194. Kluwer Academic Publishers, 1996.

[23] R. Hood, K. Kennedy, and J. Mellor-Crummey. Parallel program debugging with on-the-fly anomaly detection. In *Proceedings of IEEE/ACM Supercomputing'90*, pages 74–82. IEEE Computer Science Press, 1990.

[24] M. Hurfin, M. Mizuno, M. Raynal, and M. Singhal. Efficient distributed detection of conjunctions of local predicates. Technical Report TR-967, IRISA, 1995.

[25] M. Hurfin, N. Plouzeau, and M. Raynal. Detecting atomic sequences of predicates in distributed computations. In *Proceedings of the ACM/ONR Workshop on Parallel and Distributed Debugging* [3], pages 32–42.

[26] P. Kacsuk. Macrostep-by-macrostep debugging of message passing parallel programs. In *Proceedings of Tenth IASTED International Conference on Parallel and Distributed Computing and Systems*, pages 527–532, Las Vegas, Nevada, USA, October 1998.

[27] P. Kacsuk. Systematic debugging of parallel programs based on collective breakpoints. In *Proc. of International Symposium on Software Engineering for Parallel and Distributed Systems*, pages 83–96, Los Angeles, California, USA, May 1999.

[28] P. Kacsuk, R. Lovas, and J. Kovács. Systematic debugging of parallel programs based on collective breakpoints and macrosteps. In *Proc. of 5th International Euro-Par Conference*, pages 90–97, Toulouse, France, August/September 1999. Springer-Verlag.

[29] L. Lamport. Time, clocks, and the ordering of events in a distributed system. *Communications of the ACM*, 21(7):558–565, 1978.

[30] T.J. LeBlanc and J.M. Mellor-Crummey. Debugging parallel programs with instant replay. *IEEE Transactions on Computers*, C-36(4):471–481, April 1987.

[31] J. Lourenço, J.C. Cunha, H. Krawczyk, P. Kuzora, M. Neyman, and B. Wiszniewski. An integrated testing and debugging environment for parallel and distributed programs. In *Proceedings of the 23rd EUROMICRO Conference (EUROMICRO'97)*, pages 291–298, Budapeste, Hungary, September 1997. IEEE Computer Society Press.

[32] Y. Manabe and M. Imase. Global conditions in debugging distributed programs. *Journal of Parallel and Distributed Computing*, 15(1):62–69, May 1992.

[33] D. C. Marinescu, J. E. Lumpp Jr., T. L. Casavant, and H. J. Siege. Models for monitoring and debugging tools for parallel and distributed software. *Journal of Parallel and Distributed Computing*, 9(2):171–184, June 1990.

[34] F. Mattern. Virtual time and global states of distributed systems. In M. Cosnard et al., editors, *Proceedings of the International Workshop on Parallel and Distributed Algorithms*, pages 215–226, Amsterdam, 1989. Elsevier Science Publishers.

[35] C. E. McDowell. *Debugging and Performance Tuning for Parallel Computing Systems*, chapter Race Detection - Ten Years Later, pages 101–126. IEEE Computer Society Press, 1996.

[36] C. E. McDowell and D. P. Helmbold. Debugging concurrent programs. *ACM Comupting Surveys*, 21(4):593–622, December 1989.

[37] B. P. Miller and J.-D. Choi. Breakpoints and halting in distributed systems. In *Proceedings of International Conference on Distributed Computing Systems*. IEEE Computer Society Press, 1988.

[38] B. P. Miller and J.-D. Choi. A mechanism for efficient debugging of parallel programs. In *Proceedings of the SIGPLAN'88 Conference on Programming Language Design and Implementation*, volume 23 of *ACM SIGPLAN Notices*, pages 135–144. ACM Press, July 1988.

[39] R. H. B. Netzer. Optimal trace and replay for debugging shared-memory parallel programs. In *Proceedings of the 3rd ACM/ONR Workshop on Parallel and Distributed Debugging* [3].

[40] R. H. B. Netzer. Trace size vs. parallelism in trace-and-replay debugging of shared-memory programs. *LNCS*, 768, 1994.

[41] R. H. B. Netzer, T. W. Brennan, and S. K. Damodaran-Kamal. Debugging race conditions in message-passing programs. In *Proceedings of the Symposiun on Parallel and Distributed Tools SPDT'96*, pages 31–40. ACM Press, 1996.

[42] C. M. Pancake. *Debugging and Performance Tuning for Parallel Computer Systems*, chapter Collaborative Efforts to Develop User-Oriented Parallel Tools. IEEE Computer Society Press, 1996.

[43] C. M. Pancake and S. Utter. A bibliography of parallel debuggers. *ACM SIGPLAN Notices*, 26(1):21–37, January 1991.

[44] D. A. Reed, J. S. Brown, A. H. Hayes, and M. L. Simmons. *Debugging and Performance Tuning for Parallel Computer Systems*, chapter Performance and Debugging Tools: A Research and Development Checkpoint. IEEE Computer Society Press, 1996.

[45] M. A. Ronsse and D. A. Kranzlmuller. Rolt-MP: Replay of Lamport timestamps for message passing systems. In *Proceedings of Euromicro Workshop on Parallel and Distributed Processing*, pages 87–93, 1998.

[46] R. Schwarz and F. Mattern. Detecting causal relationships in distributed computations: In search of the holy grail. *Distributed Computing*, 7(3):149–174, 1994.

[47] M. L. Simmons, A. H. Hayes, D. A. Reed, and J. Brown, editors. *Debugging and Performance Tuning for Parallel Computing Systems*. IEEE Computer Science Press, 1996.

[48] J. M. Stone. A graphical representation of concurrent processes. *ACM SIGPLAN Notices*, 24(1):226–235, January 1989.

[49] K.-C. Tai, R. H. Carver, and E. E. Obaid. Debugging concurrent ada programs by deterministic execution. *IEEE Trans. Software Eng.*, 17(1):45–62, January 1991.

[50] A. Tarafdar and V. K. Garg. Predicate control for active debugging of distributed programs. In *Proceedings of the 1st Merged International Parallel Processing Symposium and Symposium on Parallel and Distributed Processing (IPPS/SPDP-98)*, pages 763–769, Los Alamitos, March 30–April 3 1998. IEEE Computer Society Press.

[51] A. I. Tomlinson and V. K. Garg. Detecting relational global predicates in distributed systems. In Miller and McDowell [3], pages 21–31.

[52] A. I. Tomlinson and V. K. Garg. Maintaining global assertions on distributed systems. In *International Conference on Computer Systems and Education*, 1994.

[53] J. J. P. Tsai and S. J. H. Yang, editors. *Monitoring and Debugging of Distributed Real-Time Systems*. IEEE Computer Society Press, 1995.

[54] L. Wittie. Debugging distributed C programs by real time replay. In *Proceedings of the ACM Workshop on Parallel and Distributed Debugging* [1], pages 57–67.

Chapter 6

Monitoring Parallel Programs for Performance Tuning in Cluster Environments

J. Chassin de Kergommeaux, É. Maillet and J.-M. Vincent

Abstract

This chapter surveys the issues of collecting monitoring data for performance debugging of parallel programs executed in cluster environments. The main categories of monitoring tools are either clock driven or event driven, the latter including timing, counting or tracing. The paper focuses on software tracing, deemed the most general and portable event driven monitoring technique. The lack of global clock and the tracing intrusion are identified as the two major problems hindering the quality of the traced information collected by software tracers. A global time implementation by software and an approach for compensating the software tracing intrusion are then described.

6.1 Introduction

Performance debugging is an important part of the development cycle of parallel programs since obtaining high performances is the main goal of using cluster systems. The objective of performance measurement tools is to help programmers to get the highest possible performances from their programs on their target architecture. Performance debugging usually includes several phases: monitoring to gather performance data, data analysis to correct raw data and compute performance indices and presentation of the performance indices to the programmer, usually by sophisticated visualization tools. This latter phase is presented in Chapter 8. A good survey of monitoring and visualization tools was written by Kraemer and Stasko in [13].

Performance monitoring can be used in at least two different contexts. The first one occurs when a dynamic control of the execution of a parallel program is required. In this case, data collected by monitoring tools are analyzed on line because a rapid feedback is necessary. This is the case of some tools monitoring operating systems activities, such as *xload, perfmeter, top, etc.* of Unix systems [31], used by system engineers to manage computing resources. In addition, the very long execution time of such applications — operating systems may run for days — are not compatible with data collection and post-mortem analysis of the application behavior. Monitoring tools used by real-time systems also help implementing a dynamic control of the systems. The situation is similar for monitoring tools whose objective is to help steering parallel programs on-line to improve their performances [8]. Only applications adapted for being steered can benefit from the use of such tools, for example to balance the load among the processors. Critical to such tools is the latency with which program events are transferred from the monitored program to the end-user, low-monitoring latency conflicting with low monitoring perturbations. In addition, interactivity constraints reduce the amount of analysis that can be performed on monitored data. Another use of on-line data analysis is aimed at limiting the amount of recorded data. For example, in order to analyze long running applications, Paradyn [24] performs problem detection on line, automatically or under the user's direction, without requiring to store any monitoring data. A proposal for a standard interface between on-line monitoring and analysis tools is proposed by Ludwig et al in [17].

On the contrary, to perform a global analysis of the behavior of the observed programs, during a performance debugging cycle, as much performance data as possible needs to be collected, with the lowest possible intrusion. Such constraints are best combined when monitored data can be extracted after the execution of the observed programs and data can be analyzed post-mortem. On-line and post-mortem monitoring are not contradictory since, for example, steering choices based upon on-line monitoring need to be validated with performance measures, which can be best performed using the second type of monitoring and performance data analysis. This chapter being dedicated to monitoring for performance debugging, it mainly deals with this type of monitoring activities.

In order to support performance debugging, a large number of performance indices must be delivered by performance measurement tools so that programmers can detect and reduce the overheads of their programs [1]. These indices can be divided in two main classes:

Completion times which ought to be reduced as much as possible. The objective of performance debugging is most often to reduce the completion time of a program or *makespan*. This index can be decomposed into several measures concerning the time spent by the execution of various parts of the programs such as procedures, communication protocols, etc.

Resource utilization rates indicating what percentage of resource utilisation is spent executing "useful" work. If we consider processor utilisation rates, programmers need to know what percentage of time is spent in various overheads, executing synchronization code, task creation, termination or scheduling, communications or idling. Global resource utilization rates might indicate a problem such as a low processor utilization by the application program and an important idling rate. However to correct such a problem, it is often necessary to use more detailed data. For example, an important idling rate might indicate the presence of a bottleneck, whose origin might be a lack of parallelism in the program, a poor performance of the task scheduler, an excessive use of synchronizations, etc.

The execution of a parallel program can be monitored at several possible abstraction levels: hardware, operating system, runtime system and application. Intuitively, the application level is the most significant one for parallel application programmers, since it is the only place where they can control or adjust parameters. However, it may occur that poor performances of an application can only be explained by observing the impact of programming choices on the runtime or operating systems, during the execution of the application. Being able to relate application level design or programming decisions to runtime or operating system behaviors is still a research issue and will not be dealt with in this chapter.

The organization of this chapter is the following. After this introduction, the techniques for monitoring parallel programs are surveyed. The next section focuses on tracing, deemed the most general monitoring technique for parallel programs. Software tracing is considered as the most portable and widespread tracing technique but suffers of two important drawbacks which hinder the quality of traced data: the lack of global clock in most distributed-memory systems — such as clusters where each node uses its private clock — and the overhead of tracing. Solutions to these issues are presented in the two next sections. The last section identifies performance problems which cannot be identified by tracing alone and sketches a possible detection approach, combining tracing and sampling.

6.2 Principles of parallel programs monitoring

Most monitoring tools are either clock driven or event driven [28] (see Figure 6.1).

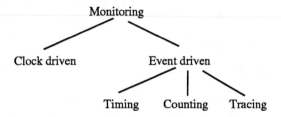

Figure 6.1: Classification of monitoring tools

6.2.1 Clock driven monitoring or sampling

Clock driven monitoring amounts to have the state of the observed system registered at periodical time intervals, by a process independent of the observed process. The periodicity of recording generally depends on the operating system (typically 20 milliseconds under Unix). The recorded information can be used on line or off line to compute global performance indices.

An example of online monitoring tool is *mon* [34], general-purpose resource monitoring system, which can be used to monitor network service availability, server problems, environmental conditions, etc. Resource monitoring can be viewed as two separate tasks: the testing of a condition, and triggering some sort of action upon failure. *mon* was designed to keep the testing and action-taking tasks separate, as stand-alone programs. *mon* is implemented as a scheduler which executes the the monitors (which test a condition), and calls the appropriate alerts if the monitor fails.

The well-known tools *prof, gprof* [7] belong to the latter category: these tools register the instruction counter value. The registered data is used to compute post-mortem global performance indices. For example, the time elapsed in a procedure of the program being executed is supposed proportional to the number of hits of the procedure in the registered samples.

Performance measurement tools based on sampling are intensively used for performance debugging of sequential programs. It is possible to observe the execution of programs at the programmers' abstraction level without being disturbed by the interaction with the operating system. However, this sort of tool may fail finding the causes of some overheads of parallel programs: global performance indices are of little help to show bottlenecks or to evaluate communication or idling times (unless a processor can be traced busy waiting). In addition, the fairly low periodicity of sampling may be unsuited to exhibit phenomena of very short durations.

6.2.2   Event driven monitoring

Event driven monitoring is triggered by the occurrences of *events*. We assume that the processes executing an application perform observable events. In this chapter, an event will be defined as an action changing the state of the monitored system, such as a procedure call or the reception of a message. Event driven monitoring aims at associating a date to each of the observed events. The observed events depend on what the programmer is interested in but, in case of parallel programs monitoring, include emissions and receptions of messages as well as "user defined" events. There exist different types of event driven monitoring approaches called timing, counting and tracing, depending on the amount of recorded information and the way it is used.

Timing

The time spent in various parts of the observed program is measured. For example, the time elapsed in a procedure can be obtained by subtracting the clock value at the beginning of the procedure to the clock value measured when it terminates. Such measurements require a low latency clock. The amounts of recorded data are limited to one counter per measured value [4, 24]. Timing intrusion depends on the number of instrumentation points but is potentially high if detailed timing is required.

Counting

The number of occurrences of the observed events is recorded into global performance indices. Counting is generally considered as minimally intrusive and involves the management of limited amounts of data [4, 24].

Tracing

Tracing is done by recording each of the observed events into a performance trace. Each record includes at least the type of the recorded event and the recording date. Additional information is also recorded depending on the type of the event. For example, if the recorded event is a message emission (reception), the record usually includes the identity of the receiver (sender) process and the length of the message.

Tracing is the most general event driven monitoring technique. It is very well suited to measure communication times – it is sufficient to record the emission and reception events — and exhibit bottlenecks — by recording where the processes executing an application spend the time. It can also be used to obtain global or detailed timing or counting information.

For example, it is possible to measure the time spent executing a procedure by recording the beginning and the end of each execution of this procedure. For all these reasons, most performance measurements tools for parallel programs executions are based on tracing [2, 9, 27, 35].

However, tracing suffers of several drawbacks. First of all, it may be very intrusive if detailed information is collected. Another problem is that the validity of the recorded data can be corrupted by the interaction with the operating system. For example, the time elapsed in a procedure is the difference between the dates of execution measured at the end and at the beginning of the procedure *only if* the process executing the procedure is not suspended during the execution of the procedure. Therefore, all tools based on tracing applications are well suited to measure performances of single-user systems but may fail obtaining exact performance data of loaded multi-users systems.

6.3 Tracing parallel programs

As defined above, tracing is the recording of performance events into a trace. As it is the case for all monitoring techniques, tracing can be performed at several levels of abstraction. There exist several tracing implementation techniques [10]: hardware, software and hybrid. The quality of the traces indicates how faithful the recorded information is. It is mainly affected by the lack of global clocks in distributed systems, which makes it difficult to order events occurring on different nodes, and the intrusion of tracing or probe effect, which changes the behavior of traced executions, with respect to untraced ones. The quality of the traces depends on the tracing technique. This section surveys the tracing techniques as well as the factors affecting the quality of the traced information.

6.3.1 Implementation techniques for tracing

Hardware tracing: hardware tracers are included in the hardware of the observed parallel system [11]. Such tracers require specific hardware developments and are for this reason considered costly. However they are not intrusive at all. Their use can be difficult for an application programmer since it may not be obvious to relate a hardware event to an algorithmic choice at the application level.

Hybrid tracing: hybrid tracers combine specific monitoring hardware with tracing software [10]. As software tracers, hybrid tracers are triggered by application level instructions. It is therefore easier to relate a traced event to a source program instruction than with a hardware tracer. The traced information is written on dedicated hardware ports, connected to a dedicated monitoring hardware, such that the monitoring intrusion remains extremely low. In addition, the monitoring hardware may include a global clock for dating registered events. Although such monitoring technique can be considered ideal for programmers because it is easy to use and delivers high quality traces, it is not widespread because of its lack of portability and its development cost.

Software tracing: software tracing is the most portable and cheapest tracing technique. It can be done without programmer's intervention, when the tracer is included in a communication library which can be used in "tracing" mode [6]. Tracing can also be done by calling a tracing library from the traced program, calls being inserted by the programmer [27] or by a pre-processor [18]. Software tracing is the most widespread

tracing technique because it is cheap and fairly easy to implement. However it makes
it difficult to obtain high quality traces because of the lack of global clocks in most
distributed memory systems and because of the intrusion caused by the recording and
transportation of the trace by the parallel system simultaneously to the execution of
the monitored program.

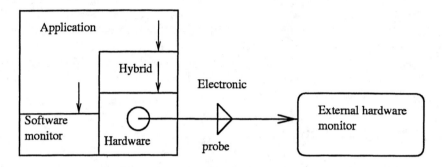

Figure 6.2: Hardware, software and hybrid monitoring techniques

6.3.2 Software tracing instrumentation techniques

Instrumentation is the insertion of code to detect and record the application events. It
can be done at several possible stages during the construction of a parallel program (see
Figure 6.3):

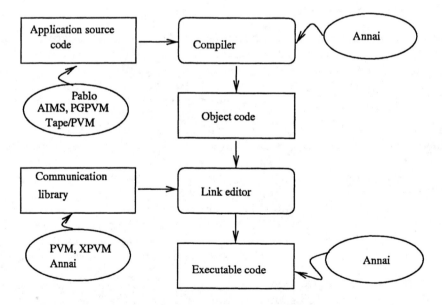

Figure 6.3: Instrumentation techniques

1. Direct source code instrumentation [19, 29, 35]: the instructions generating the events are inserted in users' programs before compilation. Insertion is usually performed by a preprocessor but it can be also done by the user, manually or through an interactive program. Although it can be implemented easily, this method has the drawback of requiring to recompile monitored programs.

2. Compile-time instrumentation gives monitoring tools access to the information computed by the compiler such as loop dependencies [2]. However it requires to have access to the source code of the compiler and to modify it.

3. Instrumentation of the communication library or of the runtime system has the advantage of requiring no modification nor recompiling of the monitored application [2, 12]. However, application specific events cannot be detected.

4. Direct instrumentation of the compiled object code is independent of the programming language and does not require any recompiling of the applications [2, 24]. Both the application and the communication library can be traced. In addition, users can dynamically adjust the grain and the localization of the instrumentation. The main drawback of this instrumentation technique is that it is not easily portable on various operating systems or hardware platforms.

6.3.3 Trace format

A trace is composed of event records. Each record contains at least the following information: type of the event, (physical) date of the event and process identification of the process having performed the event. Some records contain additional parameters of the traced event such as receiver (sender) identification and message length in case of message emission (reception) or data fields allowing users to pass information to data analysis and visualization tools. In addition to predefined event records, usually associated to synchronization or communication primitives, there might be some user-defined event allowing programmers to record whatever information they are interested in.

There is no agreement among the scientific community upon the possibility nor the necessity of defining a standard trace format. The approach consisting in using self-defined trace formats such as SDDF for PABLO [27] seems very powerful: the structure of the event records is defined in the headers of the trace files. Besides, the PICL trace format is widely used because traces can be passed to the widespread ParaGraph visualization tool [9]. It seems that converting traces from a format into another one does not raise any serious technical problem: several trace converters were already developed to convert traces collected in various formats into PICL format [18].

6.3.4 Quality of traced information

Ideally, the storage capacity of the system would be infinite, the recorded events would be dated with an infinite precision global clock and there would not be any tracing intrusion. However this is not the case in general and especially in the case of software tracing. The amount of information to be recorded may exceed the storage capacity of the system, resulting in a reduction of the traced information. The lack of global clock in distributed parallel systems may result into incoherencies between events dated with different local clocks. The intrusion of tracing may change the behavior of the observed program execution.

Buffering and data extraction

The amount of traced data depends on the number of traced events: it can be limited when tracing is restricted to communication events; it may generate a huge amount of tracing data if more detailed measures are needed or the tracing tool is misused. In any case, a potentially large amount of trace data has to be stored and extracted from the parallel system. Various trade-offs can be considered between memory overhead, resulting from the allocation of large trace buffers, and time overhead, resulting from the use of compression algorithms [20] or from the time spent transferring trace data to disk.

Dynamic reduction of the amount of traced data

There exist several approaches to reduce dynamically the amount of recorded data, based on more or less elaborate on-line analysis of the data:

1. The first class of techniques implements a dynamic change of the level of detail of the recordings. In PABLO [27], the trace recording frequency is adjusted dynamically and event tracing may be replaced by counting when the occurrence frequency of traced events becomes too high. Such dynamic adjustment of the amount of collected information is also performed by Paradyn [24]: depending on the truth value of some predicates indicating potential performance problems. In such a case, the observed program is dynamically instrumented to collect more performance data related to the problem.

2. Another technique performs dynamic statistical data clustering in order to limit the recording of event traces to representative processors from each cluster [25].

3. Another approach is based on two basic ideas: the use of "averages" to replace recording data for each instance and "formulae" to represent infinitely long sequences of values [36] — formulae representing some sort of temporal patterns, instead of the spatial patterns used in the previous method. Trace files can then be of "fixed" length, that is independent of the number of iterations and of the problem size. Event traces can be reconstructed by post processing the performance data.

Quality of time measurement

In distributed parallel systems, each processor has its own physical clock. Using the physical properties of the quartz oscillators commonly used for computer clocks, it is possible to model the local time $lt_i(t)$ measured on processor i as a linear dependence [21]:

$$lt_i(t) = \alpha_i + \beta_i t + \delta_i, \quad i \in [1, p], \tag{6.1}$$

where t represents the "absolute" or "universal" time, the constant α_i is the offset at time $t = 0$, the constant β_i (close to 1) is the drift of the physical clock, and the random variable δ_i models granularity and other random perturbations. δ_i can be assumed to be independent of the time t. This model is correct only if the physical parameters (e.g., temperature) of the environment (machine room) remain constant and t is sufficiently small to neglect crystal aging. If these constraints are not satisfied, the coefficients α_i and β_i may no longer be constant.

The lack of global clock in a distributed memory parallel system may result in incoherencies between recorded events if they are dated using the local clocks of the processors.

For example the date of reception of a message can be lower than its emission date. Such incoherencies make difficult or impossible the analysis of performance traces by performance measurement tools. On hardware or hybrid tracers, this problem is solved by using dedicated hardware [10]. On software tracers, this problem can be addressed by a software implementation of a clock correction algorithm (see Section 6.4).

Tracing intrusion

As any monitoring technique, tracing perturbates the execution of the observed parallel programs. It is hard to estimate the intrusion of tracing since it depends on the traced program and on the number of traced events. In case of hardware or hybrid tracing, it is assumed that the tracing intrusion remains limited to a few percent of the execution time. Such an intrusion can be assumed to have a negligible effect on the behavior of the observed program execution [10].

The intrusion of tracing cannot be neglected in the case of software tracing. Several proposals were done to model and compensate the tracing intrusion of software tracers [19, 20, 22, 35].

When modeling tracing intrusion, two types of perturbations are generally defined [22]:

Direct perturbations: resulting from the execution of additional event generation instructions — time spent reading the clock and building an event descriptor in memory — and trace storing on files by the instrumented processes.

Indirect perturbations: localized outside of the tracing code but resulting from the execution of the tracing code. Indeed monitoring can affect the way processes are scheduled and memory is referenced (frequency of page faults and cache misses). It can also hinder some compiler optimizations or penalize performances of I/O subsystems, including file system and network access.

Perturbation compensation models do not take indirect perturbations into account since these perturbations cannot be estimated at the application level of abstraction. However a lot of work is devoted to limit the factors influencing indirect perturbations such as the volume of the traced data.

6.3.5 Some existing software tracing tools

AIMS

AIMS [35] includes a set of tools for measuring the performances of parallel programs. The application source code is instrumented by a preprocessor performing a syntactic analysis of the program and building a call graph of procedures and loops: using a graphical presentation of this call-graph, the user can select instrumentation points. Instrumented code needs to be recompiled and linked to a library including data formating and storage procedures. AIMS includes a system for synchronizing clocks and correcting tracing intrusion based on the work of Sarukkai-Malony [30]. The amount of recorded information can also be dynamically reduced by using averages and formulae [36].

Annai

Annai [3] provides an instrumented communication library — to observe communications — as well as a compile-time instrumentation — to observe the components of the source code such as procedures, loops, etc. During the execution, users can specify "instrumentation action points", similar to breakpoints during correctness debugging, where it will be possible to change the instrumentation parameters dynamically. Annai can be used in tracing or timing mode. It is also possible to estimate the intrusion of tracing for the various components of the source program.

Pablo

In Pablo [29], the source code is instrumented directly by the user with the help of a graphical interface. In case the trace recording frequency is too high, it is automatically reduced or even tracing is automatically replaced by counting. The self defined trace format of Pablo, SDDF, was adopted for several other tools.

PGPVM

Monitoring data is collected by an instrumented version of the PVM communication library which generates traces at the Paragraph format. Post mortem clock synchronization and intrusion removal can be performed if necessary.

Tape/PVM

Tape/PVM [18–20] is a monitoring tool for PVM programs. The source code is directly instrumented using a preprocessor. A global clock is implemented by software, using the SBA technique (see Section 6.4). The tracing intrusion can be compensated post-mortem (see Section 6.5).

XPVM

XPVM [12] is a graphical interface for PVM which includes an instrumented PVM communication library generating trace data which can be used for on-line or post-mortem visualization. Trace data transmission alters the bandwidth available for the communications of the observed applications.

Tool	Instrumentation	Dynamic filtering	Global clock	Intrusion compensation
AIMS	source	yes	synchro	yes
Annai	source, compiler binary	yes		estimate
Pablo	source	yes	no	no
PGPVM	instrumented library	no	post mortem synchronization	yes
Tape/PVM	source	no	post mortem global clock	post mortem
XPVM	instrumented library	no	no	no

Table 6.1: Some existing tracing tools

6.4 Global time implementation on distributed memory parallel systems

As mentioned above, many distributed memory systems such as clusters do not have a hardware global clock. Using local clocks to date events results in errors where the sequencing order, derived from the dates of the events, could contradict the causal relationship between these events [14], which could be established using a logical clock [23]. To avoid these errors, it is possible to implement a global time in a distributed memory system by selecting the clock of one of the processors of the system as a reference clock [21]. Equation 6.1 can be derived into:

$$lt_i(t) = \alpha_{i,ref} + \beta_{i,ref} lt_{ref}(t) + \delta_{i,ref}. \tag{6.2}$$

The corrected global time on processor i, $LC_i(t)$ will therefore be estimated as:

$$LC_i(t) = lt_{ref}(t) \approx \frac{lt_i(t) - \alpha_{i,ref}}{\beta_{i,ref}}, \tag{6.3}$$

the value $lt_{ref}(t)$ in equation 6.3 being the reference clock value at time t, such as it can be computed from $lt_i(t)$, provided that $\alpha_{i,ref}$ and $\beta_{i,ref}$ are known. The coefficients $\alpha_{i,ref}$ and $\beta_{i,ref}$ need to be estimated for each of the processors of the system. The method consists in building a statistical sampling of the dates that some events — occurring on the reference processor and whose dates are measured using the reference clock — *would have* on processor i. The events used for these estimates are the receptions of "ping-pong" messages, exchanged between the reference processor and processor i (event R_{ref}^k on Figure 6.4). The statistical method assumes that the communication delays of messages sent by the reference processor to the other processors of the system are the same as the communication delays of the reply messages.

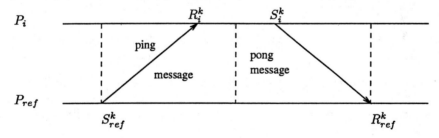

Figure 6.4: Data collection process

The expectation of the communication delay of the "ping" message is supposed equal to the expectation of the communication delay of the "pong" message. R_{ref}^k is chosen as reference event and its occurrence date, on the clock of processor i, estimated by (see Figure 6.4):

$$\widehat{lt_i}(R_{ref}^k) = \frac{lt_i(R_i^k) + lt_i(S_i^k)}{2} + \frac{lt_{ref}(R_{ref}^k) - lt_{ref}(S_{ref}^k)}{2}, \tag{6.4}$$

which is identified to $\alpha_{i,ref} + \beta_{i,ref} lt_{ref}(R_{ref}^k) + r_{i,ref}^k$, $r_{i,ref}^k$ being the residu. This method requires a recording of the four dates $lt_i(R_i^k)$, $lt_i(S_i^k)$, $lt_{ref}(R_{ref}^k)$, and $lt_{ref}(S_{ref}^k)$.

This way a sample of couples $(lt_{ref}(R_{ref}^k), \widehat{lt_i}(R_{ref}^k))$ is obtained and the coefficients $\alpha_{i,ref}$ and $\beta_{i,ref}$ are computed using linear regression techniques.

The SB (*Sample Before*) technique consists in computing the offsets and drifts of the clocks of all the processors of the system, relatively to the reference clock, before the execution of the traced application. It is then possible to give a global date to the monitored events, as soon as they are recorded. However, when an application takes a long time to execute, which is quite frequent for time-demanding parallel applications, the errors arising from approximating the drifts cannot be neglected (when they reach the order of the communication delays).

In this case, it is necessary to use the SBA (*Sample Before and After*) estimation method of $\alpha_{i,ref}$ and $\beta_{i,ref}$, which includes two series of ping-pong messages exchanges, between the reference and all the other processors, *before and after* the execution of the monitored parallel application. The use of two synchronization phases limits the global time extrapolation error. ¿From the values estimated for $\alpha_{i,ref}$ and $\beta_{i,ref}$, it is possible to correct *post mortem* the local dates of each of the events recorded during the execution of the monitored parallel program. The global time estimation error depends on the length of the synchronization phases. By adapting the length of the synchronizations to the duration of the monitored application, it is possible to get rid of all causal incoherencies (see [18] for more details).

6.5   Modeling and compensation of software tracing intrusion

Three objects are involved in the modeling and compensation process:

1. the trace file T, reflecting a perturbated application behavior;

2. the "ideal" execution trace T_0, which would be obtained by an ideal, non-intrusive instrumentation;

3. the approximated execution trace T_a, obtained by applying an intrusion compensation model to T.

In case of software tracing, in the absence of a non-intrusive hardware monitor, the only performance index which can be known about T_0 is its execution time. The importance of the intrusion of software tracing in T with respect to T_0 can be evaluated by comparing the respective execution times. Although this intrusion may remain limited to a few percent of the execution time for some program executions tracing only communications, it may become predominant as soon as detailed tracing is required, to trace the most frequently called procedures for example.

The objective of modeling and compensation methods is to transform a trace T, reflecting a perturbated application behavior, into a trace T_a, approximating as much as possible the "ideal" execution trace T_0, which would be obtained by an ideal, non-intrusive instrumentation. Only direct perturbations are taken into account in the trace correction methods. The principle of these methods is to correct post mortem the dates of the traced events to approximate the dates that these events would have if the direct perturbations caused by software tracing were negligible.

Such a correction methods must take into account the causal dependencies between events occurring in different processes, resulting from synchronizations or communications between these processes. In [22], Malony gives a correction method for several synchronization primitives such as barrier, semaphore, etc. In the remaining of this section, we present how this method was adapted by É. Maillet to the asynchronous communications of PVM in the *Tape/PVM* tracer [20].

6.5.1 Notations

The direct perturbation α is the cost in time to generate a single event and is assumed to be constant and localized at the instrumentation point (see Figure 6.5). α is assumed constant for ease of presentation only. In practice, α is likely to depend on the size of the event (i.e., its number of attributes). Generating an event for an action of interest A consists in reading the clock to get the date $t(e)$ of the start of the action, and in storing the event attributes after the end of the action. We assume that all the overhead α consists of storing the event with its attributes and that it is located *after* $t(e)$. If A is an action which has a measurable duration (e.g., blocking receive primitive), the execution time of A can be either part of the attributes of the event, or two events can be generated, one at start of A the other at end of A. This depends on the implementation of the tracing tool.

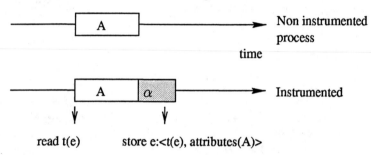

Figure 6.5: Model of elementary intrusion cost

6.5.2 Case of independent sequential processes

This is the case of a process registering local events, between two consecutive communication events (see Figure 6.6). The approximated date $t_a(e_k^i)$ of the kth registered event of process i can be estimated as:

$$t_a(e_k^i) = tb_a^i + (t(e_k^i) - tb^i) - acc^i,$$

with:

tb_a^i: approximated base date of process i. This date is used for each date correction. It is initialized at the date of the first recorded event $t(e_0^i)$. Later on it is recomputed after each communication (see below).

acc^i: accumulated perturbation of process i between the base event and the current event. For an independent sequential process (see Figure 6.6), the value of acc^i when recording the kth event is $(k-1)\alpha$.

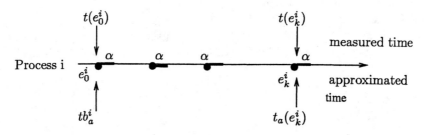

Figure 6.6: Perturbation compensation on a sequential process

6.5.3 Non-blocking send and blocking receive communication primitives

In presence of communications, it is no longer true that the perturbation at a given event e is the accumulation of all direct instrumentation delays from beginning of the process. The base date needs to be reset after each communication.

Resetting of the base date

In Figure 6.7, process P_i performs a blocking receive primitive of a message sent by P_j. Figure 6.7.a represents non traced execution. In Figure 6.7.b, the perturbations of the sender P_j delays message emission, thus increasing the blocking delay of the receiver P_i. In Figure 6.7.c, perturbations of the receiver P_i delay its posting of the request, thus reducing, or even eliminating the blocking delay. A new base date needs to be recomputed after each communication or synchronization. The base date computation algorithm, in case of non-blocking send and blocking receive primitives, such as the **pvm_send** and **pvm_receive** of the PVM communication library [32], is presented in the following.

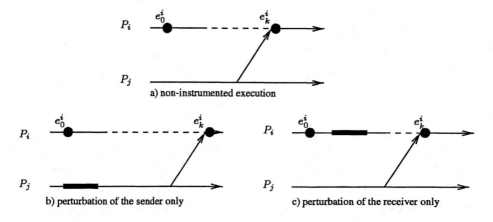

Figure 6.7: Synchronization through a blocking reception primitive: importance of the time base

Base date computation

The application level reception event can be decomposed into three different "sub-events":

SR: start of blocking receive by the receiving process.

ER: end of blocking receive after message delivery, resuming of the computation.

B: instant at which the message becomes available in the receiver's system buffers, i.e., the soonest possible instant at which the receiver can extract the message.

Information on the **B**, **SR**, and **ER** events is supposed to be stored altogether with the attributes of **ER** (they actually form one single event), which explains why a single overhead α is taken into account in the perturbation compensation algorithm (see Figure 6.8 and Figure 6.9).

Two different cases are possible, depending on whether the message arrives on the receiving node before or after the reception request **SR** of the receiving process:

1. **Before the receive request**

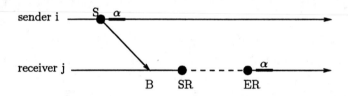

Figure 6.8: Message arrived *before* the posting of the receive request

$$t_a(ER) = t_a(SR) + DC,$$

DC being the delay of processing the incoming data (copying into a new active receive buffer in case of PVM).

2. **After the receive request**

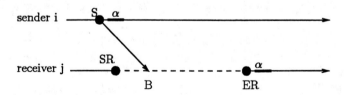

Figure 6.9: Message arrived *after* the posting of the receive request

$$t_a(ER) = t_a(B) + DC.$$

Assuming that neither the message transmission time $(t(B) - t(S))$ nor the message processing delay **DC** are affected by tracing, we get:

$$t_a(B) = t(B) - t(S) + t_a(S).$$

In both cases, the base date tb_a^j of the receiving process is reset to the approximated date of the ER event, after the communication:

$$tb_a^j \leftarrow t_a(ER) \quad acc^j \leftarrow \alpha.$$

The main problem with this algorithm is that the value of $t(B)$ cannot be measured since it is an event at the communication system level and tracing is performed at the application program level of abstraction. É. Maillet describes in [20] an algorithm allowing the correction of the date of event **ER**, depending on the relative positions in time of **B** and **SR**. In some cases, $t_a(ER)$ can be computed without needing to estimate $t_a(B)$. In the few remaining cases, an estimate of the date $t_a(B)$ can be computed from a measure of the date of $t_a(S)$, by applying an approximate cost model of the communications on the monitored parallel system.

6.5.4 Limits of perturbation compensation methods for programs behaving non deterministically

Perturbation compensation methods do not change the causal dependency relation between events and therefore do not take into account potential behavioral changes of the traced application coming from tracing. Such methods are not applicable to traces of applications using non-deterministic communication primitives. In PVM for instance, a task may request a message of any type from any other task using a **pvm_recv**(-1,-1) function call. The "execution path" of a traced execution of such a program might differ from the "execution path" of a non-traced program execution. In the example of Figure 6.10, the execution of process P_1 was heavily perturbated by tracing. If the emission date of the message sent by process P_1 to process P_2 were naively corrected, its transmission time being unaffected by tracing, the order of reception of messages emitted by processes P_1 and P_3, by process P_2, would be reversed with respect to the actual reception order of the traced execution. However, perturbation compensation methods cannot change the order of reception of messages in the corrected trace since the effects of such a change on the remaining of the traced execution could not be deduced from the traces. The only possibility to correct traces of non deterministic programs is therefore to apply a conservative approximation which keeps the order of message receptions of the corrected trace unchanged with respect to the non corrected trace.

A possible solution to the problem of non-determinism is to use a *deterministic replay* [15] mechanism, when intrusively tracing an application for performance data. Limited control information is recorded during an initial *record* execution, the intrusion caused by this recording being usually very low [5]. This information is used by subsequent *replay* execution to guarantee determinism with respect to the initial *record* execution. If performance traces are collected during a *replay* execution, a perturbation compensation method, similar to the one described above, can be used to correct on line [16] or off-line [33] the intrusion of performance tracing. In the latter case, the method aims at constructing an approximated execution trace T_a, as close as possible from the trace that would be obtained by a non-intrusive tracing of the initial *record* execution.

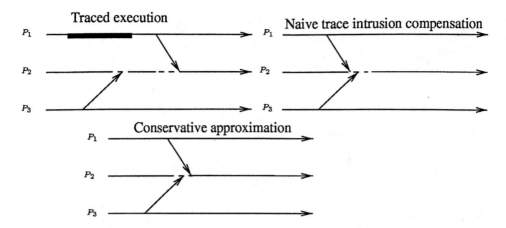

Figure 6.10: Order of message reception changed by tracing

6.6 Interaction with the operating system

Although tracing is well suited to capturing phenomena occurring at the application level such as communication delays, it may fail capturing inefficiencies of loaded multi-users systems. The reason is that tracing does not make possible to distinguish between the *ready* and *active* execution states of processes: once a process has been started, only explicit process suspensions at the application level, for example waiting for a message reception, can be detected by tracing at the application level. However, if the observed process is running on top of a multi-users operating system, it may occur that it gets suspended without any relation with an application-level event. This is the case if a higher priority process becomes activable or if the observed process has exhausted its time slice. In such cases the measured duration of the activity of some tasks is likely to exceed the actual duration of these tasks.

Such phenomenon can be captured if tracing at the application level can be coupled with measurement data gathered at the operating system level. One possible approach is to relate the counting information maintained by the operating system during the execution to the information deduced from tracing at the application level [26]. Then it becomes possible to evaluate the percentages of activity and idleness during the periods where tracing can only indicate that a thread was activable.

A similar problem may occur when other monitoring techniques are used and similar solutions may be designed. For example, in Paradyn, some performance data kept by the operating system can be mixed with the counters and timers generated from the monitoring of the observed programs. For example, the cumulative number of page faults is read before and after a procedure call to approximate the number of page faults taken by that procedure [24].

6.7 Conclusion

This chapter presents the issues of collecting monitoring data for performance debugging of parallel programs. Most monitoring tools for parallel programs are event driven, the most general event-driven monitoring technique being tracing. Among the possible tracing techniques, software tracing is deemed the most portable and widespread, although it requires to solve two difficult problems in order to obtain high quality traces: providing a precise global clock in distributed-memory systems and being able to limit or compensate the intrusion of tracing. The latter problem is specially difficult in case of programs behaving non deterministically. For such programs, a monitoring approach using execution replay techniques seems promising. Tracing alone is not sufficient to detect performance problems arising from the interaction of a parallel application with an underlying software layer such as the operating system. A possible approach to detect such problems is to combine tracing at the application level with time-driven monitoring at the operating system level of abstraction. The investigation of monitoring tools based on this approach seems a promising research track.

Acknowledgements

The authors are members of the APACHE research project supported by Centre National de la Recherche Scientifique (CNRS), Institut National Polytechnique de Grenoble (INPG), Institut National de Recherche en Informatique et Automatique (INRIA) and Université Joseph Fourier (UJF) Grenoble.

References

[1] J.M. Bull. A hierarchical classification of overheads in parallel programs. In *Proceedings of First IFIP TC10 International Workshop on Software Engineering for Parallel and Distributed Systems*, pages 208–219. Chapman Hall, 1996.

[2] C. Clémençon, A. Endo, J. Fritscher, A. Müller, and V.J.N. Wylie. Annai scalable run-time support for interactive debugging and performance analysis of large-scale programs. In L. Bougé, P. Fraigniaud, A. Mignotte, and Y. Robert, editors, *Proc. Euro-Par'96 Parallel Processing*, number 1123 in LNCS, 1996.

[3] K. M. Decker and B. J. N. Wylie. Software tools for scalable multi-level application engineering. *International Journal of Supercomputer Applications and High-Performance Computing*, 11(3):236–250, 1997.

[4] L. DeRose, Y. Zhang, and D.A. Reed. Svpablo: A multi-language performance analysis system. In *10th International Conference on Computer Performance Evaluation - Modelling Techniques and Tools - Performance Tools'98*, pages 352–355, Palma de Mallorca, Spain, September 1998.

[5] A. Fagot and J. Chassin de Kergommeaux. Systematic assessment of the overhead of tracing parallel programs. In E.L. Zapata, editor, *Proceedings of the 4th Euromicro Workshop on Parallel and Distributed processing, PDP'96*, pages 179–186, Braga, January 1996. IEEE/Computer Society Press.

[6] G. A. Geist, M. T. Heath, Peyton B. W., and P. H. Worley. PICL, a portable instrumented communication library. TN 37831-8083, Oak Ridge National Laboratory, Oak Ridge, USA, 1991.

[7] S. Graham, P. Kessler, and M. McKusik. gprof: A call graph execution profiler. In *Proceedings of the SIGPLAN'82 Symposium on Compiler Construction*, pages 120–126. ACM, 1982.

[8] W. Gu, G. Einsenhauer, K. Schwan, and J. Vetter. Falcon: On-line monitoring for steering parallel programs. *Concurrency: practice and experience*, 10(9):699–736, 1998.

[9] M. T. Heath and J. A. Etheridge. Visualizing the performances of parallel programs. *IEEE Transactions on Software Engineering*, 8(5):29–39, May 1991.

[10] R. Hofmann, R. Klar, B. Mohr, A. Quick, and M. Siegle. Distributed performance monitoring: Methods, tools, and applications. *IEEE Transactions on Parallel and Distributed Systems*, 5(6):585–598, June 1994.

[11] J.K. Hollingsworth, J.E. Lumpp, and B.P. Miller. Techniques for performance measurements of parallel programs. In T.L. Casavant et al, editor, *Parallel Computers Theory and Practice*. IEEE Computer Society Press, 1995.

[12] J.A. Kohl and G. A. Geist. The PVM 3.4 tracing facility and XPVM 1.1. In *Proc. of the 29th. Hawai International Conference on System Sciences*, 1996.

[13] E. Kraemer and J. T. Stasko. The visualization of parallel systems: An overview. *Journal of Parallel and Distributed Computing*, 18(2):105–117, 1993.

[14] L. Lamport. Time, clocks, and the ordering of events in a distributed system. *Communications of the ACM*, 21(7):558–565, 1978.

[15] T.J. LeBlanc and J.M. Mellor-Crummey. Debugging parallel programs with instant replay. *IEEE Transactions on Computers*, C-36(4):471–481, April 1987.

[16] E. Leu and A. Schiper. Execution replay : a mechanism for integrating a visualization tool with a symbolic debugger. In L. Bougé, M. Cosnard, Y. Robert, and D. Trystram, editors, *CONPAR 92 - VAPP V. Second Joint International Conference on Vector and Parallel Processing*, volume 634 of *Lectures Notes in Computer Science*. Springer-Verlag, 1992.

[17] T. Ludwig, M. Oberhuber, and R. Wismüeller. An open monitoring system for parallel and distributed programs. In L. Bougé and et al., editors, *Proc. Euro-Par'96 Parallel Processing*, volume 1123 of *Lecture Notes in Computer Science*. Springer, 1996.

[18] É. Maillet. Tape/PVM: An efficient performance monitor for PVM applications. User guide, LMC-IMAG, B.P. 53, F-38041 Grenoble Cedex 9, France, 1994. Available at ftp://ftp.imag.fr/imag/APACHE/TAPE.

[19] É. Maillet. Issues in performance tracing with Tape/PVM. In *Proceedings of EuroPVM'95*, pages 143–148. HERMES (ISBN 2-86601-497-9), 1995.

[20] É. Maillet. *Traçage de logiciel d'applications parallèles : conception et ajustement de qualité*. PhD thesis, Institut National Polytechnique de Grenoble, September 1996. In French. Available at ftp://ftp.imag.fr/pub/APACHE/THESES/.

[21] É. Maillet and C. Tron. On Efficiently Implementing Global Time for Performance Evaluation on Multiprocessor Systems. *Journal of Parallel and Distributed Computing*, 28:84–93, July 1995.

[22] A. D. Malony, A. Reed, and H.A.G. Wijshoff. Performance Measurement Intrusion and Perturbation Analysis. *IEEE Transactions on parallel and distriuted systems*, 3(4), July 1992.

[23] F. Mattern. Virtual time and global states of distributed systems. In M. Cosnard et al., editors, *Proceedings of the International Workshop on Parallel and Distributed Algorithms*, pages 215–226, Amsterdam, 1989. Elsevier Science Publishers.

[24] B.P. Miller et al. The paradyn parallel performance measurement tool. *IEEE Computer*, November 1995.

[25] O.Y. Nickolayev, P.C. Roth, and D.A. Reed. Real-time statistical clustering for event trace reduction. *The International Journal of Supercomputer Applications and High Performance Computing*, 11(2):144–159, Summer 1997.

[26] F.-G. Ottogali and J.-M. Vincent. Mise en cohérence et analyse de traces multi-niveaux. *Calculateurs Parallèles*, 11(2):211–227, 1999. In French.

[27] A. D Reed, A. U. Aydt, R. J. Noe, P. C Roth, A. K. Shields, B. Schwartz, and L. F. Tavera. Scalable performance analysis: The pablo performance analysis environment. In Anthony Skjellum, editor, *Scalable Parallel Libraries Conference*, pages 104–113. IEEE Computer Society Press, October 1993.

[28] D.A. Reed. Experimental analysis of parallel systems: Techniques and open problems. In G. Haring and G. Kotsis, editors, *Proc. 7th Int. Conference on Computer Performance Evaluation*, Vienna, Austria, May 1994. Springer Verlag.

[29] D.A. Reed, K.A. Shields, W.H. Scullin, L. F. Tavera, and C.L. Elford. Virtual reality and parallel systems performance analysis. *IEEE Computer*, 28(11):57–67, November 1995.

[30] M. Sarukkai and A.D. Malony. Perturbation analysis of high level instrumentation for spmd programs. *ACM SIGPLAN Notices*, pages 44–53, July 1993.

[31] W.R. Stevens. *Unix network programming*. Englewood Cliffs, NJ: Prentice-Hall, 1990.

[32] V. S. Sunderam. PVM: A framework for parallel distributed computing. *Concurrency: Practice And Experienc*, 2(4):315–339, 1990.

[33] F. Teodorescu and J. Chassin de Kergommeaux. On correcting the intrusion of tracing non deterministic programs by software. In *Euro-Par'97 Parallel Processing*, LNCS 1300, pages 94–101. Springer-Verlag, August 1997.

[34] Jim Trocki. Mon: Service monitoring daemon. http://www.kernel.org/software/mon/.

[35] J. C. Yan. Performance tuning with AIMS — an automated instrumentation and monitoring system for multicomputers. In *Proc. of the Twenty-Seventh Annual Hawai Conference on System Sciences*, pages 625–633. IEEE Computer Society Press, 1994.

[36] J. C. Yan and M. A. Schmidt. Constructing space-time views from fixed size trace files – getting the best of both worlds. In E.H. D'Hollander, G. R. Joubert, F. J. Peters, and U. Trottenberg, editors, *Parallel Computing: Fundamentals, Applications and New Directions*, volume 12 of *Advances in Parallel Computing*, pages 633–640, Amsterdam, February 1998. Elsevier, North-Holland.

Chapter 7

Simulation and Performance Prediction

Emilio Luque, Remo Suppi, Tomàs Margalef, Joan Sorribes
and Porfidio Hernández

Abstract

Parallel systems play a decisive role in the high performance computing scenario. However, the parallelisation of real applications is a complex task that takes a lot of time and efforts. The simulation of parallel systems is a promising approach to obtain the best trade-off between cost and performance by analysing and tuning parallel applications. This chapter analyse the possibilities and techniques for parallel system simulation in topics as performance prediction, system modelling, performance indexes, simulation techniques and an overview of some simulation tools.

7.1 Introduction

Parallel and distributed systems offer high computing capabilities that are required for many applications. However, the parallelisation of real applications is a complex task that can take a long time. During the development of a parallel application, the programmer must take care of the results generated by the program under development in order to be sure of the correctness of the program. But one must also care for the behaviour of the parallel program under development in order to obtain the best possible performance, because the main goal of parallel systems is to provide the best possible performance or more precisely the best trade-off between cost and performance. This is a new feature of parallel programming that is not considered in classical sequential programming where the programmer may rely on the compiler capabilities to optimise the code of the application.

In this context, simulation of parallel systems appears as a very promising possibility that allows the user to do all the required analysis without spending so much effort and even without completing the development of the parallel application.

In this chapter, the possibilities and techniques concerning of parallel system simulation will be analyzed in depth. In Section 7.2, the need of some performance prediction facility in the development of parallel applications is shown, focusing on the usability of simulation tools for reducing the user effort in the parallel programming cycle. Section 7.3 studies system modelling, showing the different techniques that can be found in the literature and define the main performance indexes. Section 7.4 describes the simulation techniques. Finally, Section 7.5 provides an overview of some simulation tools.

7.2   Parallel Systems and Performance Prediction

The classical sequential program development involves several phases and requires certain tools to reach the desired objectives.

- First of all the programmer must design the application.

- Then the programmer must code the application to obtain the program. This step requires the use of some editing tools.

- By using some compilers, the programmer reaches the executable program that can be executed on the target system.

However, the program development does not finish after the program coding but it requires some testing and debugging phase to be sure of the correctness of the program. If a bug is found during the testing step, the programmer must fix this bug and modify the design or the source code to solve it and reach the final correct version of the program. This classical programming cycle is presented in Figure 7.1. When parallel programming is

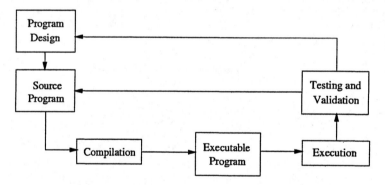

Figure 7.1: Classical sequential programming cycle

considered, the programmer must follow the same steps as in the classical sequential program in order to reach a correct program that solves the considered problem. However, there are some points that must be considered in parallel programming that were not necessary on sequential programming. For example, the programmer must specify the mapping of the tasks of the program to the processors of the system, although it is possible that the system software incorporates some facilities that do these tasks automatically.

The correct execution of the parallel program in terms of its functionality is not enough to justify the use of a parallel system and it is necessary to analyze the performance obtained from the program. Therefore, the programmer must analyze the performance results and try to improve the program behaviour to obtain the best possible performance. This is a completely new phase that must be carried out in parallel programming. Moreover, in many cases the programmer is interested in getting some information about the program behaviour before completely developing the application program:

- The programmer would be interested in knowing the behaviour of the application, before completing the development. This means that the programmer is interested in estimating the efficiency of the parallel program in order to determine if it is worthy to develop the application or the benefit obtained is too low to make all the effort of application development.

- When the application is developed or under development, in many cases the user need to test the application under different conditions (different mapping policies, different routing policies or many other possibilities) in order to determine which options provide the best performance. This analysis is very important for parallel program developers. However, all these studies are very time consuming when they are done on a real system by executing the parallel application.

- Other studies that are very interesting for parallel programmers are those related to scalability analysis. In this case, the programmer is interested in testing the behaviour of the parallel application with different number of processors or with different size input data. Concerning the number of processors, in most cases, the parallel systems available have a fixed number of processors and the programmer cannot test other systems. Moreover, it must be pointed that in many cases, the programmer is interested in testing the application with a higher number of processors to determine if it is worthy to get a bigger system or not.

All these requirements imply the necessity of some performance prediction facilities in order to allow the programmer to make all the required analysis without developing the complete parallel application and executing this application considering different conditions. Therefore, the performance prediction facilities appear as a major issue in parallel program development.

There are two main approaches to carry on performance prediction on parallel systems. These approaches are analytical prediction and simulation (Figure 7.2).

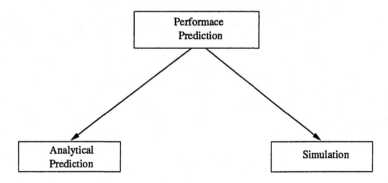

Figure 7.2: Classification of performance prediction approaches

In both cases it is necessary to develop some model of the parallel system in order to predict the behaviour of the application. These models describe the system by a set of parameters that represent the parallel system. However, very precise models including many parameters are in practice not useful because in most cases it is not possible to determine in a precise way all these parameters.

7.2.1   Analytical Prediction

Several analytical models of parallel system performance prediction have been used in the literature. These models include Markov's models, queuing theory, parameters based models and so on. However, these models are only applicable to a very reduced number of specific cases and do not provide good results when general cases are considered.

7.2.2   Simulation

Simulation is the other alternative to do performance prediction of parallel system behaviour that has been widely used. Parallel system simulation requires a representation of the parallel application and a representation of the parallel system (architecture and operating system). This topic is described in Section 7.4.

In a first step, when the parallel application has been developed and is working correctly the programmer can use some simulation tool to develop the performance analysis desired. From the developed application, a synthetic model of the application must be extracted to be used as the input to the simulator. Then, the user can modify some policy (mapping, scheduling, routing, etc.) or modify some characteristics of the system and study the performance under these new conditions. This possibility extends the parallel application development cycle by including the performance analysis after the program development (Figure 7.3). This kind of performance analysis requires the complete development of parallel application.

However, the phase of completely coding the application can be avoided if the programmer is able to provide a synthetic skeleton of the application including some parameters that characterise it. This skeleton can be used as input to the simulator. In this case, the performance prediction analysis can be done before completely developing the application. Therefore, the programmer has a more powerful prediction, because the information obtained is related to an application that has not been completely developed and this fact saves a lot of effort and time to the programmer.

Then, the application development cycle is modified by including the performance analysis phase before the step of coding the application in order to receive some feedback about the behaviour of the application. This new scheme is shown in Figure 7.4. When the programmer is actually coding the application he or she must test the correctness of the program (debugging phase), but then he or she has some useful information about the behaviour of the application. This means that this big effort of completing the development of the application is only done when it is really profitable.

7.3   Parallel System Modelling

In the previous section, it has been shown that the simulation of parallel systems is a very useful and powerful technique for parallel program development. Simulation allows the programmer to receive some knowledge about the program behaviour. However, as it has been pointed out above, simulation requires the modelling of the real system. According to the definition of Korn and Wait [26] "simulation is an experiment performed on a model".

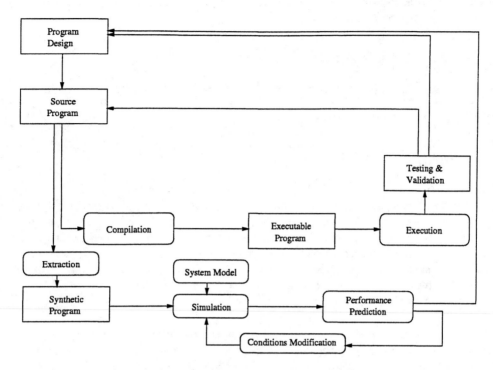

Figure 7.3: Performance analysis by simulation

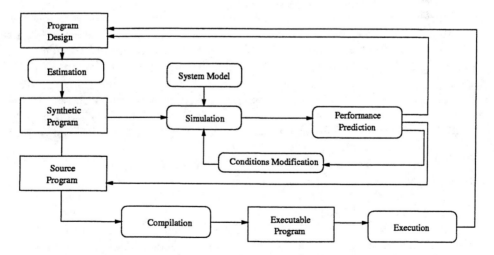

Figure 7.4: Parallel Application Development with Performance Prediction

It means that the first step to carry out a study based on simulation is to develop a model that represents the real system.

A model is the representation of the real system that is used during the experiments to extract some conclusions about the behaviour of the physical system that it is being simulated. The model can be submitted to manipulations that would be impossible to accomplish in the real system. The actions that occur on the model during the simulation can be studied and from them some properties of the behaviour of the real system or parts of the same can be extracted.

7.3.1   System Modelling

The first step towards the study of a system is building a model. It can be a formal representation of the theory or a formal expression of the empirical observation. However, it is often a combination of both. The relevance of modelling has been discussed in [15], where they affirm that the abstraction is the natural way to understand and control a given system. A model is a representation of a system. It can be a replica, a prototype, or a smaller-scale system, i.e., a simplified system abstraction that includes enough detail to allow the derivation of desired performance measures for the system to be modelled with sufficient accuracy [29, 41].

The abstraction means replacing part of the considered universe with a model having a similar structure, but simpler. Moreover modelling is an indispensable tool for the scientific procedure. A scientific model can be defined as an abstraction of the real system. It can be used for prediction or control purposes. The goal of the scientific model is to allow the analyzer to determine how one or more changes on the system can affect concrete parts or the complete system. A very important item in the model design is defining the objective function, *i.e.* the logic or mathematical function of the decision variables.

A model development involves two main tasks: the design of a system representation and the representation of the work that the system does.

Before carrying on with building the model, the designer must answer the following questions: What is the concrete level of detail to solve the problem? Are the necessary data to represent the work in this level of detail available? The task to describe the work developed by a system is called workload characterisation, and is the main key in performance analysis.

Modelling is still largely an art, in the sense that no general rules are known for systematically generating the model appropriate to each system and purpose. Instead of such rules, a set of general principles, which provide useful modelling guidelines in most situations can be shown: finality, invariance, causality, locality, simplicity, solvability, *abstraction − idealisation*, analogy, hierarchy and iteration [15].

When the model has been developed it must be compared with the real system in order to ensure that the model covers the main features of the real system. Some criteria that are pertinent for judging how well a model is suited to a particular system are: Accuracy, Precision, Completeness and Usefulness.

If the model developed is used to simulate the behaviour of the real system, it must be pointed out that the simulator must be verified and validated. The verification process implies the comparison of the model versus the simulation program to ensure that the program reproduces the model in a precise way. On the other hand, the validation process implies the comparison of the simulation results versus the real system results. Figure 7.5 summarises the modelling and simulator development cycle.

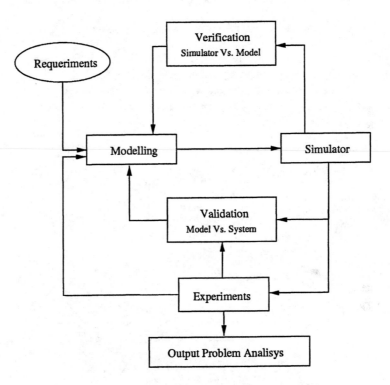

Figure 7.5: Modelling and simulation cycle

7.3.2   Model Classification

There exist a big variety of models, and there are several ways of classifying them. A preliminary classification in categories attending to the description method of the real system is the following one:

- Icon oriented or graphical models represent visually concrete aspects of the system.

- Analogous models use a set of properties to represent other set of system properties.

- Symbolic models represent the system by mathematical or logic operations that can be used to formulate a solution. These models are also called abstract models.

Another criteria for model classification is the following one:

- Parametric vs. non-parametric models: A parametric model represents a generic system in a certain class of systems; which system is intended in a given application is determined by assigning numerical values to parameters contained in the model. A non-parametric model contains no such parameters and thus represents only one specific system.

However, these are only very preliminary classifications and the main criteria for classification are the three following ones, as shown in Figure 7.6.

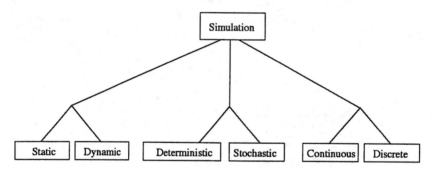

Figure 7.6: Models classification

- Static vs. dynamic models: a static model represents the system in a particular time instant. This state is representative for all the remaining states. This model is used when the time does not represent an important role in the state change of the system. On the other hand, a dynamic model represents a system that evolves in time and for each instant a different state can be obtained from the previous one.

- Deterministic vs. stochastic models: If a model does not contain any element with probabilities (random values), it is called deterministic. In this type of model, the state of the system obtained from an input data set is the same for different simulations. The same input will generate the same output for any simulation. If any characteristic of the system is represented by a random entry (or distribution function), the system is considered stochastic. A simulation under a stochastic model produces different results for the same inputs and the concept of "one simulation" loses sense. The obtained result should be used to predict the system behaviour but through analysis of a set of statistics simulations.

- Continuous vs. discrete: Continuous model where each state variable can assume any value in a certain interval of the real number line. In a discrete model the possible values of each state variable form a discrete set.

7.3.3 Performance Evaluation

The main reason to analyze a system arises from the goal of improving the system operation (performance), in some sense. The performance evaluation activity is often classified as an art rather than a science because successful performance evaluation projects cannot be produced mechanically. Every performance study requires an in-depth knowledge of the system being evaluated and a careful selection of the performance evaluation technique depending on the intended goals of that study [29].

The state of the parallel computer system, and thus system performance indexes, can be viewed from different perspectives. These different perspectives depend on the level at which the performance is considered. Figure 7.7 shows the three basic perspectives that are usually used.

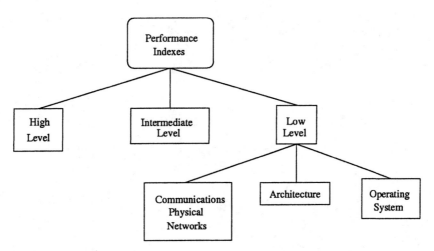

Figure 7.7: Performance indexes perspectives

High-level performance information includes information that the programmer should use to answer questions like "Should I continue working on this program's performance?". Single number metrics like program efficiency, speed-up, effectivity, etc. are included in this category. These metrics are derived by comparing the performance of a parallel algorithm to certain kinds of appropriately chosen performance standards, such as the performance of an equivalent sequential algorithm or program. Figure 7.8 shows the main performance indexes at this level.

- Speed-up $Sp := T1 \ / \ Tp$

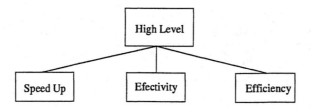

Figure 7.8: High level performance indexes

Speed-up is the ratio of the run time T1 of the sequential algorithm (prior to parallelisation) to the run time Tp of the parallelised algorithm using p processors.

- Efficiency: $Ep = Sp / p$ with $Ep \leq 1$

Concurrent efficiency is a metric for the utilisation of multiprocessor capacity. The closer Ep to 1, the better use is made of the potentially p-fold power of a p processor system.

- Effectivity: $Fp = Sp / (p \cdot Tp) = Ep / Tp$

Effectivity is the ratio between speed-up and work characterised by pTp. It measures both the absolute increase of speed and the relative utilisation of the computer capacity.

Low level performance information includes hardware and operating system features including communications on physical networks. Figure 7.9 shows typical indexes for communications on physical networks included in this low-level performance perspective.

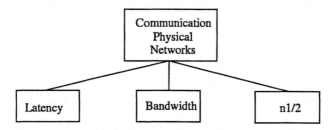

Figure 7.9: Communication performance indexes

- Latency (start-up time) is the time needed to send a 0-byte message. This time includes the time for signal travelling along the interconnection medium and the software overhead for *send/receive* the message.

- Bandwidth is the quantity of maximum information that is possible to send through the network per unity of time. This limit is the physical bandwidth of the net.

- n1/2 represents the necessary message length to achieve a performance of the half net bandwidth.

At the intermediate level there are performance data and measures that relate the problem solution method to the program-machine implementation. Examples of indexes at this level include processor utilisation, communication behaviour, workload balance, data mapping, etc.

7.3.4 Model of the Architecture

An essential question is why do we need to model the computer architecture? There is no single answer. We might need to know if a concrete architecture is amenable to execute a set of applications in a specific environment, or if such architecture is operative with a given topology. So, there are some architecture models oriented to analyze their features and functionality, while others are oriented to measure their performance and scalability. We do not always have the possibility to use the real architecture because for example, we are in the design phase and to make design decisions is necessary to measure the performance of the architecture. Sometimes we dispose of the real system but we like to know what its behaviour would be if the architecture is expanded ten times (scalability) or if the system will still be running when we introduce or eliminate elements.

The model of the architecture that has been used in the SEPP project has a representation formalism based on a directed graph. In the graph, the nodes represent the computing elements and the arcs their interconnections. The characteristics of every node and arc are given by a set of parameters. From a static point of view, the graph is a collection of interconnected resources representing the work made in the system. The movement of messages through the links and the load-execution-unload of the processes on the computing elements model the dynamic behaviour of the system.

Nodes are classified depending on the type of computing element that is modelled: processors, memory, switches and I/O processors. Processors can model systems with or without concurrent computing-communication. The parameters that characterise them are: relative computing speed, number and size of communication buffers, *send/receive* policy, access time and size of the local memory, type of CPU scheduler, input and output lists for the hardware events. The memory modules are characterised by their size and access time. The switches by their relative delay; the I/O relationship and the I/O control policy and, finally I/O processors and processors have similar parameters: computing speed, number and size of communication buffers, communication policy, I/O links and processor links.

7.3.5 Models of programs

There exists a wide range of models created to characterise parallel programs in the literature and a lot of them are tied to languages or specific tools to develop applications. Due to the scope of this book we present an introductory view about the three most important paradigms to model parallel programs: Petri nets, a data flow model and a specific model PA&AS oriented to evaluate the performance behaviour of parallel programs executed (or simulated) in a selected parallel architecture.

Petri Nets

A Petri net is an abstract, formal model of information flow. The properties, concepts, and techniques of Petri nets are developed for describing and analyzing the flow of information in systems, particularly systems that exhibit asynchronous and concurrent activities [1, 13, 29].

The representation of a Petri net as a graph is a common practice in Petri net research. The graph contains two types of nodes: circles (called places) and bars (called transitions). These nodes, places and transformations, are connected by directed arcs from places to transitions and from transitions to places. In addition to the static properties represented by the graph, a Petri net has dynamic properties that derive from its execution.

The execution of a Petri net is controlled by the position and movement of markers (called tokens) in the Petri net. Tokens, indicated by by black dots, reside in the places of the graph and their movement is directed by a set of rules: tokens are moved by the firing of transitions of the net. The transition fires by removing the enabling tokens from their input places and generating new tokens in their output places. The distribution of tokens in a Petri net defines its state and it is called the marking.

Petri nets are very useful for studying qualitative or logical properties of systems exhibiting concurrent and asynchronous behaviour. However for quantitative performance and dependability evaluation, the concept of time must be included in the definition of Petri nets. Naturally timing is associated with transitions of the Petri net.

Generalised Stochastic Petri Nets (GSPN), introduced by Ajmone Marsan, Balbo and Conte [1, 13], contain two different types of transitions. Exponential transitions fire after a certain random delay has elapsed and are drawn as empty rectangular boxes. Immediate transitions fire without delay, once they have been enabled and are drawn as thin bars. Directed arcs connect places and transitions. In the simplified form of GSPN considered here, all arcs of a GSPN have multiplicity 1. A transition fires by removing one token from all its input places and putting one token into all its output places. The firing of immediate transitions has priority over firing of exponential transitions. When more than one immediate transition could fire in a marking of a GSPN, the transition that actually fires is selected according to some appropriately determined probability.

Removing the timing specifications in a stochastic Petri yields an ordinary Petri net with priorities for which a rich theory for verifying structural properties is available. On the other hand, stochastic Petri nets constitute a formalism for defining discrete-event stochastic systems and, thus, allow a high-level description of an underlying stochastic process. As a consequence, stochastic Petri nets provide a unified modelling formalism for qualitative and quantitative analysis of discrete-event stochastic system.

Ajmone Marsan and Chiola [1] introduced deterministic and stochastic Petri nets (DSPN), as an extension to GSPN. DSPN allows the association of a timed transition either with a deterministic or an exponentially distributed firing delay. Hence, DSPN are well suited to represent system features such as time-outs, propagation delays or processor rebooting times which are naturally associated with constant delays. In recent years DSPN have became particular modelling formalism that gained considerable popularity. This popularity is because of the reduction by four orders of magnitude in the computational effort required by the numerical methods for analysing DSPN as well as because of the availability of a user-friendly software package for performance modelling with DSPN.

Data flow model

Another important modelling paradigm, oriented to performance evaluation, is data flow modelling. Data flow involves driving the program execution by the data flow, not by the instruction flow. The global data relationships in a program can be exposed and codified by static analysis methods. Such data flow, or "$def - use$" relationships, can be deduced by static, compile time analysis of the program [3].

Another interesting relationship is related to finding out, giving a program point (instruction), what data definitions are "live" at that point, that is, what data definitions given before this point are used after this point. This information is of interest, for example, when assigning index registers: data that is live at a point in a program might be profitably held in an index register at that point. The control flow graph G of a program is a connected directed graph with a single entry node n_0. G consists of a set of nodes, $N = \{n_0, n_1, \ldots n_m\}$, representing sequences of program instructions and a set of edges, E, of ordered pairs of nodes representing the flow of control. The nodes represent the data (variables and signals) and the operations. The directed edges indicate the direction of the data flow [38].

We consider per example a graph of m nodes. The graph has $N = \{1, 2, \ldots m\}$; and $E = \{(1,2), (2,3), etc.\}$. The immediate successors of a node n_i are all of the nodes n_j for which (n_i, n_j) is an edge in E. The immediate predecessors of the node n_j are all the nodes n_i for which (n_i, n_j) is an edge in E. A path is an ordered sequence of nodes $(n_1, n_2, \ldots n_k)$ and their connecting edges in which each n_i is an immediate predecessor of n_{i+1}. A closed path or cycle is a path in which the first and last nodes are the same. In order to determine which definitions affect which uses, two types of expression relationships can be distinguished: those which exist between expressions within straight line sequences of code and those which exist in the context of control flow. The basic data flow analysis method tries to see what definitions of data items reach each node from other nodes in the graph. It should be readily apparent that the set of definitions which reach a node n_i is the union of the definitions available from the nodes which are immediate predecessors of n_i. There are developed basic algorithms to show the reachability information in a general control flow graph.

PA&AS Model

A third modelling paradigm for performance evaluation of parallel applications is the one provided by PA&AS model. This programming model is entirely based on the message-passing paradigm. The programmer can define processes performing computations independently and interacting only by sending messages [36, 37]. This model is a superset of the model supported by GRAPNEL [16].

A dynamic data flow formalism is used to represent the behaviour of the parallel programs. This formalism allows modelling the dynamic behaviour of programs. In the model, a program is represented by a graph with the following characteristics (Figure 7.10):

- Finite directed graph with parallel arcs. In the graph there can exist more than one arc between two graph nodes.

- Graph nodes model the sequential code of the processes that form the parallel application.

- Arcs represent the dependency among nodes, modelling messages and synchronization.

The model is parametric and can be or not stochastic. Each node has an associated parameter SC (Figure 7.10). This parameter models the number of (sequential) instructions inside the node (computing volume). SC allows to evaluate the execution time for the simulation. This parameter can be stochastic (distribution function) or not (constant value).

Arcs have two end points (source and destination) that can be tokens or messages. They are used to *send/receive* data (messages) or synchronization signals (tokens) between nodes. Arcs possess a set of parameters to model their behaviour such as the volume of the transferred information, the *input/output* policy, etc. Input tokens have deterministic behaviour and they are used to start a node execution. The firing rule of a node is a Boolean equation that allows us to dynamically define a set of conditions to fire a node.

The *input/output* messages can have deterministic or stochastic behaviour. In the first case, a message models a communication action and it is not associated with a control sentence. In the second case it is associated with a control sentence. A control instruction

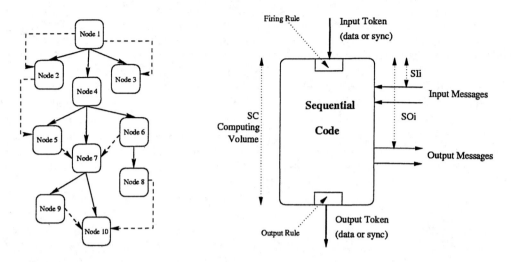

Figure 7.10: PA&AS parallel algorithm graph and node

with a communication action will have an occurrence probability. The code can contain different types of sentences (if-else, while-if, if-while, etc.) that will modify the behaviour. These conditions involve dynamic behaviour. SI_i and SO_i values model input-output communications. They have values which are percentages relative to the beginning of the code. This value models the existing code portion before I/O action. The arrival tokens always have $SI_i = 0\%$ and the departure token $SO_i = 100\%$. The model distinguishes between two message classes: blocking and non blocking messages. Each I/O message has a parameter set to describe its behaviour. A full description can be obtained in [36].

7.4   Simulation

The type of simulation that will be used in this chapter falls within the classification mentioned in Section 7.3.2 concerning discrete, dynamic and stochastic models. It is generally called "discrete-event simulation models". The deterministic models are a special case of the stochastic models and the consideration of the stochastic models does not imply loss of generality [24].

7.4.1   Discrete Event Simulation

This method is used when the state changes of the elements (entities) that compose the system occur in given times (discrete moments), as opposed to the continuous systems where the state changes occur in a continuous way.

In practice there are methodologies to study the state changes in continuous-discrete event systems by simulation. In this case, an event denotes the state change of an entity of the system. The simulation by discrete events is extremely useful due to the fact that it reduces the interval between events. A discrete event system can simulate a continuous system in an approximated way.

The simulation by discrete events is powerful to analyze a system in a computer where the state changes can be represented by a series of discrete events.

The technique adapted to model a particular system depends on the nature of the intervals between events. These intervals can be stochastic or deterministic. When they are random, the modelling technique must take into account intervals of variable magnitude. When they are deterministic, the intervals can vary according to a plan or they can all have the same duration.

In the discrete event systems the changes occur at the moment of each event. As the entity states stay constant between the events, it is not necessary to take into account the inactive time in the model. Therefore, the criterion of the "next event" for the advance of the time can be applied. Once accomplished all the changes for the time of a particular event, the time simulated to the following event is made. At this moment, the event is processed and the necessary state changes are made. In this form a simulation can disregard the inactive time between events, in contrast to the real world where it is forced to wait.

Upon modelling a system for simulation purposes, two different structures that fulfill important functions exist. One of them involves the mathematical relationships between the variables (attributes) associated with the entities. The specification of the mathematical relationships serves frequently to describe totally the the way the system state changes occur.

The logic relationships correspond to the other structures that serve to describe a system. A logic relation will be used to verify if it accomplishes a condition or not. In this case, the logic relation will describe the form in which the state change occurs in the system [28, 32, 41].

Time advance mechanisms

In addition to the distinction between discrete event systems and continuous systems, the discrete time systems should be taken into account. In the discrete event systems, the state changes occur in given time instants. These state changes, called events, cannot be uniformly distributed in the time. These events, together with the external events, form the base for the specification of the structure and behaviour of the model (static and dynamic). In contrast to the discrete event formalism, the discrete time formalism assumes that the changes in the system can occur in each time step.

However, the assumption that any entity can change its state in any time step reports serious disadvantages in the representation of the model and in terms of simulation efficiency. In a discrete event simulator the periods of inactivity are skipped over by jumping the clock from event time to event time. Fixed increment time advance does not skip over these inactive periods, which can consume a lot of computer time (Figure 7.11).

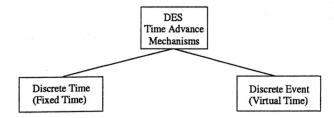

Figure 7.11: Time advance mechanisms

Figure 7.12 shows the time advance for a discrete event simulation and for discrete time simulation.

Events	e1	e2	e3		e4		e5	

Real Time

| Virtual Time | t1 | t2 | t3 | | t4 | | t5 |

Fixed Time $\delta t0$ $\delta t1$ $\delta t2$ $\delta t3$ $\delta t4$ $\delta t5$ $\delta t6$ $\delta t7$ $\delta t8$

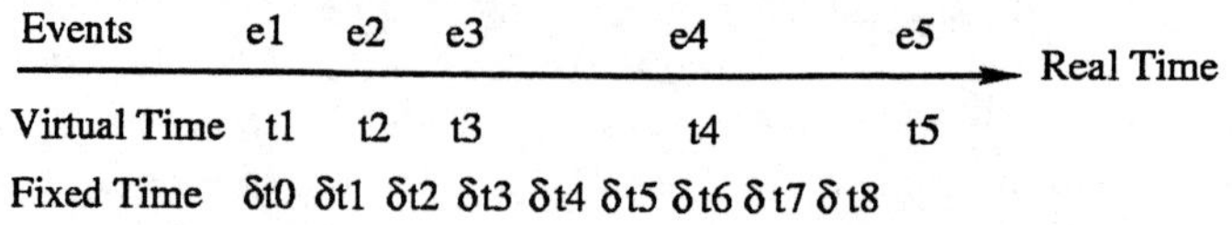

Figure 7.12: Time advance for discrete event and discrete time simulation

In Figure 7.12 it can be observed that in the discrete event simulation the virtual time advances with the events. However, in the discrete time simulation the fixed time advances step by step, and this fact implies that the second simulation will take a longer time to be computed [10, 19, 24, 41].

Parallel & Distributed Simulation

There are many complex "realistic" problems that cannot be solved by numerical or analytical evaluation. Consequently, for those cases, simulation remains the only tractable evaluation methodology. Conducting simulation experiments is, however, time consuming for several reasons. First, the design of detailed models requires in depth modelling skills and usually extensive model development efforts. Second, once a simulation model is specified, the simulation run can take exceedingly long to execute. For statistical reasons it might be necessary to perform a whole series of simulation runs to establish the required confidence in the performance parameters obtained by the simulation.

To solve these problems different approaches can be used. The most promising one is accelerating simulations using multiprocessor systems. This method implies the synchronization of logical simulation processes executing in parallel on different processing nodes in a parallel or distributed environment [17, 20].

Accelerating Simulations   In order to speed up simulation, different levels can be considered (Figure 7.13) [17, 20, 24]:

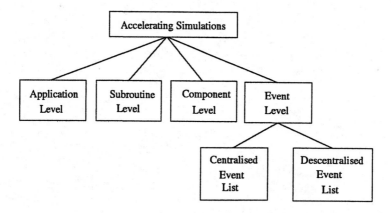

Figure 7.13: Accelerating simulations

Application-Level: The most obvious acceleration of simulation experiments with the aim to explore large search spaces is to assign independent replications of the same simulation model with possibly different input parameters to the available processors. Since no co-ordination is required between processors during their execution high efficiency can be expected.

Subroutine-Level: Simulation studies in which experiments must be sequenced due to iteration dependencies among of replicated subroutines. In this approach the degree of speedup is limited because generally, the number of processors is less than the number of parallel subroutines.

Component-Level: The previous two levels make use of the parallelism available in the physical system. A new approach is to decompose the simulation model into model components. This decomposition will reflect the inherent model parallelism. A simulator that can profit of these model characteristics will have a maximum speed up with respect to model simulation.

Event-Level, Centralised Event List (EVL): In a scheme where EVL is a centralised data structure maintained by a master processor, acceleration can be achieved by distributing concurrent events to a pool of slave processors dedicated to execute them. The master processor in this case takes care that consistency in the event structure is preserved. This approach requires knowledge about the event structure that must be extracted from the simulation model. The distribution at the event level with a centralised EVL is particularly appropriate for shared memory multiprocessors where EVL can be implemented as a shared data structure accessed by all processors.

Event-Level, Decentralised Event List: The most permissive way of conducting simulation in parallel is at the level where events from arbitrary points of the space-time are assigned to different processors, either in a regular or an unstructured way. A higher degree of parallelism can be expected to be exploitable in strategies that allow the concurrent simulation of events with different time-stamps. Approaches following this idea require protocols for local synchronization, which may increase communication costs depending on the event dispersion over space and time in the simulation model.

Logical process simulation A common approach in all simulation strategies with distribution at the event level is to divide a global simulation task into a set of communicating logical processes, trying to exploit the parallelism of the model components with the concurrent execution of these processes.

The logical process simulation can be viewed as the co-operation of an arrangement of interacting logical processes, each of them simulating a subspace of the space-time. In general, a region would be a spatial part of the process network topology. A set of conditions can be observed for the logical process simulation:

- A set of logical processes (LPs) can execute event occurrences synchronously or asynchronously in parallel.

- The communication system provides the possibility for LPs to exchange local data, but also to synchronize local activities.

- Every logical process has assigned a region as part of the simulation model, upon which a simulation engine operating in event driven mode executes local events and advances the local virtual clock.

- Each logical process has access only to a statically partitioned subset of the state variables.

Two kinds of events are processed in each logical process: internal events (without effect to another logical process), and external events that can have effect to the local states of other logical processes. Basically two strategies have been proposed for the logical process simulation: conservative or optimistic. These types of simulation are different in the position with respect to the advancement of event executions. Both are based on the sending of messages carrying causality information that has been created by one logical process and affects one or more other logical processes (Figure 7.14).

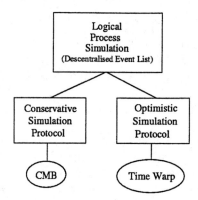

Figure 7.14: Logical process simulation

In the first case, the conservative protocol prevents the causality errors by blocking until there is the chance to process an "unsafe" event. In the optimistic protocol, the process executes all available events and undoes the simulation if it detects that premature processing of local events is inconsistent with causality conditions produced by an other logical process [17].

Conservative simulation Protocol   The conservative strategy is based on the work of Chandy and Misra and Bryant [11] (CMB protocol). In CMB protocols the causality of events across logical processes is preserved by sending time-stamped event messages that include a copy of Local Virtual Time (LVT) of the process.

A logical process with the conservative protocol is allowed to process safe events only. The protocol will process events with the guarantee that it does not receive an external message with time-stamp $< LVT$ (time-stamp "in the past"). For this reason, all events (internal and external) must be processed in chronological order. This guarantees that the message stream produced by the protocol is in turn in chronological order.

The main problem of this protocol is the possibility of deadlock: each logical process is waiting for a message to arrive, however, awaiting it from an logical process that is blocked itself. Moreover, the cyclic waiting of the logical process involved in deadlock leaves events unprocessed in their respective input buffers, the amount of which can grow unpredictably, thus causing memory overflow (this is possible even in the absence of deadlock). Several methods have been proposed to overcome the vulnerability of the CMB protocol to deadlock, falling into the two principle categories: deadlock avoidance and deadlock *detection/recovery*.

Deadlock avoidance The deadlock state can be prevented by modifying the communication protocol based on the sending of null messages [34] (messages that imply a null event -event without effect-).

A null message is not related to the simulated model and only serves for synchronization purposes. Essentially it is sent on every output channel as a promise not send any other message with smaller time-stamp in the future. It is launched whenever a logical process processed an event that did not generate an event message for some corresponding target. The receiver can use this implicit information to unblock their situation and process the next events.

This protocol modification is very easy to implement but it can put a dramatic number of null messages in the communication net with serious effects upon the simulation performance. Several optimisations of the protocol exist to reduce the frequency and amount of null messages, *e.g.* sending them only on demand (upon request), delayed until some timeout, or only when an logical process becomes blocked [4, 9].

Deadlock detection and recovery An alternative to the CMB protocol avoiding null messages has also been proposed by Chandy and Misra [12], allowing deadlocks to occur, but providing a mechanism to detect it and recover from it. Their algorithm runs in two phases:

- Parallel phase, in which the simulation runs until it deadlocks,

- Interface phase, which initiates a computation allowing some logical process to advance LVT.

They prove that in every parallel phase at least one event will be processed generating at least one event message, which will also be propagated before the next deadlock. A central controller is assumed in their algorithm, thus violating a distributed computing principle. To avoid a single resource (controller) to become a communication performance bottleneck during deadlock detection, any general distributed termination detection algorithm or distributed deadlock detection algorithm could be used. Different approaches to this idea can be obtained from [34].

Different improvements to the conservative protocol have been proposed in Conservative Time Windows [30].

Optimistic Logical processes Optimistic logical processes simulation strategies, in contrast to conservative ones, do not strictly adhere to the *localcausalityconstraint* (lcc). This protocol allows the occurrence of causality errors and provides a mechanism to recover from lcc violations. In order to avoid blocking and safe-to-process determination which are serious performance pitfalls in the conservative approach, an optimistic logical process progresses its simulation (and by that advances LVT) as far into the future as possible, without warranty that the set of generated (internal and external) events is consistent with lcc. For this reason, the possibility exists of the arrival of an external event with a time-stamp in the local past of the logical process [17].

Time Warp The most important work in optimistic logical process simulation was done by Jefferson and Sowizral [23] in the definition of the Time Warp (TW) mechanism. Time Warp employs a rollback (in time) mechanism to take care of proper synchronization with respect to lcc. If an external event arrives with time-stamp in the local past, -out of chronological order- (straggler message), then the Time Warp scheme rolls back to the most recently saved state in the simulation history consistent with the time-stamp of the arriving external event and the mechanism restarts simulation from this state.

One of the most important drawbacks of the rollback part is that the protocol requires a record of the logical process history with respect to the simulation (internal and external events). The protocol has to keep sufficient internal state information, (state stack), which allows for restoring a past state.

Because the arrival of event messages in increasing time-stamp order cannot be guaranteed, two different kinds of messages are necessary to implement in the synchronization protocol. First the usual external event messages (positive messages). Opposed to positive messages there are another type called negative messages (antimessages), which are transmitted among logical processes as a request to annihilate the prematurely sent positive message generated on the base of a causally erroneous state. In order to control the size of the simulated information on a logical process, the algorithm will periodically calculate the minimum time-stamp that circulates in the network. This time is the Global Virtual Time and gives the minor time-stamp for all logical process. For this reason, a logical process is able to free all the past state of the simulation as far as the GVT.

Lazy Cancellation   In the original Time Warp protocol, a logical process receiving a straggler message initiates sending antimessages immediately when executing the rollback procedure. This behaviour is called aggressive cancellation. As a performance improvement over aggressive cancellation, the lazy cancellation policy does not send an antimessage immediately upon receipt of a straggler. Instead, it delays its propagation until the re-simulation (after rollback) has progressed to the time of positive sent message. If the re-simulation produced a positive message equal to the previous one, the antimessage has not to be sent [22]. Lazy cancellation thus avoids unnecessary cancelling of correct messages. This improvement has the drawback of additional memory and bookkeeping overhead (potential antimessages must be maintained in a rollback queue) and delaying the annihilation of actually wrong simulations. An improvement of this idea is the Lazy Reevaluation. Some different modifications to the protocol in order to break cascades of rollbacks are proposed in [17, 33].

Optimistic Time Windows   A similar idea of "limiting the optimism" to overcome potential rollback overhead is to advance computations by "windows" moving over simulated time. In the original work of Sokol, Briscoe and Wieland [35], the moving time window (MTW) protocol, neither internal nor external events with time greater that the size of the time window are allowed to be simulated. If some events do not satisfy this condition, they are postponed for the next time window. Naturally, the protocol is in favour of simulation models with a low variation of event occurrence distances relative to the window size. The main drawback of this protocol is to determinate the size of the window and the assumption of approximately uniform distribution of event occurrence times in space.

The latter is addressed with the adaptive Time Warp concurrency control algorithm (ATW) proposed by Ball and Hyot [5], allowing the window size to be adapted at any point t in simulation time. ATW aims to temporarily suspend event processing if has observed a certain amount of lcc violations in the past.

7.4.2 Other types of simulations

Even though the greater emphasis in this chapter has been for the discrete event simulation, there exist other simulation types that present a considerable importance within the simulation field.

A brief description of these methods is given in the following sections indicating the main contrasts with respect to the simulation directed by events. In particular the continuous simulation, the discrete and continuous combination and finally the Monte Carlo simulation will be discussed.

Continuous Simulation

In the model of this type of simulation, the state variables changed in a continuous form with respect to the time. Generally, the continuous simulation models imply differential equations that return the change of the state variables with respect to the time. If the differential equations are simple, these can be solved analytically generating the values for the variables for all the values of the time as function of the values of the state variables at time $= 0$. For most continuous models, the analytical solutions are not possible. However, different integration methods (e.g., Runge Kutta) can be used to integrate differential equations numerically giving specific values for the variables at time 0. At present there are a set of languages to facilitate the tasks of generating continuous simulation models [10]. Moreover, other languages exist for discret simulation which incorporate blocks or components that allow to include in the same experiment elements modelled under continuous or discrete principles [10, 41].

Discrete and continuous simulation combination

Due to the fact that some systems can not be considered as continuous or discret, the need arises of incorporating both elements in a model and this is called "combined discrete-continuous simulation". [10, 24] describes the principal elements of a system with such characteristics.

There exist three principal bases that can occur between the discret and the continuous change of the state variables:

- A discret event can cause a discret change in the state variables in a given time.

- A discret event can cause the relationship governing a continuous change in the state variables in a given time.

- A state variable achieving a threshold can cause that a discret event will be or not processed.

Monte Carlo Simulation

The Monte Carlo Simulation (MCS) is defined as a scheme that employs random numbers (stochastic variables) and it is used to solve stochastic or deterministic problems where the time step does not play a decisive role. Because of this, the MCS is defined generally as a static simulation method. The MCS is widely used to solve problems in statistics that cannot be solved in analytical form. A detailed discussion of MCS can be obtained from [28].

Finite Elements Simulation

This type of simulation is applied when the model can be split into a set of objects of fixed size and can be determined by the actions imposed to these objets (inputs and outputs). The inputs are the outputs generated by the neighbours elements and under these inputs, the element will produce a set of outputs that will have effects on the neighbour elements. This type of simulation has the advantage of permitting a high scalability — accuracy ratio when one increases the the number of elements that form the system to simulate. This simulation is used in deformation models of surfaces or topographic models that describe irregular surfaces. The principal disadvantage of this type of simulation is that for a given system, the task of obtaining, for each object, all the inputs (generated by contiguous elements) and outputs (that will affect the contiguous elements) can be very complex and sometimes impossible to perform. In terms of the simulation these systems are characterised by requiring large calculation capabilities.

Trace Driven Simulation

This simulation type uses a previously generated trace in order to obtain the events that will be simulated. There are simulators that can run in a mixed mode: events generated internally and events obtained from the previous trace.

7.5   Simulation Tools

Aspects like bottleneck identification, comparisons of alternative *mapping/data* distribution strategies, suitability of a parallel algorithm for a given multiprocessor system, scalability and sensitivity analysis are covered by a great variety of tools available to the programmer of parallel applications. Existing tools for performance prediction are still in the research stage. In this section, we will show tools that help the users in the performance prediction of parallel applications using simulation as a common framework to model the non-deterministic nature of parallel systems, such as interprocess communication events, contention for shared resources, and program structures.

The existing parallel system simulation tools can be divided in two significant groups, as shown in Figure 7.15.

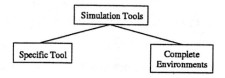

Figure 7.15: Simulation tools classification

In Specific tools for particular evaluation, the efforts are directed to the design of simulation tools that provide to the user some performance indexes related to some particular feature of parallel *hardware/software* design. Complete environments for performance studies of parallel applications include some simulation tools to study general aspects of parallel system design.

7.5.1 Specific tools for particular evaluation

In this section, we present some of the tools related to different problems derived from the parallel computing area that do not appear in serial processing. The following list does not aim to be an exhaustive relation of available tools. It is only a sample of the variety of fields where the simulation techniques can be applied.

Scheduling and Mapping

DIMEMAS [27], allows the user to evaluate the influence of sharing processors between sequential and parallel applications. It is a trace driven simulator that reconstructs the behaviour of parallel programs from a set of traces that characterise each application.

Networking

CLASS [2], is a software package for the simulation of connectionless services in ATM networks, implemented like a time driven, slotted, synchronous simulator written in *C* language. A formal grammar called NICE and its parser was generated with the help of YACC. This grammar allows a fairly easy description of the network to be simulated.

Simulation of NOW system

This method simulates the system heterogeneity at different levels [39]. It provides direct simulation on the target workstations, on the pair processor-memory model, computation abstraction using analytical models.

Performance Analysis and Simulation Tools for specific systems

ATExpert [25] is a tool developed by Cray Research Inc. that graphically displays the performance of parallel programs. Several experts systems simulate parallel execution and help the user for tuning his application.

Modelling and evaluation in MIMD Architecture Design

MERMAID [7] focuses on the construction of simulation models for MIMD multicomputers in order to evaluate them and to give estimations of the system's performance.

PROTEUS [6] is an execution driven simulator for MIMD multiprocessors. It is designed to simulate the total system, including application program, network and memory.

Complete environments for performance studies of parallel applications

In this section, a summary of relevant characteristics of a set of complete environments considering the simulation component is presented

N-MAP [18], as part of the CASPE environment, supports an automatic parse and translate step. It generates a simulation program from a skeletal SPMD program. The programmer expresses just the constituent and critical performance parts, subject to an incremental refinement. The design is discrete event simulation.

EUCLID [8] simulator runs a sequentially organised uniprocessor computer. This net is defined through a set of elements called terminals (memory, *input/output*), processors and relations between the terminals and processors. The system inputs are: topology, algorithm to execute, and priority access, and provide simulation information and statistics of the processing. This system has been used with success in multiple buses architectures. Its principal disadvantage is the complexity in the representation formalism.

PERFORM [21] is a tool that implements a new methodology of performance prediction for FORTRAN 77 programs on complex RISC microprocessors. It simulates the effect that load and store operations have on the register sets, cache memories and main memory of the target system. The simulator emulates the execution of each instruction with many host instructions and modifies its internal machine in accordance with the instruction-driven simulation.

AXE-BDL [40] is an event driven simulation environment within the AIMS toolkit. It is useful for tuning parallel and distributed programs on a variety of platforms.

Q+ [14] has Montecarlo simulation capabilities and also interfaces for analytic tools in a discrete event simulation system. It has been used to model many systems in *AT&T* Bell Labs. Ranging in size from large national telecommunication networks to microprocessors internals, from one node to several thousands.

PSEE [31] is an environment for the evaluation of parallel architectures. This tool has been oriented to educational areas. The system allows describing both simulations of the algorithm behaviour and its assignment to different processing elements of the parallel architecture, as well as to estimate its performance using different executions, scheduling and routing policies.

7.6   Conclusion & Future Trends

Parallel systems play a decisive role in the high performance computing scenario. However, the parallelisation of real applications is a complex task that takes a lot of time and efforts. The simulation of parallel systems is a promising approach to obtain the best trade-off between cost and performance by analysing and tuning parallel applications. In this chapter the possibilities and techniques for parallel system simulation have been analyzed in depth. This task has been carried out by considering four main topics:

- Parallel Systems and Performance Prediction.

- Parallel Systems Modeling.

- Simulation.

- Simulation Tools.

Simulation has been and is being used as a successful tool to reduce time and efforts in many fields including Engineering, Physics, Biology, Chemistry... In the particular field of parallel/distributed processing, simulation is also a useful tool that can be used in several ways to allow the user/programmer to analyze the behaviour of its application before doing the complete effort of program design and development.

In Section 7.2, the use of simulation tools for reducing the parallel programming cycle has been shown. These aspects are the basic background to reach some performance prediction on the parallel applications. The system modelling techniques that can be found in the literature and the main performance indexes necessary to evaluate the performance of the parallel applications was presented in Section 7.3.

However, although a lot of work has been done to develop models and tools for simulation of parallel/distributed systems, this is still a very active field since the new computing capabilities offered by parallel and distributed systems will introduce new possibilities, but also new problems that will require a lot of work. On one hand, the new capabilities will allow the introduction of more accurate models that take into account more realistic conditions and produce more precise solutions. These models are not feasible with the actual monoprocessor systems due to the enormous amount of work required to reach some solution. On the other hand, the use of parallel and distributed simulation implies the study and analysis of all the techniques related to process communication and syncrhonization in a distributed system.

In this context, Section 7.4 describes traditional methods of Discrete Event Simulation (DES) but also innovative techniques (Parallel DES) that will represent the most active research field in simulation techniques in the next years.

Acknowledgements

This work has been supported by the CICYT under contracts TIC 95-0868 and TIC 98-0433.

References

[1] M. Ajmon Marsan, G. Balbo, G. Chiola, G. Conte, S. Donatelli, and G. Franceschinis. An introduction to generalised stochastic petri nets. *Microelectronics and Reliability*, 31:699–725, 1991.

[2] M. Ajone and R. Agno. Simulation of atm computer networks with class. In *Lecture Notes in Computer Science 794*, pages 159–179. Springer-Verlag, 1994.

[3] F. Allen and J. Cocke. A program data flow analysis procedure. *Communications of ACM*, 19(3), March 1976.

[4] W. Bain and D. Scott. An algorithm for time synchronization in distributed discrete event simulation. In *Proceedings of the SCS Multiconference on Distributed Simulation*, pages 30–33. SCS, 1998.

[5] D. Ball and S. Hoyt. The adaptative time-warp concurrency control algorithm. In *Proceedings of the SCS Multiconference on Distributed Simulation*, volume 22–1, pages 174–177. SCS, 1990.

[6] E. Brewer. Proteus: A high-level performance parallel architectute simulator. Technical report, MIT, 1991.

[7] J. Brummen and A. Pimentel. Mermaid: Modelling and evaluation research in mimd architecture design. Technical report, Deptartment of Computer System. Univerty of Amsterdam, 1994.

[8] J. Butler. A facility for simulating multiprocessor. *IEEE Micro*, pages 32–44, 1996.

[9] W. Cai and S. Turner. An algorithm for distributed discrete-event simulation. the carrier null message approach. In *Proceedings of the SCS Multiconference on Distributed Simulation*, volume 22–1, pages 3–8. SCS, 1990.

[10] F. Cellier. *Continuous System Modelling.* Springer Verlang, 1991.

[11] K. Chandy and et al. Distributed simulation: A case study in design and verification of distributed programs. *IEEE Transactions on Software Engineering,* 5:440–452, 1979.

[12] K. Chandy and J. Misra. Asynchronous distributed simulation via a sequence of parallel computations. *Communications of the ACM,* 24:198–205, 1981.

[13] G. Chiola, M. Ajmon, G. Balbo, and G. Conte. Generalised stochastic petri net models: A definition on the net level and its implications. *IEEE Transactions on Software Engineering,* 19:89–107, 1993.

[14] A. Cynthia and L. Funka. Interactive visual modeling for performance. *IEEE Software,* pages 58–68, 1991.

[15] W. Delaney and E. Vaccari. *Dynamic Models and Discrete Event Simulation.* Marcel Dekker Inc., 1989.

[16] G. Dózsa, P. Kacsuk, and T. Fadgyas. GRADE: A graphical programming environment for PVM applications. In *Proceedings of Euromicro Workshop on Parallel and Distributed Processing,* pages 347–354. IEEE Press, 1997.

[17] A. Ferscha. *Handbook of Parallel and Distributed Computing.* McGraw-Hill, 1995.

[18] A. Ferscha and J. Johnson. Performance Prototyping of Parallel Applications in N-MAP. In *2nd International Conference on Algorithms & architectures for Parallel Processing,* pages 84–91. IEEE CS Press, June 1996.

[19] G. Fishman. *Concepts and Methods in Discrete Event Digital Simulation.* Wiley & Sons Inc., 1973.

[20] R. Fujimoto. Parallel des. *Communications of the ACM,* 33(10):30–35, 1990.

[21] T. Hey, A. Dunlop, and E. Hernández. Realistic parallel performance estimation. *Parallel Computing,* 23:5–21, 1997.

[22] D. Jeferson and P. Reiher. Supercritical speedup. In *Proceedings of 24th Annual Simulation Symposium,* pages 159–168, 1991.

[23] D. Jefferson and H. Sowizral. Fast concurrent simulation using the time warp mechanism. Technical report, RAND Corporation, 1982.

[24] A. Keith and et al. *System Modelling and Computer Simulation.* Dekker Inc., 2nd edition, 1995.

[25] J. Kohn and W. Wiliams. Atexpert. *Journal of Parallel and Distributed Computing,* 18:205–222, 1993.

[26] G. Korn and J. Wait. *Digital Continuous System Simulation.* Prentice Hall, 1978.

[27] J. Labarta, S. Girona, and T. Cortés. Analyzing scheduling policies using dimemas. *Parallel Computing,* 23:23–34, 1997.

[28] A. Law. *Simulation Modelling and Analysis.* McGraw Hill, 1991.

[29] C. Lindemann. *Performance Modelling with Deterministic and Stochastic Petri Nets.* Wiley and Sons, 1998.

[30] B. Lubachevsky. Bounded lag distributed doscrete event simulation. In *Proceedings of the SCS Multiconference on Distributred Simulation*, volume 19–3, pages 183–191. SCS, 1988.

[31] E. Luque, R. Suppi, and J. Sorribes. Psee: Parallel systems evaluation environment. In *Proceedings of the* 5th. *International PARLE Conference*, volume 1, pages 696–699, 1993.

[32] M. Macdougall. *Simulating Computer Systems: Techniques and Tools.* MIT Press, 1990.

[33] V. Madisseti, J. Walrand, and D. Messerchsmitt. Synchronization in message-passing computers: Models, algorithm and analysis. In *Proceedings of the 1989 Winter Simulation Conference*, pages 296–305, 1989.

[34] J. Misra. Distributed discrete-event simulation. *ACM Computer Surveys*, 18(1):39–65, 1986.

[35] L. Sokol, D. Briscoe, and A. Wienland. Mtw: A strategy for scheduling discrete dimulation events for concurrent execution. In *Proceedings of the SCS Multiconference on Distributed Simulation*, volume 19–3, pages 34–42, 1988.

[36] R. Suppi and E. Luque. *Parallel System Evaluation Environment User's Guide.* Computer Architecture and Operating Systems Group. University Autonoma of Barcelona, 1998. http://www.caos.uab.es/coper.html.

[37] R. Suppi, E. Luque, J. Sorribes, E. Cesar, M. Serrano, and J Falgueras. Performance prediction of parallel systems by simulation. *Computers and Artificial Intelligence*, 17(5):52–60, 1998.

[38] R. Walker and R. Camposanto. *A Survey of High-Level Synthesis Systems.* Kluwer Academic Publishers, 1991.

[39] Z. Xu. Simulation of heterogeneous networks of workstations. Technical report, Computer Sciences Department. University of Madison, 1995.

[40] J. Yan, S. Sarukai, and P. Mehra. Visualization and modeling of parallel and distributed programs using the aims toolkit. *Software-Practice and Experience*, 25(4):429–461, 1995.

[41] B. Zeigler. *Multifaceted Modelling and DES.* Academic Press, 1987.

Chapter 8

Performance Visualization

George R. Ribeiro Justo

Abstract

This chapter discusses the main concepts and techniques that characterize peformance visualization tools. To better categorize the concepts, a taxonomy is proposed which can assist both visualization tool developers and users. The fundamental aspect of the taxonomy is to consider not only the performance visualization concepts and methods but also the software engineering process in which they usually take place.

8.1 Introduction

A typical parallel program design is characterized by a large collection of (independent) processes, which execute their (internal) computation in parallel but also need to synchronize and communicate. This design usually leads to a program, the behavior of which is more complex than its sequential counterpart. Another important issue in the design of a parallel program is that the performance of a parallel program plays a more important role in its design process than that of a sequential program. This means additional levels of complexity that the designer has to deal with in order to understand the behavior of the program and the many other factors that may affect its performance. In the case of parallel programs running in heterogeneous networks of workstations, performance analysis becomes even more difficult, as there are more possibilities of mappings the processes to the various processors.

To support parallel program designers in constructing, displaying and analyzing visual representations of the various factors that may affect the behavior of their programs, researchers and practitioners have developed visualization tools. A visualization tool can be used on its own or as part of a complete environment for the design and performance evaluation of parallel programs.

In this chapter, the main concepts and techniques that characterize these tools are described and classified. It is not the objective of this chapter to present a complete survey of visualization tools currently available but to give the reader an introduction to the most important concepts involved in performance visualization and present examples of tools and environments that use them. To better categorize the concepts and tools, a taxonomy is also proposed. The fundamental of the taxonomy is to consider not only the concepts and the methods involved in performance visualization but also the software engineering process in which performance visualization usually takes place. This approach enables visualization tool developers and users to understand and quantify the practical advantages and disadvantages of using a particular concept or tool.

8.2 Taxonomy of Performance Visualization Tools and Concepts

The general performance visualization process consists of recording (observed) events about the program behavior and factors that influence its performance and after that presenting the results in a visual form for analysis. A taxonomy of visualization tools must take into account this whole process, even though some activities are not necessarily carried out by the visualization tools themselves, for example the recording of the events. The focus of the taxonomy, however, is to enable tool developers and users to have a general insight of the visualization process and the tools. More details about how to observe the program by monitoring its execution or by simulating its behavior can be seen in Chapter 6 and Chapter 7 respectively.

To take into account the user view, the visualization process must also consider the software engineering process applied to the development of parallel programs, as the users of visualization tools are usually parallel program developers. Unfortunately, most of these models and frameworks, which allow us to characterize program development methodologies and their processes, are based on traditional (sequential) program development. Little has been done to systematically characterize methods applied to parallel program development. Attempts have been made in presenting surveys of methods and tools [12] but there are no frameworks or models similar to those applied to sequential programs. There are many reasons for this, the main one being the lack of life-cycle or software process models that describe the development of parallel software. An exception is the work presented in [24], which proposes the characterization of the parallel program development and presents a formal framework, specified in Z [25], to describe tools and methodologies. This chapter is not aimed at presenting a formal model for the visualization process but borrows from the work presented in [24] the role that performance visualization may play in the development of parallel programs and includes that element in the taxonomy described in Section 8.7. Another interesting view is that presented in [13], where prototypes for performance analysis are proposed at each stage of the development. Each prototype focuses on a particular state of the program development and the performance issues related to that stage.

To summarize, a general performance visualization process usually involves the following main stages:

Data generation: The stage when performance statistics and (execution) event trace files are generated. The main issues at this stage are the instrumentation of the program to generate the required data and the format of the files. In this respect, visualization tools[1] can be classified according to the time the data is generated and the format of the files in which the data is stored.

Data displaying: This is the stage when the data generated in the previous stage, about the program behavior and performance, is processed and displayed. The level of detail

---

[1]For simplicity, the term visualization tool will be used to refer to both a specific performance visualization tool or an environment which supports performance visualization.

presented and the visual representations are the key issues to be considered at this stage. In this case, the tools can be classified according to different aspects that range from the type of program development concepts covered, such as process distribution and the communication structure, to the level of detail, such as abstract application aspects or more detailed hardware aspects. These considerations indicate the role of the tool in the software development process. For example, a visualization tool which does not provide information about hardware performance is not appropriate for use during the mapping stage (allocation of processes to processors) of the development [4], as the user will not able to infer whether the chosen mapping is improving or reducing the program performance.

Data analysis and user interaction: At this stage, the user (program designer) analyses the program behavior and performance according to the data displayed. The key issues here are how the tools can simplify the analysis by supporting animation, replay or other types of user interaction.

In the following sections, each stage described above is discussed in more detail together with the criteria for classification. A summary of the classification is depicted in Figure 8.1. These criteria are further evaluated with examples of how tools are classified.

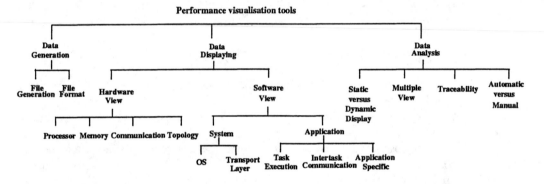

Figure 8.1: Classification tree of visualization tools.

8.3 Data Generation

The key activities during this stage are how the program is instrumented to generate the required data for visualization and how the data is stored. The instrumentation is not essential for the Visualization process and tools. More important are the format of the data files and how the data is generated. The data file formats indicate what type of information the visualization tool can produce and its openness, that is; how easy it is to integrate it with other tools. How the data is generated, by monitoring the program execution or predicting its behavior, designates what type of analysis can be carried out with the data.

8.3.1 Data File Generation

The most common approach to trace (or statistics) file generation is to collect data during the program execution and store the data into the trace file. These are the key criteria usually used to classify the visualization tools according to data generation, as illustrated in Figure 8.1. Although the trace file is generated during the program execution, the data is only displayed after the execution has terminated when the whole file has been created. This approach is therefore known as "post-mortem". In the real-time approach, on the other hand, the data is displayed as it is generated. A technique usually applied is to replace the trace file with a data stream such as sockets, which can then be connected to the Visualization tool to receive the data as soon as it is generated. This approach is used, for example by Pablo [19]. XPVM [33] also allows events to be routed to it by the PVM [26] kernel during the application run time. The third approach is to allow both modes, post-mortem and real-time generation, but the user selects one of them before the trace is generated. Pablo and XPVM support this approach.

Another important issue is how the trace file is generated. One approach is to observe the (real) execution of the program applying a monitoring instrumentation, as described in Chapter 6. Another approach is to use some modeling technique to predict the behavior and performance of the program. The prediction can be done using an abstract model of the algorithm [34] or a simulation model [3], as described in Chapter 7.

Certain visualization tools are built to work specifically with real execution or prediction. XGecko [28] is a visualization tool used to display the trace files and statistics generated by Transim [7], a performance prediction and prototyping tool [7]. Tools, like PVMVis [29], allow the visualization of both trace files generated after real execution and simulation.

8.3.2   Data File Format

The data required for performance and behavioral analysis are usually categorized into two main groups: statistics file and event trace file.

The statistics file contains samples of various parameters, which are important for analysis. Some of these parameters are generic, for example, processor utilization but some of them depend on the programming model and the requirements of the visualization tool.

The (event) trace file stores detailed information events about the program execution, so they are usually larger than the statistics files. The events allow not only performance analysis but (run-time) behavioral analysis of the program.

Tools like PVMVis [3] and AIMS [2] use two files but other tools, such as ParaGraph [8], depend solely on the event trace file and the statistics must be computed by the visualization tool, using the trace file.

The key criterion for classifying a visualization tool is whether its file format is generic (and standard) or specific. The trace file can be specific to a particular tool or programming model. XGecko uses the trace file generated by Transim [7], a specific simulation tool.

There is no general or standard proposed format for the statistics file but there are several proposals for the trace file. SDDF (Self-Defining Data Format) is a general data meta-format used by Pablo [19]. SDDF is a performance data description language that specifies both data record structures and data record instances. Converters are also available for translating other formats to SDDF, so the traces file produced in other formats can be visualized by Pablo.

The PICL format [5] was developed for use with the Portable Instrumented Communication Library (PICL). It is a portable format that does not depend on a particular programming model or machine. ParaGraph [8] is the most well-known visualization tool which uses this format. Other examples include nupshot [2].

The TAPE/PVM format [17] is used to record event traces of PVM [26] applications.

Although it is not specific for a particular tool, it focuses on the PVM model. This format is used by PVMVis [3]. A converter to PICL is also available, enabling TAPE/PVM trace files to be visualized by ParaGraph. More details on trace forms were presented in Chapter 6.

8.4 Data Displaying

This is the main stage in the visualization process when the trace and statistics files are presented to the user in their visual form. Since both hardware and software affect performance, the visualization tools usually provide a large variety of information, allowing the tools to be classified in various groups, as depicted in Figure 8.1. In the following sections, each important concept is discussed in detail and we also present examples which illustrate how they are applied by particular visualization tools.

8.4.1 Hardware View

Since performance bottlenecks were originally thought to be a consequence of limitations or misuse of hardware resources, the earliest visualization tools were focussed on providing the users with visual abstractions about the various hardware factors that usually affect the performance of a parallel program. The best way to identify and categorize the most import concepts (abstractions) related to the hardware of a parallel system is to assume a general parallel computing model. In a message-passing (hardware) model [4], a collection of *processors* are responsible for carrying out local computation, making use of their local *memory*, and they may exchange data and synchronize using *communication channels*, put together according to a certain *topology*.

Processor

The key objective in obtaining good performance at processor level is to maximize the *utilization* of each processor and maintain a good *load balance* amongst all processors. A simple utilization display is presented by PVMVis [3] using curves indicating utilization as a function of time. ParaGraph [8] has a utilization count display that depicts the state of each processor (busy, idle or overhead — that indicates that the processor is executing in the communication subsystem), as a function of time. Most visualization tools also use colors to denote the state of the processors but with different meanings. In XGecko [28], red denotes a busy processor but in ParaGraph it means that the processor is idle.

Kiviat diagrams are used by ParaGraph [8] to represent load balance (see Figure 8.2). A kiviat diagram is a wheel-like display and each spoke represents a processor. A shaded hub reaches up each spoke. The height of the hub at each spoke denotes the processor's utilization percentage (zero indicates completely idle and one completely busy). For examples, the diagram in Figure 8.2 indicates, for example, that processor 2 has been more utilized than processor 1.

Memory

Memory access is not as important to a message-passing model as it to a shared-memory model but it can have a serious effect on the performance, especially with respect to cache behavior [1]. For this reason, cache performance analysis is becoming important and visualization tools are necessary. The EDPEPPS environment allows the cache performance

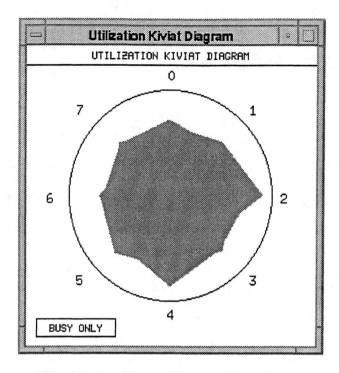

Figure 8.2: ParaGraph utilization kiviat diagram.

analysis via the **Chronos** tool , as described in Chapter 19. However, PVMVis does not support the visualization of the cache performance results.

The underlying principle of cache is to exploit the inherent temporal and spatial data locality existing in most code. A miss usually occurs when data required by the processor is not stored in the cache. The number of cache misses is therefore an important indicator of performance. Cache performance analysis can focus on different types of cache miss. For example, a *capacity miss* occurs when the cache size is too small to store enough data and a *conflict miss* occurs because of the cache mapping function [27]. Performance analysis tools can enable the designer to identify or evaluate the code with respect can assist in showing visual representations of behavior or statistics.

The Cache Visualization Tool (CVT) [27] is one of the few existing visualization tools. CVT focuses on the visualization of cache behavior of *selected* code sections rather than on identifying critical code sections. Two main types of displays are provided. The cache model display represents a cache as a grid where each box denotes a cache block or cache line (a set of words with consecutive addresses). The second type of display presents statistics on cache behavior (e.g., per cache line and per cache area). Statistics displays also include misses, which can be displayed in different forms such as ratios, cumulated and non-cumulated.

Since cache misses usually happen when using large amount of data, cache analysis usually involves code that uses arrays. In the case of CVT, unique colors are used to represent each array both in the cache display and statistics. The CVT displays for three arrays represented by white, green and read respectively is illustrated in Figure 8.3. The distribution of the arrays in the cache is shown in Figure 8.3a) and Figure 8.3b) presents the number of misses when accessing each array.

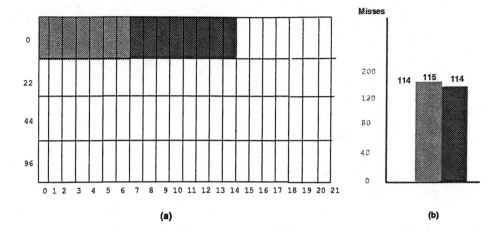

Figure 8.3: Overview of CVT displays (a) cache display (b) number of misses display.

Communication

Inter-processor communication has a crucial influence on the overall performance of a parallel program. Excessive and unnecessary communication can lead to bad utilization of processors because of the overheads associated with the communication or the waiting time for messages to arrive. The major factors to be considered are therefore the volume and frequency of communication.

Several curves can be used to illustrate the volume of communication as a function of time. PROVE [14] host communication window, illustrated in Figure 8.4a) is a typical example of graph which displays the communication among the hosts, especially the rates and the amount of data transferred between the host computers (processors). In addition, some types of displays represent other factors related to communication, such as the average size of the message queues and even the contention of the network. Please see Figure 8.4b) for an example of this type of display provided by PVMVis [29]. The x-axis shows the number of collisions and the y-axis the percentage of packets for each number of collisions.

The frequency of the communication can be depicted together with the processor utilization in a spacetime diagram. Processor activity is represented by horizontal lines and inter-processor activity by diagonal lines. This type of display is provided by ParaGraph [8].

Topology

This type of display usually summarizes the processor utilization/load-balance together with the communication graph representing the topology of the underlying machines. In many cases, the visualization tool only allows a limited fixed number of topologies. XGecko [28] displays Transputer grids, where the nodes denote the Transputer processors and the lines the channels amongst them. Colors are used to indicate the state of the processor and channels, as illustrated in Figure 8.5. The figure illustrates a typical tree configuration.

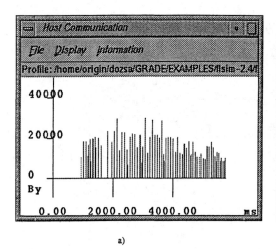 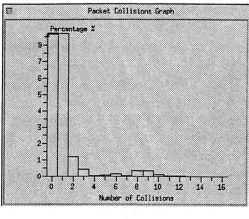

a)   b)

Figure 8.4: a) PROVE host communication display b) PVMVis network collisions display.

ParaGraph [8] provides a network display that depicts details of a number of networks, including message routing. It also indicates the volume of pending messages in a physical link enabling the user to detect bottlenecks.

8.4.2 Software View

The principal reason for performance visualization is to enable the program designer to understand the program's behavior and how it relates to its performance. The ultimate objective, however, is to optimize or improve the program performance. This means that the visualized results should be associated with the original design.

Although this property is desirable, it does not mean that visualization tools always make this association clear. This property is discussed further in Section 8.5. Here the focus is on the general concepts used in the visualization of the software components of a parallel application.

To close the gap between the different levels of abstractions, namely, the one associated with program design and the one associated with performance results, the approach taken is similar to that followed in the hardware view seen in the last section, using in this case a model of the software components. The model may range from a general one to an application specific one. Certainly, a specific model facilitates the designer's task, as the visualization tool can provide results close to the program design (application). The BSP profiling and prediction performance tool, for example, is specific for the BSP model [11]. A general model, however, can lead to more generic visualization tools, such as ParaGraph [8], but can make the designer's work more difficult, as they become responsible for associating the performance results to their design. The main concepts applied to the classification can be seen in Figure 8.1.

To enable a taxonomy which covers a large range of visualization tools, one can assume a general model of computation for message-passing systems, similar to that assumed for the hardware view presented in the Section 8.4.1. A parallel program model [4] consists of one or more *tasks*, executing concurrently, and encapsulating some *local computation* and data.

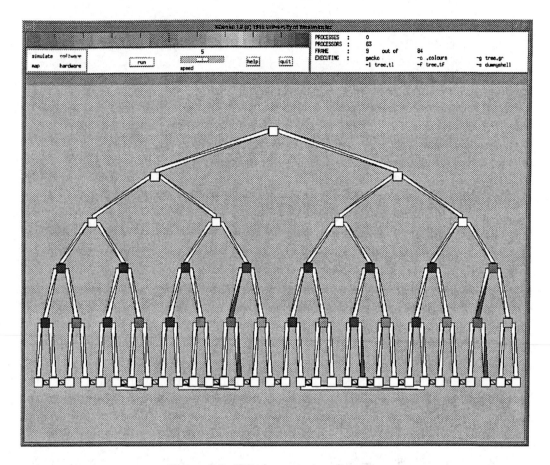

Figure 8.5: XGecko mapping diagram.

Each task is uniquely identified and can *interact* with other tasks by *sending and receiving messages*.

Another important issue is the level of detail (abstraction) provided by the tool. This may vary from high-level abstraction (application level) to low level abstraction (software system level). The general model described above can consist of several layers of software, which comprise distinct levels of abstraction for the tasks and their interaction. At the highest level, the application level, the interactions are modeled according to the message passing models. The model is further refined into lower levels where the model is realized or implemented. This lower level of abstraction can be decomposed into the operating system layer, to provide process (task) management, and the transport layer, to provide communication.

System Level

The key aspects at this level are the management (scheduling) of the tasks and their communication.

Operating System: The management of processes (tasks) includes the creation and schedul ing of processes, usually provided by the operating system. An example is presented in [31], showing the effects of scheduling mechanisms utilizing time slices, priorities, preemption, and multiple processors, especially with respect to the dispatching of processes in operating systems.

Transport Layer: The transport protocol can play an important role in the communication performance of a parallel program. The reason is that well-known protocols like TCP/IP can add a high overhead to the communication in comparison to less reliable UDP. One reason can be the size and the management of packets. Visualization tools, for example PVMVis [29], provide graphical statistics on the average size of packets and number of packets lost. This information helps the designer to identify bottlenecks in the network software.

Application Level

The application or program design level is the abstraction level closest to the program designer, and therefore the most important. At this level the designers should be able to relate the results to their own design. Assuming the general programming model described above, the key concepts are each task (internal) computation and its concurrent execution, together with the interactions, both in terms of synchronization and communication.

Task Execution: A task execution time should measure not only the elapsed time taken to execute the internal computation but also any overhead time incurred because of communication, synchronization or scheduling. In other words, similar to the processor utilization displays, the execution of a task is divided into states indicating whether the task is *busy*, performing its internal computation, is *idle* or is in an *overhead* state, carrying out some computation which is not part of its algorithm. Bar charts or similar representations depict the execution of each task, separating the time spent in each state, as a function of time. The utilization display in XPVM [33] summarizes the space-time view at each instant by showing the aggregate number of tasks computing, in overhead or waiting for a message (see Figure 8.6).

The behavior window is the central window of the PROVE tool [14] and created on the startup of the program (see Figure 8.7). The behavior graph is a two-dimensional representation of the program. The horizontal axis represents the program time while the executed tasks are arranged along the vertical axis. Each task is represented by a horizontal line that shows the time during which the task was executed by a processor. The thick horizontal lines have several sections colored differently showing the stages of the process (e.g., computation and communication,). The number of tasks and the total program run time are displayed at the top of the window.

Special displays can combine task execution information together with hardware utilization. The ParaGraph task display usually follows this approach. The task count display, for instance, shows the number of processors that are executing a given task at the current time and the task Gantt display indicates the current task being executed by the corresponding processor as a function of time.

Inter-task Communication: Inter-task communication can affect the program's performance in two main ways, namely, the communication cost itself and also the direct or indirect synchronization it imposes on the task's execution. The communication cost includes overheads and routing. Synchronization reflects itself on the time a task can

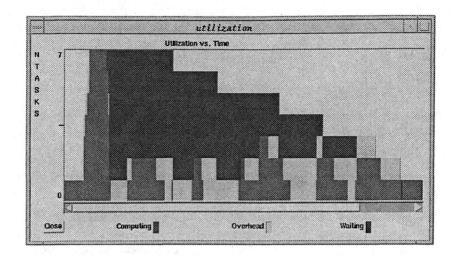

Figure 8.6: XPVM utilization display.

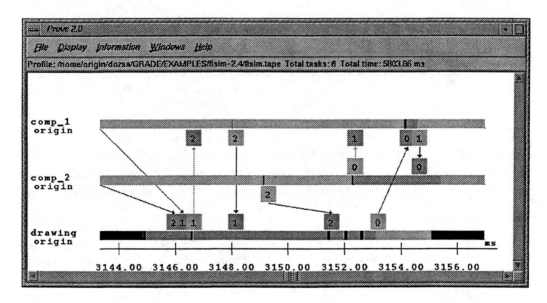

Figure 8.7: PROVE behavior display.

become idle waiting for messages to arrive. To avoid this problem, the design should provide enough parallel slackness [11], in order to guarantee that each processor has enough work to do when one task becomes idle. To support the designers, the visualization tools should provide information about the cost and volume of inter-task communication with respect to each task.

A common display results from the combination of the task utilization display with the inter-task communication display, enabling the designer to identify the ratio of computation and communication of each task and their respective communication activities. In PVMVis [29], a bar chart diagram shows each task and its state, including the communication time, as a function of time. Inter-task communication is represented by vertical lines between the communicating tasks (see Figure 8.8).

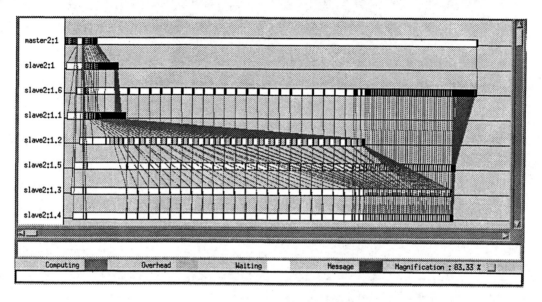

Figure 8.8: PVMVis task bar chart display.

Application Specific Visualization: Some visualization tools add extra information to the typical displays previously described. For example, PROVE [14] introduces more detail about the task state, indicating the type of action the task is performing. Similarly, in PVMVis [29], the task bar chart display (see Figure 8.8) includes information about the PVM communication operation performed by each task.

The xmtool [30] is a graphical performance analysis tool which allows the user to visualize various aspects of a WPAMS (Workstation Parallel Application Management System) application [15, 30].This is achieved largely with one construct called *pardo* (a kind of parallel while do statement), which can be inserted in a C or Fortran program in place of a normal loop construct. Performance visualization within xmtool [30] is based on statistics about the number of *pardo*'s that appears in an application code. In addition, the user can visualize details of each task such as execution-time, memory usage, and calls to the WPAMS control program. The xmtool main window is illustrated in Figure 8.9.

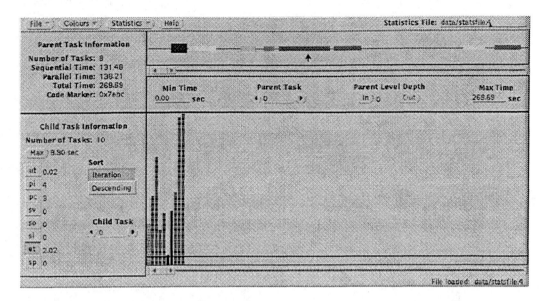

Figure 8.9: Overview of xmtool main window.

A BSP computation basically consists of a sequence of parallel super-steps, where each super-step is a sequence of steps carried out on local data, followed by a synchronization barrier where the non-local data accesses take place [11]. The performance visualization include bars representing the elapsed time of the task that takes the longest time to perform its local computation phase of a super-step and the time taken to perform communication [11]. The SP tool displays the details of each superstep (see Figure 8.10).

In XPVM [33], as illustrated in Figure 8.11, the space time display shows the status of all tasks indicating whether they are executing useful user computations, executing PVM system routines for communication, task control, etc., waiting for messages from other tasks or communicating with other tasks.

8.5 Data Analysis and User Interaction

To facilitate the daunting task of identifying and correcting performance imbalances or bottlenecks, visualization tools provide several mechanisms. They can be used to classify visualization tools as presented in Figure 8.1. They usually tend to assist the designer who ultimately is responsible for both the analysis and modification of the design. There are, however, a few exceptions where automatic detection and correction is provided. There are also some techniques, which guide the user during the performance analysis [20].

8.5.1 Static versus Dynamic Display

The most common mechanism is the use of animation and step-by-step inspection of the program execution. Animation can be applied to any level of the abstraction. For example, the hardware animation of XGecko [28] shows how the states of the processors (busy, idle

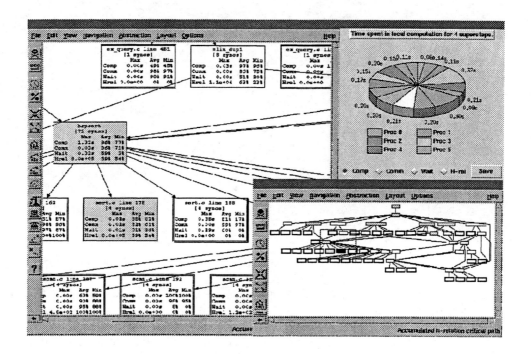

Figure 8.10: Snapshot of the SP profiling and prediction performance tool.

or communicating) and communication channels (busy or idle) change. The user can have
a snapshot of the hardware at any instant of the execution.

The most common display, however, is the task bar chart (provided for example by
PVMVis [29], PROVE [14] and xmtool [30]), which shows step-by-step the behavior of each
task together with their interactions (synchronization or communication).

Application-specific tools also provide mechanisms to enable the animation of the design
itself. For example, both PVMVis [29]and PROVE [14] are associated with a specific visual
language (see Chapter 2 for more details on visual languages), which then enables the
designer to have an animation of the original design. Note that the kind of animation referred
to here is based on the trace file and not real execution. This allows the combination of this
display with other visualization displays providing powerful mechanisms for performance
analysis.

8.5.2   Multiple Views

The designer may need to combine information on different aspects of the program behavior
and performance to identify and eliminate a performance bottleneck. This means that

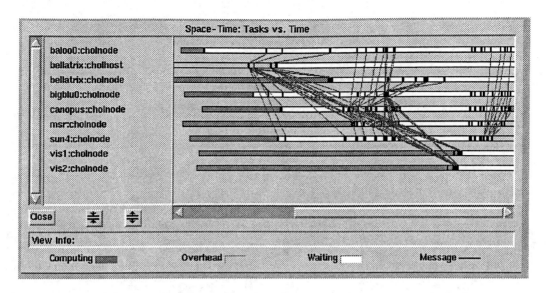

Figure 8.11: XPVM space-type display.

visualization tools can combine displays to enable the designer to have different views of the program performance simultaneously. A good example is the combination of the design animation, as provided by PVMVis [29] and PROVE [14], with the task bar chart, which gives the current state of the task together with a history of their execution.

In general, however, the designer may need to go into several levels of abstraction, starting from the application level, passing by the system level and terminating at the hardware level. Please see Figure 8.12 for an example of the PVMVis window, which combines the design animation (top left), the task bar chart (bottom left) and also statistics of the CPU utilization and the network (top and bottom right respectively).

8.5.3 Traceability

Multiple viewing displays are not sufficient to enable the identification of a particular design element, which can be a statement, function or line of code, that may be causing a performance bottleneck. Most visualization tools provide some tracing facility, which allows trace back (or drill-down) to the line of code or operation being executed. XPVM [33] provides good tracing capability by indicating the PVM operations being executed by the tasks. In the case of visual programming design, such as those supported by PVMVis [29] and PROVE [14], it is also possible to trace a graphical element instead of a line of the code. This facility can be more effective when combined with a multiple viewing facilities. So, the designer can combine step-by-step animation with views of different abstraction levels of the program and related that information to specific design elements.

8.5.4 Automatic versus Manual Analysis

The use of multiple displays described in the previous section is certainly the right direction towards performance analysis but in the end the designer still has to process all the information and identify the performance problem in the design. To reduce this activity,

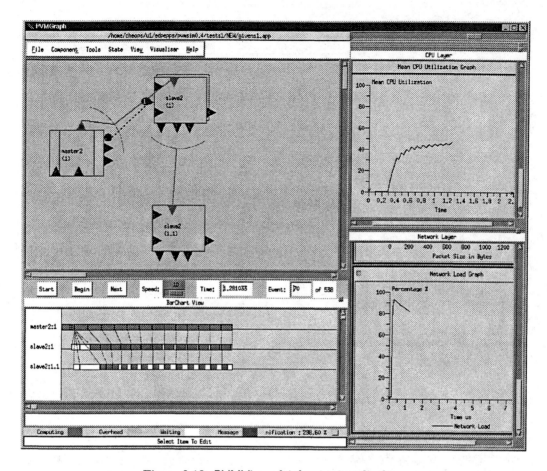

Figure 8.12: PVMVis multiple viewing display.

automatic support can be used. A generic automatic performance analysis environment is described in [6]. The key component is a meta-tool named EARL [32], which consists of a new high-level trace analysis language and its interpreter which allows the ease construction of new trace analysis tools. The approach taken is to enable the abstraction and filtering of information obtained from the trace files.

Paradyn [18] is another example of a tool, which automatically tries to locate performance bottlenecks. The approach is to control the program instrumentation to search for performance bottlenecks, starting with general issues related to synchronization and memory delays and subsequently including instrumentation to identify particular problems. It maintains a knowledge base of performance bottlenecks and their causes, which is used to locate the bottlenecks.

Despite its importance, automatic and intelligent performance analysis is still an open problem, as Reed *et al.* suggest [23]. One of the reasons suggested by the authors is the behavior of most parallel applications which is poorly understood to be modeled using traditional decision mechanisms such as decision tables or trees. A solution seems to be the use of fuzzy logic, which is more applicable than tradition techniques to modeling the conflict goals present in the resource management problem. *Autopilot* [23] uses intelligent decision procedures, based on configurable fuzzy logic rules for decision making, that determine how and when the system should dynamically adjust resource allocation policies and system parameters to maximize performance.

8.6   Human Computer Interaction Issues

Ultimately, performance analysis is usually carried out by a human user, so *user friendliness* becomes an important property for visualization tools. There are many issues to consider when designing user interfaces but in terms of visualization tools the main issues are the use of color and aesthetic elements to simplify the presentation of complex performance and program behavior information, and how to deal with the problem of "visual explosion".

As previously discussed, color plays an important and essential role in performance visualization as it can simplify the presentation of information. Color spectrum can be used to indicate states of a processor or a process, in particular emphasizing states which can cause performance bottlenecks. XGecko [28] provides a color scale that denotes the load percentage of the processor or processes. The user can modify it by specifying value ranges for the colors, depending on the level of detail required. In general, however, few colors are used to indicate the main states, for example, in PVMVis [29] red indicates idle, green denotes busy and blue and yellow signify sending and receiving a message respectively.

Another important human interaction issue of a visualization tool is how to deal with visual explosion caused by the amount of information display. A task bar chart for a complex application is presented in Figure 8.13a). The mechanisms usually used to solve that problem are zooming and filtering. Zooming enables the user to focus on particular parts of the display. In general most tools provide some support for this activity, as illustrated in Figure 8.13b), where the user is responsible for manually changing the display. Filtering (or more specific techniques such as clustering [23]) tries to reduce the amount of information presented to the user by focusing on particular parameters or the region of the design.

8.7   Software Engineering Taxonomy of Visualization Tools

In general, visualization tools are classified according to their displays but for the designer is also important to understand in which stages of the design the visualization tool can be used.

A rapid prototyping development model for parallel and distributed programs based on performance analysis is presented in [13]. The key principle of the model is that complete algorithms, outline designs, or even rough schemes can be evaluated at a relatively early stage in the development life-cycle, with respect to possible platform configurations and mapping strategies. Modifying the platform configurations and mapping will permit the prototype design to be refined, and this process may continue in an evolutionary fashion through out the life-cycle. Our interest here, however, is the issue of what information is necessary and how to detect performance bottlenecks.

The proposed model is based on a general software process for parallel and distributed systems, which identifies the main activities and artifacts in the development and defines the information needed for performance analysis at each stage of the design (see Figure 8.14).

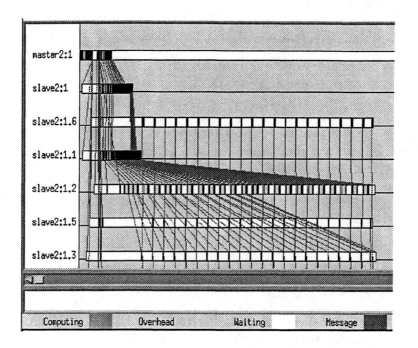

a)

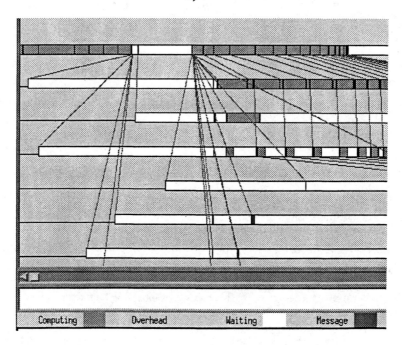

b)

Figure 8.13: Visual explosion.

That information can be applied to a taxonomy of visualization tools according to which display can provide the required information for each stage of a parallel program development.

Decomposition: The process starts with the identification of the main tasks of the design. The artifact generated by this step is a collection of task nodes. Initially, approximations of each task's (*total*) workload can be defined, in terms of timing equations if a performance prediction tool is used [3], together with an (*ideal*) mapping[2], as suggested in PCAM method [4]. The designer focuses on processor efficiency (utilization). A processor utilization display is, therefore, the most appropriate for this type of analysis. Also, as the behavior of each task is not described in detail, a general task display can be used to analyze load balancing. These displays are provided by ParaGraph [8] and PROVE [14].

Behavior: The next step is the definition of each task (general) behavior. The behavioral description consists of defining how the processes react to events (messages) they receive and which events they generate. The resulting artifact is also a collection of tasks but some of them with their behavior only partially defined. Each task (*total*) workload is refined by replacing part of it with real code. The designer can then have more insight into processor efficiency and scheduling. In this case, in addition to the processor utilization display, the designer needs a task display, which specifies the ratio computation and communication of each task. Also important is a display depicting the behavior of a task. A task bar chart, with application specific information, could be used in this instance, as provided by PVMVis [29] and PROVE [14]

Communication: The following step in the design is the definition of the communication structure. This corresponds to the description of the relationships between the tasks. The resulting artifact is usually a connected graph, where nodes denote tasks and edges represent communication channels. At this stage, the designer evaluates the communication network instead of individual processors. Issues such as message size, network load and contention are considered here. To support this analysis, statistics about the network are essential. The amount of statistics depends on the level of abstraction of the analysis. This means that systems level information can also be important. In this case, PVMVis [29] network statistics displays can be used. To evaluate the communication structure of the design, a task graph or bar chart can also be used. ParaGraph [8] provides several useful communication displays. Statistic on communication volume amongst processors can be visualized by PROVE.

Mapping: The *ideal* (initial) mapping must be refined to a more realistic one, taking into account the components' behavior and the communication network. The designer is also encouraged to evaluate and compare different mapping strategies. XGecko [28] provides a specific mapping display. To achieve a good mapping, knowledge of the hardware is also necessary. Statistics on (CPU) utilization and cache (memory) usage are important. ParaGraph [8] also provides several processor utilization displays.

Refinement: Similar to the behavior definition stage, where the remaining timing equations are replaced with the sequential algorithms and specific communication actions. The designer can therefore have a more realistic view of the tasks and their final implementation. Application level displays can be usually used. Both PVMVis [29] and

---

[2]The designer can use as many processors as possible. This assumption is later reviewed.

Program Development Stages	Tools
Decomposition	PROVE, ParaGraph
Behavior	PVMVis, PROVE
Communication	PVMVis, ParaGraph, PROVE
Mapping	XGecko, ParaGraph
Refinement	PVMVis, XPVM

Table 8.1: Classification of visualization tools using a software engineering approach.

XPVM [33] provide application specific displays about PVM operations executed by each task.

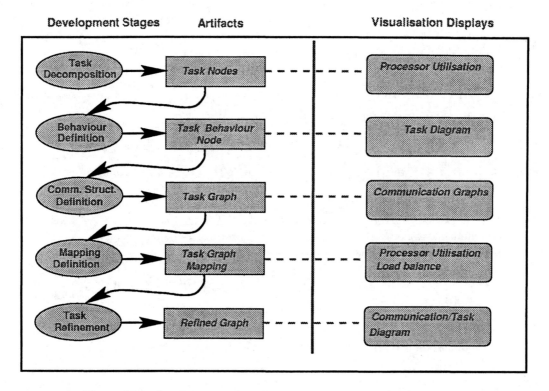

Figure 8.14: A software engineering taxonomy of visualization tools.

Note that the above stages are complementary and are not necessarily carried out in sequence. Instead, as new information is added, the results of the analysis are revised and re-evaluated. Modifications of the design or evaluation of different alternatives are important parts of any approach to performance analysis. Software engineering and performance engineering activities should occur concurrently.

See Table 8.1 to understand how the above taxonomy can be applied to some existing tools previously described.

8.8   Summary and Future Trends

This chapter has introduced the main concepts in performance visualization together with a taxonomy, which can assist both visualization tool developers and users to classify them. The starting point is to understand the performance visualization process, which consists of the generation of the event trace and statistics files about the program's behavior and performance, followed by the displaying of the results and finally the analysis. During the file generation, the key issue is the file formats that can be specific to a particular tool or generic, providing more portability and a facility for integration with other tools. In spite of much effort, there is not at the present an international standard for trace file format.

Data displaying is the key stage of the visualization process. The level of detail and amount of information provided depend on particular tools but there are general accepted displays, such as processor utilization, task and message displays.

The common approach for the analysis is still manual, where the user employ the various displays and tries to identify the performance bottlenecks. Attempts to provide automatic and intelligent analysis are still emerging as research topics.

In terms of future trends a clear picture has not emerged yet but there are new development in the use of virtual environments [21, 22], which will provide more sophisticated visual representations by using multi-media technology. The most complex problem, however, is still the difficulty in providing automatic performance analysis. Current development in intelligent agents can provide exciting new developments in visualization tools , where models of users or problems can be specified for gathering and tracing information about performance bottlenecks, advising users when a problem will possibly happen.

8.9   Further Reading

Surveys of visualization tools and parallel development environments are present in the literature [2, 9, 12, 16, 34]. More recently, a high-level abstract model for performance visualization has been proposed in [10]. The object of the model is to explain and relate the most important concepts and principles involved in performance visualization. A recent paper by Reed *et al.* [23] summarizes recent approaches for performance analysis and lists open research topics.

References

[1] J Bourgeois. Cpu modelling in edpepps. EDPEPPS Technical Repor 35, University of Westminster, London, U.K, 1997.

[2] S. Browne, J. Dongarra, and K London. Review of performance analysis tools for mpi parallel programs. Available at http://www.cs.utk.edu/ browne/perftools-review/, 1997.

[3] T. Delaitre, G. R. Ribeiro-Justo, F. Spies, and S Winter. A graphical toolset for simulation modelling of parallel systems. *Parallel Computing*, 22(13):1823–1836, 1997.

[4] I. Foster. *Designing and Building Parallel Programs.* Addison-Wesley, 1995.

[5] G. A. Geist, M. T. Heath, B. W. Peyton, and P. H. Worley. A users' guide to PICL, a portable instrumented communication library. Technical Report ORNL/TM-11616, Oak Ridge National Laboratory, Oak Ridge,TN, USA, October 19990.

[6] M. Gerndt, M. Pantano, B. Mohr, and F. Wolf. Automatic performance analysis for cray t3e. In *7th Workshop on Compilers for Parallel Computers (CPC'98)*, Linkping, Sweden, June29–July1 1998.

[7] E. Hart. *TRANSIM: Prototyping Parallel Algorithms.* University of Westminster Press, 1994.

[8] M. Heath and J. E. Finger. Paragraph: A tool for visualizing performance of parallel programs. The National Center for Supercomputing Applications, University of Illinois at Urbana-Champaign, available at http://www.ncsa.uiuc.edu/Apps/MCS/ParaGraph/manual/manual.html, 1997.

[9] M. Heath, A. D. Malony, and D. T. Rover. Parallel performance visualization: From practice to theory. *IEEE Parallel & Distributed Technology*, 3(4):44–60, 1995.

[10] M. Heath, A. D. Malony, and D. T. Rover. The visual display of parallel performance data. *IEEE Computer*, 28(11):21–28, 1995.

[11] J. D. Hill, S. Jarvis, C. Siniolakis, and V. Vasilev. Portable and architecture independent parallel performance tunning using a call-graph profiling tool. In *6th EuroMicro Workshop on Parallel and Distributed Processing (PDP'98)*. EEE Computer Society Press, 1998.

[12] I. Jelly and Gorton. I. Software engineering for parallel systems. *nformation and Software Technology*, 36(7):379–380, 1994.

[13] G. R. Justo, P. Vekariya, T. Delaitre, M. J. Zemerly, and S. C. Winter. Prototype-oriented development of high-performance systems. In *Proceedings of 2nd International Workshop on Software Engineering for Parallel and Distributed Systems*, pages 74–84, Boston, USA, May 1997.

[14] P. Kacsuk, J. C. Cunha, G. Dózsa, J. Lourenço, T. Antão, and T. Fadgyas. A graphical toolset for simulation modelling of parallel systems. *Parallel Computing*, 22(13):1747–1770, 1997.

[15] W. Karpoff and B. Lake. PARDO: A deterministic, scalable paradigm for distributed computer systems and workstation clusters. In *Supercomputing Symposium'93*, June 1993.

[16] E. Kraemer and J. T. Stasko. The visualization of parallel systems: An overview. *Journal of Parallel and Distributed Computing*, 18(2):105–117, 1993.

[17] E. Maillet. *Tape/PVM: An Efficient Performance Monitor for PVM Applications: User Guide.* Grenoble, France, 1995. LMC-IMAG, ftp://ftp.imag.fr/ in pub/APACHE/TAPE.

[18] B. P. Miller, M. D. Callaghan, J. M. Cargille, J. K. Hollingsworth, R. B. Irvin, K. L Karavanic, K. Kunchithapadam, and T. Newhall. The paradyn parallel performance measurement tools. *IEEE Computer*, 28(11):37–4, 1995.

[19] A. D Reed, A. U. Aydt, R. J. Noe, P. C Roth, A. K. Shields, B. Schwartz, and L. F. Tavera. Scalable performance analysis: The pablo performance analysis environment. In Anthony Skjellum, editor, *Scalable Parallel Libraries Conference*, pages 104–113. IEEE Computer Society Press, October 1993.

[20] A. D. Reed and R. L Ribler. Performance analysis and visualization, computational grids: State of the art and future directions. In I. Foster and C. Kesselman, editors, *High-Performance Distributed Computing*. Morgan-Kaufman Publishers, August 1998.

[21] D. A. Reed, Foster Padua, A., D. B. I. T., Gannon, and B. P. Miller. Delphi: An integrated, language-directed performance prediction, measurement, and analysis environment. In *Frontiers '99: The 9th Symposium on the Frontiers of Massively Parallel Computation*, Annapolis, MD, USA, 1999.

[22] D.A. Reed, K.A. Shields, W.H. Scullin, L. F. Tavera, and C.L. Elford. Virtual reality and parallel systems performance analysis. *IEEE Computer*, 28(11):57–67, November 1995.

[23] R. A. D. Reed, A. U. Aydt, L. DeRose, C. L. Mendes, R. L. Ribler, E. Shaffer, H. Simitci, J. S. Vetter, D. R. Wells, S. Whitmore, and Y.g Zhan. Performance analysis of parallel systems: Approaches and open problems. In *Joint Symposium on Parallel Processing (JSPP)*, pages 239–256, Nagoya, Japan, June 1998.

[24] G. R. Ribeiro-Justo, M. d'Inverno, and P. Howells. Formalising high-performance systems methodologies. *Journal of Systems Architecture*, 45:441–464, 1999.

[25] J. M. Spivey. *Understanding Z, A Specification Language and Its Formal Semantics*. Cambridge University Press, 1998.

[26] V. S. Sunderam. PVM: A framework for parallel distributed computing. *Concurrency: Practice And Experienc*, 2(4):315–339, 1990.

[27] E. van der Deijl, G. Kanbier, O. Temam, and E. D. Granston. A cache visualization tool. *IEEE Computer*, 7:71–78, 1997.

[28] P. Vekariya. Development of prototype visualisation tool. EDPEPPS Technical Repor 2, University of Westminster, London, U.K., 1995.

[29] P. Vekariya. EDPEPPS: An environment for the design and performance evaluation of portable parallel software - extended graphical/visualisation tool. EDPEPPS Technical Report 40, University of Westminster, London, U.K., 1997.

[30] D. Watters. xmtool: A post-processing tool for the myrias PAMS environment. Master's thesis, School of Computer Science, University of Westminster, London, UK, 1994.

[31] I. H. Wettstein. Visualization of process scheduling 1.0. Available at http://www.ask.uni-karlsruhe.de/cgi-bin/sisy/program, 1994.

[32] F. Wolf and B. Mohr. EARL: A programmable and extensible toolkit for analyzing event traces of message passing programs. Interner Bericht FZJ-ZAM-IB-9803, Forschungszentrum Julich, April 1998.

[33] XPVM Web site. Available at http://www.netlib.org/utk/icl/xpvm/xpvm.html.

[34] M. J. Zemerly, T. Delaitre, and G. R. Ribeiro-Justo. EDPEPPS: An environment for the design and performance evaluation of portable parallel software - literature review (2). EDPEPPS Technical Repor 32, University of Westminster, London, U.K., 1997.

Chapter 9

Quality Issues of Parallel Programs

Henryk Krawczyk and Bogdan Wiszniewski

Abstract

Quality evaluation of parallel programs does not imply a simple distinction between "good" and "bad" programs and requires experimental analysis of various quality attributes, based on characteristics and measurable metrics. This chapter presents models for quality evaluation of parallel software and describes related methods and tools for developing, testing and maintaining high quality parallel programs.

9.1   Introduction

Mass production of software decreased the responsibility of individual programmers for finished products. This is particularly visible with the decline of the traditional *waterfall model* of software development and the rise of an alternative *iterative enhancement* model.

The waterfall model has been criticized for not being able to cope with changing product specifications and design, the poor feedback from customers, the lack of risk assessment incurred by the changing market demand and no provision for ongoing tests of the evolving product [5]. Unlike waterfall, the iterative model is "stepwise" and stimulates ready to use programming paradigms, template solutions, etc., which force developers to reuse life-cycle experience and products [5].

The iterative development model adopted in SEPP is suitable for comprehensive prediction, measurement and management of quality of evolving parallel software products. Therefore the development of this chapter is not confined only to parallel program testing techniques and tools, which although important for *measuring* quality of software by observing its behavior, do not address exhaustively all relevant quality issues. First of all, we have identified all important contributors to the final quality of a software product. It has been indicated that such a quality is a derivative of the development process quality, the underlying computer environment quality, a programming platform quality, as well as the quality of tools and maintenance procedures being used. Based on that perspective, a unified view on software quality is proposed by using a small set of common quality attributes. Procedures for evaluating these attributes form a framework for *quality testing*, which along with technically oriented *engineering testing*, and customer oriented $\alpha-$ or $\beta-$

testing constitutes the domain of software testing. Finally, by selecting one specific attribute, *dependability*, we have explored the issue of quality testing and demonstrated its appropriateness for developing quality programs using SEPP tools, described further in the book.

9.2   General view on software quality

Assuring desired quality of software products requires a thorough analysis of various quality attributes with regard to the physical distribution and operational characteristics of the code. Testing, which concentrates on bug detection by exercising, observing and evaluating the program's operational behavior, certainly provides the means for checking on the program code quality. Due that view, developers who aim at designing high quality software usually attempt to make it *testable*, thus provide a "quality" product as well as define a "quality" process [3].

Ideally, testing is a three-step activity consisting of the program text *analysis* in order to determine test data and expected results, *execution* of the program code to collect actual results, and *evaluation* to compare actual results with the expected ones. Our experience with parallel programs, however, indicates that such a traditional focus on product quality is rather narrow and partial [22]. We argue that checking on the behavior of such programs involves a variety of quality attributes rather than just detection of concrete errors.

Quality attributes provide a basis for evaluating software products in terms that are understandable to target users. Measurable representation of each attribute is based on *characteristics* — they are functions determined by developers in a series of experiments aimed at measuring concrete values of *metrics*. Relationships between attributes, characteristics and metrics are described with quality trees, introduced further in this Chapter.

Consider Figure 9.1 in which three major contributors to the commonly understood notion of "program quality" have been outlined. One is the *programming platform*, which supports the development cycle of a parallel software intended to be a solution to some realistically stated application problem. Programming platforms provide various communication mechanisms, data abstraction, exception handling, diagnostics, etc., along with programming, testing and debugging tools.

Another contributor shown in Figure 9.1 is the *development process*, which concentrates on the precise *problem definition*, development of the adequate *solution strategy* and application of the relevant *verification/validation* procedures to obtain a quality product. Development processes achieve that goal by adopting techniques which help to eliminate most errors quite early during program design and implementation, like software reuse, simulation, visual programming or rapid prototyping. Finally, the *computing environment* delivers basic means for parallel and distributed computing, including processors and communication channels, processing nodes and clusters, operating system kernels and system software to make user programs running fast, recover from hardware failures, tune-up or reconfigure hardware to serve the current program needs as far as possible.

On top of this we may specifically distinguish the additional insight into the overall product quality, brought by its prolonged maintenance history. This is not a part of the development process, nor the computing environment, as users concentrate on exploiting and maintaining concrete products. Nevertheless, user satisfaction and acceptance of product services is strongly influenced by both the computing environment and the final product quality accepted by developers upon its release.

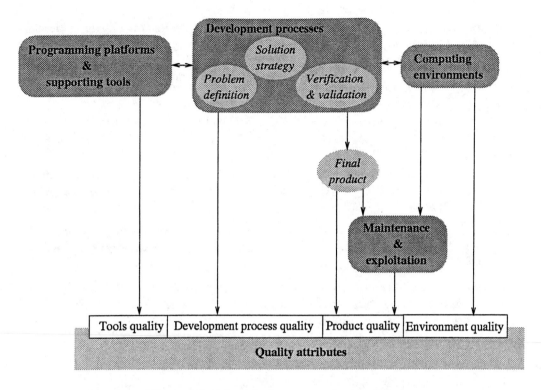

Figure 9.1: A broad view on product quality

9.2.1   Development process quality

Development process includes all human activities from problem definitions to final product. Several attempts have been made [22, 23] to establish a generic design process. The most recent attempt is the ANSI/IEEE St.1016 document [17]. There are four general approaches [1] to develop a software design architecture:

- *Normative*, which entails adopting an established architecture that has proven effectiveness in prior similar situations and follow-up policies, standards, and practices instituted by a company, a client or a standardization body.

- *Rational*, which is implicitly embodied in the scientific method already used.

- *Argumentative*, which implies using techniques like brain-storming, concurrent design or design teams, along with extensive outside audits and reviews.

- *Heuristic*, which relies on applied common sense, rules of thumb, experience and good, commonly accepted, engineering judgment.

An effective design effort spent on parallel software uses a blend of four approaches. However, evolution of this process is a very complex and tedious task, so in practice one has to concentrate on some standard solution, for instance the Capability Maturity Model (CMM) [8]. This model incorporates all elements of the quality paradigm, i.e., methods, techniques, tools and theory, and provides details about how to apply them in developing software. CMM includes guidance for recognizing, defining, measuring, analyzing and continuously improving processes of software development. There is already a substantial evidence of the business benefits of this methodology and a growing understanding of the factors that contribute to a successful improvement effort. CMM is organized into five, so called " maturity" levels:

1. *Initial* — software processes are characterized in an ad-hoc manner and success depends on individual competence and effort.

2. *Repeatable* — basic project management processes are established to tract *cost, schedule* and *functionality,* and some discipline is in place to repeat earlier successes and similar projects.

3. *Defined* — the software process for both management and engineering activities is documented, standardized and integrated into some obvious approach for the organization concerned.

4. *Managed* — detailed measures of a software product (explained in Section 9.2.4), and the software process characteristics, like productivity, time to market, cost and risk, etc., are collected in a controlled way.

5. *Optimizing* — continuous process improvement is facilitated by quantitative feedback from the process and from piloting innovative idea and technology.

A practical guidance on how to introduce CMM into software organization is beyond the scope of this book. We concentrate here only on design techniques which explicitly allow for parallel software quality improvement. This is the case of the SEPP project, adopting *iterated design* to identify, control and improve key development processes for parallel software.

The priority processes concerned are: *design, simulation, execution, analysis* and *monitoring* [28]. First of all, design in SEPP is not confined to a set of decisions determining the final shape of a software product. Instead, an interactive design based on visual programming is used (see Chapter 2), which allows for simulation and prototyping of alternative solutions (see Chapter 7 and Chapter 8). Simulation involves experimentation with the architectural design of the program, including its component processes, control flow and data structures, as well as timing relations governing communication channels. Analysis of the program structure and its simulated behavior provides a feedback for refining its design. Criteria taken into account here are performance and dependability. Special assignment techniques (see Chapter 3 and Chapter 4) allow to increase program efficiency, while testing [21] (see Chapter 5) and debugging [4] improve its dependability. If the analysis indicates that the program is mature enough for real experiments, its code is automatically generated (see Chapter 11). The program code behavior is then analyzed, with the use of monitoring tools [9], to provide additional feedback for enhancing and further modifying its design. When analysis indicates that the program (product) has attained a sufficient acceptance level the last successfully completed development step is considered final.

9.2.2   Programming platform and tools quality

As indicated before, standard platform mechanisms and tools, when appropriately used, can significantly improve the overall product quality. The basic principles and methodology of

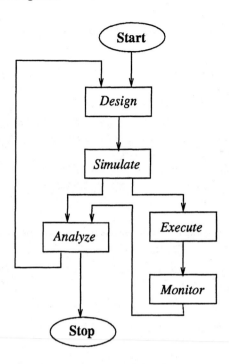

Figure 9.2: Iterated development in SEPP

the evaluation technology follow from the ISO/IEC 9126 standards [16]. These principles concern software applications as well as software engineering tools, which also constitute "software". The possible evaluation criteria for platforms and their tools form the following groups [10]:

1. *General features* — functional aspects, flexibility, understandability of implemented ideas, easy to learn and use software libraries.

2. *Visual aspects* — graphical user interface and animations.

3. *Modifiability* — coding aspects of flexibility and robustness, i.e., possibility of additional coding (re-usability) and integration between the tool and the product.

4. *Efficiency* — capability of a given tool to analyze complex software.

5. *Experimental facilities* — variety and characteristics of experiments analyzed by the tool.

6. *Financial features* — the cost and technical characteristics of the tool, including price, installation and maintenance.

7. *Correctness and exactness of analysis* — distance between the analyzed reality and the inherent platform model describing this reality.

8. *Pedigree* - references to the origin of the tool and its prominence, how widely it is used, reputation of its suppliers, etc.

9. *Integration degree* — possibility of cooperation with other tools to create complete development systems.

10. *Statistical facilities* — the available range of certain statistical calculations on historical data offered by tools.

Evaluation of a programming platform and its underlying tools is indirect, i.e., requires prior selection of *benchmark* application problems with predefined quality characteristics. These characteristics should cover criteria listed above.

In the FASET project [24] a concrete evaluation methodology was proposed for programming platforms, libraries and their supporting software tools. For the platform libraries two main attributes have been considered:

1. *Learnability* — a set of factors that bear on the effort needed for understanding and mastering the underlying platform language.

2. *Functionality* — a set of factors that bear on the capability or effort for describing and modifying provided functions and data types.

For the platform tools two attributes have been explicitly considered:

1. *Functionality* — a set of factors that bear on the existence of a set of specified function tools and services.

2. *Usability* — a set of attributes that bear on the effort needed for using particular tools.

9.2.3   Computing environment quality

A computing environment is created by a system architecture, i.e., hardware, and the operating system making it work, i.e., software. *Standard ISO900x*, where $x=1,2,3,4$ [15] determines basic quality requirements that may be considered here:

1. Management responsibility.

2. Quality system principles.

3. Quality marketing (contract review).

4. Quality documentation and records.

5. Quality production (process control).

6. Product verification, auditing and corrective actions (inspections and testing).

7. Product safety and liability.

8. Control, measuring and test equipment.

9. Handling and post production functions.

10. Personnel training.

They concern the entire manufacturing process and are well formulated for hardware. Many companies making computing equipment have already some kind of ISO quality certificate. We limit our attention here just to performance and dependability, in which we have been interested since distinguishing quality attributes of programming platforms and products (programs) earlier in the chapter.

High performance means both high speed of computations (measured with MIPS and MFLOPS), as well as system scalability, i.e., increase in speed-up with regard to the number processors used in parallel.

Dependability can be achieved by adopting hardware redundancy, and fault-detection with possibly fault-correction mechanisms implemented by the operating system. Quality of such a fault-tolerance mechanism may be evaluated with the fault-injection testing described later in the chapter. A generic metric applicable here is the *user outage time*, which is the sum of all user outage time periods related to the underlying equipment failures [22].

9.2.4 Product quality

ISO/IEC 9126 [16] specifies six main quality attributes for evaluating software products. They are the following:

1. *Functionality* — number of functions of the software product which are well utilized.

2. *Usability* — human effort required to learn how to operate and to use the product.

3. *Reliability*, or *dependability* (explained later) — product capability to execute correctly all of its functions.

4. *Efficiency* — execution of the product functions without wasting time or resources.

5. *Maintainability* — possibility of fault identification and fault removal of the product.

6. *Portability* — an effort required to transfer the product from one programming platform or computing environment to another.

Each quality attribute can be expanded into a set of factors, which can better characterize the product under examination. Moreover, each factor can be measured in a different way, so it can be expressed by various metrics. Unfortunately, although many attributes, factors, and metrics have been proposed and used, no one is widely accepted. Moreover, they depend on many other parameters related to the class of product applications, a design methodology and a programming platform. In a case of parallel and distributed software applications we narrow the above set of attributes in a way described below.

Instead of *reliability* and *maintainability* we consider the more general *dependability* attribute, which means capability of a product to execute correctly even in the presence of faults. We exchange the *portability* attribute for the more general *flexibility* attribute, including *re-usability* and *modifiability*. Similarly, we exchange *efficiency* for *performance*, which jointly describes hardware and software efficiency — what is essential for parallel and distributed programs. Up to this point we have considered attributes related to four major components of quality identified in Figure 9.1. These attributes correspond to one another across these components, although specific details of the relationships may vary, depending on the class of a particular application problem [22]. One possibility is shown in Table 9.1.

The attributes listed there are refined into factors represented by characteristics. In order to determine the latter a few suitable metrics are selected from several candidates for each respective factor. Thus obtained *quality tree* is defined, so that each metric rating criterion is given and grading levels, e.g., *reject (0)*, *marginal (1)*, *good (2)*, and *excellent (3)*, are considered.

Let us denote by γ_i the rated point, by δ_i the required point, and by w_i the weight for an i-th metric, and by n the number of metrics within a factor. Then the *measured (ML)* and *required (RL)* levels can be defined in the following way:

$$ML = \sum_{i=1}^{n} \gamma_i \cdot w_i \qquad (9.1)$$

$$RL = \sum_{i=1}^{n} \delta_i \cdot w_i \qquad (9.2)$$

The *achieve score (AS)* can be expressed as follows:

$$AS = \frac{ML}{RL} \cdot 100\% \qquad (9.3)$$

Quality attributes and factors can be selected in various ways, according to particular criteria, e.g., life cycle of the target software tools, some important properties of programming platforms, etc. Therefore such an estimation constitutes a "qualitative" approach.

Product	Process	Platform	Environment
functionality	completeness	maturity	stability
performance	accuracy	efficiency	speed
dependability	adequacy	fault-tolerance	reliability
flexibility	re-usability	portability	configurability
usability	simplicity	generality	accessability

Table 9.1: A selection of corresponding quality attributes

9.2.5   Quality related activities

Owing to the new paradigms — including parallelism and distribution — software manufacturing became more complex and overwhelmingly productive, therefore industry turns towards standardization of all issues relevant to *product*, as well as *process* quality standards [23]. These issues split into four main streams of activities, comprising quality assessment, productivity, control and assurance, as shown schematically in Figure 9.3.

Quality assessment evaluates quality of software components based on physical evidence gathered during experiments with the binary code in a specially selected testing environment (or the product target environment), as well as by means of static analysis using inspections, walkthroughs and audits of partial or final product source code, documentation, etc.

Quality prediction is a forecast of certain quality characteristics during the design phase to look for values that are feasible and realistic with respect to the existing project resources. It provides developers with the basis for evaluation and monitoring trends during further product development. Owing to the extremely complex process of predicting behavior of

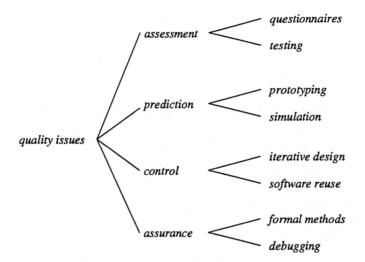

Figure 9.3: Streams of quality related activities

parallel (distributed) systems consisting of reusable components and reconfigurable computing environments, experimentation plays also a dominant role there. When a binary code is not yet available for experimentation, thus for "physically" measuring product quality, developers have to develop prototypes, for example by means of *exploratory programming* involving program skeletons, or *simulation* with specialized tools, before attempting any real code implementation.

Quality control is the ongoing evaluation of software components against predetermined (predicted) values of metrics that are considered important, in order to identify components that fall outside quality limits. The purpose of such a "control" is to allow developers to identify product components that have unacceptable quality sufficiently early to take corrective actions. This is the case of *iterated design*, which enables measuring various quality characteristics of a product not yet fully complete in a series of simple experiments, which enable close monitoring of the development process. Moreover, such experiments also facilitate gradual development of tests capable of assessing (demonstrating) the evolving product quality. Quality control may also rely on software *reuse* - when developers are offered alternative template solutions provided by various programming platforms libraries and exhibiting various quality levels.

Quality assurance serves as the traditional mechanism to ensure product quality, in software, as well other manufacturing industries. It is aimed at ensuring compliance with standards and development procedures, and often relies on formal methods based on a well-defined formal specification language. In practice, however, this language does not have to be explicitly given. More important is that the model used to describe final product properties can precisely define notions like *consistency* and *completeness*, thus enable proving that specifications are *realizable*, program implementation is *correct* and certain properties of a software product hold - without necessarily running the code to determine its behavior. An alternative, or rather a complementary measure to formal quality assurance methods (used early in the product development process to prevent bugs) is *debugging*, which actually localizes and eliminates bugs that may still remain in the program code at the end of the development cycle, even after the most rigorous bug prevention measures taken during design and implementation.

Testing and debugging is the simplest case of the *software process improvement* — the latter of course comprises all quality attributes.

9.3   The concept of quality testing

IEEE Standards, e.g., ANSI Std. 829, 983, 1008 and 1012 documents [11–14], determine principles of software testing. According to this document, software testing breaks down into three parts (see Figure 9.4):

1. Development and engineering testing concentrates on the code level, involving module (unit) and integration testing.

2. Internal quality assurance (system) testing, which operates on user interface, and in the case of parallel programs, evaluates functionality, usability, performance, dependability, and flexibility, based on the opinion of a selected group of internal testers, who are regular members of the designing team.

3. External (α and β) testing, which relies on external testers recruited from among actual and potential end users of the product, and validates product either in the developer's environment (α-testing) or in the customer's environment (β-testing).

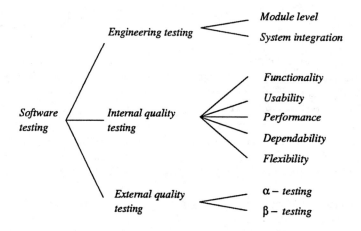

Figure 9.4: Parts of software testing

While engineering testing is relatively well explored and has been investigated for years [2], quality testing is still an open issue with respect to the selection of quality attributes, measurement procedures, standards for specific application areas, etc. We investigate these issues below in some detail to give a complete overview of quality testing principles and strategies.

Each kind of testing can be supported by some kind of a specialized tool, different with respect to what metrics are used for evaluation — either partial products of each single iteration step, or the final product (see Figure 9.2). In the case of engineering testing the fundamental approach uses static and dynamic analysis of the product [22]. External α-testing engages some testing tools and relies on suitable experiments described later in the chapter. β-testing, oriented towards a target environment may repeat certain experiments run during α-testing, but also defines new experiments to check quality characteristics, considered to be the most important ones for a given class of users. Automated usage of data collection and reporting of testing results is strongly recommended in such cases. Collected information may be sent over to various experts for proper evaluation. In this chapter we concentrate on internal quality testing and emphasize its essentials concerning parallel and distributed testing.

Preparation and planning for the test phases should begin early in the development cycle and be the major concern throughout the development process. Appropriate software criteria for two levels of engineering testing can be the following [26]:

- *Interface integrity* — exercise both human-machine interfaces and internal interfaces, using specifications and operational timeliness as sources for test cases.

- *Functional validity* — confirm the specifications, particularly those embedded in acceptance criteria.

- *Data contents* — test local and global data structures, data protection features, access protocols, and integrity preservation features to expose all weaknesses.

- *Functional performance* — test the performance requirement on the basis of performance specifications and analyze all exceptional conditions and threats.

9.3.1 Traditional views on testing and debugging

Testing normally means a process of experimenting with a system (program) code for selected input data, state or condition, and comparing actual outcome with the expected outcome in a controlled and systematic way to demonstrate the presence of the required function and the absence of unwanted effects. Since testing provides a natural means to exercise a program code behavior in an attempt to measure or assess its quality it may be viewed as a process of exploring *how good* is (or will be) the system or its component.

The task of testing is discovering bugs in a program, while locating and removing bugs involves yet another process known as *debugging*. Bugs are not always obvious, because knowing that the program is incorrect does not imply knowing the bug. Different bugs may manifest in the same way, and one bug may have many symptoms. Debugging requires repeated executions of a product piece of code for small detailed tests in order to observe patterns in program behaviors. By inspecting selected variables, states or conditions immediately during program execution, and in a highly interactive manner, various manifestations and symptoms can be systematically observed in order to develop and verify a hypothesis about the reason for a particular bug.

The goal of software testing and debugging is to devise tests that can exercise the code in a meaningful and systematic way, so that any deviation from the original specification can be detected and localized, and yet all the related activities completed within a reasonable time predicted by the project timetable. These activities are generally known to be difficult and error prone even for intuitively simple sequential programs. This is because the volume of tests may grow arbitrarily large. One reason for that is the presence of loops in computer programs, and another is interleaving of computations if a program can run in parallel to other programs. SEPP has addressed and solved a number of issues resulting from these two facts within the framework of structural testing. Structural testing is an implementation-based approach, which derives test cases most commonly from the program code, but also can be based on the system architecture and the high-level design. The motivation for concentrating on this kind of sources of deriving test cases has been to develop automatic testing tools for the parallel software.

The list of problems addressed by SEPP with this regard has been the following:

1. *Analyzing possible interleavings of computations performed by programs running in parallel.* A space of possible states or behaviors in a set of parallel programs is potentially infinite. How to examine such an infinite space in order to determine whether a program (parallel system) has certain desirable properties?

2. *Recognizing events and states occurring in a set of programs that run in parallel.* Intuitively, parallel program execution represents a sequence of events that causes transformations in the program state. How to relate specific events to specific changes in state? What is the relationship between individual actions of processes and erroneous states?

3. *Halting and resuming parallel program execution at specific points.* In a typical implementation, a breakpoint replaces selected program statements with a trap back to the monitoring tool. When the monitoring tool detects a breakpoint in one process, it can halt this process immediately, but it must notify all the other processes in the system using messages. How to deal with the unpredictable interval between the time of a trap and the time at which other process can be notified about that? Shall all other processes be allowed to continue to execute until receiving that notification?

4. *Eliminating the probe effect caused by the monitoring software.* Using breakpoints introduces delays that can alter the execution of the parallel program under test, and thereby hide error symptoms. On the other hand, a monitoring medium is required to record specific data values at specific execution points. How to cope with the uncertainty inherent in this situation?

5. *Detecting error symptoms based on the recorded information.* Techniques are needed to support experiments, where the user makes a hypothesis regarding the cause-and-effect relationship between the program and an error condition, monitors the result, and repeats the process. How to interact with such a "living" code? What should be the way to present information to the user?

6. *Designing and rapid prototyping of test cases.* Even a thorough analysis of the related parallel program specifications and code may overlook some crucial state configurations. There should be a mechanism for experimenting with various tests before actually running them in a target system. How to utilize collected information to refine existing tests or design new ones? Is it possible to run tests in a non-intrusive manner, so that errors could be detected as early as at test design?

These problems have been investigated and solutions to them implemented in a form of a testing tool STEPS. We defer technical details of these solution until Chapter 16. Here we wish to concentrate on the role which traditional testing and debugging has in assuring and evaluating product quality.

9.3.2   Quality testing framework

Quality testing of parallel programs necessitates direct measurement of various program characteristics, requiring collection of far more specific data than in ordinary testing. Consider Figure 9.5 and note that the parallel *application program* under test is running in its *environment* in the presence of a specialized *monitoring system*. The program under test is provided with various data values, being delivered to its component processes "at place" and "in time" prescribed by the specially selected execution (test) scenario. Such a scenario determines also which program environment parameters should be actively *controlled*, and which just *observed* during each experiment.

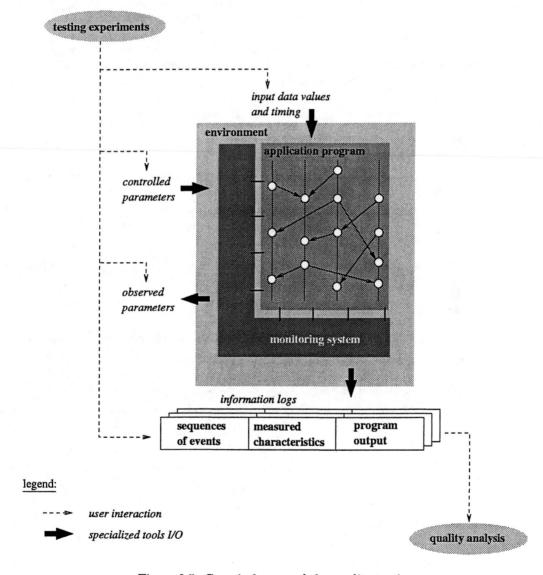

Figure 9.5: Generic framework for quality testing

All the information that is considered relevant is collected by the monitoring system and truthfully *logged* for further processing and evaluation. Although in principle, the framework for quality testing is similar to the one typically used by the traditional testing, procedures governing its use get more complex for the former. This is because evaluation procedures in traditional testing concentrate only on estimating *test coverage*. Parallel program behavior modeled with tokens moving through a set of flowgraphs representing component processes, as it has been implemented in STEPS (see Chapter 16) for example, provides a *structural abstraction* that allows testers to realize and evaluate sequences of concrete events such as: data and control flow during communication events, message buffer changes, object status changes, etc. That structural abstraction level emphasizes only the syntactic aspects of program behavior, as it relies mostly on the program text.

Quality testing instead estimates coverage of quality attributes assessed during experiments. This requires emphasizing the semantic aspects of test experiments from the standpoint of each respective contributor to the product quality indicated in Figure 9.1. Therefore, on top of the structural abstraction we want to define a more general form of scenarios that can completely describe certain functional properties of distributed programs. In consequence, we are able to define a variety of specialized estimation procedures for determining both functional and non-functional quality characteristics of the program under test.

9.3.3   Quality testing strategies

Based on Table 9.1 we wish to distinguish five basic classes of generic quality testing strategies. Each strategy concentrates on a single quality attribute specific to the final software product, i.e., we define a whole range of *functionality, usability, performance, dependability,* and *flexibility* testing strategies. Each strategy is further characterized in Table 9.2 by considering topics indicated already in Figure 9.5:

1. What input values, timing, objects, pieces of information and other *data* to use in experiments?

2. What *parameters* to control and observe during experiments?

3. What results, metrics and other *output* specific to the program under test to collect?

4. What other info to *log*?

5. What *tools* and techniques to use?

Testing	Data	Parameters	Output	Log	Tools	Remarks
Functionality	Representative subset of input data	Configuration, initialization	Completeness, correctness	Anomalous functions	Specification, documentation	Review (reading)
Usability	Representative subset of user functions	Different kinds of users	Time spent on interaction	Unclear operations	Questionnaires, certification	Inquiring expert users
Performance	Random data	Program granularity, program structure, application class	Processing and communication time	Start and end time of events	Simulator, mapping, monitoring tools	Histograms
Dependability	Specific and average input data	Time conditions, probes, fault injection	Sequences of events, output data, time related parameters	Events and behavior at various levels, the number of bugs vs. testing time	Simulator, tester, debugger	Independent teams
Flexibility	Predicted changes or enhancements	Different platforms and environments	Required modifications and frequency of modifications	Questionnaires, re-use and re-engineering	In accordance to new platforms and environments	Standards needed

Table 9.2: Principles of quality testing strategies

The last column in Table 9.2 includes remarks on some specific issues. Note that since functionality relies on specification analysis (mostly a "reading" technique), a reasonable use of any tools is limited — unless a very formal specification language and its supporting tool are used. Usability in turn can be best assessed by expert, i.e., experienced and knowledgeable, users. The only "tool" recommended here is a questionnaire — its form and content usually cannot be generated automatically and requires a great deal of understanding and professionalism by the responsible staff. On the other hand, performance testing can be automated very well. Besides specialized tools, like simulators, mapping tools and monitors, other more general tools for processing collected result may be used — even simple spreadsheet tools capable of drawing automatically histograms and other figures based on recorded data. Finally, dependability should be assessed as often as possible by independent teams, to eliminate bias or misunderstanding incurred sometimes to the product by a development team.

9.3.4   Visualization of quality attributes

Visualization of quality attributes, characteristics and metrics is very important for quick understanding and comparison of different software products.

There are many ways for representing each particular quality metric. The most popular are diagrams and histograms represented with rectangles or curves showing the most important tendencies, typically *rise* and *fall*. General rules of good visualization are the following:

1. Context clarification, i.e., point of view from which information is presented, the relationships between real information and used constructs.

2. Scaling and composition determining multidimensional and multivariate representations, macroscopic and microscopic views and their compositions to enhance visual relationships among the views and to present more global information.

3. User perception and interaction, i.e., suitable feedback loop between users and visualization tools, shape, color, motion, animation and repetition.

4. Extraction of information based on reduction and filtering, clustering and separation techniques.

Each software tool can have its own way for information visualization. In the case of software quality visualization we want to show only two representative solutions: one based on the notion of a *quality tree*, and another on a *pie-chart*.

A quality tree identifies relationships between *attribute*, *factors* and *metrics*, where quality attributes define software quality by indicating factors and representing them with metrics. Each metric must be "generable" in practice, i.e., an algorithm for effective collection of parameters and their subsequent utilization has to be provided. Detailed description of parameters, metrics and related factors that contribute to the overall parallel program quality is beyond the scope of this book. Here we may just illustrate the general idea with a simple example — a more complete description of quality trees for parallel and distributed software can be found in [22].

In Figure 9.6 we have identified the *usability* attribute using the *operability, understandability* and *learnability* factors. For example, the understandability factor can be measured with two specific metrics: one metric expressing the degree of easiness of understanding the

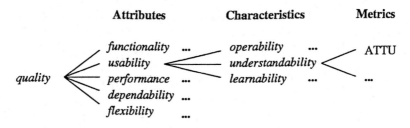

Figure 9.6: The quality tree

concept of the software product (program) by its target user, and another metric expressing the degree of easiness of understanding by the user the basic functions (commands, services) provided by the product. Both metrics mentioned here may rely on *benchmark tests*, which are dedicated to novice, as well as expert users. This allows one to obtain respectively top and bottom estimations of effort spent on completing benchmark applications in a given period of time. One metric that should certainly be measured here is the *Average amount of Time To Understand (ATTU)* metric.

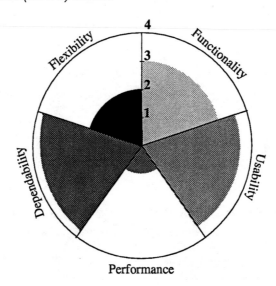

Figure 9.7: The pie-chart representation

A "pie-chart" (see Figure 9.7) may refer to general attributes, like the ones listed in Table 9.1, as well as just a few factors specifically corresponding to one attribute. Observe that a weight for each attribute is represented by its angle and an achieved score is represented by its radius — scaled in four grades: 1 (reject), 2 (marginal), 3 (good), and 4 (excellent).

Using calculations with Formulas 9.1 and 9.2 the measured results can be judged visually as a degree of filling respective sections of the chart. If a weight equal to or greater than the average is assigned to the attribute, and if the achieved score is not less than three quarters of the radius, then the attribute is judged as "acceptable" when the weight of the attribute is less than the average. The attribute may be judged as acceptable, even if the achieved score is less that three but not less than two quarters of the radius. This allows one to interpret quality of the analyzed product quite easily.

9.4   Benchmarks for dependability testing

Dependability is a property that allows reliance to be justifiably placed on the functions or services delivered by an application. Below we concentrate only on two aspects of dependability, namely *reliability* and *fault-tolerance* (see Figure 9.8).

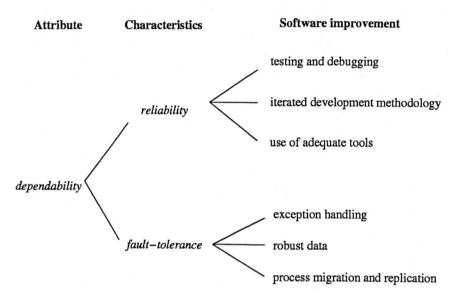

Figure 9.8: Improving dependability of applications

We assume that reliability is not understood as the probability of a correct functioning of the program, but rather the number of residual bugs hidden in the application after its testing and debugging process. It depends on the used design methodology, completeness of testing tools, as well as the tools properly supporting each single step in the iterated software development cycle. Ways of software improvement with regard to reliability characteristics have already been outlined in Section 9.2.

Fault tolerance, as a complementary technique to reliability, means capability of an application to run its functions correctly, in spite of the occurrence of residual bugs. Many mechanisms are available to increase fault-tolerance, as most of the existing parallel and distributed platforms offer diagnostic and exception handling support. Exception handling is, supported by many programming languages, allowing definition of exception conditions and implementation of procedures to handle all classes of errors discussed in Section 9.4.1. Besides exception handling, developers can use specialized mechanisms to control input data in order to assure their robustness, i.e., to avoid data from outside the program application domain. Data robustness is the principal responsibility of the target user.

The computing environment may also support process migration or replication to contribute further to fault-tolerance by resuming processing of tasks at fallen units on another, redundant units. Process migration and replication uses ordinary mechanisms suitable for load balancing, which in turn is aimed at increasing the overall program performance.

In the next three sections we outline typical errors of parallel applications, four testing strategies for detecting them, and one evaluation strategy for the fault tolerance mechanisms.

9.4.1 Classes of parallel software bugs

We distinguish three classes of parallel software errors, namely *data*, *processing*, and *timing* errors.

Data errors (DTE)

Data errors can be linked to four aspects of data items: *content, structure, attributes*, and *state*. *Data content* refers to the actual bit pattern stored in bytes constituting an object instance. It has no meaning unless it is interpreted according to the object semantics. If the bit pattern is corrupted or misinterpreted a data error occurs.

Data structure refers to a number and a particular arrangement of bytes implementing an object in a computer memory. If a chunk of memory implementing the same object instance represents at least two alternative structures a potential for data error exists.

Data attributes refer to the meaning of a particular object. This meaning is usually determined by the object's type or class; it is generally illegal to combine objects of incompatible types. Type violations that escape detection by the underlying language compiler originate or cause data errors. They most often occur at interfaces, including the human interface being usually behind a parallel program's access to the external world.

Data state refers to the history of using a given instance of some object, combining the object's methods (services) with private data components hidden behind them. If after a series of requests for object services it reaches a state (its private data assume values) considered to be wrong for any further (intended) use of the object, a data error occurs.

Processing errors (CPE, CNE)

The principal responsibility of any process in a parallel program is *data processing*. This involves acquiring data from outside, producing new values, and delivering results to the right place on time and in an orderly manner. Processing errors can be linked to two aspects of control flow paths going through processes constituting a parallel program: a *computation* performed by assignment statements taken by a path, and a *control predicate* being a conjunction of predicates of all decision statements taken by that path.

A *computation error (CPE)* occurs if during experimentation any path of any process produces an incorrect result, despite having correctly placed and evaluated decision statements. A *control error (CNE)* occurs when any path of any process has been executed for some input data, but although having correctly placed and executed assignment statements, this path should not be followed for this particular input data.

Processing errors are usually combined in complex ways. For example, a computation error before a conditional statement in some path may affect predicate evaluation, thus introduce a control error later in that path. A control error may cause directing control flow to a wrong path, giving a reason to a computation error there, and so on, i.e., a processing error at one point of a program can cause another path error somewhere else in that program. Such a cumulative effect of the whole series of processing errors may have arbitrary many manifestations, according to the underlying program semantics and structure; nevertheless, the original reason for a bug can always be related to one of the two "canonical" representations of processing errors.

A processing error is *time dependent* if for some decision statement, in which it occurs, there is at least one more alternative transition (not necessarily in error) for which the relevant predicate may evaluate to *true*. Time dependent processing errors occur because of timing errors that may exist in a program.

Timing errors (TME)

When relative timing of parallel actions or data being transmitted is incorrect we say that *timing errors* occur. They usually cause the following problems:

- data are received from a wrong process,

- wrong data are received,

- data are sent to a wrong process,

- wrong data are sent,

- a process waits unusually long for data to be sent or received.

Since output variables of one process may be input variables to another process, all the problems listed above can be explained in terms of assignments involving special variables, which are *communication buffers*. According to this interpretation any *send* action is for assigning a communication buffer of a receiving process with data provided by the sending process. Similarly, a *receive* action is for reading data from a communication buffer of the respective receiving process. If data sent by one process can be eventually received by another process the respective send and receive actions are called *matching* [22].

The following phenomena may give reasons to timing errors:

1. *Races at send* actions, where two or more receive actions match the same send action.

2. *Races at receive* actions, where two or more send actions match the same receive action.

3. *Deadlocks*, where receive actions have no matching send actions.

While deadlock are commonly considered "bad" and are to be avoided, races are often intended to speed-up communication or increase reliability. Serious problems occur, however, when races are not intended.

9.4.2   Basic testing strategies

We distinguish four basic testing strategies for parallel programs:

1. *Random testing (RT)* corresponds to the general concept of "black-box" testing, when the program is run with as little intrusion as possible [2]. Input data are defined by the user or tester based on the user's manual. Each experiment may be repeated many times, without any guarantee on repeatability. Time dependent phenomena, in the program as well as in its environment may occur arbitrarily and in an unpredictable

way. This strategy is the easiest one to implement, as most often it relies just on observing the regularly used product. Presence or absence of errors may be inferred only upon comparing results from various executions, therefore the level of error coverage is low. An advantage is that the "probe effect" is virtually nil and all kinds of parallel programs, especially those with dynamically created and terminated processes.

2. *Structural testing (ST)* attempts to identify a set of *global states* of a program using first static analysis of its text, and then tests systematically all transitions of interest between such states [27]. All processes are executed in a deterministic mode, according to the pre-defined test scenario. This strategy is most difficult to implement, but time dependent phenomena may be replayed in a reproducible way, and in a "slow-motion" fashion, to demonstrate the presence or absence of errors. The probe effect is irrelevant here, although a disadvantage is a possible state explosion during static analysis.

3. *Controlled execution (CEX)* testing concentrates on a single process in an attempt to detect races [6]. This strategy requires implementing control on each process message queue to withhold messages coming to the process at some execution point and observe whether more than one message may be received at this point. It is rather easy to implement, but a disadvantage is that communication statements that can be "controlled" in this way must be blocking.

4. *Controlled environment (CEV)* testing is similar to random testing in that there is no intrusion into the program code [19]. However, various time related parameters of the program environment are controlled in order to run the program under modified conditions to demonstrate the presence or absence of time dependent errors. There are two ways of achieving that: one is by changing from execution to execution the allocation of process to computation nodes, and another is changing time delivery of messages. CEV has all the advantages of RT, i.e., simplicity, low-complexity and non-trivial re-execution ability, and is quite easy to implement.

Based on our current experience gained in SEPP we characterize the four strategies listed above using the types of bugs considered before (see Table 9.2). Note that although evaluations for CEX and CEV are the same, CEV is different from CEX in that its implementation does not introduce any "probe effect" to the program under test. Besides that the implementation of all these four strategies is straightforward, using a generic framework shown in Figure 9.5.

				strategy
bugs	RT	ST	CEX	CEV
DTE	3	3	1	1
CPE	3	4	2	2
CNE	2	4	2	2
TME	1	2	3	3

Rating:
1 (reject), 2 (marginal),
3 (good), 4 (excellent)

Table 9.2: Evaluation of testing strategies

9.4.3   Evaluation of fault-tolerance mechanisms

Fault-tolerance mechanisms used in parallel programs with dependability requirements need special testing strategies, based on fault-injection techniques. Faults are inserted into both the hardware and software components of a target system, or just its simulation model. Effects of each inserted fault have to be adequately monitored and recorded.

Fault-injection testing is typically used to functionally test a prototype during the development cycle. When a product (system) is completed and ready for deployment, fault-injection is used to observe the behavior of its code in the presence of a given set of faults. In both cases information about the quality of system design and the level of dependability actually achieved can be obtained.

The injected faults should cover basic types of errors characterized before, i.e., data, processing, and timing errors, and also take into account the following:

- *Locality*, attributing anomalies either to the program, its platform or environment.

- *Latency*, representing time intervals between insertion and observation of individual faults.

- *Frequency*, characterizing average occurrence of a fault over a given time interval.

- *Severity*, describing the magnitude of the fault effects on program behavior.

As indicated already in Figure 9.5, data collected in *information logs* can be processed further with specialized quality analysis tools [20].
There are two basic fault injection approaches:

- *Code injection*, directly dealing with the source code or the object code corrupting binary code or data structures.

- *State injection* achieved through altering the state behavior of a running parallel program code. Modification are made in the operating system, processors, storages, dynamic states of running processes, messages, etc., as well as in specific service, administration, and maintenance commands.

Based in this technique and with the support of the testing framework shown in Figure 9.5 we are able to evaluate various quality metrics, and also find some useful relationships between metrics, e.g., a correspondence between performance and dependability.

9.5   Future trends in quality testing

9.5.1   Development strategies

Development of parallel software products is partially automated, but their quality depends not only on technical aspects but first of all on human activities, which are rather not systematic in spite of many existing rules and recommendations aimed at formalizing development processes. Further work will concentrate on standardization of the overall development effort, in order to eliminate misunderstanding of quality issues and to integrate existing standards into one coherent framework. As far as the CMM model is concerned, experts will probably attempt to define concrete certification procedures for each level of process development maturity. This is a tedious task requiring a lot of time and effort. Examples include the SM-CMM v2 approach [25], and *Software Process Improvement and Capability dEtermination (SPICE)* [7], which define common roles for software process assessment (SPA) and software process improvement (SPI), as shown in Figure 9.9.

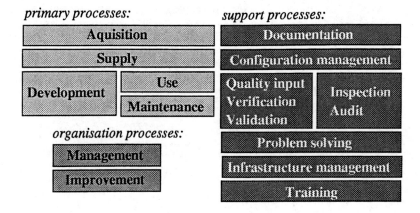

Figure 9.9: SPICE life cycle processes

The framework for SPA is the following:

1. Encourages self-assessment.

2. Addresses the adequacy of management of the assessed processes.

3. Takes into account the context in which the assessed processes operate.

4. Produces a set of ratings (as process profiles).

5. Is appropriate across all application domains and organizations of all possible sizes.

The framework for SPI is the following:

1. Defines priorities of the considered improvement. This improvement must be compliant with the company's business goals to ensure top management commitment and business levels.

2. According to the Pareto analysis, those 20% improvement actions must be identified which will bring 80% of the improvement benefit.

3. The entire project must be "measurement goal" driven, because without measurements developers are not able to decide about success or failure objectively.

4. A proper improvement culture must be established, which gives people a feeling to actively participate in the establishment of a continuously improving organization.

5. To ensure compliance with the standards of the standard template for action planning provided a framework for doing all of such planning works.

These activities concern all life cycle processes, as defined by the ISO Std.12207 document [18].

9.5.2   Generic tools for quality testing

A rapid development of various tools to support quality testing is a fact. Problems arise on how to use these tools for preparing and performing experiments, and how to analyze the collected information. In our opinion these two problems will play a growing role in quality testing. Diversity of tools will lead to their closer integration into a generic, standard frame, which may support creation and maintenance of specialized databases with historical data (see Figure 9.10).

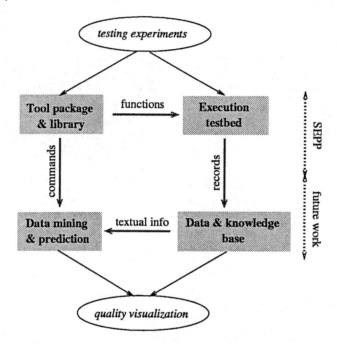

Figure 9.10: A quality testing frame

These databases will be widely used to make a complete evaluation of all important quality attributes — specific to the development process as well as to the partial and final products of various steps in the iterated development model. Some further standardization with this regard seem to be inevitable, first of all to define interfaces between the main components of the postulated frame.

References

[1] A. Behforooz and F.J. Hudson. *Software Engineering Fundamentals*. Oxford University Press, 1996.

[2] Boris Beizer. *Software Testing Techniques*. Van Nostrand Reinhold, 1990.

[3] G. Boloix. A software system evaluation framework. *IEEE Computer*, pages 17–26, December 1995.

[4] J.C. Cunha, J. Lourenço, and V. Duarte. Using DDBG to support testing and high-level debugging interfaces. *Computers and Artificial Inteligence*, 17(5):429–439, 1998.

[5] M.A. Cusumano and R.W. Selby. How Microsoft builds software. *Comm. of the ACM*, 6(40):53–61, 1997.

[6] S.K. Damodaran-Kamal and J.M. Francioni. Testing races in parallel programs with an OtOt strategy. In *Proc. of the SHPC Conference*, pages 702–709, 1994.

[7] A. Darling. SPICE – software process improvement and capability determination. *Software Quality Journal*, 2:209–224, 1996.

[8] J. Herbsleb, D. Zubrow, D. Goldenson, W. Hayes, and M. Paulk. Software quality and capability maturity model. *Comm. ACM*, 6(6):30–40, June 1997.

[9] L. Hluchy, M. Dobrucky, and J. Astalos. Hybrid approach to task allocation in distributed systems. *Lecture Notes in Compuetr Science*, 1277:210–216, 1997.

[10] V. Hlupic. A comparative evaluation of ten manufacturing simulation packages. *Journal of Computer and Information Technology*, 5(1):21–32, January 1997.

[11] IEEE. *IEEE Standard for Software Test Documentation (Std. 829)*.

[12] IEEE. *IEEE Guide for Software Quality Assurance Planning (Std.983)*, 1986.

[13] IEEE. *IEEE Standard for Software Verification and Validation Plans (Std. 1012)*, 1986.

[14] IEEE. *IEEE Standard for Software Unit Testing (Std. 1008)*, 1987.

[15] ISO. *Quality Management and Quality Assurance Standards (Std. 9001)*, 1991.

[16] ISO. *Process Model of Quality Evaluation and Measurement (Std. 9196)*, 1992.

[17] ISO. *Recommended Practice for Software Design (Std. 1016)*, 1993.

[18] ISO. *Life Cycle Processes (Std. 12207)*, 1995.

[19] H. Krawczyk, B. Krysztop, and J. Proficz. Time controlled environment for testing distributed applications. In *Proc. DAPSYS'98*, Pudapest, 1998.

[20] H. Krawczyk, Sikorski, S. M., Szejko, and B. Wiszniewski. A tool for quality evaluation of parallel and distributed software applications. In *Proc. 3rd Int. Conf. Parallel Processing and Applied Mathematics PPAM'99*, pages 413–426, Kazimierz Dolny, Poland, 1999.

[21] H Krawczyk and B Wiszniewski. Structural testing of parallel software in steps. In *Proc. 1st SEIHPC Workshop*, Braga, Portugal, 1996. COPERNICUS Programme.

[22] H. Krawczyk and B. Wiszniewski. *Analysis and Testing of Distributed Software Applications*. Research Studies Press Ltd., UK, 1998.

[23] John J. Marciniak, editor. *Encyclopedia of Software Engineering*. John Wiley & Sons, 1994.

[24] T. Miyoshi and M. Azuma. An empirical study of evaluating software development environment quality. *IEEE Trans. Software Eng.*, 19(5):425–435, May 1993.

[25] M.C. Paulk. SW-CMM v.2: Feedback and proposed changes. *Process Newsletter*, (7):5–10, Fall 1996.

[26] L. Ryan. Software usage metrics for real world software testing. *IEEE Spectrum*, 35(4), April 1998.

[27] A. Szczerba and B. Wiszniewski. A tool for testing communication events in TCP/IP environments. In D'Hollander et al., editors, *Parallel Programming: State of the Art and Perspectives*, pages 362–376. Elsevier Science - North Holland, 1996.

[28] S. Winter and P. Kacsuk. Software engineering for parallel processing. In *Proc. 8th Symp. on Microcomputer and Microprocessor Applications*, pages 285–293, Budapest, Hungary, 1994.

Part II

Tools and Environments

Chapter 10

The **GRADE** Graphical Parallel Programming Environment

Péter Kacsuk, Gábor Dózsa and Róbert Lovas

Abstract

GRADE is a graphical programming environment that supports the entire development cycle of parallel applications using the PVM communication library. It contains a set of fully integrated tools including a graphical editor, a code generator, a mapping toolbox, a distributed debugger, a monitoring tool, a performance visualisation tool and a parallel architecture simulator. GRADE provides unique and complete solution for efficient and easy development of parallel programs and it accelerates the re-engineering procedure of sequential programs for parallel computers significantly.

10.1 Introduction

As local area networks and clusters have become a basic part of today's computing infrastructure, more and more people encounter the possibility to exploit the available computational power of heterogeneous network of computers as well as PC/workstation clusters.

The most widely used paradigm for implementing applications on such distributed systems is the message-passing (MP) concept, and it is expected to be the most common approach for the next few years. The main reasons of its popularity are the simplicity of the concept and the fact that message-passing paradigm closely corresponds the way in which data are actually moved around in a distributed memory computer thus, MP libraries can be implemented very efficiently in such systems. Moreover, sequential languages (mainly C and FORTRAN) familiar to most application programmers can be used to perform the bulk of the computation.

Although there are quite a few MP systems (e.g. PVM, MPI) that enable the execution of parallel programs in heterogeneous environments, the lack of proper (i.e., user-friendly) support for development of such applications prevents most of the potential users from dealing with parallel programming.

To cope with the extra complexity of parallel programs arising due to inter-process communication and synchronization, we have designed a visual programming environment called GRADE (GRaphical Application Development Environment). Its major goal is to provide an easy-to-use, integrated set of programming tools for development of general message-passing applications to be run in both heterogeneous and homogeneous distributed computing systems. The central idea of GRADE is to support each stage of the parallel program development life-cycle by an integrated graphical environment where all the graphical views applied at the separate stages are related back to the original graph that defines the parallel program and which is designed and edited by the user.

The parallel program development life-cycle supported by GRADE is shown in Figure 10.1. Rectangles represent activities of the life-cycle and the grey ovals inside the rectangles represent the tools that support the corresponding activity in the GRADE environment. Except for the PVM library (represented by white ovals) all the other libraries (grey ovals outside the rectangles) and the tools were developed in the SEPP and HPCTI projects.

The first stage of the life-cycle is the program design which is supported by the GRAPNEL (GRAphical Process NEt Language) language and the GRED graphical editor. In GRAPNEL, all process management and inter-process communication activities are defined graphically in the user's application. Low-level details of the underlying message-passing system are hidden. GRADE generates all message-passing library calls automatically on the basis of the graphical code of GRAPNEL. Since graphics hides all the low level details of message-passing, GRADE is an ideal programming environment for application programmers who are not experienced in parallel programming (for example, for chemists, biologists, etc.). GRAPNEL is a hybrid language: while graphics is introduced to define parallel activities, textual language parts (C/C++ or FORTRAN) are used to describe sequential activities. The GRED editor helps the user to construct the graphical parts of GRAPNEL programs in an efficient and fast way. GRAPNEL programs edited by GRED are saved into the so-called GRP file which contains both the graphical and textual information of GRAPNEL programs.

The second stage is mapping which can be done either by a very simple, user written mapping table or by a more sophisticated automatic mapping tool. The mapping information is also inserted into the GRP file.

The third step is the pre-compilation of GRAPNEL programs. This stage has the goal to translate the graphical language information of the GRP file into MP library function calls and to generate the C/C++ or FORTRAN source code of the GRAPNEL program. For the time being, only C/C++ source code is generated by the GRP2C pre-compiler. For the sake of flexibility MP library function calls are not called directly in the resulting C code, rather an internal library, called GRAPNEL Library is introduced.

Beside generating the C/C++ source code, GRP2C also creates a cross-reference file in order to support symbolic debugging as well as a *makefile* to facilitate compiling and linking.

The fourth step is compiling and linking. Here a standard C/C++ compiler and linker are used. The GRAPNEL, Tape/PVM and PVM libraries are linked to the C/C++ source code of GRAPNEL programs. Notice that the Tape/PVM library can be omitted if performance monitoring is not needed. In a heterogeneous cluster of different kinds of workstations executables are generated for each machine type. This approach has the advantage that the programmer does not have to worry about updating executables on each different computer whenever the design of the parallel program has been changed. It has to be mentioned here that the third and fourth steps of the life-cycle are merged into a single step from the point of view of GRADE users.

Having the necessary executables for the parallel/distributed computing system, the next stage is validating and debugging the code with the help of the DDBG debugger [1, 3]. It

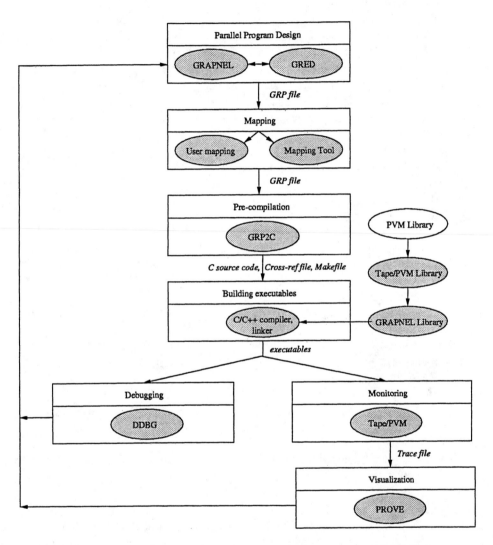

Figure 10.1: Program Development Life-cycle Support in **GRADE**

is important to emphasize that debugging information is related directly back to the user's graphical code. Step-by-step execution is possible both at the usual C instruction level and at the higher graphical icon level. This feature significantly facilitates parallel debugging which is the most time-consuming stage of parallel program development.

After debugging the code, the next step is performance analysis. First, it requires performance monitoring that generates an event trace file at program execution time and then, performance visualisation that displays performance oriented information by several graphical views. Performance monitoring is performed by the Tape/PVM monitor and its output trace file is processed by the performance visualisation tool PROVE.

As Figure 10.1 shows, any correctness or performance bug requires a step back to the program design stage where the error can be corrected in GRAPNEL by the GRED editor. When the code is bug-free the executables can be run any platforms supported by GRADE.

The GRADE system currently consists of the following tools as main components:

- GRED: A graphical editor to design parallel applications. The editor supports the syntax of the graphical language GRAPNEL.

- GRP2C: A pre-compiler to produce the C/C++ code with PVM function calls from the graphical GRAPNEL program.

- Mapping tools: Several mapping algorithms have been implemented and integrated into GRADE as a mapping toolbox to facilitate distribution of processes among the available processors [2].

- DDBG : Distributed debugger that support testing and debugging of GRAPNEL applications.

- Tape/PVM[1] [4] : monitoring tool to collect event traces during execution time of PVM and GRAPNEL applications.

- PROVE: A visualisation tool to analyse and interpret Tape/PVM trace file information and present them to the programmer graphically.

- Simulator: A parallel architecture simulator has also been integrated for performance prediction purposes [5].

The current chapter explains the concept of GRAPNEL in Section 10.2. The detailed description of the main features of GRAPNEL are given in Section 10.3. The GRED graphical editor is described in Section 10.4. The other tools of GRADE are described in the subsequent chapters: the GRP2C pre-compiler and the structure of the GRP file in Chapter 11, mapping and load balancing tools in Chapter 12, the DDBG debugger in Chapter 13, the Tape/PVM monitor and the PROVE visualisation tool in Chapter 14. There is also a mapping tool and architecture simulator which are integrated with GRADE. They are explained in Chapter 12 and Chapter 15, respectively. Finally, Chapter 17 gives a case study as a summary to explain how to use GRADE for program development.

---

[1]Tape/PVM is a monitoring tool for PVM programs having been developed at LMC-IMAG, Grenoble, France.

10.2 The concept of GRAPNEL

There has been several attempts to support parallel programming with graphical user interfaces and particularly with graphical languages. A collection of such languages and their programming models have been summarized and compared in Chapter 2. One of those languages is GRAPNEL that has been developed in the framework of the SEPP/HPCTI projects.

There are several parallel programming paradigms that are successfully used in real-life application programs. The two main such paradigms are the shared memory concept and the message passing approach. In the design of a parallel programming language, the first decision point is the selection of the programming paradigm the language will support. In case of GRAPNEL, the message passing approach (and particularly PVM) was chosen since this paradigm can be easily used for the whole range of parallel systems like supercomputers, clusters and even metacomputing systems.

The main motivation of designing GRAPNEL was to hide the low level details of the underlying message passing library (i.e., PVM) by an easily conceivable graphical user interface that can help the user both in the design, compilation and debugging stages of parallel program development. However, graphical languages have the danger that the usage of too much graphics can reduce the readability of the program and results in the opposite effect for which they were designed. Hence, keeping the right balance between graphics and text is a decisive factor in the applicability of a graphical language. Accordingly, GRAPNEL applies graphics only at those levels where parallelism appears and every other code could be written in a well known textual language like C/C++ or FORTRAN.

GRAPNEL is based on a hierarchical design concept that can support both top-down and bottom-up design methodologies. A GRAPNEL program has three hierarchical layers which are as follows from top to bottom:

1. Application layer is a graphical layer which is used to define the component processes, their communication ports as well as their connecting communication channels. Shortly, the Application layer serves for describing the interconnection topology of the component processes.

2. Process layer is also a graphical layer where several types of graphical blocks are applied: loop construct, conditional construct, text block, input/output activity block and graph block. These blocks can be arranged in a flow-chart like graph to describe the internal structure of processes.

3. Text layer is used to define those parts of the program that are inherently sequential and hence a textual language like C/C++ or FORTRAN can be applied at this level. These textual codes are defined inside the text blocks of the Process layer.

The top-down design method can be used to describe parallel activities of the application program. At the top level the inter process communication structure can be defined and then in the next layer the internal structure of individual processes can be specified. In this level and in the Text layer the bottom-up and top-down design methods can be used in a mixed way. In the case of the top-down design method, the user can define the graphical structure of the process and then uses the Text layer to define the C/C++ or FORTRAN code for the sequential blocks. In the bottom-up design approach the user can inherit code from existing C/C++ or FORTRAN libraries and then will build up the internal process structure based on these inherited functions.

This hybrid hierarchical language approach has many advantages compared to a pure textual message passing program as well as compared to a completely graphical approach. Advantages compared to a pure textual message passing program are as follows:

1. The programmer does not have to learn the syntax of PVM. The graphical notation is much simpler and easier to learn than the notations of an MP library like PVM.

2. The **GRAPNEL** pre-compiler can check systematically and automatically the correctness of communication protocols between communicating processes. This checking is impossible in PVM though incorrect protocols are the main source of programming errors in message passing parallel programs.

3. The separation of parallel and sequential code by hierarchical layers facilitates the re-engineering of existing sequential programs into parallel ones.

4. Graphical debugging can be applied at the Application and Process layer and is much more convenient and user friendly than textual debugging.

Advantages compared to a completely graphical approach:

1. A completely graphical approach would result in huge graphs that would be very difficult to understand by the programmer. The separation of parallel and sequential code results in screen size graphs that can be easily conceived by the user.

2. A completely graphical approach would require to rewrite existing sequential codes into a graphical one. It would prevent the user from applying of existing libraries.

3. A completely graphical approach would mix up sequential and parallel code segments which would make design, debugging and code maintenance much more difficult.

10.3   The **GRAPNEL** language

The GRAPNEL programming model is based on the message passing paradigm. The programmer can define processes which perform the computation independently in parallel, and interact only by sending and receiving messages among themselves.

10.3.1   The Process Model

A process can be either a single unit or a member of a process group. Similarly to MPI, the process group is an ordered collection of processes, and each process is uniquely identified by its rank number within the group. Process groups can be used in two important ways. Firstly, they can be used to specify which processes are involved in a collective communication operation, such as a broadcast. Secondly, they can be used as an abstraction mechanism to support the structured design at the level of processes, i.e., processes which perform logically the same task, or a more or less independent subtask, can be put physically into a group to be managed together. Since the process groups can be nested (a group may contain further groups), they support the hierarchical design of the distributed application and facilitate to locate communication related errors during the testing and debugging phase. Recall that PVM supports the process group concept and hence GRAPNEL was also designed to support this concept.

PVM supports dynamic process creation but MPI-1 does not. The Occam experience showed that static process creation is sufficient to program any parallel algorithm and hence for the sake of simplicity GRAPNEL was designed as a static language like.

To manage the most often used regular process topologies, predefined topology templates are supported by GRAPNEL. In these regular arrangements only the representative process types of the topology must be defined by the user, the arrangement itself is generated automatically at runtime based on size parameter(s). This feature also supports to test and debug the application in a relatively small size and then the homogeneous topology[2] can be expanded without violating the correctness of the program.

10.3.2 The Communication Model

Communications among processes are either *point-to-point* or *group* communications, and can be *synchronous* or *asynchronous* ones. Communication operations always take place via communication ports which can belong to either processes or groups, and which are connected by channels. Every port of a process has its own protocol to ensure that the form of the transmitted data is the same at both the sender and receiver sides. The programmer must define the protocol explicitly by writing the appropriate list of data types to be delivered by the port.

Inside a process the *Communication Input* and *Output Action* nodes represent the two fundamental types of the communication operations which can be characterized by two features:

1. How many ports of the process are involved in the operation (one or more)

2. What type of operation is applied

The following different types of operations are available:

1. **Simple input** or **output** action (CAI or CAO). One or several ports participate in the communication, so data can be received from or sent to one or several other processes (or process groups).

2. **Alternative input** action (CAIALT). Several ports participate in the input operation, so data can be received from several other processes, but only one message must be selected from the alternatives.

The first type corresponds to the usual point-to-point *send-receive* instruction pairs applied in general in the MP systems. The second type represent an extremely important higher level operation, it corresponds to the ALT construct of Occam and the wild-card message tag of PVM and MPI.

Collective communication operations can be performed by defining special compound ports to a process group. Via these *group ports*, all members in the group can be accessed by an outer process. Applying this technique the following types of collective communication operations become available:

- **Broadcast** $(1 \rightarrow n)$. The outer process can send the same data to each process in the group.

---

[2]Homogeneous means that processes which constitute the given regular topology have the same code (i.e., SPMD code)

- **Scattering** $(1 \rightarrow n)$. The data sent by the outer process is scattered among the processes of the target group, i.e., each process in the group receives its own different data from the sender process.

- **Gathering** $(n \rightarrow 1)$. Every process in the group sends its own different data to the receiver process.

- **Reduce** $(n \rightarrow 1)$. A reduce port performs global computations like choosing the minimum from the values sent by the member processes, or computing the sum of them, etc.

10.3.3 The Process

In GRAPNEL the most fundamental unit of the language is the *process* which manifests at two levels:

- Application Layer

- Process Layer

Every process has two graphical views: one for describing the communication connections (ports and channels) to the other processes (Application Layer), and one for describing the internal structure of the process (Process Layer).

The Application Layer

At this level a process is represented by a rectangle icon with caption (see Figure 10.2).

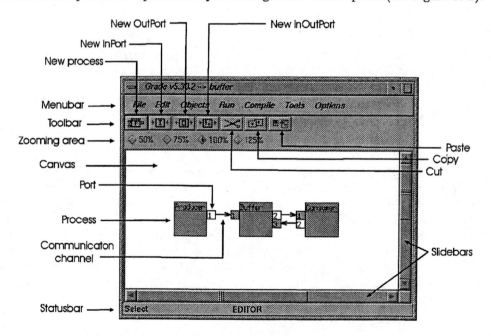

Figure 10.2: The Application Window of the GRED Editor

Attached to the edges of the process icon several small rectangles are used to represent the communication ports. Each port must be connected to a port of another process (or process group) by directed arcs (channels) representing the direction of message transfers. If there is an arc between two processes (or groups), they can communicate with each other during the execution of the program, otherwise, they cannot. There are three types of communication ports due to the direction of the data flow (Figure 10.2):

- input (represented by green boxes)
- output (represented by grey boxes)
- inout[3] (represented by half green-half grey boxes)

Each port has its own protocol which should ensure that the structure of the transmitted data always consistent concerning the sender and the receiver processes. The protocol is defined by a list of data types. The data structure of the message transferred by the port should match to this list of data types. For example, the list `int[3];float[2];` represents a protocol in which first, three integer numbers and then two float numbers should be packed in the message. If two ports are connected by a communication channel, their protocols should be the same and this equivalence is checked by the compiler.

The Process Layer

The internal structure of any process can be described at the Process Layer using graphical symbols to represent the control flow. Only those parts of the control flow must be specified in a graphical way that are related to communication operations. The point is that all communication instructions are represented by icons thus, if communication occurs in a specific branch of a conditional construct than the whole conditional construct must be defined graphically. Similarly, if communication is needed inside a loop, the whole loop construct must appear in a graphical way. Graphical code of an example process is shown in Figure 10.3.

These drawings can seem to be unnecessary or uncomfortable for those who are experienced in ordinary textual programming, but it takes the great advantage of shortening dramatically the debugging phase of program development. Using these kinds of graphical views of processes the programmer can track the whole application much more efficiently and can locate communication related errors faster than debugging the textual source code line by line.

Each graphical symbol possesses a corresponding piece of textual C/C++ code fragment to define the low level semantics of that symbol. The available icons to construct the graphical code of a process are listed as follows.

Loop Construct   This icon is used for any loop constructs in the program e.g. 'for', 'while' and 'do' structures (Figure 10.3). The icon consists of two arrows wrapping the body of the loop like parenthesis. The loop condition should be defined at the begin loop icon in the case of 'for' and 'while' loops and at the end loop icon for 'do' loops.

Conditional Construct   The icon of conditional constructs is used for any conditional structure like 'if' or 'switch' (Figure 10.3). The conditional expression should be defined on the upper triangle of this icon.

---

[3]The *inout* port is simple a graphical abbreviation of an input-output ports couple.

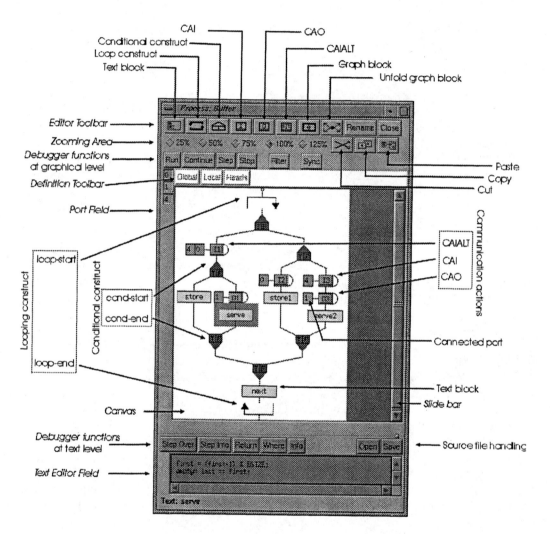

Figure 10.3: Process Window of the **GRED** Editor

Communication Action   Inside a process, the Communication Action (CA) symbols are used to perform input and output operations via the appropriate ports. The CA symbols can be divided into two fundamental groups:

- Communication Action Input (CAI) and

- Communication Action Output (CAO).

Actually, the graphical symbols for input (CAI) and output (CAO) are very similar and - in the simplest case - consist of two icons (a main and a satellite one) (see Figure 10.3). The main icon represents the sending or receiving actions of the communication, while the satellite icon represents a port of the process (which is defined at the Application Layer). The satellite icon defines the communication protocol and the main icon defines when to use the protocol and on which data. It is possible to use both synchronous and asynchronous output communication actions.

In GRAPNEL it is possible to express input/output operations from/to several processes simultaneously. In this case, the main icon has more satellite icons denoting that the process receives data from or send data to all processes connected to the ports represented by satellite icons. In the text code belonging to the main icon the following expression must be defined for each port denoted by satellite icons:

PORT *port-identifier* : *data-description*;

So the port must be identified firstly – because there are more ports connected to the main icon – and then the variables are defined where the data should be stored or should come from (i.e., *data-description*).

GRAPNEL contains an additional special CA symbol, called Alternative Communication Input Action (CAIALT, see Figure 10.3). In the case of Alternative CAI the main icon has several satellite icons, so the process can receive data from several other processes but only one message must be selected from the alternatives. In the text window belonging to the main icon, the programmer must define a similar expression for each port denoted by satellite icons like in the case of an ordinary CAI, but now they can contain an additional field to define guard conditions:

PORT *port-identifier* : GUARD *logical expression*: *data-description*;

If there are several ports whose guard conditions are satisfied (the logical expression is evaluated to true) and on which a message appears, the selection will be non-deterministic.

Blocks   Blocks are used to support the structured program design at the Process Layer. They own code fragments which can be two different types:

1. Text Block: The code fragment is written in textual way (in C/C++)

2. Graph Block: The code fragment is drawn using graphic symbols

If the code fragment, the user wants to put into a block, does not contain any CA (Communication Action) the Text Block[4] can be used (see Figure 10.3) otherwise, the Graph Block must be applied (see Figure 10.4). Graph Blocks can be nested and they have the same satellite icons as we have seen at the CA symbols because in this case the Graph block itself denotes the sending and/or receiving operations at that level.

[4]The Text Block is also called SEQ (sequential) block in GRAPNEL terminology.

10.3.4   Process Groups and Group Ports

Process groups were introduced both in PVM and MPI. In the case of GRAPNEL, they can help the user in two respects:

1. Sub-graph abstraction: structured process topologies can be constructed by defining compound nodes (i.e., sub-graphs) to get a clear view of large process communication graphs. The role of process groups, in this sense, is quite similar to that of graph blocks applied in the Process layer.

2. Group communication: scope of a communication operation can be extended to a whole group by defining communication ports for process groups (i.e., *Group ports*).

Groups are often used as container objects for processes that are logically separated from the rest of the application (e.g., they solve a separate sub-problem together). In such a case, it might be necessary to access several or even all members of that group in one communication step in order, for instance, to distribute some initial data for them or to collect their results. To support such communication operations, the user can define group ports. All member processes of a group can be accessed via such group ports without drawing the channels to the member processes individually.

Similarly to graph blocks, process groups can be nested, too. The user can create new groups inside existing ones without any limitation regarding the number of levels in the hierarchy.

In order to support efficient translation of frequently used collective communication and computation operations into PVM or MPI code, GRAPNEL provides *multicast, scatter, gather* and *reduce* type of ports for such operations.

10.3.5   Communication Templates

A communication template describes a group of processes that have a pre-defined regular interconnection topology. The user only has to define the actual size and all the processes and channels comprising the group are created by the system automatically. The most relevant difference between a communication template and a simple process group is the ability to change the number of member processes without modifying the graphical code of the application. GRAPNEL defines such communication templates for the most common regular process topologies like Process Farm, Pipe, 2D Mesh and Tree. Similarly to process groups, templates can have group ports, too.

10.4   GRED

GRED is a graphical editor that supports the construction of GRAPNEL programs. It is important to note that the GRED editor supports only a subset of the GRAPNEL language due to the limited manpower being available in the SEPP/HPCTI projects. Thus, the user cannot create currently process groups, group ports and communication templates with the help of GRED.

According to the three levels of GRAPNEL, GRED offers basically three different types of windows for editing parallel programs. These windows are introduced in top-down order as follows.

10.4.1 Application Window

This window is used to define the top level graphical description of the parallel application. Processes, communication ports and connections among the processes must be defined graphically. In Figure 10.2, a sample window of this type is depicted. It contains the following main areas: Menubar, Toolbar, Zooming area, Canvas, Slidebars and Status bar.

The Application Window plays the role of the central console of the whole GRADE system and hence its menubar serves both to perform various editing actions (e.g., to create new applications, to save and open existing ones, to modify process graphs, etc.) and to activate the different tools of GRADE (e.g., the distributed debugger and the performance visualizer).

The canvas, where the interconnection topology of the application program can be drawn, is the central part of the Application Window. In Figure 10.2, there are three processes represented as filled rectangles supplied with a name field showing the names of the processes (Producer, Buffer, Consumer). Small squares clung to them are ports connected by lines representing communication channels.

The toolbar can be used to perform different editing actions like creating processes, ports and channels, or moving existing processes to new locations. All these activities are executed only by simple mouse operations. Newly created processes and ports are automatically assigned with identifier numbers that can be easily modified by the user to a symbol. Creation of processes and ports are supported by buttons of the toolbar. The location of a new process is determined by a mouse clicking in the canvas. Newly created port icons are automatically arranged around the selected process to ensure the best possible layout of the graph (i.e., to minimize channel crossings).

Processes together with their ports and connected channels can be easily moved to new positions by simple mouse operations. Cut/copy/paste mechanism is provided as well with respect to processes or ports. Notice that in the case of copy, the complete internal structure (if already defined) of the copied process will be replicated and passed to the new copy of the process. The scrolling and zooming of the communication graph are also supported and it is rather necessary when the graph tends to be too large.

10.5 Process Window

After finishing the definition of the communication layout of the application program in the Application Window, the next step is the definition of the internal structure of the component processes. The Process Window serves for graphically describing the message-passing related parts of the control flow of individual processes as shown by Figure 10.3 for the process Buffer of Figure 10.2.

The Process Window of a process can be opened by a double mouse click on the process icon in the Application Window. The Process Window contains eight main areas: Editor Toolbar, Zooming area, Debugger Toolbars, Definition Toolbar, Port Field, Canvas, Text Editor Field and optional Slidebars (used only if the size of the process graph is bigger than that of the Canvas).

The Editor Toolbar provides buttons for defining the various graphical structures than can be applied at the process level. These structures are: Text block, Loop construct, Conditional construct, CAI (Communication Action Input), CAO (Communication Action Output), CAIALT (Communication Action Alternative Input) and Graph block. The icons of these graphical structures are shown in Figure 10.3. The creation of a new graphical structure happens by simple mouse clicks. The two compound structures, the Loop construct and the Conditional construct, are always defined by two icons: by a begin icon and by an end icon. The begin and end icons are always placed in pairs by the editor. Notice that the drawing of the process graph does not require any real drawing activity. By simply using the mouse, graphs of any complexity can be constructed. Every icon is placed automatically on the canvas, i.e., the layout of the visual control flow is always generated by the system. It is one of the main achievements of **GRED** which makes the construction of process graphs extremely easy and fast.

The editor also helps the user to find the matching begin and end icons of the loop and conditional constructs: when the user clicks on the begin icon of a loop or conditional construct the whole graph of the selected construct including its begin and end icons is highlighted.

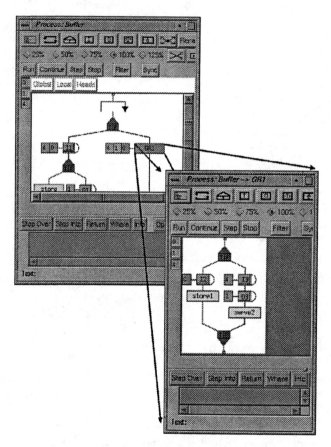

Figure 10.4: Sample Graph Block in **GRED**

In order to support the structured design of the visual control flow and to keep the size of the process window smaller than that of the screen size, the Graph block symbol is provided to fold parts of the graph into a single icon. Such a Graph block can be considered as a graphical macro instruction and they can be nested arbitrary deeply. Recall that a Graph block always contains communication operations since otherwise it could be replaced by a Text block. The contents of a Graph block icon can either be unfolded in place of the icon by means of the Unfold graph block button or a new (Graph Block) window can be opened for it as shown by Figure 10.4. Notice that the structure of the Graph Block Window is very similar to that of the Process Window. The only difference is that the Definition Toolbar is omitted in the Graph Block Window since it does not represent a stand-alone process and hence global/local data or header file definitions are not needed here.

When a Process Window is created for a process, all the ports of the process defined in the Application Window are inherited and placed as buttons in the Port Field (left edge) of the Process Window. They can be attached either to communication action icons to define the target/source of the communication or to Graph blocks to make them accessible inside those blocks. Whenever a communication action (CAI, CAO or CAIALT) is placed in the process graph the necessary port(s) should be connected to it. As in other cases, it can be done by mouse clicking. The editor automatically prohibits to connect input ports to CAO icons and output ports to the CAI and CAIALT icons. Such on-line editor checks significantly reduce the likelihood of making errors in coding parallel programs.

The Text Editor Field of the Process Window serves to define the necessary textual code for the icons of the graphical structures. It is obvious that the Text block contains textual code. However, even for the other graphical structures some short of textual code is necessary. In the begin icon of for/while loops, we have to define textually the usual loop expression, i.e., the loop variable, its range of values, etc. In the begin icon of the Conditional construct, the branch conditions should be defined. In CAI and CAIALT icons, the variables where the incoming message to be stored should be defined textually. In the case of CAIALT, additionally, guards can be defined for the possible input ports. In a CAO icon, the variables should be defined whose values will be sent through the attached port. Textual code belongs to the ports, as well. Their role is to describe the port protocols. Selecting an icon of the process graph will load its associated textual code to the Text Editor Field where the user can edit it.

Note that in case of large textual code parts that might belong to Text blocks the user has the opportunity to invoke an arbitrary external text editor by double-clicking on the corresponding icon. The type of this external editor can be defined through some specific UNIX environment variables thus, the programmer may use his/her favorite text editor (e.g., emacs, vi, etc.).

Any subgraph of the process graph can be selected either by a simple mouse click (if it consists of a structure) or by a series of mouse clicks (if it consists of several structures). For example, a loop containing arbitrary complex subgraph can be selected by a simple mouse click on the begin icon of the loop. The selected subgraph can be removed or a copy of it can be saved by another click on the appropriate button. In both cases the subgraph can be inserted to any arc of the process graph in two steps. First the arc should be selected by a mouse click on the arc, then a mouse click is needed to the 'Paste' button. Notice that in such case, not only the subgraph is placed to the selected arc but all the associated textual codes are copied, too. This feature of GRED significantly facilitates and accelerates the construction of even large process graphs.

Zooming and scrolling of the graphs are also possible by buttons of the Zooming area. Furthermore, the Process Window has three special buttons in the Definition Toolbar (labeled 'Global', 'Local' and 'Heads'). They can be applied to invoke text editors to define global/local data or header files for the process. Finally, the buttons of the Debugger Toolbars are used during debugging and their role is explained in Chapter 13.

10.6   Conclusions

The most important advantages of the GRADE environment that make it unique among the existing message-passing based program development systems are summarized as follows. First of all, graphics hides all the details of underlying low-level message-passing libraries and this fact implies two important consequences.

1. The learning curve of the system is not steep. One of the ultimate goal of the GRADE developer team was to facilitate spreading high performance computing technology by approaching non-professional programmers (e.g., mathematicians, physicists) who have large problems to solve but who are familiar only with ordinary sequential languages (i.e., FORTRAN, C) and do not want to deal with the details of parallel programming. Easy learning is also important if education is concerned and the GRADE system has already involved in several practical courses at various universities to aid teaching of parallel and distributed software engineering.

2. Fast prototype design is ensured that is ultimate for efficient development of industrial applications. A prototype program in GRADE is the graphical skeleton code of the application in which text blocks contain simple delay instructions instead of real complex computations. The user can easily modify such skeleton code by means of the graphical editor to study various potential solutions of a problem before elaborating the details of the implementation.

Furthermore, GRADE is a fully integrated development environment that covers all relevant phases of the development life-cycle (planning/coding, correctness debugging, performance analysis/debugging) of parallel programs. In all of these phases, the same high-level graphical user interface is provided for the user. As a result, runtime events collected by either the debugger or the monitor can always be related directly back to the user's graphical code.

The main limitation of GRAPNEL is its static nature, i.e., dynamic process creation is not possible. It is painful in the case of algorithms where processes could be created in a recursive way. For example, the well-known divide-and-conquer parallelization style requires recursive structures. Nevertheless, the problem can be avoided by constructing statically the necessary process structure for a certain depth and afterwards inside the leaf processes (at the deepest level) sequential recursion can be used. With similar techniques most of the problems requiring dynamic process creation can be solved by an equivalent static solution scheme.

References

[1] J.C. Cunha, J. Lourenço, and V. Duarte. Using DDBG to support testing and high-level debugging interfaces. *Computers and Artificial Inteligence*, 17(5):429–439, 1998.

[2] L. Hluchý, M. Dobrucký, and J. Astalos. Hybrid approach to task allocation in distributed systems. *Computer and Artificial Intelligence*, 17(5):469–480, 1998.

[3] J. Lourenço, J.C. Cunha, H. Krawczyk, P. Kuzora, M. Neyman, and B. Wiszniewski. An integrated testing and debugging environment for parallel and distributed programs. In *Proceedings of the 23rd EUROMICRO Conference (EUROMICRO'97)*, pages 291–298, Budapeste, Hungary, September 1997. IEEE Computer Society Press.

[4] E. Maillet. Issues in performance tracing with Tape-PVM. In J. Dongarra et al., editors, *Proc. Second European PVM User's Group Meeting, Lyon*, pages 143–148. Hermes, 1995.

[5] R. Suppi, E. César, J. Falguera, M. Serrano, J. Sorribes, E. Luque, G. Dózsa, P. Kacsuk, and T. Fadgyas. Simulation in parallel software design. *International Journal of Parallel and Distributed Systems and Networks*, 1(2):85–92, 1998.

Chapter 11

GRAPNEL to C Translation in the **GRADE** Environment

Dániel Drótos, Gábor Dózsa and Péter Kacsuk

Abstract

The chapter explains the internal structure and representation of GRAPNEL programs as well as the transformation mechanism by which a GRAPNEL program is translated to a C/C++ source program by the GRP2C pre-compiler. Various logical layers of GRAPNEL applications are also discussed including the interface between the GRAPNEL and the PVM level communication instructions.

11.1 Introduction

The GRAPNEL [3] language and its editor GRED [4] are described in Chapter 10 in detail from the point of view of potential users. The current chapter explains the internal structure and representation of GRAPNEL programs as well as the transformation mechanism by which a GRAPNEL program is translated to a C/C++ source program. This chapter also reveals how the PVM [1] function calls are automatically inserted into the C/C++ source code generated from GRAPNEL programs.

Readers who are interested only in the use of the GRADE programming environment can skip this chapter. Reading of this chapter is highly recommended for those who wish to learn about the techniques by which graphical programs can be translated into conventional textual languages extended with calls to communication libraries.

11.2 Layers of **GRAPNEL** programs

GRAPNEL programs can be represented by several layers as shown in Figure 11.1. In the current section we summarize the role of the various layers and the transformation mechanisms between the layers.

11.2.1   GRAPNEL layer

GRAPNEL provides the top layer of the GRADE system where the user can construct his/her parallel program by a graphical editor GRED. At this layer the program is represented graphically as described in Chapter 10. This representation is easy to understand for the program developer but it is difficult to interpret by programs like parsers. Because of this difficulty GRED saves the graphical program in a plain text file, called GRP file, which is used by the tools of the GRADE system. GRED is also able to read back GRP files and restore graphical representation on the screen. The GRP file is an internal form of the GRAPNEL program containing information on both the graphical and textual parts. The detailed description of the GRP file is given in Section 11.3.

11.2.2   C-source layer

The GRP file is translated into C-source by the GRAPNEL pre-compiler called GRP2C. The goal of this translation is that all the graphical information which represents C code should be replaced with the equivalent C source code. However, those graphical information that are relevant only for drawing the GRAPNEL graphs on the screen without representing any C code (for example X-Y co-ordinates of graphical nodes) are omitted during this translation. Notice that, while the GRP file is completely equivalent to the original GRAPNEL code, the C-source generated by the GRP2C pre-compiler is not.

11.2.3   GRAPNEL API layer

Because the communication layer upon which GRAPNEL programs run can be implemented by different kinds of message passing systems, another software layer is required which hides all dependencies on communication layer. This layer is an Application Programming Interface (API) and because its physical representation is a code library, it is called as GRAPNEL Library. This API layer can support interfacing to a message passing system, e.g. PVM, MPI ([2]), or a direct interface to an operating system. This API consists of GRAPNEL (or shortly: GRP) functions. Higher layers of the GRADE system and particularly, the generated C-sources use these GRP functions to start processes and send messages.

An API for PVM is already available and support for other systems such as MPI and the QNX operating system is planned to be developed.

The API has a very important functionality: it creates trace information during execution of the developed GRAPNEL program. Every time when the higher layer calls a GRAPNEL function to start a process or send a message, the corresponding API function makes a record in the trace-file. The API functions do not implement their own trace generation methods but they use the tracing tool Tape/PVM in order to produce trace-files. After the execution the generated trace-file can be visualised by PROVE as described in Chapter 14.

11.2.4   Message passing layer

This layer should be a widely used communication system. PVM is a good choice because it has been ported to many operating systems. Because this layer hides operating system dependencies the GRADE system can be hardware and operating system independent.

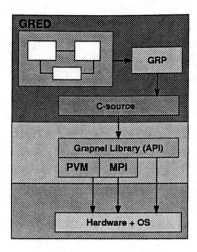

Figure 11.1: Layers of GRAPNEL programs

11.2.5 Hardware layer

The lowest layer is the computer hardware and its operating system. GRAPNEL uses the message passing paradigm so the operating system should support messages between processes. Most systems do it but in some cases it is difficult to use different interprocess communication systems of different OSs. Generally we use a special software layer (i.e., PVM) on top of the operating system which hides the differences in the message passing facilities.

11.3 Text representation of **GRAPNEL** applications: GRP files

GRAPNEL applications are represented by mixed graphical icons and textual code segments on the screen. In order to store such applications on the disk or to produce their executable code they are saved into the so-called GRP files. GRP files are plain text files that contain all necessary information about GRAPNEL programs. The exact syntax of these files are defined in BNF form (see Appendix 1). The next subsections give a brief summary about their contents.

11.3.1 GRP File Format

GRP files have human readable format. They store information in a well structured hierarchical way. Different hierarchical levels are always enclosed by braces. This hierarchical structure is depicted in Figure 11.2. The top level structure is the "Application" that consists of two main parts: "HeaderPart" and "ProgramPart". They are used for storing information related to the whole application and to the individual processes, respectively. Note that the BNF description defines another part called "ScreenPart" but it is not currently used.

The "HeaderPart" consists of two main sections: "Editor" and "Mapping". Both sections contain various "Groups". In order to be flexible, the GRP syntax does not fix the number

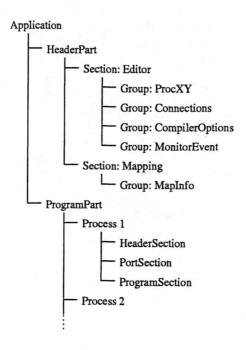

Figure 11.2: Hierarchical Structure of GRP Files

or names of such "Groups". "Groups" in the "Editor" section that are currently used by GRADE are as follows.

- "Group: ProcXY": stores information about what are the processes comprising the application and what are the physical locations of their icons in the GRED editor.

- "Group: Connections": defines the communication channels that are established among various application processes.

- "Group: CompilerOptions": defines the necessary options to be passed to the compiler during application compilation. These include access paths for extra include files or libraries that are referred to in the text part of the corresponding GRAPNEL code.

- "Group: MonitorEvent": information about what program events the user is interested in during monitoring. Monitoring is done at the graphical level of GRAPNEL programs so, various groups of graphical code elements can be selected here to be monitored at run-time.

The other important section in the "HeaderPart" is the "Mapping" section. It contains only a single group called "MapInfo" that defines how the GRAPNEL processes are to be distributed among available machines and processors.

To summarize, the "HeaderPart" contains all information about the application except definitions of the internal structure of the individual processes that are described in the "ProgramPart" of the GRP file. Both the internal program graph of the processes and their C source code attached to the various nodes of the graph are stored in the "ProgramPart". In fact, the "ProgramPart" is a list of process descriptions. Processes are separated in this list by the keyword "Process" followed by the numerical ID and the name of the particular process. Description of a process consists of three sections: "HeaderSection", "PortSection" and "ProgramSection".

The "HeaderSection" contains the definition of program variables and include files as plain C code defined by the user. "PortSection" defines the type and protocol of ports. Though the BNF definition provides the possibility to describe connections to other ports (i.e., channels) here as well, they are rather defined in the "Connection Group" of the "Editor" section (see above) in order to ensure that the same process may easily be included into different applications. (Further support for such re-use of processes is explained in Section 11.3.2 in detail.) Finally, the "ProgramSection" defines the code of a particular process including a text representation of the graphical code and the C source code belonging to various nodes of the GRAPNEL process graph.

In "ProgramSection", each node of the graphical code of a process is described by an individual "ProgItem"structure. A "ProgItem" structure is defined by five attributes: type, numeric ID, name, parameter list and C source code. Type corresponds to the type of graph node in the GRAPNEL code thus, it can be SEQ for sequential block, CAI for a receive (i.e., input) node, IFB for the top icon of a conditional construct, etc. The numeric ID is automatically generated by GRED and it is guaranteed to be unique in a particular process. The name attribute can be an arbitrary string defined by the user on construction of the graph. The C source code attribute describes the C/C++ code defined by the user for the particular node.

Finally, the most interesting attribute is the parameter list that is mainly used to describe the spatial relations among different nodes of the code graph. For this purpose, several "Cin" and "Cout" parameters are defined for each "ProgItem" structure that are referred to as "Connection" in the BNF description (see Section 11.7). "Cin" and "Cout" parameters denote incoming and outgoing control lines of the corresponding node in the graph, respectively. The actual number of such parameters depends on the type of the node, e.g., a "ProgItem" that describes a SEQ node (i.e., sequential block) has exactly one "Cin" and one "Cout" parameters while an IFB node (i.e., begin node of a graphical 'if' construct) has one "Cin" and two "Cout".

A connection parameter is identified by a numerical ID that appears right after the "Cin" or "Cout" keyword. Control line segments among graph nodes have unique numerical IDs and these line IDs are referred to in braces after the connection ID of "Cin" and "Cout" parameters. Thus, two "ProgItems" describe two nodes connected by a control line in the program graph if the ID of the control line appears in braces in parameter lists of both items. This way, the order of "ProgItems" structures is irrelevant in the GRP files since the program graph is reconstructed by matching the connection parameters. An example program graph and its corresponding GRP file are explained in detail in Section 11.4.

Furthermore, the parameter list of a "ProgItem" contains "Port" parameter(s) as well if the corresponding node denotes inter-process communication (i.e., CAI, CAO or CAIALT nodes). Such "Port" parameter defines the port via which data transfer is to take place together with the data to be transferred. In case of communication node, the list may contain additional parameters that can affect the execution behaviour of the communication operation, e.g., a send operation can be either "BLOCKED" or "UNBLOCKED" and a guard expression can be assigned to any send or receive action.

11.3.2   Naming Convention of GRP Files

GRP files are interpreted by a parser that is integrated both into the GRED editor and the
GRP2C code generator. This parser enables a GRAPNEL application to be split into several
GRP files. Thus, different parts of the same application can be stored in separate files.
According to the two distinct levels of the graphical code, information that must be saved
into GRP files can be divided into two main groups. The first one concerns the global view
of the application including the application level GRAPNEL code while the second one deals
with local information about individual processes. Each process is saved into an individual
GRP file that has the name "*process-name*.prc" where *process-name* is the user defined
name of the particular process. All global information about an application are saved into
a separate GRP file named "*appl-name*.app" where *appl-name* is the user defined name of
the application.

Saving local information of processes into separate files supports the re-use of process
codes across different applications. By using the GRED editor, the user can open individual
process files belonging to other GRAPNEL applications to insert those processes into the
program being edited. Furthermore, it is also possible to save the code of any process individually, e.g., to store it in a "process warehouse" directory for later use in other GRAPNEL
applications.

11.4   Example GRP Files: The Bounded Buffer Application

A simple example program is presented in this section to illustrate how the contents of GRP
files look like in practice. The whole application consists of three processes as it is depicted
in Figure 11.3. Process *Producer* produces data items and sends them to the *Buffer* process
that stores those items in a fixed size buffer. If this buffer is full, *Buffer* process stops
receiving items. In parallel, process *Consumer* sends requests to the *Buffer* to get new
items to consume. If the buffer is empty, the *Consumer's* request is not accepted by *Buffer*.

As explained in the previous section, such an application is saved into four separate
GRP files. One file describes the application related global information (*buffer.app*) and
each process has its own GRP file containing the text representation of its GRAPNEL code.
For the sake of brevity, only two of these files are discussed (*buffer.app* and *Consumer.prc*)
in the rest of this section.

The contents of the *buffer.app* file describing the application related global information
is listed as follows.

```
 1 Application: buffer
 2 {
 3 HeaderPart
 4   {
 5     Section: Editor
 6       {
 7         Group: ProcXY
 8           {
 9             Producer = 0,1;
10             Consumer = 6,1;
```

```
11                      Buffer = 3,1;
12                  }
13              Group: Connections
14                  {
15                      Producer= 0, "Buffer", 0;
16                      Consumer= 0, "Buffer", 1, 1, "Buffer", 4;
17                      Buffer= 0, "Producer", 0, 1, "Consumer", 0, 4, "Consumer", 1;
18                  }
19              Group: CompilerOptions
20                  {
21                  }
22              Group: MonitorEvent
23                  {
24                  }
25          }
26      Section: Mapping
27          {
28              Group: MapInfo
29                  {
30                      Producer="originf";
31                      Consumer="indigof";
32                      Buffer="ultra10f";
33                  }
34          }
35      }
36 }
```

The lines in this file are numbered for simplifying the explanation. The name of the GRAPNEL program is defined in the first line following the keyword "Application". Line 2 and line 36 contain the pair of braces that enclose the toplevel structure of the GRP file, i.e., the "Application" part. At line 3 the "HeaderPart" begins followed by its first section called "Editor" at line 5. Group "ProcXY" starting at line 7 defines the name of processes belonging to this application as well as the user defined location of their icons in the application window of the GRED editor.

The next group beginning at line 13 describes the channel connections among processes. Communication connections of each process are defined as a list in a separate line. The user defined name of the process is the head of the list followed by an equal sign. Each channel of that process is described then as three consecutive elements in the list: an integer value, a string and another integer value. The string is the name of the partner process connected by the channel and the two integers are the IDs of ports at the corresponding ends of the channel. For example, line 15 defines the single channel of the *Producer* process that joins port 0 of that process to port 0 of *Buffer* process.

The rest of the groups in the "Editor" section (i.e "CompilerOptions" and "MonitorEvent" starting at line 19 and 22, respectively) contain no information thus, this application requires no special compiler options and no filtering of monitor events is defined by the user.

The "HeaderPart" ends with the "Mapping" section (line 26) that contains mapping information in the "MapInfo" group (line 28). In each line of this group, the name of a GRAPNEL process is given followed by the name of the processor on which that process is to be executed. For instance, in line 30 process "Producer" is assigned to host "originf".

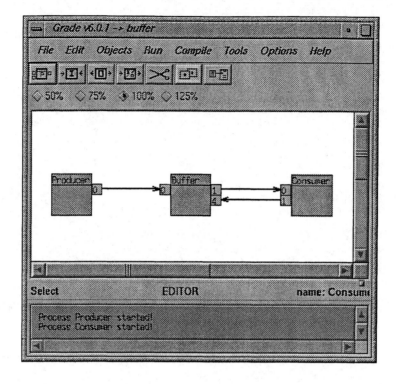

Figure 11.3: The Bounded Buffer Application

GRAPNEL code of process "Consumer" is depicted in Figure 11.4 and the GRP file describing it is listed as follows.

```
 1 Application: buffer
 2 {
 3 ProgramPart
 4 {
 5   Process 2 : Consumer
 6   HeaderSection
 7   {
 8     Heads {#@GRP@#    #@GRP@#}
 9     Global {#@GRP@##
10             define MAX 100
11             int i;
12             double item, request = 1.0;
13             #@GRP@#}
14     Local {#@GRP@#    #@GRP@#}
15   }
16   PortSection
17   {
18       InPort 0: data
```

```
19          { Proc:; PortID:; Type double[{#@GRP@# 1 #@GRP@#}];}
20        OutPort 1: request
21          { Proc:; PortID:; Type double[{#@GRP@# 1 #@GRP@#}];}
22     }
23     ProgramSection
24     {
25       DUMMYB: 115 "" {Cout 1: {1}}
26       LOOPB: 119 "LOOP-START"
27       {
28         Cin 1: {1}
29         Cout 2: {2}
30       }
31       {#@GRP@#  for(i= 1; i <= MAX; i++)  #@GRP@#}
32       CAO: 121 "O1"
33       {
34         BLOCKED
35         Cin 1: {2}
36         Cout 2: {3}
37         Port 1:  {#@GRP@#  request  #@GRP@#} ;
38       }
39       CAI: 122 "I1"
40       {
41         BLOCKED
42         Cin 1: {3}
43         Cout 2: {4}
44         Port 0:  {#@GRP@# item #@GRP@#} ;
45       }
46       SEQ: 123 "print"
47       {
48         Cin 1: {4}
49         Cout 2: {5}
50       }
51       {#@GRP@#
52        grp_printf("Item %d: %f consumed.\n",i,item);
53        #@GRP@#}
54       LOOPE: 120 "LOOP-END"
55       {
56         Cin 1: {5}
57         Cout 2: {6}
58       }
59       {#@GRP@#   #@GRP@#}
60       DUMMYE: 116 "" {Cin 1: {6}}
61     }
62 }
63 }
```

As every GRP file, this one starts with the top level "Application" part (at line 1) defining the name of the application to which the file belongs[1]. Braces in lines 2 and 63 enclose the body of this part which practically means the whole contents of this file. Since the file

---

[1]If the user imports a process from another application, the name of the former application is simply ignored when loading the process file

describes the code of an individual **GRAPNEL** process, "HeaderPart" misses here. Instead, the "ProgramPart" starts at line 3 that contains the description of process "Consumer" having the numerical ID 2 (see line 5).

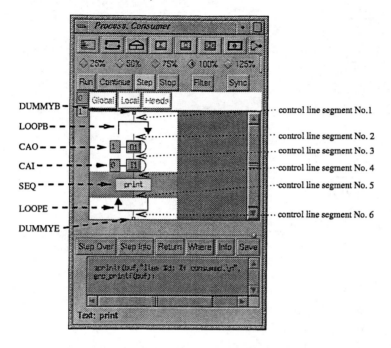

Figure 11.4: **GRAPNEL** Code of the Consumer Process

As it is mentioned already, the GRP description of a process consists of three sections: "HeaderSection", "PortSection" and "ProgramSection".

The "HeaderSection" of the "Consumer" process ranges from line 6 to line 15. It contains the definition of program variables and include files as plain C code defined by the user. C code segments are always enclosed by a pair of the following special character sequence "#@GRP@#". This sequence usually does not appear in normal C code thus, the parser can use them to identify the beginning and the end points of arbitrary user defined C code fragments in the GRP files. As it can be seen in the list of "Consumer.prc", no include statements or local variables are present for this process (see line 8 and 14, respectively) but three global variables (*i, item, double*) and one constant (*MAX*) are defined following the "Global" keyword in lines 9-13.

The "PortSection" begins at line 16 and ends at line 22. Process "Consumer" has two ports: an output port to send requests to "Buffer" and an input port to receive the requested data items (see port 1 and 0, respectively, in Figure 11.3). Description of a port in the GRP file consists of three main parts as follows:

- A keyword that defines the type of the port (i.e., "InPort", "OutPort" or "InOut-Port").

- The numerical ID and user defined name of the port,

- Port connection information of the port and the user defined protocol.

For example, line 18 and 19 contain the description of the only input port of the "Consumer" process. The numerical ID and name of this port are 0 and "data", respectively, as it can be seen in line 18. The next line describes the connection information and the protocol within braces. As mentioned already, connection information is usually defined in the "HeaderPart" so it is omitted here, i.e., partner process and port ID following the keywords "Proc" and "PortID", respectively, are left empty. The protocol is described as a list of types with size information. Each item in the list begins with the keyword "Type" followed by the actual type name. Size information (i.e., how many items of the particular type are used) is defined as a general C expression within square brackets after each type name. In line 19, the protocol list consists of only one item that defines a double type with size 1.

The rest of this GRP file (i.e., "ProgramSection" ranging from line 23 to 61) contains the text form of GRAPNEL code of the "Consumer" process. Each node in the graphical code has its corresponding "ProgItem" structure in the GRP description. Control line segments connected to the top and bottom of a node are indicated by "Cin" and "Cout" parameters, respectively.

To help understanding the correspondence between graphics and the text of the GRP files, types of different icons in the code and the internal numerical IDs of the control line segments are shown on the left and right sides, respectively, of the editor window in Figure 11.4.

The first and last node of the code graph in Figure 11.4 have type "DUMMYB" and "DUMMYE", respectively, and they are created by the GRED editor automatically to denote the start and end points of the graphical code. They are described as "ProgItem" structures in lines 25 and 60. The numerical ID of "DUMMYB" item is 115 and its parameter list describes only one out line (i.e., "Cout 1") that is associated with control line segment No. 1 as it is denoted within the braces. Since "DUMMYB" and "DUMMYE" nodes are used only for internal administrative purposes, no user defined code can be attached to them thus, "ProgItem" information in line 25 ends with the parameter list.

The first "real" node of the program graph (i.e., node representing real program code) is a "loop begin" node that is described in line 26. Type of the node is "LOOPB", the numerical ID is 119 and the user defined name is "LOOP-START". The parameter list indicates that control lines segment No. 1 and No. 2 connects to the top and to the bottom of the node (see "Cin" and "Cout" parameters in line 28 and 29), respectively. User defined C code attached to this node closes the description of the "ProgItem" structure in line 31.

The rest of the nodes are coded similarly in the GRP file. As extra information, line 34 and 41 indicate that both CAO and CAI nodes (i.e send and receive nodes) perform blocked communication operations, i.e., they stop the execution of the process until the data transfer has been carried out via the corresponding communication channel.

11.5   Translating graphical elements into C source files

After defining the structure of the GRP files, we summarize how the GRP2C pre-compiler generates standard C source code from the GRP files. The programs generated by the pre-compiler can be compiled with any standard C/C++ compiler and can be executed in the usual way.

Code generation consists of two phases. In the first phase the pre-compiler scans the GRP files and collects information about the elements of the program such as processes, ports, connections, etc. It is done by the parser part of the pre-compiler and it is available as a separate library which contains a class hierarchy (the parser has been written in C++). This class library is used by other tools of the GRADE environment, such as GRED, in order to read in and handle GRP files or manipulate them in other ways (Figure 11.5).

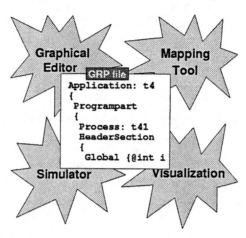

Figure 11.5: GRP file used by GRAPNEL system

When all the requested information about processes, ports, and other program elements are collected from the GRP files, the second phase of the translation can be done. The second phase is responsible for source code generation. The GRP2C pre-compiler creates one file for every process. The generated source files are unique executable C programs containing the necessary GRAPNEL Library calls to realize inter-process communication defined by the user in the graphical code.

Basically, each icon in the graphical code has its own text code fragment in the generated source file. In case of text blocks, the pre-compiler simply copies the user defined contents of those blocks into the generated file. In case of communication actions, such as input, output and alternative input nodes, the situation is a bit more complicated since the user defines only the list of variables participating in the message transfer and the port protocol and it is up to the pre-compiler to generate all C instructions performing the corresponding communication.

To illustrate the second case, let us examine the C instructions generated for a graphical send operation. For instance, the graphical code of process "Consumer" (see Figure 11.4) contains a CAO node to send a message via port 1. As it can be seen from the corresponding GRP file (line 21), this port protocol is defined as:

```
double[1]
```

and the list of variables attached to the icon consists of a single item (line 37):

```
request
```

which is a variable of type double defined in line 12.

The generated C code fragment corresponding to this CAO icon is listed as follows.

```
/* @@@BB(79): Source of block 79 (CAO). Line= 116. */
```

```
grp_pre_send(&Channs[to_receiver_0], Magic | MagicBlocked);
grp_pack(&request, (1), DOUBLE);
grp_post_send(&Channs[to_receiver_0], Magic | MagicBlocked);
/* @@@BE(79) End of source of block 79 (CAO). Line= 128. */
```

Names of GRAPNEL Library functions have the common prefix `grp_`. Three of them are used to realize such a send operation:

- `grp_pre_send()`: prepares the internal send buffer

- `grp_pack()` : packs the data to be sent into the send buffer

- `grp_post_send()` : sends the packed message (and waits for an acknowledgment in case of synchronous communication)

Data to be sent and the target of the particular communication are passed to these general functions as actual parameters.

11.6 Conclusions

Availability of powerful programming environments for heterogeneous networks is getting more and more important. GRADE provides a complex programming environment where the programmer can concentrate on high level abstractions without worrying about the low level details of communication primitives. Currently the GRADE environment supports PVM as target systems and it runs on UNIX hosts. The GRED editor generates GRP files from GRAPNEL programs and the GRP files are further translated into C source files by the GRP2C pre-compiler. Graphical symbols are language independent so it is possible to modify the pre-compiler tool to generate source files for other programming languages. The development team is going to support FORTRAN which is the most widely used language in high performance computing. New GRAPNEL API implementations are going to be developed as well to support more message passing systems for example, QNX operating system. Supporting the QNX operating system can be important for industrial real-time applications.

11.7 Appendix 1. BNF description of the GRP file format

Note: all reserved words (character strings between "" in the BNF definition) are case independent.

```
GRPfile::= AppList.
AppList::= Application | AppList Application.
Application::= "APPLICATION" ":" ID "{" AppPartList "}".
AppPartList::= AppPart | AppPartList AppPart.
AppPart::= HeaderPart | ProgramPart | ScreenPart.

HeaderPart::= "HEADERPART" "{" HeaderSList "}".
HeaderSList::= | HeaderSList HeaderSection.
HeaderSection::= "SECTION" ":" SectionName "{" GroupList "}".
```

```
SectionName::= "EDITOR" | "MAPPING" | "DEBUG" | "MONITOR" | "HARDWARE".
GroupList::= | GroupList Group.
Group::= "GROUP" ":" ID "{" ParamList "}".
ParamList::= | ParamList Param.
Param::= ID "=" ParamValueList ";".
ParamValueList::= ParamValue.
ParamValueList::= ParamValueList "," ParamValue.
ParamValue::= IntNumber | FloatNumber | StringParam.


ProgramPart::= "PROGRAMPART" "{" ProgramSList "}".
ProgramSList::= | ProgramSList Process.
Process::= "PROCESS" ProcessNumID ":" ID
           "HEADERSECTION" "{"ProcHgroupList "}"
           "PORTSECTION" "{" ProcSgroupList "}"
           "PROGRAMSECTION" "{"ProcPgroupList "}".
ProcessNumID::= | IntNumber.
ProcHgroupList::= | ProcHgroupList ProcHgroup.
ProcHgroup::= PhgName CSuorce.
PhgName::= "GLOBAL" | "LOCAL" | "HEADS".
ProcSgroupList::= | ProcSgroupList ProcSgroup.
ProcSgroup::= PortType IntNumber ":" PortName PortDefToPort.
PortName::= ID | IntNumber.
PortType::= "INPORT" | "OUTPORT" | "INOUTPORT".
PortDefToPort::= | "{" "PROC" ":" PortDefToProcID ";" "PORTID" ":"
                 PortDefToPortID ";" TypeList "}".
PortDefToProcID::= | ID | IntNumber.
PortDefToPortID::= | IntNumber.
TypeList::= | TypeList PortDataType.
PortDataType::= "TYPE" DataTypeDef ";".
DataTypeDef::= | DataType | DataType "[" DataTypeNum "]".
DataTypeNum::= IntNumber | CSource.
Datatype::= "CHAR" | "INT" | "FLOAT" | "DOUBLE" | ID.


ProcPgroupList::= | ProcPgroupList ProgItem.
ProgItem::= ProgItemType ":" IntNumber StringParam "{" ParamsOfPrgItem "}"
          PrgItemSource.
PrgItemSource::= | PrgItemSource CSource.
ProgItemType::= "SEQ" | "CAI" | "CAO" | "CAIALT" | "IFB" | "IFE" |
                "SWITCHB" | "SWITCHE" | "LOOPB" | "LOOPE" | "GRAPHIC" |
                "DUMMYB" | "DUMMYE".
ParamsOfPrgItem::= ItemOptionList ConnList PortParamList
                   ItemListOfGraph.
ItemOptionList::= | ItemOptionList ItemOption.
ConnList::= Connection | ConnList Connection.
PortParamList::= | PortParamList PortParam.
ItemListOfGraph::= ProcPgroupList.
ItemOption::= "BLOCKED" | "UNBLOCKED" | ItemGuard.
ItemGuard::= "GUARD" "=" CSource.
Connection::= ConnectionType IntNumber ":" "{" ConnectionTo "}"
              ConnectionSource.
ConnectionType::= "CIN" | "COUT".
ConnectionTo::= IntNumber.
```

```
ConnectionSource::= | CSource.
PortParam::= "PORT" IntNumber ":" PortGuard PortSourceList.
PortGuard::= | "GUARD" "=" CSource.
PortSourceList::= | PortSourceList PortSource ";".
PortSource::= | CSource.
```

References

[1] A. Geist, A. Beguelin, J. Dongarra, W. Jiang, R. Manchek, and V. S. Sunderam. *PVM: Parallel Virtual Machine – A Users' Guide and Tutorial for Networked Parallel Computing.* MIT Press, 1994.

[2] W. Gropp, E. Lusk, and A. Skjellum. *Using MPI : Portable Parallel Programming with the Message-Passing Interface.* MIT Press, 1994.

[3] P. Kacsuk, G. Dózsa, and T. Fadgyas. Designing parallel programs by the graphical language GRAPNEL. *Microprocessing and Microprogramming*, 41:625–643, 1996.

[4] P. Kacsuk, G. Dózsa, T. Fadgyas, and R. Lovas. The GRED graphical editor for the GRADE parallel program development environment. In *Proceedings of HPCN'98: High-Performance Computing and Networking*, pages 728–737, Amsterdam, The Netherlands, April 1998.

Chapter 12

The Mapping, Scheduling and Load Balancing Tools of **GRADE**

Ladislav Hluchý, Miroslav Dobrucký, Viet Dinh Tran and Ján Astaloš

Abstract

In this chapter we describe the integration of the GRADE environment with mapping, scheduling and load balancing tools. The scheduling and mapping tools consist of different scheduling and mapping algorithms which aim to find sub-optimal solution for the schedule and mapping vector. A dynamic load balancing tool is based on a semi-distributed algorithm and it co-operates with the distributed monitoring system which provides the information about availability of resources in distributed systems.

12.1   Introduction

The optimization environment of GRADE based on the theoretical aspects described in Chapter 3 consists of a DSM&S - distributed static mapping and scheduling tool and a DLB - dynamic load balancing tool.

This chapter describes how these tools are used to distribute the processes among processors to achieve optimal performance goals, such as minimizing execution time, minimizing communication delays, and/or maximizing resource utilization. In this chapter the integration of these tools in the GRADE environment is described.

For the static mapping and scheduling the objective functions (see Section 3.2.3 in Chapter 3) are used to evaluate the optimality of the allocation/scheduling of a task graph (TIG/DAG) onto a process graph (cluster of workstations).

For the dynamic task allocation the semi-distributed approach was used (see Chapter 4) based on the division of processor network topology into independent and symmetric spheres. DSM&S and DLB tools are controlled by the user window interface and they are integrated together with a software monitor (Tape/PVM) in the GRADE environment.

12.2 Integration of **DSM&S** and **DLB** Tools in the **GRADE** Environment

The block scheme in Figure 12.1 represents the integration of the GRADE environment with DSM&S and DLB tools and with the software monitor Tape/PVM (see Chapter 14 - measurement of computational load and communication costs).

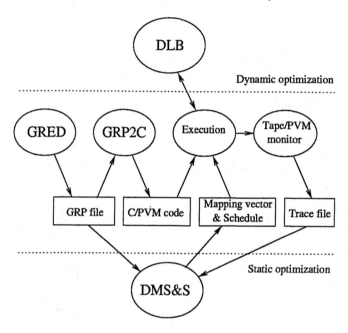

Figure 12.1: Block scheme of the GRADE integration

Having created a parallel application program (using the graphic editor - see Chapter 10), which is stored in the GRP file of the GRAPNEL code, the DSM&S tool analyzes this file and extracts the non-weighted task graph DAG/TIG. Then if there is the trace file generated (by the Tape/PVM monitor used in a previous application run), it is also analyzed for getting an evaluated DAG/TIG. The first not-well balanced run can use non-accurate mapping, e.g. PVM (Parallel Virtual Machine) default strategy.

Other internal mapping information such as the hardware-topology graph, the chosen method and mapping results are read or written directly from/to GRP-file by the DSM&S tool.

Next the DSM&S tool generates the mapping vector or the schedule. They are used at run time and specify the allocation of parallel tasks onto cluster of workstations or the ordering of tasks (via arranging their start time), respectively.

The user can choose any sequence of compiling and mapping/scheduling before the application run, because the application will use a mapping vector or schedule at run-time.

If the user is not willing to specify an application mapping, the default PVM mapping policy is used or the user can activate the DLB tool, which will try to better exploit parallel computing resources. If the application has dynamic behavior, i.e., the number of parallel processes is not known at compile time, the DLB tool can improve the hardware resource utilization during run time.

In Figure 12.1 the Tape/PVM monitor is a client-server instrumentation system for logging the communication activities in PVM programs for post-mortem visualization using for example the well known ParaGraph tool. It can be enabled without adding explicit start-up code to the original program. Instead of Tape/PVM other monitoring tools, such as PG_PVM, can be used.

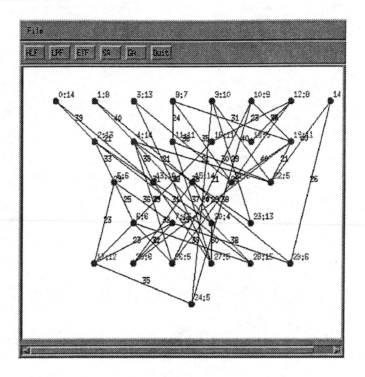

Figure 12.2: The DAG viewer of the scheduling tool

12.3 The Scheduling Tool

The scheduling tool uses the GRP-file as the input for the description of the DAG graph to be scheduled and creates an output file where the results (*schedule*, i.e., the location and time vector) are stored.

As the scheduling tool starts, it reads the DAG configuration and shows it in the scheduling main window (Figure 12.2). Each node is annotated with two numbers, the first being the identification number of the node, the second being the execution time of the node; each edge is labelled by its communication time.

The scheduling tool can recommend the most suitable algorithm on the basis of the DAG characteristics, or the user can choose one of the implemented scheduling algorithms (HLF, LPF, ETF, SA, GA, see Chapter 3) by clicking on the appropriate buttons above the viewing area. The time for generating the schedule by scheduling tool is different for heuristic and iterative methods. For example, SA and GA with 10000 iterations take about

2 minutes for scheduling, and heuristic algorithms take only a fraction of a second (on a Pentium 150 MHz computer).

The chosen algorithm will generate a schedule, shown by Gantt diagram form in a new window (Figure 12.3). In the window, each processor is represented by a row, which contains all nodes executed on the processor, and horizontal axis gives time (in ms).

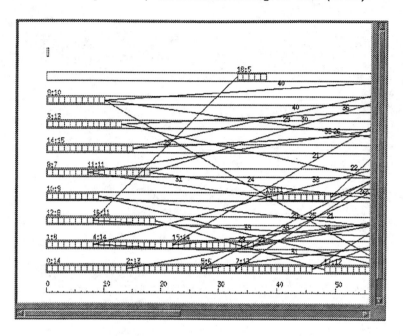

Figure 12.3: The schedule viewer of the scheduling tool

12.3.1   Experimental results

All algorithms have been implemented in Linux. In order to compare the efficiency of the algorithms, the stop condition in simulated annealing and genetic algorithm is the number of iterations. Using number of iterations as stop condition has another advantage: we can see the dependence of quality of solutions on the number of iterations. In the following text, GA1000 means genetic algorithm with 1000 iterations. DAGs used in experiments are randomly generated with a given number of nodes, number of edges, range of values of nodes (computation costs) and range of values of edges (communication costs). In the following text, DAG(100, 200, 10, 5, 3, 1) means a DAG with 100 nodes with values from 5 to 10 and 200 edges with values from 1 to 3.

Optimal scheduling algorithms are those by which the minimum *makespan* (execution time of application program represented by the DAG) is achieved.

Figure 12.4a shows the average makespan of 1000 different DAGs(50, 100, 20, 14, 6, 2) on 4 processors scheduled by different algorithms. The average granularity (the execution time / communication time ratio) of DAGs is about 4. They represent a class of small DAGs with large granularity.

For these DAGs, GA10000 produces the best solution. SA10000 produces a slightly

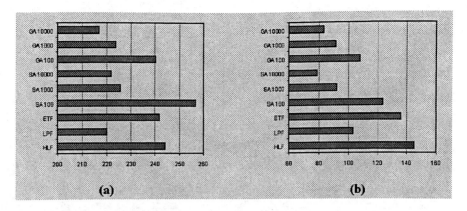

Figure 12.4: Comparison algorithms for DAGs(50, 100, 20, 14, 6, 2) (a)
and DAGs(50, 100, 6, 2, 20, 14) (b)

worse solution then GA10000. Among heuristic algorithms, LPF is the best. The solution of LPF is comparable with the solution of GA and SA.

Figure 12.4b shows the average execution time of DAGs(50, 100, 6, 2, 20, 14) on 4 processors. They represent a class of small DAGs with small granularity. For these DAGs, SA1000 produces the best solution. Heuristic algorithms are inefficient in this case. The reason for the inefficiency of heuristic algorithms is that heuristic algorithms always choose the first idle processors for tasks regardless of communication. When granularity is small, because of the large communication time the location of task is more important than the execution order.

Figure 12.5 shows the average execution time of DAGs(1000, 2000, 20, 14, 6, 2) and DAGs(1000, 2000, 6, 2, 20, 14) on 20 processors. They represent classes of large DAGs with small and large granularity. Although heuristic algorithms are inefficient with small granularity, in both cases heuristic algorithms produce better solution than statistic algorithms. The reason of inefficiency of statistic algorithms is that the number of searched solutions (the number of iterations) is too small in comparison with the entire solution space. We can see the dependence of the quality of solutions (i.e., schedule) on the number of iterations in Figure 12.6.

Figure 12.6a shows the dependence of the makespan produced by statistic algorithms on the number of iterations for DAGs(50, 100, 6, 2, 20, 14). We can see that while the number of iterations is small, GA is slightly better than SA. When the number of iterations is large, SA produces better solutions than GA. The makespan decreases more quickly when the number of iterations is small. When the number of iterations is large, the makespan decreases very slowly. We can predict that if the number of iterations increases continuously, the makespan converges to the optimal solution. Note that in the chart, the number of iterations increases geometrically.

Figure 12.6b shows the dependence of the makespan on the number of iterations for DAGs(1000, 2000, 6, 2, 20, 14). For these large DAGs, the makespan still reduces very fast at the end. If we compare Figure 12.6b with Figure 12.6a, we can see Figure 12.6b just looks like the beginning of Figure 12.6a. It means that the number 102400 iterations are not large enough to reach the level of saturation. The algorithms need more iterations to produce a "good" solution. It can explain why statistic algorithms shown in Figure 12.5 are

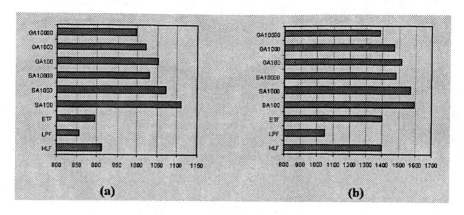

Figure 12.5: Comparison algorithms for DAGs(1000,2000,20,14,6,2) (a)
and DAGs(1000,2000,6,2,10,14) (b)

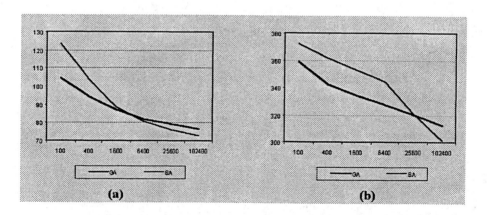

Figure 12.6: The dependence of the solution quality of SA and GA on the number of iterations for DAGs(50, 100, 6, 2, 20 , 14) (a) and DAGs(1000, 2000, 6, 2, 20, 14)
(b)

inefficient.

12.4   The Distributed Static Mapping Tool (DSM)

The DSM tool was developed as a distributed parallel program running in PVM environment. DSM uses the GRP-file (GRAPNEL code, see Figure 12.1) as the input for the description of the TIG graph to be mapped and creates an output file in which the result (the mapping vector) is stored. The DSM tool uses various mapping methods (diffusion method, simulated annealing, heuristic move exchange and greedy methods, see Chapter 3).

Having started, DSM spawns its copies on all the current PVM-host processors (Figure 12.7). Only the main process (the master) manages the input and output data (stored in files; SW graph means DAG/TIG). Other copies act as co-workers (slaves) and communicate with the master and also with each other.

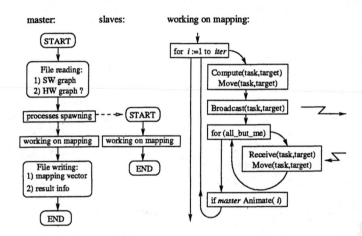

Figure 12.7: The implementation of distributed static mapping (DSM)

The diffusion mapping method works iteratively (Figure 12.7). After each iteration, the computed data are interchanged among all DSM processes. This implementation is synchronized, because the information about each location has to be up-to-date in all the DSM processes. After the last iteration is done, all results are present in the master and they do not need to be collected.

The simulated annealing mapping method uses another parallelization possibility - a processing pool (Figure 12.8). The more parallel processes, the better quality of the mapping can be achieved. Each processor ($me \in [0, n-1]$) optimizes mapping method almost independently using sequential simulated annealing[1]. To get the new mapping vectors (map), the random generators (starting with different value for each processor) are used, thus the search space for finding optimal mapping vector is better covered. In certain randomly chosen moments (with the probability $Probab.cross$) the partial result (map) from a randomly chosen slave (who) is sent to the master ($me = 0$). Then the genetic algorithm (cross-over, mutation...) is performed (in the master) on two partial solutions (master's one and that

---

[1]T in Figure 12.8 denotes temperature and is understood as iterative step

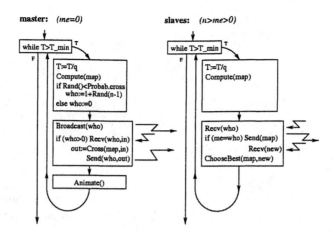

Figure 12.8: The distributed simulated annealing with the genetic approach

one received from chosen slave *who*). The result is returned to the slave and the better partial solution is chosen.

In Figure 12.9 the user interface window is depicted. The tool can be started immediately by clicking the OK/restart button, because some default method is chosen automatically. Or the user can play with it by choosing another mapping method, by inspecting PVM (number of actually running hosts by clicking the HW button) and s/he can watch the mapping progress in a separate window (Figure 12.10) which appears after pressing the View button. The mapping results like the load imbalance, the communication cost and also task allocation on processors are shown and can be changed by choosing another mapping method and restarting the mapping process if the user likes it.

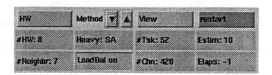

Figure 12.9: XPMAP

12.4.1   Comparison of the static mapping methods

For better imagination of how fast versus effective are the static mapping methods that we had implemented, Table 12.1 shows the comparison of these methods. We compare one greedy G method (if a task is placed somewhere it cannot be moved elsewhere, and takes and places largest task first), that runs only sequentially (very fast, but with pure results), with the diffusion method D (see Section 3 in Chapter chapthree:subsec:clust), the Heuristic move-exchange method H and Simulated Annealing with the genetic approach S. For the experimentation a hardware platform was used consisting of four PCs (200MHz Pentium Pro and three Pentiums 200MHz) connected by fast ethernet (100Mbit).

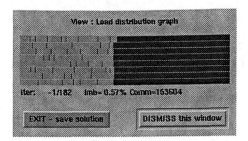

Figure 12.10: XPMAP-view

We have used 5 random-generated SW-graphs, which differ in their size (number of tasks T from 50 to 800, number of communication channels C from 192 to 5148) and whose computational task load and communicational channel load are random-generated in the interval from 5 to 15.

Sequential methods are running on the master which is approximately 2.5 times faster than slaves. As it can be seen (Table 12.1, section *Sequential*), the H method works very slowly (especially for large graphs), although it gives better (smaller) imbalance and minimizes communication. The winner seems to be the S method, although also the diffusion method D works very similarly.

In the right part of Table 12.1 (section *Distributed*) results of the distributed mapping are given. Here the time consumption is the average CPU usage time per workstation because of the heterogeneity of our cluster of workstations.

With the distributed version (supported by the genetic approach for the S method) better solution is possible (bold values in Table 12.1). To get the same quality by sequential version (mainly for S and H methods) at least 4 times more CPU-usage time is required for it.

SW-graph		Sequential				Distributed		
		G	S	D	H	S	D	H
T=51	CPU time[s]	0.00	0.03	0.06	1.29	0.08	0.03	2.12
C=192	Imbalance[%]	0.89	0.03	0.49	0.24	0.03	0.49	**0.03**
	Comm.[kB]	7.82	7.55	7.38	6.84	**7.15**	7.50	6.99
T=101	CPU time[s]	0.00	0.11	0.10	27.5	0.20	0.08	28
C=433	Imbalance[%]	0.45	0.12	0.37	0.08	**0.08**	**0.22**	**0.05**
	Comm.[kB]	18.2	18.6	17.6	17.8	**18.4**	18.5	17.9
T=201	CPU time[s]	0.00	0.62	0.34	362	0.79	0.21	851
C=1099	Imbalance[%]	0.29	0.13	0.23	0.05	**0.11**	**0.05**	0.05
	Comm.[kB]	287	252	282	235	257	288	237
T=401	CPU time[s]	0.00	2.01	1.41	7395	2.70	0.78	—
C=1711	Imbalance[%]	0.21	0.03	0.13	0.02	0.05	0.19	—
	Comm.[kB]	680	628	683	600	**623**	685	—
T=801	CPU time[s]	0.03	9.38	5.80	—	12.31	2.65	—
C=5148	Imbalance[%]	0.09	0.04	0.03	—	**0.03**	0.06	—
	Comm.[kB]	1470	1341	1473	—	1349	**1467**	—

Table 12.1: Static mapping method results

12.5   The Dynamic Load Balancing System (DLB)

Our DLB system is divided into two parts (Figure 12.11), Distributed Monitoring System and Dynamic Load Balancing Tool. The main reason was to avoid multiple monitoring of the same information in multi-user environment.

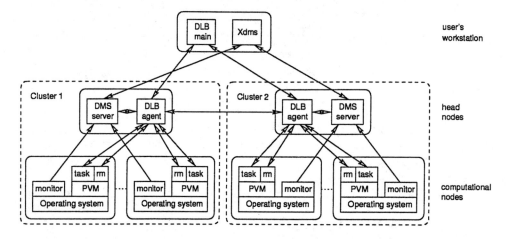

Figure 12.11: Functional design of Dynamic Load Balancing system

12.5.1   Distributed Monitoring System (DMS)

The main purpose of DMS is to provide information about availability of resources (CPU, memory, communication links) in distributed systems. Since our target distributed environment PVM has no support for monitoring of processes which belong to other users and neither support for monitoring of network connections, DMS is designed as a set of daemons accessible via Remote Procedure Calls (RPC). Monitoring of communication links (sockets) is needed by preemptive load balancing methods (process migration profitability determination). It requires OS kernel modification because it is not provided by default. Kernel modifications include notification of process creation/termination, socket opening/closing and socket counters. The monitoring information is provided in one system call and in binary form, thus avoiding the overhead of checking each single process.

The structure of DMS is designed to be suitable for large scale distributed computer systems (clusters of clusters). Each cluster has one DMS daemon (DMS server in Figure 12.11), which collects information from monitors (process and socket monitors) running on each node. Monitors check processes and sockets in regular time intervals and they report changes to the DMS daemon. In order to reduce information inconsistency, process (socket) creation and termination are reported immediately. Besides information about processes and communication links, DMS monitors utilization of system resources (memory, swap, etc.).

The main information needed for every dynamic load balancing method (except of the simplest ones) is an estimation of host (processor) response time for the near future, i.e., host performance prediction. Since the process performance depends on many factors (instruction mix, memory access patterns, code optimization), the only suitable way how to determine the performance is to use the appropriate benchmark. But on-line monitoring cannot use periodic benchmarking because of high intrusiveness. In our approach we try to get the result of benchmark without really benchmarking the host during application run-time. It is based on assumption that if we know maximal host performance and we find out a percentage of CPU time that can be allocated to a new process, we can estimate the possible performance of the new process. It requires good knowledge of OS process scheduler and the information about CPU requirements and priority for each process running on the host. The algorithm is based on modeling the situation that would happen if a new process with specific priority was launched.

CPU time is recursively allocated to processes with lower CPU need than they potentially can have. After eliminating these processes, the rest of CPU time is divided between CPU-intensive processes and new processes according to their priorities. New processes launched in the last interval (without information about CPU needs) are considered to be CPU-intensive (worst case). Maximal CPU time available is counted from CPU consumption of running processes plus idle time, thus terminated processes are excluded. The result is relative CPU availability and the client (load balancing, visualization, application) can use it with the appropriate value of maximal available performance.

DMS clients can obtain information from DMS server via libDms library call. It can be a full process/socket information or relative CPU availability for a given host. The user can observe the information using X-windows client called xdms (Figure 12.12). Xdms has four folders (host list, process list, link list and host CPU availability chart). In the host list, the information about hosts is displayed, that is CPU, memory and swap availability, number of processes and standard values of system load (in 1, 5 and 15 minutes, see Figure 12.12). Multiple hosts can be selected and will be displayed in other folders. The process list contains the information about memory and CPU consumption of processes (Figure 12.13). In the link list, cumulative information about communication between pairs of processes is displayed along with the communication rate (Figure 12.14). CPU availability chart (Figure 12.15) shows history of CPU availability for selected hosts.

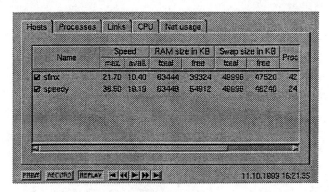

Figure 12.12: Xdms client window

12.5.2 Dynamic Load Balancing Tool

We have implemented a semi-distributed load balancing algorithm based on Ahmad's approach (see Chapter 4). Our Dynamic Load Balancing (DLB) system consists of a set of

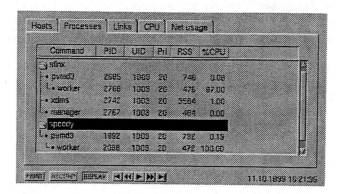

Figure 12.13: Process list

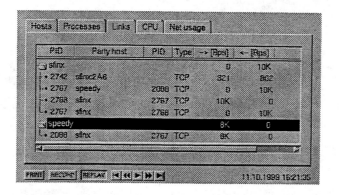

Figure 12.14: Link list

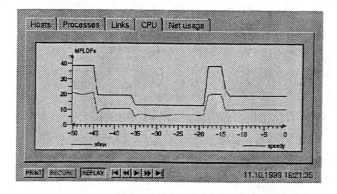

Figure 12.15: CPU availability chart

DLB agents, each serving a set of PVM hosts (sphere). Partitioning of a system into spheres depends on the size and interconnection of the system. The hosts that are more tightly coupled (i.e., laying on the same network segment) should be located in the same sphere. The implementation of DLB in PVM environment is based on PVM support for resource management. The resource manager (*rm* in Figure 12.11) is a PVM plug-in process that catches requests for spawning new tasks and can decide where the task will be placed. The choice is made by the DLB agent that is serving the *rm*.

The DLB agent selects the node with the best performance; if the sphere is overloaded, it can ask another agent to create the task in a remote sphere. If a set of tasks is requested, it is divided according to the hosts' performance. The agent can be called from a task, enabling the load balancing at application level which is important mainly in data-parallel applications. The manager process can distribute work to workers more accurately, and consequently avoids synchronization delays. The agents are autonomous, but they can be controlled by theDLB main process (Figure 12.16). Interaction between DMS and DLB systems is described in Figure 12.11.

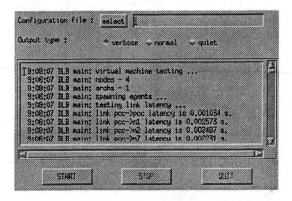

Figure 12.16: DLB main window

12.6 Conclusion

In this chapter the diffusion method for static mapping for a distributed system was proposed. Implementation in a distributed form using PVM was described. Together with the diffusion method also augmented simulated annealing, "heuristic move-exchange" and several methods for faster mapping (greedy methods) were implemented. Dynamic task allocation based on the semi-distributed approach was described as the DLB tool. Two-phase optimization for allocation of task graph on distributed systems was supposed: in the first phase the distributed static task allocation is done (before runtime) and then during runtime the dynamic task allocation is executed which balances the utilization of computing resources among processors. The user is provided with a X-window interface XPMAP allowing to choose a static mapping method and switch on/off the dynamic task load balancing.

The implementation is performed on the UNIX operating system (Solaris, IRIX, Linux, [2, 3]) and PVM 3.3. DSM&S and DLB tools were integrated in the GRADE environment. Randomly generated graphs for testing the DSM&S and DLB tools were used, testing was also done for an irregular distributed simulation problem (WaTor, [1]) and water flow modeling.

Acknowledgements

This work has been supported by the Slovak Scientific Grant Agency within Research Projects No.2/4102/97-99.

References

[1] G. Fox, M. Johnson, G. Lyzenga, S. Otto, J. Salmon, and D. Walker. *Solving Problems on Concurrent Processors*, volume I, General Techniques and Regular Problems. Prentice-Hall International, 1988.

[2] L. Hluchý, M. Dobrucký, V.D. Tran, and J. Astaloš. Mapping and scheduling tools for distributed environment. In M.Jelšina and J.Kollár, editors, *Proc. of Sci. Conf. with Intl. Particip. Computer Engineering and Informatics*, pages 120–125, Herl'any, Slovakia, October 1999, 1999.

[3] L. Hluchý, M. Dobrucký, V.D. Tran, and J. Astaloš. Optimization tools for distributed environment. In R.Wyrzykowski et.al., editor, *Proceedings of 3-rd Intl. Conf. on Parallel Processing and Applied Mathematics PPAM'99*, pages 387–397, Kazimierz Dolny, Poland, September 14-17, 1999.

Chapter 13

The **DDBG** Distributed Debugger

José C. Cunha, João Lourenço and Vítor Duarte

Abstract

This chapter presents the main issues involved in the design of the DDBG distributed debugger. DDBG provides basic support for state based debugging of distributed C/PVM processes. Due to its flexible architecture, DDBG enables the implementation of several debugging methodologies for deterministic re-execution and systematic state exploration. This is achieved through its integration with other tools in a parallel software development environment. The chapter describes how DDBG was integrated with two tools of the SEPP/HPCTI environment: the STEPS testing tool and the GRED graphical editor.

13.1 Introduction

As described in previous chapters, the SEPP/HPCTI projects have promoted the design and implementation of tools supporting visual graph-based parallel program development, including mapping and load-balancing, simulation, monitoring, testing and debugging tools. The main goal of these projects was to achieve an integrated environment that would ensure a suitable degree of consistency among the above mentioned tools.

As discussed in Chapter 5, the debugging activity relies on the observation and control of a computation in order to identify, locate and correct so-called program bugs. In a brief summary, the following issues characterize the main dimensions of the distributed debugging activity:

1. *Observation and control of distributed computations.* The construction of consistent global states of a distributed computation is a fundamental requirement to support the meaningful evaluation of local and global predicates, which involve state variables in multiple processes. Concerning control of the distributed computation, coordinated actions such as step-by-step execution and breakpoint marking must be applied to individual processes, as in sequential debuggers, and to collections of distributed processes.

2. *Program analysis and testing.* Distributed computations exhibit a very large space of alternative computation paths that should be explored during debugging. Deterministic

re-execution schemes have a limitation here because they only allow to try the recorded trace that happened during a previous computation and this trace may be the wrong one to inspect. So, the identification of the desired traces that should be inspected under re-execution should be the result of applying a testing tool. This aspect also relates to the ability to specify suitable global predicates that should be submitted to an evaluation by the underlying system. So a debugger needs to be complemented by program analysis and testing tools.

3. *User level interfacing, program behavior interpretation and visualization.* This includes several aspects:

(i) Due to the complexity of the distributed computations we need to provide high-level views to the user (high level debugging) that are close to the abstraction levels at which the application is specified or programmed. This is opposed to the low-level view of debugging where system or language (sometimes assembly-level) concepts are explicitly visible to the user.

(ii) Such views may be supported through the provision of graphical and visual interfaces. Graphical user interfaces (GUI) support the already conventional windows and menu based access to debugging commands and replies. Visual debugging is another aspect that concerns the suitable interpretation and visualization of the relevant events of a distributed computation, ranging from simple space-time diagrams to more sophisticated views offered by interactive visualization tools.

(iii) Internal consistency of the debugging tool means all the debugging functionalities (for inspection and control of the distributed computation) are accessible through the graphical and visual presentation interfaces as well as through text based command consoles and text based message displays. Also, the user should be able to selectively enable/disable such graphical/visual views for subsets of processes, communication channels, or any other components of a distributed program. Furthermore, it should be possible to consistently observe/control a distributed computation at the desired abstraction level, by changing from high level to low level debugging and vice versa.

The above dimensions cannot be supported by an isolated debugging tool as it is virtually impossible to anticipate all possible requirements posed by each user at each point in time. Several complementary tools should be considered to support each individual aspect and they should be able to cooperate with the debugging tool, as illustrated by the following simplified list:

1. *A debugging console* providing access to the control and inspection commands, in the form of a textual command line oriented interface, and/or in the form of a graphical user interface with a set of associated buttons, plus a text window to display the program source code, as well as several information displays for the computation status.

2. *A graphical display* for the representation of a higher level view of the program structure (e.g., a graph-based view) such that it is possible to perform debugging commands at a higher level of abstraction, and to hide a more detailed view of the internal state transitions in each process.

3. *A visualization tool* that displays the evolution of processes or threads in space-time diagrams.

4. *A testing tool* that allows the generation of specific testing scenarios identifying suspect computation paths that must be subject to a more detailed inspection under debugging control.

13.2 Design Issues for a Distributed Debugger

Two main requirements arise when designing a distributed debugging tool:

(i) Mechanisms for the observation and control of distributed computations. This includes two dimensions, depending on the level of observation that is required at each point during debugging. One level concerns the observation of individual process or thread states. The other level concerns the observation of global states.

(ii) Frameworks to support testing and debugging methodologies. This concerns the support provided by the distributed debugging tool to guide the user along the steps of identifying and precisely locating bugs.

There are two main possibilities to try to meet the above requirements:

(i) A self-contained autonomous debugging tool. It incorporates mechanisms and strategies for all the above aspects into a single debugging architecture. Such aspects are perhaps more easily made transparently accessed by the user which is an advantage of this approach. It may also more easily provide a uniform user interface. However, in general this kind solution is tied to a specific parallel or distributed programming model and/or to a specific debugging methodology (if any). Due to the self-contained design, it becomes difficult to adapt the tool to distinct abstractions and/or testing and debugging methodologies.

(ii) A minimal distributed debugging architecture with a facility for integration of extended services. This approach allows to separate, on one hand, the basic low level debugging mechanisms for observation and control, and the higher level mechanisms that may relate to higher level abstractions. On the other hand it allows to separate the mechanisms from the debugging methodologies or strategies that one wants to enforce in each case.

The DDBG distributed debugger that was developed within the SEPP project is an example of the second approach. The basic mechanisms supported by DDBG are of the following kinds:

(i) Observation and control of multiple distributed sequential processes.

(ii) Tool integration based on an interface library.

13.2.1 Observation and control of distributed processes

Concerning the observation and control mechanisms, DDBG offers the following main functionalities:

(i) Control of the debugging session. This includes commands to start or finish a debugging session, to put a process under debugger control, and to remove a process from the debugging environment.

(ii) Control of the process execution. This includes commands that directly control the execution path followed by a process, once it is under debugger control.

(iii) Process state inspection and modification. This includes commands to inspect the state of a process in well-defined points which are reached due to the occurrence of breakpoints or other types of events (process stopped or terminated). The information that can be accessed includes process status, variable and stack frame records, and source code information.

Such functionalities provide direct support to state based interactive debugging of distributed processes (see Chapter 5). All other aspects such as deterministic re-execution, systematic state exploration, and correctness predicate specification, must be provided as extended services and implemented through tool integration.

13.2.2   Tool integration

Besides text and graphic based user interfaces which give access to the debugging commands, DDBG allows direct access to its services through an interface library that can be linked to each client tool. Each client tool typically provides some high level debugging functionality and/or supports some testing and debugging methodology that in the end must rely upon DDBG basic mechanisms. So the concept underlying the DDBG design is to enable an open architecture on top of a low level built-in distributed debugging framework. This concept was the basis of our experimentation during the SEPP project, and several distinct kinds of tool integration were achieved with reasonable success, as described in the following sections.

In order to support easy integration of the debugger with other tools in a parallel software engineering environment, a well-defined debugging interface must be provided to be used by high-level tools, namely graphical interfaces and graphical program editors, runtime support systems for distinct parallel and distributed language models, and testing and high-level debugging tools.

Concerning such interface to high-level tools, the following aspects must be taken under consideration:

(i) *Concurrent access from multiple separate client tools.* Multiple tools can independently and concurrently issue debugging commands over the same target application. Thus they all share the same information concerning the program state and have the same abilities to issue inspection and control commands.

(ii) *Dynamic attachment and detachment of client tools to the debugging engine.* Client tools can join and exit the debugging process dynamically, having their own life cycle independent of the DDBG debugger life cycle.

(iii) *Support for heterogeneity.* Heterogeneity is supported at multiple levels: hardware, operating system, programming language and model, as the client-server architecture accepts plug-and-play node level debuggers that are used to access each individual target application process.

In order to allow access by distinct client tools, the DDBG interface provides a bidirectional interaction scheme supporting an asynchronous operation mode. In fact, many client tools such as editors and graphical interfaces exhibit an event-driven behavior. The debugging interface primitives that are invoked by each high-level tool must support a non-blocking semantics because some debugging commands don't provide an immediate answer. On the other hand, the communications interface must support the passing of the output information coming from such non-immediate debugging commands back to the user tool (e.g., a graphical editor). A simple solution to this problem is to provide a library function that allows the user tool to poll a communication channel that is associated with this interaction with the debugging system. An alternative solution is to support a facility for the handling of asynchronous events by the client tool such that the invocation of a previously specified handler can be triggered by the arrival of the debugging information.

Multiple simultaneous client connections should be supported by the debugging system, so that multiple cooperating tools can be accessing the debugging environment for inspection and control of the distributed program execution.

A mapping service of high-level process names onto low-level system process identifiers allows to integrate client tools which support distinct high level abstractions such symbolic virtual process identifiers. Conceptually, it is up to any client tool to interpret its abstract entities and convert them to low level DDBG entities. This can also be achieved by some intermediate tool, with the advantage of allowing the clear separation of concerns when designing the high level client tool. An example of this approach is described in Section 13.4.3.

As a consequence of the above aspects, DDBG has no built in fixed user interface. In SEPP, we have implemented a command line user interface giving access to all the debugging functionalities. We have also implemented an unsophisticated graphical user interface that is consistent with the user views being offered by other tools in the environment. As far as SEPP project was concerned, this graphical user interface only allowed selective inspection of the variables of each distributed process. This approach is opposite to the usual approach of having highly sophisticated graphical user interfaces for a parallel and distributed debugger (e.g. TotalView [7]), but lack of integration support mechanisms.

13.2.3 Characteristics of DDBG

How do we classify DDBG according to the dimensions of Chapter 5?

(i) *Debugging methodologies.* DDBG directly supports state based interactive debugging of distributed processes. It can support all other methodologies through tool integration. Within SEPP, we have implemented *systematic state exploration* of C/PVM programs using DDBG, through the integration of DDBG and the STEPS testing tool (see Chapter 16).

(ii) *Debugging at distinct phases of development.* DDBG directly supports on-line dynamic analysis and control of distributed processes. This can be used to observe and enforce specific testing scenarios. It can also be used to "manually" check dynamic program behavior, through the user interfaces. Off-line analysis is not directly supported by DDBG. However, these facilities can be integrated with DDBG.

(iii) *DDBG observation model.* DDBG is a state based distributed debugger. It supports observation and control of individual distributed processes. It can be used to support global observations and global control of distributed computations, through an adequate integration with other tools. Namely, deterministic re-execution and controlled re-execution facilities were achieved for C/PVM programs within SEPP, based on the tool integration of STEPS and DDBG.

(iv) *Debugging at multiple (hierarchical) levels of abstraction.* Due to the support of multiple concurrent client tools and to the minimal design of its architecture, DDBG naturally supports multiple levels of observation and control of a distributed computation. This is illustrated in the following through the integration of GRED (see Chapter 10) and DDBG.

13.3 The **DDBG** Parallel and Distributed Debugger

In this section we briefly describe the architecture and interface library which were developed for the DDBG distributed debugger within the SEPP project.

13.3.1 Architecture

Figure 13.1 illustrates the DDBG architecture, where three different types of processes are involved in a debugging session: client processes, DDBG processes and target application processes.

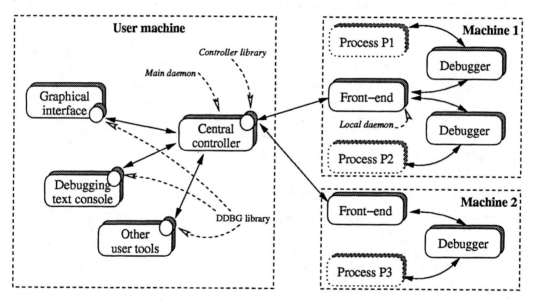

Figure 13.1: The **DDBG** distributed debugger

DDBG has a basic client-server architecture which follows the lines of the p2d2 design [8]. The reader may find a more detailed presentation of DDBG in [4]. A brief summary is presented here.

The client processes are depicted in Figure 13.1 as user interfaces or other user tools. These processes are linked to the *DDBG Library* that provides access to all DDBG debugging functionalities.

The target processes belong to the application being debugged. This application can have multiple processes spread on multiple nodes, with different hardware and operating systems. Heterogeneity concerns are handled by DDBG at the level of its internal communication layer (the SEPP implementation of this layer uses PVM for interprocess communication, and UNIX sockets for the interactions between each client tool and the central controller). Heterogeneity is also handled by allowing multiple possible types of local node debuggers to be integrated into DDBG architecture. SEPP implementation relied upon GNU GDB as the only local node debugger supported.

The DDBG architecture internally consists of several component processes:

(i) *Central Controller.* It coordinates the handling of the client requests, converts them into a set of commands and distributes them to the relevant local node debuggers. It is also responsible for processing the local node debuggers' replies, and sending them back to the client processes as returns to the calls of functions of the debugging library.

(ii) *Local Front-ends.* There is one of these processes in each node. Besides some local interpretation of the debugging commands, it locally distributes them to the local debuggers, and gets the answers back so that they mat be conveyed to the central controller.

(iii) *Local Node Debuggers.* A system-dependent sequential debugger, for a specific programming language and the underlying hardware. There is a local node debugger attached to each process of the target application processes, that applies the inspection and control commands to that process.

13.3.2 Interface Library

Any user tool can access the DDBG system as a client process that uses an interface library to interact with the central debugging controller. The interface library supports functions for the control of the DDBG system and for supporting the interfacing with other tools, and functions supporting distributed process control and state inspection. The latter type of functions are currently adapted from identical functions provided by the GNU GDB debugger, but they operate upon multiple distributed processes. The functions for distributed process control and state inspection include support for debugging commands that control the execution of each individual process in a detailed way, including step by step execution, handling breakpoints and watchpoints, and displaying or modifying local process information (variables, status, stack frames, current breakpoints). A detailed definition of these functions is presented in [1, 2].

There are functions to support, respectively, the initialization and the cleanup of the debugging environment. The initialization also establishes a connection between each user tool and the central controller, that is used for further interaction with DDBG. It also sets up an interprocess communication channel that is used for the passing of delayed output information between the DDBG and the user tool. This channel can be inspected by invoking another interface function with a non-blocking semantics, corresponding to a design requirement that was discussed in a previous section.

There are also functions supporting the dynamic attachment and detachment of application processes to new debugger instances, as well as to obtain information about new components (e.g., newly spawned application processes) in the debugging environment.

In the implemented prototype for the debugging of C/PVM programs, an user application or tool may use specific *Process ID's* (strings) to identify the processes. In order to support the mapping between the user processes symbolic names and the PVM task names, a name mapping function is provided allowing to associate a *tid*, a PVM task identifier, to a given process identifier. This allows any of the library primitives, as well as the corresponding user consoles, to refer to string process identifiers, besides PVM *task ID's* (integers). This solution currently solves the name mapping problem and it is used by the current interface of the GRAPNEL and DDBG. A similar functionality was implemented for the STEPS-DDBG integration.

13.4 Interfacing the DDBG Debugger with Other Tools

In this section we briefly discuss our experimentation with the interfacing of the DDBG system and two high-level tools of a parallel software engineering environment: the GRED and the STEPS tools. More detailed descriptions of these tools and interfaces is given in Chapters 10 and 16 and in several references [3, 5, 6, 9–12].

13.4.1 User Interfaces

Graphical and text-oriented debugging user interfaces are two examples of client processes, not being part of DDBG by themselves, but which are included in the SEPP distribution. Besides a command line console that gives access to all the interface library functions, it is possible to interface any kind of graphical user interface to the DDBG system. The SEPP prototype provided a X-based window interface for the interactive display of selected process variables.

13.4.2 Graphical Debugging in GRED with the DDBG Debugger

The GRAPNEL model, a graph-based parallel programming language (see Chapter 10), supports a structured style for designing parallel applications. In order to allow the debugging commands and the output information from the debugger to be directly related to the GRAPNEL model, an integration of GRED and DDBG was developed in SEPP. The main goal was to ensure that only GRAPNEL abstractions should be handled by the user at this level.

Two main issues are considered in this integration:

(i) The design of the high-level user interface, with the specification of the adequate set of debugging commands, and its coherent integration within the GRED level abstractions. A detailed description of such interface can be found in [9]. The distinctive aspect is that the information on specific debugging commands is directly related to the GRAPNEL source program, e.g., by highlighting corresponding entities in the graphical representation, and their corresponding lines of source code in the textual program representation [5, 10].

(ii) The design of the interface between GRED and DDBG. For each debugging action invoked on the GRED editor, corresponding DDBG primitives are invoked, and process names are converted as previously explained. GRED was linked to the DDBG library and so it became a client tool that could be integrated into the DDBG architecture.

The GRED-DDBG interface (Figure 13.2) and its SEPP implementation relies upon an UNIX socket-based communication protocol to interact with the DDBG system, but this is hidden in the interface library functions that send commands to the debugger. Output debugging information is asynchronously passed back to GRED handler routines through a socket that is polled by the editor, in an event-driven mode. A DDBG interface library function allows GRED to get that information.

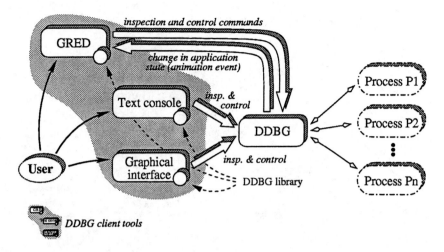

Figure 13.2: The Integration of GRED and DDBG

Two-level (or hierarchical) debugging is allowed, so that the user may switch between high level debugging through the GRED interface (see Chapter 10) for a structural level debugging view, to the low level debugging of individual processes, for a component level, textual debugging view of the C/PVM program, directly invoking DDBG commands through the DDBG user interface.

13.4.3 Tool Composition for Testing and Debugging

The SEPP project introduced an interesting approach to support testing and debugging methodologies. Instead of a monolithic approach based on a single testing-and-debugging tool, several specific tools were separately designed and then their developers worked together towards the combination of such tools.

Program analysis and testing of parallel programs were investigated by our partners of the Technical University of Gdansk. They have independently developed a testing tool called STEPS [11] (Chapter 16), that generates selected execution scenarios for a given parallel (C/PVM) program. After the generation of a testing scenario by the STEPS tool, and through a suitable integration with the debugger, it is possible to submit an user controlled execution of the paths under test, allowing the user to inspect program behavior at the desired level of abstraction and with the guarantee of reproducible execution. The user is allowed to run a complete test scenario until the end or alternatively it is possible to follow a step by step execution controlled by breakpoints. This is achieved by converting the information associated with the specification of each testing scenario onto corresponding information and commands known to the DDBG debugger. Such conversion is supported by an interface component between the STEPS and DDBG tools.

One should note here that the main goal of tool composition or integration is to obtain a new functionality as a result of the integration of two distinct tools, each with its own functionality. Moreover this should be achieved with no change (or a minimal change) to each tool.

The above goal was achieved in the integration of STEPS and DDBG through the development of an interfacing component, the **DEIPA** tool, as described in Figure 13.3.

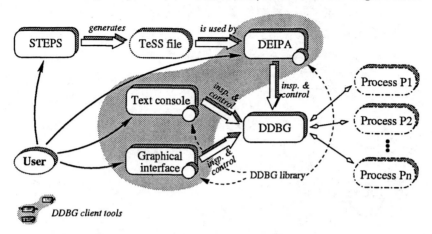

Figure 13.3: The **DDBG** distributed debugger

DEIPA

The **DEIPA** tool (Deterministic (Re-)Execution and Interactive Program Analysis) [12] has an interactive console allowing the user to issue the following types of commands:

(i) Opening and closing intermediate **TeSS** files containing the specification of sequences of global computation states that must be followed under actively controlled execution (see Chapter 16).

(ii) Running the program under the control of **DDBG**, until the next global breakpoint is reached or until the end. Global step-by-step execution from one global breakpoint to the next one is also allowed.

DEIPA interprets each line of the **TeSS** file and is responsible for the local interpretation of these commands (e.g., in case of open or close) or for the generation of corresponding sequences of **DDBG** commands, e.g., in case of the global step command.

The internals of the **DEIPA** tool, e.g., concerning the handling of virtual process identifiers, or the detailed interpretation of the **TeSS** file are not described here, but can be found in [12].

Observation of a distributed computation at the level of global states is possible, as the **STEPS-DDBG** integration does in fact implement global breakpoints. The **DEIPA** tool controls program execution until a global breakpoint is reached. Then the user can switch to the **DDBG** console and perform a state based observation of individual processes, using specific **DDBG** commands. This integration of **DEIPA** and **DDBG** is the result of the **DDBG** architecture allowing multiple concurrent tools.

13.5   Conclusions

We have shown how the **DDBG** distributed debugger has been designed under the influence of specific interfacing requirements posed by high-level parallel software development tools.

We described the SEPP working prototype and its use to support the integration with the GRED and the STEPS tools.

Several significant results were obtained:

(i) High level graphical debugging of GRAPNEL programs was achieved through the implementation of a GRED debugging interface (see Chapter 10) on top of the DDBG debugger.

(ii) Hierarchical debugging of GRAPNEL programs was achieved by allowing simultaneous access to the GRED and the DDBG user interfaces, providing a facility to switch from structural, graphic based, views of the application, to process level, textual based views of individual application components.

(iii) Systematic state exploration of C/PVM programs is supported, based on a testing, active control and debugging approach (see Chapter 5, Chapter 9 and Chapter 16) that was obtained through the integration of STEPS and DDBG. Besides enabling the mentioned testing approach, this integration also ensures deterministic re-execution of the enforced paths.

(iv) Observation of a distributed computation (C/PVM) at the level of global states, as the STEPS-DDBG in fact implements global breakpoints, and followed by a state based observation of individual processes, using specific DDBG commands. The latter aspect is the result of the DDBG functionality of allowing multiple concurrent tools.

The DDBG experience showed the great importance of a flexible distributed debugging architecture that support the requirements for tool integration.

Further work includes improvements on the architecture, its intensive evaluation by real end users, and its integration into other parallel and distributed computing frameworks, namely to support the debugging of component based and metacomputing applications.

Acknowledgements

This work was partially supported by the Centre for Informatics and Information Technologies (CITI) and the Department of Informatics (DI) of FCT/UNL, by the PRAXIS XXI SETNA-ParComp (Contract 2/2.1/TIT/1557/95), and by the French Ambassy — INRIA/ Portuguese ICTTI and the Hungarian/Portuguese Governments cooperation protocols.

References

[1] J. C. Cunha, J. Lourenço, and T. Antão. DDBG: A distributed debugger – user's guide. Technical report, Departamento de Informática, FCT-Universidade Nova de Lisboa, Portugal, 1996.

[2] J. C. Cunha, J. Lourenço, and T. Antão. A debugging engine for a parallel and distributed environment. In KFKI Hungarian Academy of Sciences, editor, *Proceedings of the 1st Austrian-Hungarian Workshop on Distributed and Parallel Systems (DAPSYS'96)*, pages 111–118, Misckolc, Hungary, October 1996.

[3] J. C. Cunha, J. Lourenço, and T. Antão. Integrating a debugging engine to the GRAPNEL environment. Technical Report HPCTI Project, COPERNICUS Programme, 3rd Progress Report, University of Westminster, London, UK, 1996.

[4] J. C. Cunha, J. Lourenço, and T. Antão. An experiment in tool integration: the DDBG parallel and distributed debugger. *Euromicro Journal of Systems Architecture*, (11):897–907, 1999. Elsevier Science Press.

[5] G. Dózsa, T. Fadgyas, and P. Kacsuk. GRAPNEL: A graphical programming language for parallel programs. In *Eighth Symposium on Microcomputer and Micropocessor Applications*, pages 285–293. IEEE Press, October 1994.

[6] G. Dozsa, P. Kacsuk, and T Fadgyas. Development of graphical parallel programs in PVM environments. In *Proceedings of the 1st Austrian-Hungarian Workshop on Distributed and Parallel Systems (DAPSYS'96)*, pages 33–40, Miskolc, Hungary, October 1996.

[7] Etnus Inc., Framingham, MA. *TotalView User's Guide (v3.9.0)*, June 1999. http://www.etnus.com/.

[8] R. Hood. The p2d2 project: Building a portable distributed debugger. In *Proc. of SPDT'96: SIGMETRICS Symposium on Parallel and Distributed Tools*, pages 127–136, Pennsylvania, USA, May 1996. ACM Press.

[9] P. Kacsuk, J. C. Cunha, G. Dózsa, J. Lourenço, T. Fadgyas, and T. Antão. A graphical development and debugging environment for parallel programs. *Parallel Computing*, 22(1997):1747–1770, 1997. Elsevier Science Press.

[10] P. Kacsuk, G. Dózsa, and T. Fadgyas. Designing parallel programs by the graphical language GRAPNEL. *Microprocessing and Microprogramming*, 41:625–643, 1996.

[11] H. Krawczyk and B. Wiszniewski. Object-oriented model of paralel programs. In *Proc. 4th EUROMICRO Workshop on Parallel and Distributed Processing*, pages 80–86, Braga, Portugal, 1996. IEEE Computer Society.

[12] J. Lourenço, J.C. Cunha, H. Krawczyk, P. Kuzora, M. Neyman, and B. Wiszniewski. An integrated testing and debugging environment for parallel and distributed programs. In *Proceedings of the 23rd EUROMICRO Conference (EUROMICRO'97)*, pages 291–298, Budapeste, Hungary, September 1997. IEEE Computer Society Press.

Chapter 14

The **Tape/PVM** Monitor and the **PROVE** Visualization Tool

Péter Kacsuk, J. Chassin de Kergommeaux, É. Maillet and J.-M. Vincent

Abstract

This chapter presents the monitoring and visualization tools developed in the SEPP project. The main characteristics of the Tape/PVM monitoring tool are a precise and causally coherent event dating and a minimal perturbation of the analyzed applications. The trace is analyzed and visualized by the Prove visualization tool. The most salient characteristics of Prove are the click-back and click forward facilities, to relate the source code of parallel applications with the visualizations of their executions. Another important feature is the zooming facility, to combine high-level visualizations giving a global view of parallel applications behaviors with the ability to delve into details when it is necessary.

14.1 Introduction

Performance visualization is a new branch of program development not used in the case of sequential programs. Performance visualization aims at discovering performance bottle-necks in logically correct parallel programs. Such bottle-necks can lead back to previous stages of the parallel program development according to the nature of the bottle-neck. Performance visualization is based on intensive run-time monitoring. In the GRADE parallel program development environment two tools have been integrated in order to realize performance visualization support. These tools are:

- Tape/PVM monitor

- PROVE visualization tool

The current chapter describes these tools and their usage in the GRADE program development environment.

14.2   Structure of performance visualization systems

Performance visualization systems typically consist of four stages as shown in Figure 14.1. The first stage, the source code instrumentation stage, serves for instrumenting the code with the necessary calls to the operating system or to the underlying extended communication library. The second stage serves to collect trace events during the execution of the parallel program. These collected events are typically stored in one or several log files that are analysed after the execution of the program. This third stage, called trace analysis stage is important in order to establish the physical or logical timing order of the collected events. Finally, the ordered events are visualised by several display views in order to give easily conceivable explanation of the nature of parallel program execution.

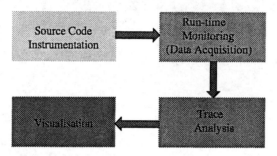

Figure 14.1: Stages of performance visualization

Performance visualization systems can be classified according to how they support the four stages of performance measurement. Source code instrumentation is decisive concerning the convenient use of the system or simply from the point of view of usability. Scalability is another important aspect of performance visualization systems.

Scalability is strongly related to the second and third stages of performance visualization. A tool is scalable if it enables the analysis of large, long running parallel programs. It requires special techniques to avoid the generation of too large trace files at run-time. Finally, versatility is another key issue that defines the various display views that the performance visualization system can provide as well as the interoperability with other visualization tools. In the next sections we give a detailed description of all these three aspects and show how they are supported by the Tape/PVM monitor and the PROVE visualization tool in the GRADE programming environment.

14.3   Source code instrumentation

Source code instrumentation has four major components that should be considered in classifying performance visualization systems:

1. Instrumentation mode

2. Filtering

3. Support for monitoring modes

4. Support for click-back facility

The instrumentation mode can be manual or automatic. All the state-of-the-art performance visualization systems provide automatic instrumentation. It means that the user has not to touch the source code, it is the task of the compiling/linking system to transform the original source code or to call extended instrumented communication libraries that support run-time monitoring. In the case of GRADE it is the GRP2C pre-compiler and the GRAPNEL Library that are responsible for supporting automatic code instrumentation. The GRAPNEL Library can call either instrumented PVM or MPI library calls for tracing communication events. It also provides instrumented calls for the graphical blocks of GRAPNEL enabling the GRAPNEL graphical block level event generation and visualization.

Filtering means that the user can specify for the compiling/linking system the interesting program components for which the run-time events should be generated and collected. The lack of such a facility makes the trace file unnecessarily big. Oppositely, filtering makes the trace file customisable to the particular interest of the programmer. The size of the trace file is one of the most crucial problem of performance visualization systems and hence all facilities that can reduce its size are worth supporting. In GRADE, filtering is supported at the level of GRAPNEL as a built-in feature of GRED. In a pull-down menu all the GRAPNEL graphical block types can be filtered. In default, PROVE will collect events on the entry and exit point of each GRAPNEL graphical block. However, if the user is interested for example, only in the SEQ, CAI, CAO and CAIALT blocks, he can filter out all the other graphical blocks (LOOPS, LOOPE, etc.) by the Filter Types pull-down menu as shown in Figure 14.2. Moreover there is a possibility to individually turn on or off filtering on each graphical block of the GRAPNEL program. In this way, the programmer is able to customise the monitoring system to his particular interest and to focus on the events most interesting for him.

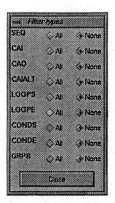

Figure 14.2: Filter Types pull-down menu

Basically two monitoring modes are supported in performance visualization systems. The first one is the collection of individual events, the second one is the collection of statistical information. The former one is supported by Tape/PVM. The current version of PROVE cannot provide statistical information. However, in the new version of GRADE, called P-GRADE (Professional GRADE) both the monitoring system and PROVE will support the collection and visualization of statistical information. The application of statistical information helps in reducing the size of the trace file and hence its usage is highly advantageous.

Although, the click-back facility is one of the most important facilities of performance visualization systems, there are only very few systems that support this feature. The general problem with performance visualization systems is that they provide various graphical views on the program execution based on collected events but they cannot explain which part of the source code is responsible for the generation of the visualised events. The click-back facility applied in advanced tools is a remedy for the problem. It means that when clicking on a visualised event, the system can highlight the part of the source code that is responsible for the generation of the event.

The click-forward facility is the opposite of the click-back facility and it means that when clicking on a source code line, the visualization tool can indicate on its graphical views which events were generated by the selected source code line.

The pair-wise use of click-back and click-forward facilities ensure the perfect identification of the role of program components during the parallel program execution.

The click-back facility of GRADE is illustrated in Figure 14.3. The vertical time bar in the space-time diagram of PROVE in Figure 14.3 is used to realize the click-back facility. The time bar selects the interesting or relevant moment of the execution time. Clicking on the cross point of any process line and the time bar will result in highlighting (making red) the corresponding process in the application window and the corresponding graphical block in the process window. Vice versa, clicking on a graphical block in the process window, the time bar will move in the space-time diagram to the next event that was generated by the selected graphical block.

The click-back facility of PROVE is strongly supported by the Tape/PVM monitor. In order to allow users to quickly find the statement in their source code that generated a particular event, Tape/PVM's events contain the line number of that statement and the identifier of the source code file. In fact, the user's source code is instrumented by Tape/PVM's pre-processor (*tapepp, tapeppf*) which knows the name of the file it processes and the current line number. Each time a probe is inserted into the user's code (at a call of a PVM library function, for instance) the information about file name and line number is given to that probe (in a way similar to Aims [8]). Thus, a visualization tool, like PROVE, can feature source code click-back based on Tape/PVM traces.

14.4   Data acquisition

Data acquisition is realized by the Tape/PVM run-time monitoring system. Tape/PVM[1] is a tool to generate event traces of PVM applications for post-mortem performance analysis, e.g., discrete event simulation and visualization. It comprises the tool to generate the traces, as well as a utility to transform the traces into the PICL format. It also contains a library of C functions which allows to easily read the generated traces.

Trace generation and post-mortem analysis of traces are two different research areas, each with its own specific problems. The main problem of trace analysis is the design of an appropriate model and a simulator based on that model. The simulator takes a trace file (set of events) as input and reconstructs the successive global states of the system on which the traces were generated. Such a simulator can be coupled with a visualization tool to give a global view of the system under study. However, the simulation is only as accurate as its input - the trace file. Such a trace file has to be representative of what really happened in the parallel system under study. Thus, the main problem in designing a tracing tool is

---

[1]The manual and Tape/PVM's distribution are available at ftp://ftp.imag.fr/imag/APACHE/TAPE

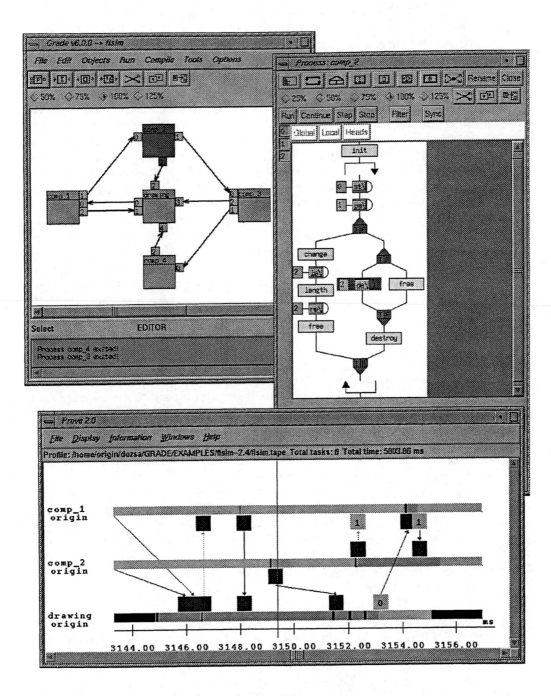

Figure 14.3: Click-back facility in PROVE

to guarantee the representative quality of the generated traces. The design of Tape/PVM particularly focused on the following two points:

1. Precise, causally coherent event dating,

2. Minimal perturbation of analyzed applications.

Some existing tracing tools for PVM focus on trace visualization and "real-time" interaction rather than on the representative quality of the generated traces. XPVM [3] for example, is a graphical console and monitor for PVM. It uses the event collection mechanism integrated in PVM V3.3.0 or later. Events are routed to XPVM by the PVM kernel during run-time of the instrumented application. Thus, XPVM can update its views in "real time". XPVM can also be used for post-mortem trace analysis using the events of previous executions saved into a file. However, whatever the mode in which XPVM is used, real-time or post-mortem, its traces represent potentially perturbed applications due to on-line event message routing. These messages increase the load of the network which can infer a change in behaviour of the observed application (in fact, many parallel applications are non-deterministic). In addition, the tracing mechanism of the PVM kernel relies on a globally synchronized system clock. Not many systems have a global time reference which is sufficiently accurate to avoid dating anomalies.

In Tape/PVM a non-intrusive, statistical method is used to estimate a precise global time reference [5] (see Chapter 6 for more information on global time implementation in Tape/PVM). Rather than doing post-mortem tachyon removal, an a priori tachyon prevention is achieved through the use of a global time reference. Dated events are causally coherent. However, the estimated global time is only available at the end of the instrumented application which prohibits on-line dating. This is not a drawback because Tape/PVM is intended for post-mortem trace analysis only. In addition to this, at generation, an event is not routed to a central collector task, like in XPVM, in order to avoid additional network load. Instead, the events are stored in local event buffers, which are flushed to local event files. The collection of events into a single file is only done at the end of the user's application to avoid interfering with it.

The problem of perturbation of parallel applications due to the presence of a tracing tool is a difficult one. The approach of Tape/PVM is similar to the one adopted in the Aims environment [8]. Although intrusion can be reduced by careful implementation of the tracing tool, it can not be eliminated. The main causes of intrusion are the flushing of local event buffers, the accumulation of the delays of each individual event generation, as well as the additional messages exchanged by the tracing tool. To limit the intrusion due to Tape/PVM the following techniques are used:

- On-line compacting of events. This allows a gain of about 50% with respect to a non-compacted text representation of events. The number of buffer flushes is significantly reduced and so is the perturbation of the application.

- The number of messages exchanged by Tape/PVM is reduced to a minimum. Only events like *PVM_addhost* and *PVM_ kill* which change the configuration of the parallel virtual machine need such additional messages.

- The additional tasks used by Tape/PVM (for global control, for clock synchronisation) are not active while the instrumented user application is running.

14.5   Trace analysis

The third stage of performance visualization is devoted to trace analysis. The physical clocks of the processors in a distributed system are usually non synchronized or even in the case of synchronisation they can be drifted to each other. Hence the data collected at run time and time-stamped by the ticks of the physical clocks cannot be considered as strongly and precisely ordered. The first task of the data analysis is to create an at least logical ordering among the collected events. The most frequently used ordering criteria is based on the happened-before relation introduced by [4]. In the GRADE system the Tape/PVM monitor is applied which guarantees the physical ordering of events in the trace file according to a non-intrusive, statistical clock synchronisation algorithm [5].

The trace analysis phase should also support some displaying features that are most relevant for the user. Such facilities are zooming and filtering. Zooming means that the user can focus on any part of the whole execution and the visualization view shows the selected part in a much more detailed way. The zooming facility of PROVE is shown in Figure 14.4 and Figure 14.5 for the same program that is shown in Figure 14.3. Total view of the complete program is given in Figure 14.4 but in such a condensed figure the details of communication and other events cannot be observed. A zoomed version of Figure 14.4 is shown in Figure 14.5 where only three processes were selected in the time interval of 3144–3156. Notice that such a zoomed figure can give details on the ports applied in the communication events as well as on the change of state of processes during and among communications. The different colours in the horizontal process bars represent different process states like idle, waiting for communication and busy.

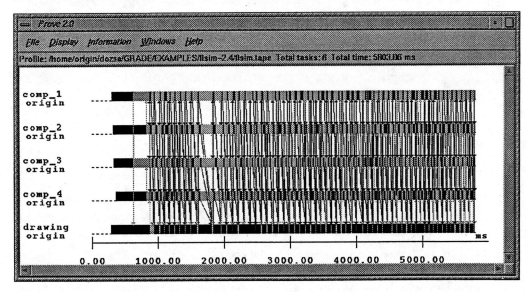

Figure 14.4: The complete space-time diagram of the flight simulation program

The role of post-mortem filtering is different from the role of the filtering during code instrumentation. Post-mortem filtering helps in selecting relevant information from the collected data similarly to the zooming feature. However, filtering is more selective than zooming and hence it can help in selecting the required processes, processors, communication

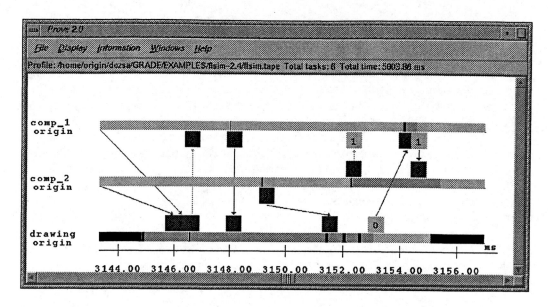

Figure 14.5: The zoomed space-time diagram of the flight simulation program

events, etc. and to visualise only these selected events and units. In order to help the user in selecting post-mortem filters and to rearrange the order of processes and processors in the space-time diagram PROVE provides the dialog window shown in Figure 14.6.

14.6   Visualization

Most performance visualization tools (Paragraph [2] Pablo [7] VAMPIR [6]) provide a significant number of various display views to visualise the various aspects of program execution. The current version of PROVE gives detailed space-time diagram which describes the communication aspects of parallel processes as well as the change of their state in time. It also shows on which processor the processes were executed and when they were created on the processor. The space-time diagram of PROVE is shown in Figure 14.4 and Figure 14.5.

PROVE provides three additional windows for statistical purposes. One of them shows the processor utilization by representing process states in a common window. When all the processes that were executed on a particular processor are shown by the Process State Window, the utilisation of the selected processor is well demonstrated. The other two statistical windows are related to communication. The Process Communication window shows the amount of process communication as function of time. The Host Communication window displays the amount of communication among selected hosts in the communication network or among selected processors in a parallel computer. The time range of the three windows are jointly synchronized together with the space-time diagram. The statistical windows are shown in Figure 14.7.

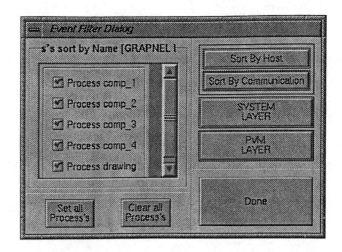

Figure 14.6: Event filter dialog window in PROVE

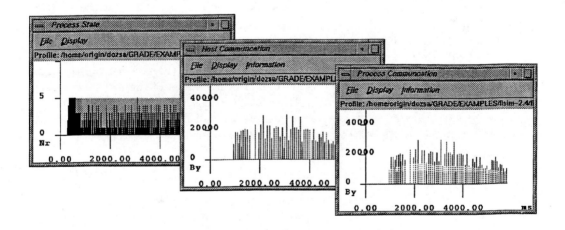

Figure 14.7: Statistical windows of PROVE

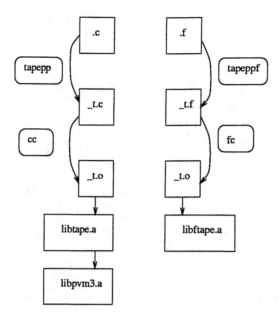

Figure 14.8: Tape/PVM system architecture

14.7   Tape/PVM instrumentation architecture

So far we have described Tape/PVM and PROVE from the user's point of view. In the current section we give some insight into the Tape/PVM instrumentation of GRAPNEL programs which is practically hidden from the user. The only feature which is important for the user is the way how to set the Tape/PVM instrumentation option when he/she starts the GRADE system.

In Chapter 11, it is explained how to generate C source code from GRAPNEL programs and how to extend them with the necessary PVM or MPI function calls through GRAPNEL Library functions. In the current section we show how to create the necessary instrumentation for the Tape/PVM trace generation system. The main idea of the instrumentation is that every PVM call is replaced in a pre-processing phase with its instrumented version taken from the Tape/PVM library. Instrumenting a parallel application for Tape/PVM comprises three phases which will be discussed in the following subsections.

14.7.1   Pre-processing phase

Tape/PVM proposes a trace format along with a series of tools operating on this format. Users are also allowed to define their own trace format. In this section we assume pre-processing is done in order to generate traces in the Tape/PVM format.

The Tape/PVM software distribution contains special pre-processing tools which can automatically insert instrumentation points (*probes*) in C and Fortran application source files[2]. The pre-processing phase consists essentially of inserting a call to the Tape/PVM initialization function (*tapestart* or *tapefstart*) and in *intercepting* calls to the PVM library.

---

[2]User code pre-processing is required because Tape/PVM does not use PVM's run-time event collection mechanism.

For each PVM library function there is an associated intercepting function which records the trace information before passing control to the actual PVM function.

The Tape/PVM pre-processor is called *tapepp* or *tapeppf* depending on whether you want to instrument C or Fortran code. Use

$$tapepp[f] \ [options] \ source.(f \mid c)$$

to create an instrumented source code. The resulting instrumented source file is called *source.t.(f | c)*[3]. The *tapepp* tools associate a unique source file identifier to each source file they processed and keep these identifiers in a database. The generated Tape/PVM events contain pointers to the line number and file identifier which contain the statement that generated the event. Thus, analysis tools based on Tape/PVM traces can feature source code click-back.

14.7.2   Compiling phase

The instrumented source files (*_t.(f | c)*) are compiled like the non instrumented files with few exceptions:

- The _t.c files need a special include file.

- Due to instrumentation insertion, the _t.f file may contain lines longer than the 72 characters allowed by standard Fortran (a special option has to be used in order to permit longer lines - unfortunately, there is no standard way in Fortran to do so).

14.7.3   Linking phase

Like the PVM library, the Tape/PVM library comprises two modules: a main library *libtape.a* and the associated Fortran interface library *libftape.a*. The dependencies between the different modules are shown in Figure 14.8. The name of the instrumented executable has to be the same as the name of the corresponding non-instrumented executable suffixed by _t. When intercepting *PVM spawn* calls, Tape/PVM automatically suffixes the task's name by _t. If this naming convention is not respected, all the *spawns* in the instrumented application will fail.

14.8   Tape/PVM as a stand-alone tool

The Tape/PVM monitor can be used independently from GRADE as a stand-alone tool for monitoring PVM programs and its output can be connected to stand-alone visualization tools like Paragraph. The trace format output by Tape/PVM is close to the PICL format [1]. A tool (*t2p , t2np*) can be used to transform the traces to the PICL format so that they can be visualised with Paragraph [2]. A special feature of *t2p* is that it models the overhead due to buffer flushes by the "overhead" state. Thus, with Paragraph, the overhead due to buffer flushes is clearly outlined on the "Task Gantt Chart" so that users can study the intrusion by comparing different executions using different buffer sizes (which can be parameterised in Tape/PVM). *t2p* also takes into account the overhead due to packing (unpacking) data in (from) messages. Visualization of group operations in Tape/PVM is fully supported.

---

[3] *(f | c)* means that the extension is either .f or .c.

14.9   Conclusions

The Tape/PVM monitor proved to be easily integrated into the GRADE programming environment. Besides, it can be used as a stand-alone monitoring tool for PVM programs. The main features of Tape/PVM are as follows:

- Trace of events at user application level (PVM library calls) through function call interception.

- Pre-processor to instrument user source code (C or Fortran) automatically (instrumented source code has to be recompiled).

- User defined events (like *printf*).

- An event contains the line and file number of the instruction which generated the event (source code feed-back).

- Selective tracing using *source code module groups* and *event types*.

- Precise, causally coherent global time reference.

- On-line event compacting (gain up to 50% with respect to text storage) to limit event buffer flushes.

- Includes a C library which allows to read Tape/PVM traces easily.

- Can generate PICL traces for use with Paragraph.

The PROVE visualization tool is strongly integrated with the Tape/PVM monitor and also with other tools of the GRADE program development environment. Such a strong integration enables the unique click-back and click-forward facilities of PROVE.

Acknowledgements

Tape/PVM was developed in the framework of the APACHE research project, supported by Centre National de la Recherche Scientifique (CNRS), Institut National Polytechnique de Grenoble (INPG), Institut National de Recherche en Informatique et Automatique (INRIA) and Université Joseph Fourier (UJF) Grenoble.

References

[1] G. A. Geist, M. T. Heath, Peyton B. W., and P. H. Worley. PICL, a portable instrumented communication library. TN 37831-8083, Oak Ridge National Laboratory, Oak Ridge, USA, 1991.

[2] M. T. Heath and J. A. Etheridge. Visualizing the performances of parallel programs. *IEEE Transactions on Software Engineering*, 8(5):29–39, May 1991.

[3] J.A. Kohl and G. A. Geist. The PVM 3.4 tracing facility and XPVM 1.1. In *Proc. of the 29th. Hawai International Conference on System Sciences*, 1996.

[4] L. Lamport. Time, clocks, and the ordering of events in a distributed system. *Communications of the ACM*, 21(7):558–565, 1978.

[5] É. Maillet and C. Tron. On Efficiently Implementing Global Time for Performance Evaluation on Multiprocessor Systems. *Journal of Parallel and Distributed Computing*, 28:84–93, July 1995.

[6] W. E. Nagel, A. Arnold, M. Weber, H. Hoppe, and K. Solchenbach. VAMPIR: Visualization and analysis of MPI resources. *Supercomputer 63*, 12(1):69–80, 1996.

[7] R. A. D. Reed, A. U. Aydt, L. DeRose, C. L. Mendes, R. L. Ribler, E. Shaffer, H. Simitci, J. S. Vetter, D. R. Wells, S. Whitmore, and Y.g Zhan. Performance analysis of parallel systems: Approaches and open problems. In *Joint Symposium on Parallel Processing (JSPP)*, pages 239–256, Nagoya, Japan, June 1998.

[8] J. C. Yan. Performance tuning with AIMS — an automated instrumentation and monitoring system for multicomputers. In *Proc. of the Twenty-Seventh Annual Hawai Conference on System Sciences*, pages 625–633. IEEE Computer Society Press, 1994.

Chapter 15

Parallel System Simulation Toolset (PA&AS)

Remo Suppi

Abstract

The design and development of a parallel application can be focused by two different points of view: 'design of parallel program, execution and monitoring, analysis and redesign' and 'design of parallel program, simulation, analysis and redesign'. The first one is the most conventional form, but presents several disadvantages such as: full code must be written, a long timescale in the developing cycle, difficult tuning and debugging, etc. The second approach allows effective design decisions with acceptable performance of the resulting system in such aspects as: parallel algorithms & architectures, scalibility, tuning, etc. This chapter describe the Parallel Architecture and Algorithm Simulation toolset (PA&AS) that has been designed in the framework of the EC-SEPP project (CIPA- C193-0251). These simulation tools allow the user to get information and conclusions about the performance and behaviour of the parallel system under study using simulation.

15.1 Introduction

Parallel architectures and distributed systems appear as a promising approach due to the need of large processing capabilities required by complex applications. This potential however is still constrained by the great complexity in the utilization of such systems for most of the users. This fact is due to dependencies and relationships that appear in parallel/distributed computing where some processes must communicate and synchronize to each other. These new features were not present in sequential programming in monoprocessor architectures. All these new factors are quite complex and make more difficult all the tasks related to analysis and performance evaluation.

The performance evaluation of a parallel system can be based on a set of indices such as execution time, utilization of the processors, volume of communications, maximum traffic capacity, message latency, average number of messages, etc. However, the user must distinguish if these measures provide the required information to estimate the efficiency of the parallel system. Moreover, other factors such as the selection of a parallel algorithm, implementation, process allocation on the architecture (mapping), execution order of processes (scheduling) and routing policy increase the difficulty of analyzing performance evaluation.

The simulation constitutes an evaluation method that offers a trade-off solution between validation - monitoring and efficiency. Therefore, it is presented as a valid alternative for the different studies that satisfy the required performance indices.

The simulation method is guided to characterize the elements that take part in a parallel system, to model and to obtain a valid representation for them. Using these models the simulator is able to obtain performance results without the real implementation and/or execution [5].

Some important advantages of simulation methods to evaluate parallel computer systems are the following ones:

- Rapid prototyping for user's applications.

- Characterization of the architecture scalability.

- Analysis of the different machines behavior to measure the matching degree between algorithm and architecture.

- Performance evaluation of the parallel approach.

- Saving time with respect to the analytic methods.

Basically, simulation involves modelling and there are three types of entities to be defined: real system, model and simulator. These entities cannot be properly understood in isolation but must be seen in their relation to each other [3, 5].

There are two fundamental kinds of correlations: modelling deals with the relationships between real systems and models, while simulation refers to the relationships between models and computers. The modelling relation concerns the validity of a model as a representation of a real system. The simulation relation concerns the faithfulness with which the simulator executes the instructions intended by the model. A difficult choice in the design of the simulator is the degree of detail adopted to describe the real system (parallel architecture and parallel algorithm). Simulator performance and model precision are interdependent and require a trade-off solution.

A dynamic data flow programming approach for the parallel program model has been selected to model the parallel algorithm. This algorithm model is oriented to the functionality model. The functionality model is based on the independence between the sequential code of each node and its firing rules. This modeling formalism is described in Chapter 7.

Parallel architectures are modeled by directed graphs. The nodes represent hardware modules: processors, switches, and I/O elements and the arcs represent the interconnection network between hardware modules. The hardware nodes have a set of parameters to model their characteristics (processing speed, memory size, number of I/O channels, etc.) and the hardware links are modeled by their communication speed and buffer size (see Chapter 7).

The approach to model the operating system running in a multiprocessor system is to model the basic activity of a replicated microkernel that exists in each monoprocessor. This operating system model includes some submodels: memory, process and input/output management and file systems control that add an overhead in execution time for each process.

The Parallel Architecture and Algorithm Simulation toolset (PA&AS) has been designed in the framework of the Software Engineering for Parallel Processing project (EC Copernicus Project CIPA-C193-0251). The main objective of this project is to provide tools for programming and evaluating parallel machines from a performance point of view and also to provide an appropriate set of tools for non-professional users.

Section 15.2 shows the relation of PA&AS with the other GRADE tools (Chapter 10) as well as the set of tools included in this toolset. A description of the simulator structure, the static-dynamic behavior, simulation tool interface and an example in order to validate the results of the simulation tool is developed in Section 15.3. Finally, the conclusions are presented in Section 15.4.

15.2 The GRADE environment and the simulation toolset

The PA&AS toolset is a part of the GRADE environment (see Chapter 10) [1]. In this environment there are several interactions with the other tools (Figure 15.1). Basically, the interaction is in defining the interconnection from resources used by the simulator and generated by others tools.

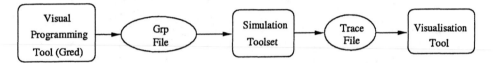

Figure 15.1: Grade Environment

There are three tools interrelated with the simulation toolset:

- Visual Programming Tool (GRED): This tool provides a programming environment that allows the user to develop the parallel application in a visual way. The simulation environment must extract the synthetic graph of the parallel application in order to simulate its execution. On the other hand the results of the simulation must be used by the replay tool to animate the simulated execution on visual programming screen (Chapter 10).

- Automatic Mapping Tool: This tool generates the allocation policy applying different strategies (see Chapter 12). The result is a file containing the assignment of processes to processors. It must be pointed out that this allocation file can also be modified by the Mapping editor tool of the simulation environment.

- Visualization: the simulation tool provides the trace file from simulated execution. This trace files must be used as input by the visualization tools.

The simulation toolset includes six tools (Figure 15.2):

- Event Driven Simulator.

- Replay Tool.

- Hardware Editor.

- Mapping Editor.

- Graph and Parameters Editor.

- Parameters Estimation Tool (includes extractor tool).

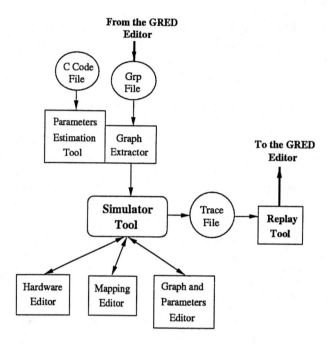

Figure 15.2: Simulation Toolset

Simulator : it corresponds to a discret event-driven simulator that uses synthetic descriptions of a parallel program and a parallel architecture. As a result, it shows the behaviour of the parallel program executed on the parallel architecture. It needs several external inputs: a synthetic program graph file (the simulator accepts a file generated by the Visual Programming Tool), a hardware file, a routing and a mapping file. The synthetic program graph consists of a set of processes with communication actions and their parameters in order to model the static and dynamic behaviour. However, it is also possible to extract the synthetic graph from the graph file description (GRP file, see Chapter 11) using an extractor tool. The hardware file contains a description of the parallel architecture (processors, links, memory, ...) and the corresponding parameters. The routing file describes the intermediate processors used by the messages sent between processes not assigned to the same processor. Finally, the mapping file gives information about how processes are allocated to processors.

Replay Tool : it corresponds to a trace-driven simulator capable of reproducing the execution of a parallel program on different architectures. As input, it uses a trace file consisting of a list of events recorded by the simulator tool or a monitoring tool during the execution of the parallel program on the target system. The replayer has a graphical interface that will show and control, in a graphical and interactive way, the results generated either by the simulator or by the monitoring tool. It uses as external input, a trace file, that includes all events generated by the simulation tool. Moreover, the replay sends the animation message to the Visual Programming Tool (GRED) in order to show these events in the graphical representation of the user program.

There are some additional tools that support the simulation environment:

Hardware Editor : This editor allows the user to create and/or modify the hardware specification. Using this tool, the user can select a regular topology or can specify whatever architecture he/she wants. It is also possible to include the hardware parameters (processing and communication speed,etc) and to specify the routing step between pairs of processors.

Graph and Parameters Editor : With this tool the user can modify the structure of the synthetic graph or their parameters in order to manage minor modifications in the application graph.

Mapping Editor : The user can assign processes to processors using this tool. The user can select a manual or automatic assignment. When the automatic assignment is selected, the Editor calls another program that computes a static mapping policy using clustering strategies and provides this assignment to the Mapping Editor.

Parameters Estimation Tool : This tool accepts as input the C code generated by the Visual Programming Tool and using estimation concepts extracts a set of parameters (without execution of the binary code) necessary to fulfill the parameters of the graph extracted from the application user code by the extractor tool. These parameters include: size of sequential code for each event, probabilities of loops or communication actions, iteration numbers and size of iteration loop, arrival and departure point of communication actions, etc.

15.2.1   Shared files and data

The simulator interacts with the others tools by exchanging the following files and data:

- Grp.File: The Extractor Tool reads the grp.file to obtain all the necessary information about the graph application described by the user, basically processes and communication actions, and writes the Graph.file.

- Trace.File: This file is generated by the Simulator and has all recorded events produced during the simulation runtime. This file is generated according to two formats: an internal format used by the replay tool to animate the simulated execution onto visual programming graph screen; and a standard format (npicl [6]) used as input to a standard performance visualization tool (i.e., Paragraph).

- Graph.file: this file is extracted from Grp.File and has all elements of the user application. The Parameters Estimation tool uses the code from Grp.file and fulfills the necessary parameters inside this file.

- Hw.file: This file is produced by the Hardware Editor and has the architecture description. This description is produced from a topology library (regular architectures) or by the user description in the HW editor.

- Mapping.file: This file is generated by the Mapping Editor. The Mapping editor uses the results of the hand selected mapping policies to produce this file. Moreover, the Mapping Editor also includes an interface to receive the results of the automatic mapping tool.

- Communication Messages: The Replay Tool reads the trace.file (generated by the Simulation Tool) and generates the corresponding messages sent to the Visual Programming Tool (GRED editor) for the animation of the parallel application.

15.3   Simulator Structure

The objective of the following paragraph is to describe the design, specification and implementation of a discret event simulator for a parallel computing system whose model was described in Chapter 7. As initial point, the design is guided towards a multicomponent simulation model. In this model the simulator have several functional units and these units will simulates the behaviour of some parts of the real system.

This condition implies a set of advantages as follows:

- Deadlock free simulator: in spite of the fact that deadlock could exist in the system to simulate.

- Simulator functionality can be updated in an easy form.

- Simple implementation of the simulator code with the advantages of partial tests (debugging) support and by units.

- Modular validation of the simulator.

The simulation model is based on the objectives of modularity and hierarchy. The methodology employed for the formal specification is to analyze the elements of the model and to develop a simulator that satisfies the simulation conditions of the model. It is important to note that this design must be applicable to a monolithic simulator (data and simulator on the same machine) as much as to a distributed one (replicas of the simulator with distributed data).

15.3.1   Functional description

The first step within the functional description of the discret event simulator is to identify the different events that exist on the physical system. The second step is the design of the simulator that could handle these events.

The execution of a parallel application (processes) on a parallel architecture generates the following events:

- Creation/destruction of a process on the processor memory.

- Process ready to be executed on a processor.

- Partially ready process.

- Beginning/end execution of a process.

- Blocked/not blocked process.

- Send/receive message with blocking/not blocking.

- Send/receive synchronization.

- Verify if send/receive has ended.

- Verify if there is available message.

- Waiting until a message is available.

The parallel architecture generates the following events:

- Hardware element free/busy

- Routing step (beginning/end) with/without concurrent execution.

- Load/unload of a process in the processor memory.

- Block/unblock of a process by the condition of link buffer full/empty.

- Task assignment to a processor.

- Load balancing/migration of task of a processor to another.

- Local manager of CPU.

- Basic input/output.

- Hardware failure.

It should be taken into account that some of these events are interrelated events; that is to say, they are consequence of the same action. For example, a process that sends a blocking message will block if and only if there is not enough memory capacity to store the message associated with the link that will be used to send the message.

15.3.2 Static Description

Taking into account the types of events, the different units that will handle them within the simulator can be identified. The relationship between the different modules is shown in Figure 15.3.

The modules are independent and communicate through shared lists. Each list belongs only to one module that has read rights only for this list. The remaining modules can access this list with write rights only.

The functionality of each unit is the following:

- Algorithm and Architecture Control Unit: The main task of this unit is to load and to manage the different elements used during the simulation runs: the elements of the architecture and the parallel application processes. Furthermore, this unit must load and control the result files (trace file) generated during the simulation. As an entry, this unit receives the specification files for parallel application and the parallel architecture.

- Blocking Unit: This unit stores the processes that can not send/receive their messages and are waiting for these events to take place.

- Execution Unit: This unit controls the simulation time and decides the advance of the simulated time. This unit processes the elements of the model and distributes the events toward the remaining units. Its role is fundamental since is the only one that takes decisions on the events to simulate and controls the work of the others units. In other words this unit accomplishes, in addition toits own work, the coordination of the work of the remaining units of the simulator. It receives, as a parameter, the global execution policy.

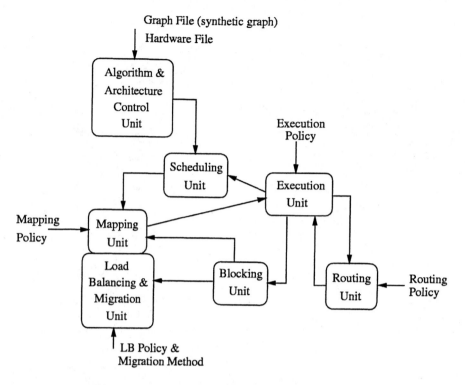

Figure 15.3: Simulation tool: Internal description

- Routing Unit: The objective of this unit is to route the messages of the processes through the links of the architecture, so that they arrive to the destination processor according to the routing policy. It receives, as a parameter, the selected routing policy.

- Mapping Unit: This unit identifies the processes and assigns them to the hardware elements according to an established assignment policy (static policy). It receives, as a parameter, the mapping policy to use.

- Load Balancing and Migration Unit: This unit has the goal of simulating the load balancing that is produced on a parallel architecture when a load balancing-migration policy exits (dynamic policies). It receives as parameter the load balancing policy and the migration method.

- Scheduling Unit: The function of this unit is to control the activation of the processes' fire rules that form the parallel application and to change the state of a process when is ready to be executed.

15.3.3   Dynamic Description

Three basic control loops exist in the simulator :

- Execution Unit - Scheduling Unit - Mapping Unit.

- Execution Unit - Blocking Unit - Load Balancing and Migration Unit.

- Execution Unit - Routing Unit.

In the beginning, the user introduces the name of all the files and selects the firing nodes of the application. The Algorithm and Architecture Control Unit controls the loading of these files. Each unit, when is active, reads on its owned list, processes the information (events) and writes in the lists of the other linked units. The activity of a unit ends when it processes all the information in the lists. All the units can write into the trace file to store the events generated during their execution.

It is important to note that the dynamic characteristics of the simulation with respect to the data coherence is maintained by a parameter ("instance") that is added to each activation of a node and/or message. This condition can be necessary when loop-backs exist or when a node produces messages more rapidly than the service time of the destination node. This situation can mean loss of coherence in the data when the destination node receives data from different nodes and these are accumulated to the same input. The instance identification allows the node to wait or process the messages in the indicated order (all those of the same instance). This characteristic allows a behavior such that, using a load balancing policy (dynamic), the nodes activated with the same value of instance could be relocated for execution on another processor reducing the execution time of the parallel application.

15.3.4 The Simulation Tool Interface

The graphical output of the simulation tool is shown in the Figure 15.4.

The simulator interface is divided in four zones containing the following:

- Control Area: this area has the "quick access menu" and icons.

- File Area: identify the simulation and configuration files and the execution policy selected.

- Show Area: This area shows the processed events at simulation runtime.

- Information Area: include the information area and the status area. These two areas show information about the simulator status and the simulation process.

Control Area There are two different zones (Figure 15.5): The upper zone containing the different menus and the main tool controls. The lower zone has the icons and the different fast access controls. The simulation tool offers five different menus:

File : The user can select the different application files (input files and trace file) and call the extractor tool (see Section 15.2).

Simulation Options : this option allows to choose between the different simulation options (the global execution policy, traces files in NPICL format [6] and files of GRAPNEL processes)

View : From this option the user can select the event filter that will be used to generate visual information (show area) or trace information (trace file)

Run : This menu allows to start and to stop the simulation, as well as to select some parameters (the initial processes of the simulation, number of simulation runs)

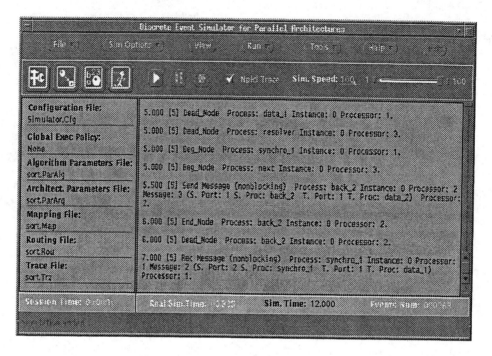

Figure 15.4: Simulation tool window

Figure 15.5: Simulation tool control area

Tools : Through this menu the user has access to tools integrated within the simulation environment. These tools are: The Hardware Editor, the Graph Editor, the Mapping Editor, Parameters Estimation Tool and the Replay tool.

Help : Calls to the Web Browser to show the simulator help.

In lower zone of the bar control area there are icons that allow the user to perform some tasks without using the menu options: access to different tools and simulation controls (start, pause, stop or modify the simulation speed).

File Area This zone (Figure 15.4 -left area-) of the screen gives information on some options that the user has selected for the simulation. This area offers the following information: configuration file, active global execution policy, algorithm, architecture, routing and mapping inputs files and output trace file.

Show Area This area (Figure 15.4 -right area-) shows the events generated by the animation while they are processed. The shown events must be previously selected with the *view* button. The format of events is the following: *TimeEvent Type Auxiliary Data*. The most common auxiliary data are the source process identifier, the source processor and the message identifier.

Information Area This area (Figure 15.4 -botton area-) shows the user the simulation state and the different information messages: session time, real simulation time (in seconds), simulation time and the number of generated and information messages.

The simulation tools (simulator and editors) are executed under the Xwindow environment. A detailed guide for these tools can be found in the *Simulation User Handbook* [4].

15.3.5   Validation of the simulation tool

An important aspect of the simulations tool is the simulation validation, i.e., to verify the behavior of the simulator with respect to a real application. A Master-Slave (M&S) parallel program implemented on PVM [2] has been used to carry out this analysis (Figure 15.6). The process *main* creates the process *master* and the number of *slaves* processes. *Master* sends a message to each *slave* process. Each slave after receiving the master message performs the following task: reads the message from the master, calculates the message CRC (cyclic redundant code), updates the message with this value and sends the message to the right neighbor. This cycle is repeated "n" (n=number of slaves) times.

The procedure to follow will be:

- Real execution of the M&S with the objective of obtaining the parameters for the synthetic graph.

- Simulation of this application and parameters adjustment.

- Analysis of the results and conclusions about the precision as well as considerations on the adjustment of the parameters.

It is important to note that the "first step" is necessary only once to extract the main parameters of the application. With these parameters the user can change in the simulator tool the architecture, the mapping, the routing or redefine the structure of the graph (i.e., add more slaves to test the scalability of the algorithm). These measures have been

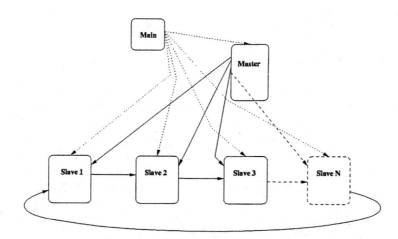

Figure 15.6: Master-Slave program diagram

accomplished under optimum operation conditions (without net load and with the minimal influence of the operating system).

Figure 15.7 and Figure 15.8 show the differences of the results of the simulation (average value of 1000 simulation runs) with the real execution results (average value of 100 executions) for M&S on the same processor and each process on a different processor, respectively. The Figure 15.9 shows the error between the real and simulation measures for both cases.

As it can be observed the differences between real and simulated execution data, it can be asserted that the data obtained by simulation are a valid representation of the real program. The conclusion is that the simulation model is a valid representation of the real system; that is to say, this reproduces the behavior with a sufficient accuracy to satisfy the objectives of the analysis.

In Figure 15.9 the greater error is produced when the Master and the Slaves are in different processor. To reduce this error it would be necessary a most accurate adjustment of the parameters of the architecture since in the simulated example the connection between the processors has been considered as a two-way link with infinite capacity, while the real link is a LAN net (Ethernet) and there are some other communication packets (netload greater than 0).

As a final test, a prediction has been made with the simulator for the execution of 16 slaves and thereafter it has been verified by the real execution of the program. The obtained results are:

- Average execution time by simulation (100 simulation runs): 1444.3506 seconds.

- Average of the real execution time of the application on a cluster of Sun machines (100 executions): 1344.2072 seconds.

- Error: 7.45%

The difference between the simulation and the real execution is due to the local CPU scheduling algorithm. An adjustment of the parameters that models it, would cause a decrease on the error. As a final point of the experiment one can conclude that the proposed objectives have been fulfilled with very good results.

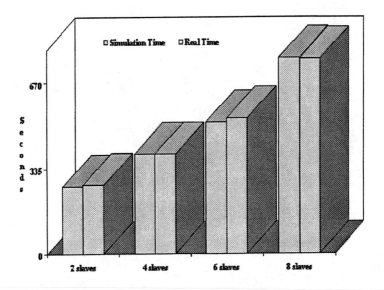

Figure 15.7: Master-Slave application (all process in the same processor)

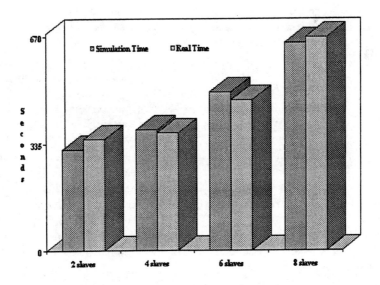

Figure 15.8: Master-Slave application (each slave in a different processor)

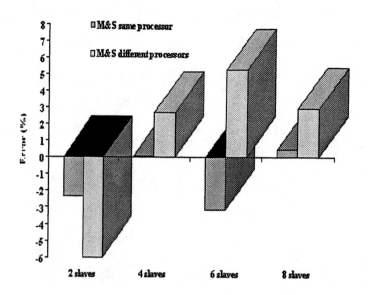

Figure 15.9: Error between real and simulated execution

15.4 Conclusions

The design and development of a parallel application can be focused by two different points of view: 'design of parallel program, execution and monitoring, analysis and redesign' and 'design of parallel program, simulation, analysis and redesign'. The first one is the most conventional form, but presents several disadvantages such as: full code must be written before the cycle is completed, a long timescale in the developing cycle, difficult tuning and debugging in middle and big size problems, etc. The second approach allows effective design decisions with acceptable performance of the resulting system in such aspects as: parallel algorithms & architectures, scalability, tuning, etc. In this sense, a set of tools has been developed. These tools allow the user to get information and conclusions about the performance and behaviour of the parallel system under study. For the second approach the most important tool is the Simulator Tool. This tool allows the user to 'execute' the parallel application on a parallel architecture in a simulated way. This simulation generates useful information about performance evaluation to make decisions on the design. The simulator offers real time visualization, using the GRED User Interface as graphical interface.

The simulator tool has been developed in CAOS Group, University Autonoma of Barcelona (Spain). Binaries, references and User's Manuals can be obtained from www.caos.uab.es/coper.html (Solaris 2.x). The author wishes to thank to Eduardo Cesar, Fernando Cores and Francesc Garcia for their contribution in the development and implementation of the simulator environment.

Acknowledgements

This work has been supported by the CICYT under contracts TIC 95-0868 and TIC 98-0433.

References

[1] G. Dózsa, P. Kacsuk, and T. Fadgyas. GRADE: A graphical programming environment for PVM applications. In *Proceedings of Euromicro Workshop on Parallel and Distributed Processing*, pages 347–354. IEEE Press, 1997.

[2] A. Geist, A. Beguelein, J. Dongarra, W. Jiang, R. Mancheck, and V. Sunderam. *PVM Users's Guide and Reference Manual*. Engineering Physics and Mathemathics Division. Oak Ridge Laboratory, 3.3.10. ornl/tm-12187 edition, 1998.

[3] E. Luque, R. Suppi, and J. Sorribes. Psee: Parallel systems evaluation environment. In *Proceedings of the 5th*. *International PARLE Conference*, volume 1, pages 696–699, 1993.

[4] R. Suppi and E. Luque. *Parallel System Evaluation Environment User's Guide*. Computer Architecture and Operating Systems Group. University Autonoma of Barcelona, 1998. http://www.caos.uab.es/coper.html.

[5] R. Suppi, E. Luque, J. Sorribes, E. Cesar, M. Serrano, and J Falgueras. Performance prediction of parallel systems by simulation. *Computers and Artificial Intelligence*, 17(5):52–60, 1998.

[6] P. Worley. A new picl trace file format. Technical report, Oak Ridge Laboratory, 1992.

Chapter 16

STEPS — a Tool for Structural Testing of Parallel Software

*Henryk Krawczyk, Piotr Kuzora, Marcin Neyman, Jerzy Proficz
and Bogdan Wiszniewski*

Abstract

STEPS is a tool for structural testing of parallel software which incorporates static and dynamic analysis and a visual interface to ease the process of finding errors in parallel C programs with inter-process communication based on standard PVM library calls. The version of the tool described in this chapter has been implemented on Sun Microsystems machines running Solaris with X-Windows and Motif, various GNU system facilities and Quintus Prolog.

16.1   Introduction

The goal of software testing is to devise tests that can exercise the code in a meaningful and systematic way, so that any deviation of its actual behaviour from the expected one can be detected, and yet all the testing activities completed within a reasonable time. These activities are particularly difficult for

parallel and distributed programming for cluster computing, owing to the inherent non-determinism of computations performed simultaneously by many processes. The STEPS addresses a number of issues resulting from this fact within the framework of structural testing, which derives test cases directly from the program code. The tool has been implemented for PVM based parallel programs written in C and solves the following problems:

1. *Analysis of possible interleavings of computations performed by programs running in parallel.* A space of possible states or behaviour cases in a set of parallel programs is potentially infinite. STEPS exploits the fact that computations performed by different processes are physically separated, owing to distribution of memory and processing units, thus can avoid combinatorial explosion in determining whether a system assumes a specific state of interest.

2. *Recognition of events and states occurring in a set of programs that run in parallel.* Intuitively, parallel program execution represents a sequence of events involving *processing* and *communication* operations, where message passing operations are the primary events of interest during monitoring. STEPS uses information logs and breakpoint traps to bring execution of a program under test to some *global* state of interest. With this regard STEPS implements the generic framework for quality testing outlined in Figure 9.5in Chapter 9. In doing that, the tool relies on a high level abstraction of communication events identified in the program code by the means of static analysis of parallelism. These abstract events combine the notion of local data, state and condition of individual component processes into a composite (global) state.

3. *Halting and resuming parallel program execution at specific points.* Owing to the specific combination of static analysis for identifying potential communication events, logging of communication actions, and then deterministically "re-executing" the program, STEPS can achieve the effect of "freezing" program execution at a specific state even when the order of messages is not preserved by communication channels.

4. *Minimization of the intrusion incurred by the monitoring software.* Using breakpoints introduces delays that can alter the execution of the parallel program under test, and thereby hide error symptoms. On the other hand, a monitoring medium is required to record specific data values at specific execution points. STEPS introduces the notion of a test scenario that specifically relates test data, timing of processes, and the composite state of processes under test. This is possible owing to the static analysis of parallelism preceding a real program execution; results of this analysis indicate potential communication events and enable producing special test scenario scripts to force a parallel program to execute in a deterministic fashion. Various scenarios can be designed by direct interaction between the user and the running code.

5. *Detection of error symptoms based on the recorded information.* STEPS supports experimentation in which the user can make hypotheses regarding the cause-and-effect relationship between the program and observed error conditions, can inspect variables and re-execute the program repeatedly many times. The tool captures dynamic execution information and presents it to the user for analysis and evaluation in a truly interactive manner.

6. *Design and rapid prototyping of test cases.* Even thorough analysis of the related parallel program specifications and code may overlook some crucial state configurations. STEPS implements a mechanism for experimenting with various tests before actually running them in a target system, i.e., enables rapid prototyping of test scenarios. It is essential for dealing with programs, whose behaviour is hard to predict or observe.

STEPS represents the program source code with a certain static control structure modeled with a control flowgraph, which consists of interconnected nodes corresponding either to a block of sequential processing statements, or to a communication event involving a possibly small set of matching "send" and "receive" actions [5]. Execution of parallel program processes is modeled with control flow tokens progressing along certain execution threads, visiting graph nodes and interacting with other tokens. Various positions of tokens at the respective threads represent composite states of corresponding processes. Detection and control of composite states is implemented by STEPS with breakpoints installed in the specially *instrumented* code; this installation is transparent and can be modified by the user any time.

Test scenarios considered by STEPS are aimed at exercising paths through individual component processes. A path through a process consists of a sequence of statements executed by that process when going from its one local state to another. Each path has an associated *path condition* and a *path computation*, both being functions on input variables. Selection and execution of paths attempt systematic testing for the set of data, processing and timing errors, defined in Chapter 9.

Processing errors are reproducible, i.e., for the same input data a program will always behave in the same way. Races depend on relative timing between processes, thus actions of various processes may take sporadically different precedence over one another in various program executions, even for the same set of input data. Deadlocks result in a program inability to continue by executing blocking actions of its component processes, a situation that may be caused by races or sudden death of some of its critical processes. STEPS attempts detection of any such kind of error.

Upon selecting processes and events for testing, the tool asks the users to decide what paths and in what order to execute. It assists users in determining the feasibility of paths being selected, provides control over individual movements of control flow tokens, and collects data needed by users to assess test results. Thus defined test scenarios can be re-executed to allow observing patterns of program behaviour.

16.2 A framework for structural testing

As indicated schematically in Figure 16.1, the structural testing methodology implemented by STEPS combines three levels of representation of parallel programs: dynamic program states assumed by the program *run-time code*, decision statements specified by the program *source text*, and *communication events* in which component processes may participate.

Structural testing splits in STEPS into complementary streams, which although addressing their specific issues at distinct representation levels, they jointly constitute a coherent framework. The key concept here is to use static and dynamic analysis to support one another, in order to simplify the main activities of each stream. These streams have been indicated schematically with arrows connecting the three program representation layers mentioned before.

In order to observe a particular behaviour exhibited by a parallel program, testers have to be able to detect communication events during program execution. Event detection is based on information logs and requires two steps: monitoring of communication actions, and scanning the log entries. STEPS performs *event prediction* based on the program source text in order to identify special *monitoring states* requiring detection during experiments. Transitions between monitoring states indicate at what communication actions special monitoring probes (breakpoint traps) shall be installed.

STEPS supports interactive selection of paths through individual component processes and implements symbolic interpretation that mimics a real program execution. Testers may determine *timing relations* between selected paths and *select test data* that satisfy entry conditions for selected paths. Each thus designed test scenario is subsequently implemented by STEPS in a form of a test scenario script. The binary program code is dynamically *instrumented* according to the predefined scenario — breakpoint traps are inserted and special testing procedures associated with them in a form of dynamic trap (software interrupt)

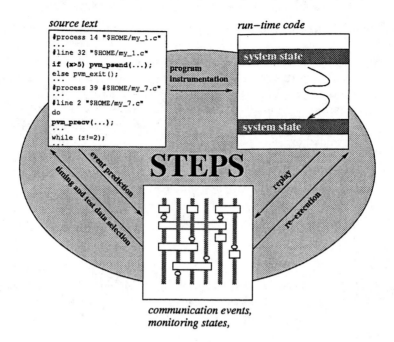

Figure 16.1: Levels of analysis in STEPS

handlers. Testing procedures can fetch processes with input data and enforce specific timing relations of communication actions.

A program under test is started and executed according to a certain test scenario designed by the user. Typically, the first scenario developed by the user is just an initial one in a whole series forming a "cycle". It usually calls for *random* execution of the instrumented program code for any input data provided by the user. During execution, a program behaviour is recorded to the log for further inspection and analysis, and used as input for designing new scenarios. Events are retrieved from log entries and *replayed* on a screen. Static analysis of a program text and dynamic analysis of its run-time code representation enable stepping back and forth through the program dynamic states, inspecting and modifying variables of individual tokens (processes), as well as modifying order of state transitions in protocol machines of communication events. These operations involve *re-execution* of the program binary code from some initial state down to a specific program state of interest and are performed interactively by the user — who is able to design new testing scenarios based on previously executed ones and prototype them before any actual code execution. Throughout the rest of this chapter we will illustrate all the streams of activities mentioned above with a detailed example.

16.2.1   Identification of communication events

The STEPS uses finite state *protocol machines* to represent the dynamic behaviour of parallel processes engaged in any communication event of interest. A detailed analysis of parallel programming primitives in PVM indicates that there is a relatively small set of *classes* of protocol machines.

There are two types of communication actions for sending in PVM: *point-to-point*, when a single process sends a single message to some other process, and *broadcast* or *multicast*, when a single process sends a single message to a group of processes. Communication statements for sending are *buffered*, therefore a sender may proceed without blocking — it always puts a message into the buffer regardless of the state of the receiver.

There are also two types of communication actions for receiving in PVM, either *blocking* or *non-blocking*. In each case, a receiver may want to receive a message from a specific sender or just any sender.

Based on that, STEPS considers three basic classes of application protocols, depending on the number of processes participating in a single communication event: *one-to-one*, in which exactly two processes communicate, *many-to-one*, in which several processes communicate with exactly one process, and *one-to-many*, in which exactly one process communicates with several processes.

Consider for example two source code files `sender.c` and `receiver.c` of a program implementing a simple *Go-back-N* scheme of two processes *sender* and *receiver*, listed below:

```
/* sender.c */
#include <stdio.h>
#include <pvm3.h>
main()
{ int sid, rid;/* ids of sender and receiver */
  int OK;      /* a flag */
  int ack;     /* NACK=-frame#, ACK=frame# */
  int first;   /* frame awaiting ACK */
  int last;    /* frame awaiting ACK */
  int cn;      /* no of frames awaiting ACK */
  int Max;     /* max ACK buffer */

  first=0; last=0; Max=10;
  sid = pvm_mytid();
  printf("sender=%x\n",sid);
  OK = pvm_spawn("receiver",0,0,"",1,&rid);
  if (OK !=1)
   printf("cant start receiver\n");
  else
   while(OK)
   {cn=last-first; /* current buffer count */
    while (cn < Max)
    {last++; /* send next frame */
     cn++; /* increment buffer count */
     pvm_initsend(PvmDataDefault);
     pvm_pkint(&last,1,1);
#line 41
     pvm_send(rid, 1);
     printf("sending frame#=%d\n",last);
    }
#line 44
    pvm_recv(rid,2); /* wait for ACK */
    pvm_upkint(&ack,1,1);
```

```
    printf("receiving ack=%d\n",ack);
    if (ack < 0) /* NACK for frame#=-ack */
     last=-ack; /* retransmit from here */
    else
     first=ack; /* shrink ACK buffer */
   }
   pvm_exit(); exit(0);
}


/* receiver.c */
#include <stdio.h>
#include <pvm3.h>
main()
{ int sid, rid;/* ids of sender and receiver */
  int OK=0;    /* a flag */
  int ack;     /* frame# to be acknowledged */

  sid = pvm_parent(); /* who is the sender */
  rid = pvm_mytid(); /* who am I */
  while (TRUE)
#line 27
   {pvm_recv(sid,1); /* wait for frame */
   pvm_upkint(&ack,1,1);
#line 29
   if (check(ack) == OK) /* corrupted */
    ack=-ack;
   pvm_initsend(PvmDataDefault);
   pvm_pkint(&ack,1,1);
#line 33
   pvm_send(sid, 2); /* send acknowledgement */
   }
   pvm_exit(); exit(0);
}
```

There are two pairs of matching send-receive statements. One pair consists of statement **pvm_send()** at line #41 of the sender process and statement **pvm_recv()** at line #27 of the receiver process; they are handling the transfer of successive top frames from the sender's retransmission buffer, each one indicated by index **last**. Another pair consists of statement **pvm_send()** at line #33 of the receiver process and of statement **pvm_recv()** at line #44 of the sender process; they are handling positive and negative acknowledgments for each frame received by the receiver and determine the size of the retransmission buffer.

The two cooperating processes may exhibit stochastic behaviour observed by the tester, owing to the varying timing relations between sender and receiver, as well as the randomness of the **check()** function call performed by the receiver for each received frame in line #29. We will show later on that this particular implementation of the *Go-back-N* scheme has an error; its detection is possible because of the facility for generating test scenario scripts provided by STEPS.

In order to analyze the behaviour of a parallel program, STEPS performs static reachability analysis to identify matching communication statements and to determine the class of application protocol for each respective communication event. For our example *Go-back-N* implementation STEPS identifies two *one-to-one* communication events and displays them as shown in Figure 16.2.

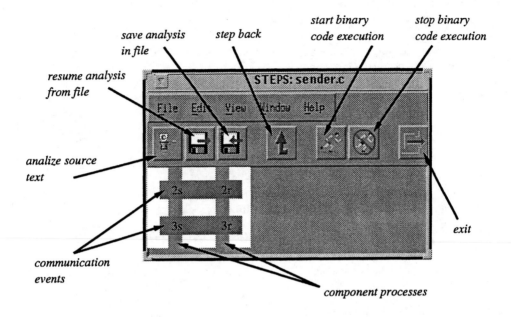

Figure 16.2: Identification of communication events

This is a standard control panel of STEPS, which enables all principal streams of activities indicated in Figure 16.1 [3]. It can be seen that in this particular example internal details of the identified (predicted) events are hidden from the user's view. Of course, all the necessary instrumentation of the code is done by STEPS automatically to enable logging of send and receive actions in each respective communication event during a real code execution. The related events are pairs of matching send and receive actions, denoted respectively as {sender.c:41,receiver.c:27} and {sender.c:44,receiver.c:33}, and displayed briefly as event #2: {2s,2r} and event #3: {3r,3s}. The numbering of events being identified by STEPS during event prediction is automatic, where event #1 always refers to the first spawning of component processes of the analyzed application.

16.2.2   State analysis

STEPS enables detection of parallel program states by utilizing the structuring concept of communication events. This is done in two steps, as specified below. Step 1 involves inserting breakpoint traps into the run-time code to register execution of all respective send and receive statements identified during static analysis of parallelism of the source code. Subsequent execution of so instrumented code yields a log file that is scanned in Step 2:

1. A monitoring process registers to the log file all actions of each component task in the following way:

(a) for each send statement a triple (P_i, s_j, n_k) is registered to the log, where P_i is the relevant `id` number of a sending process, s_j is a unique identifier of the current execution of a relevant send statement, and n_k is a line number of that statement in a source code of the sending process;

(b) for each receive statement a triple (P_i, r_j, n_k) is registered to the log, where P_i is the relevant `id` number of the related receiving process, r_j is a unique identifier of the matching send statement received along with the regular message by the receive action, and n_k is a line number of a relevant receive statement in a source code of the receiving process;

2. Log file created in Step 1 is scanned and the registered log entries interpreted to identify communication events:

(a) the left-most triple not yet analyzed is picked-up,

(b) a set of triples that match a triple picked-up at the previous step is searched and found eventually,

(c) using the results of prior static reachability analysis it is possible to determine the pair of matching triples correponding to each communication event.

For the example *Go-back-N* program a log generated by STEPS (a plain ASCII file readable with any common text editor) may look like this:

```
Log Begin
process #1: send( 1 ) line nr: 41
process #1: send( 2 ) line nr: 41
process #1: send( 3 ) line nr: 41
process #1: send( 4 ) line nr: 41
process #1: send( 5 ) line nr: 41
process #1: send( 6 ) line nr: 41
process #1: send( 7 ) line nr: 41
process #1: send( 8 ) line nr: 41
process #1: send( 9 ) line nr: 41
process #1: send( 10 ) line nr: 41
process #2: receive( 1 from process nr 1 ) line nr: 27
process #2: send( 1 ) line nr: 33
process #2: variable ack = 1
...
Log End
```

It can be seen that in this particular execution of our example program, process #1 (sender) executed its send statement ten times, before process #2 (receiver) was able to execute its receive statement the first time. Further lines of this file indicate the entire execution history of the program instrumented by STEPS.

If specifically requested by the user, STEPS may also register values of specified variables. In this case variable `ack` in the example `receiver.c` process was watched. Watching values of variables, along with registering timing of cooperating processes are two important elements of test scenarios, explained later in more detail.

STEPS is able to *replay* any recorded log file arbitrary many times in a "slow-motion" fashion in the following way:

1. Tokens are displayed on the screen at the initial communication events recorded in the log,

2. The log content is scanned from left to right, and

   (a) the left-most token that according to the respective log entry has to be moved from its current position is found and marked,

   (b) Step 2a is repeated until no new unmarked tokens can be added to the set of marked tokens,

   (c) marked tokens are unmarked and moved to their new positions.

3. Replay is stopped if the log end is reached, otherwise it continues from Step 1.

Using this procedure, STEPS can display a sequence of consecutive states of the parallel program, each one represented by a specific token configuration. For the example program STEPS replays a sequence of state transitions from the log listed before as shown in Figure 16.3. By using the basic STEPS menus STEPS explained before in Figure 16.2, the sequence of token movements may be replayed repeatedly for visual inspection to observe any "anomalous" pattern of behaviour. It also may be explored for alternative behaviour cases by stepping back and choosing different order of individual token movements. This issue is addressed in STEPS as an interactive design of test scenarios.

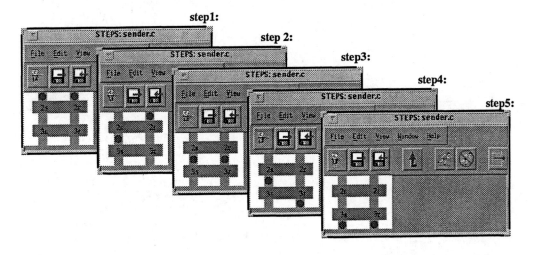

Figure 16.3: Step by step replay of states from the information log

16.3   Design of test scenarios in STEPS

STEPS supports interactive design of test scenarios with the minimum impact on the related processes (see Figure 16.4). First, the *static analyzer* of the PVM text identifies all potential communication events before actually running a program. Paths and data values are selected interactively by the user with the *symbolic interpreter*, according to the syntax of ANSI C.

If a program under test is executed without any specific scenario in mind, i.e., in a random execution mode mentioned before, states reported by the *dynamic analyzer* are registered to a special log file. Upon program termination (or the user's break) the log is interpreted and the corresponding sequence of global program states is retrieved as a sequence of respective token positions. While visualization of token movements aids the user in inspecting program behaviour recorded to the log, formal representation of this behaviour in a machine readable form is essential for STEPS to reproduce program execution for further tests. Such a machine readable representation of a test scenario produced by STEPS is called a *test scenario script (TeSS)*. TeSS scripts provide an input to the *dynamic analyzer*, which is capable of re-running the program from the beginning up to one of the composite states selected by the user from the sequence of states identified by the scenario.

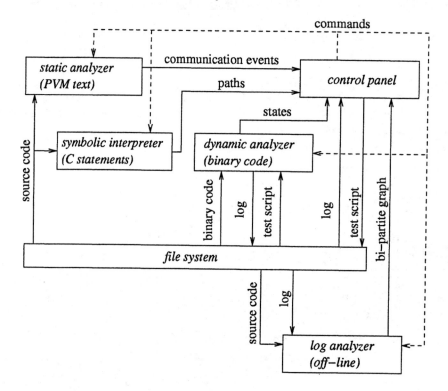

Figure 16.4: Architecture of STEPS

16.3.1 Test preparation

Upon arriving to the selected composite state, all component processes are stopped and *symbolic interpretation* is started to find a transition from the current state to some *target state* of interest. This analysis is interactive, as it is up to the user to decide what paths and in what order to execute. STEPS assists the users in collecting test data and timing information that is necessary to build up a test scenario script.

For example, after the initial execution of the *Go-back-N* program during which all values of ack recorded in the log were positive, one may want to exercise the program for some

corrupted frames. According to the specification of *Go-back-N*, the sender should in such a case retransmit a series of frames starting from the frame number (value of `last`) equal to the most recent negatively acknowledged frame number.

The respective scenario can be designed using the existing log by modifying the value of variable *OK* tested by the receiver in its main loop. Therefore at some state of the program under test its execution shall be suspended and the value of `OK` in the receiver process will be forced to change. The STEPS window enabling that is shown in Figure 16.5; by pressing button **TRUE** one may change a way the program was executing so far.

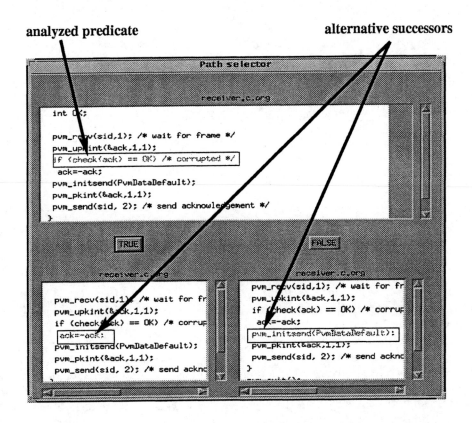

Figure 16.5: Predicate interpretation in line #29 of `receiver.c`

A new test scenario script, shown in Figure 16.6 is generated automatically. Note that this script tells STEPS to override the content of variable `OK` with the value of 1 when the component processes, namely sender (process #1) and receiver (process #2) reach their respective lines #44 and #29.

16.3.2 Test execution

The example TeSS script shown in Figure 16.6 specifies the sequence of composite states of the *Go-back-N* program that guarantees a deterministic execution of the required scenario. Triple (`trap_type,process_no,line_no`) specifies the line and process where the relevant

```
START_FILE:
sender
INITIAL:
[{ (1,1,41) }],
[{ (2,1,41) }],
[{ (1,1,44) }],
[{ (1,1,44),(1,2,27) }],
[{ (1,1,44),(2,2,27) }],
[{ (1,1,44),(1,2,29,[1,1,"OK","1"]) }],
[{ (1,1,44),(1,2,33) }],
[{ (1,1,44),(2,2,33) }],
[{ (2,1,44),(2,2,33) }],
[{ (1,1,41),(2,2,33) }],
[{ (2,1,41),(2,2,33) }],
[{ (2,1,41),(1,2,27) }],
[{ (2,1,41),(2,2,27) }],
[{ (2,1,41),(1,2,33) }],
[{ (2,1,41),(2,2,33) }],
[{ (1,1,44),(2,2,33) }],
[{ (2,1,44),(2,2,33) }],
[{ (1,1,41),(2,2,33) }],
[{ (2,1,41),(2,2,33) }];
```

Figure 16.6: An example TeSS script

breakpoint trap has to be inserted. Each line of the script containing a field [{ . . . }] contains a list of triples determining the next target state for all processes to be exercised. Upon trapping each respective process at the relevant breakpoint specified by the same line of the TeSS script, STEPS installs new breakpoint traps in all processes specified by process_no and line_no fields of the respective triples from the next script line. Breakpoints from the "old" line are removed and then processes are resumed until they hit breakpoints from the "new" line. Upon hitting selected breakpoints additional operations may be performed, in this case overriding the value of OK in the receiver process with the value of 1. Consecutive lines of the TeSS script specify steps that processes #1 and #2 must go through.

There are two types of breakpoints in TeSS scripts: type "1" for trapping a specified process_no *before* executing the statement at a given line_no, and type "2" for trapping it *after* the respective statement execution. Distinction of these two types is necessary to handle communication with blocking statements; it can be seen in Figure 16.6 that all actions involving execution of the PVM function call pvm_recv() in either process, i.e., line #44 in process #1 (sender) and line #27 in process #2 (receiver), use both types of breakpoints to properly register "entry to" and "exit from" the blocking action.

Processes #1 and #2 in our example have been forced to go through the repeated transmission of the last received frame. The line before overriding the value of OK in TeSS tells STEPS to stop process #1 before executing reception of ACK and to allow process #2 to complete its reception of a current frame. The next line tells STEPS to keep process #1 still stopped at line #44, while process #2 is forced to pass the corruption test via the negative ACK alternative. Further lines of the TeSS script in Figure 16.6 will eventually make sure process #1 to receive the negative ACK and continue transmission of the next series of frames. However, it is expected that the first frame number in the next series should be equal to the last negatively acknowledged frame.

16.4 Test evaluation

The notion of a test scenario implies examining concrete values of data objects assumed at specific points of program execution, as well as respective timing of events related to these points. Usually all potentially possible timings of actions that lead to the specific computation of a value expected by the tester at some point have to be exercised. This is particularly important in checking on *races*, when two or more processes compete in sending or receiving messages.

16.4.1 On-line inspection

The *Go-back-N* example program involves only one-to-one communication events, therefore races are not the problem here. Nevertheless, it may exhibit stochastic behaviour, due to the randomness of function check() detecting corrupted frames.

Consider again the TeSS script listed in the previous section. Running it by STEPS gives some reason to suspect bugs in the example program. Our concern here is the first frame number that is retransmitted by the sender upon receiving a negative acknowledgement. The on-line inspection mechanism provided by STEPS enables both reading and modifying variables of component processes and supports effective error detection. Consider Figure 16.7, showing the respective dialog windows displayed by STEPS at two consecutive program states depicted in Figure 16.3 respectively as "step 4" and "step 5".

The content of the "step 4" window in Figure 16.7 indicates that the most recently received frame #2 (by the the receiver process) has been corrupted. By proceeding with the sender process just one state further, i.e., to the point where the value for the next frame number is calculated, and opening the inspector window on sender again ("step 5") the error is revealed. The retransmitted frame number at this point of execution should be equal to 2 instead of 3. This is because of the bug in the line in file sender.c, where variable last is assigned -ack, instead of -ack-1.

16.4.2 Off-line log analysis

Besides the on-line interpretation of respective log entries, when visualizing the dynamic behavior of particular scenarios, the recorded data can be processed further on in an off-line fashion to provide concrete evidence on errors and their origins in the program under test. One objective is to detect incorrect data values at specific execution points, like the sequence of frame numbers being sent by the sender in our example *Go-back-N* program. Owing to the textual form of logs generated by STEPS this can be done with any text processing tool — from just a plain text editor, up to a more sophisticated analyzer based on LEX and YACC.

Another objective of such a log analysis is to identify communication actions that are involved in incorrect or incomplete communication events. These include races and deadlocks. The respective windows provided by STEPS for this kind of analysis are shown in Figure 16.8. This form of presentation treats a log as bi-partite graph $G(S, R)$, where vertices from sets S and R form respective sets of matching send and receive statements.

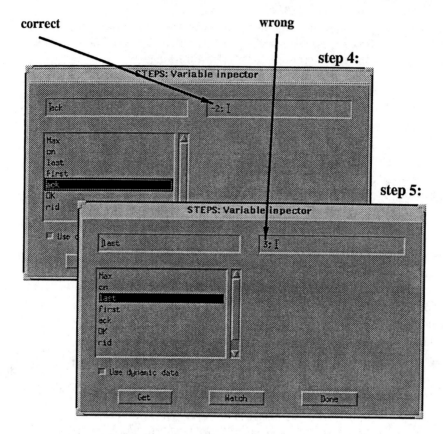

Figure 16.7: Inspecting variables of sender

STEPS presents the results of log analysis in a form shown in Figure 16.8. Left and right columns indicate respectively all send and receive actions recorded to the log. Edges connect all send-receive pairs, which according to the log content are "matching". If during experiments all respective communication events were completed correctly, i.e., each sent message was eventually received, all respective nodes in the displayed bipartite graph are connected. This is the case of Figure 16.8a. If during experiments some communication events are not completed the respective edges are missing from the graph. Observe in Figure 16.8b that in this particular execution receiving a message sent by receiver (line #33) was not recorded during the experiment. It may indicate problems with executing sender between its lines #41 and #44.

16.5   Generation of test scenario scripts

To this end we have illustrated the process of designing a single test scenario. Generation of TeSS scripts for a series of test scenarios, which combine various sets of input data, specific timing relations of selected processes and sequences of *reachable* states of the program may be quite sophisticated. Fortunately, STEPS supports automatic generation of test scenario scripts, based on both static and dynamic analysis, as shown in Figure 16.9.

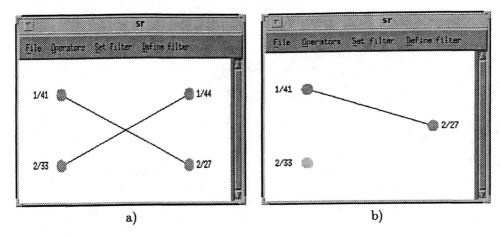

Figure 16.8: Off-line analysis of process actions: (a) matching actions, (b) a blocked action.

Static analysis is used as a vehicle for predicting communication events and determining timing relations between component process by moving individual tokens with a mouse pointing device in a test window shown in Figure 16.3. This is possible upon completion of token movements replay by **STEPS**.

A single token movement changes the corresponding process state, thus defines a new global state. A sequence of token movements in Figure 16.3 indicates in fact a sequence of the global parallel program states. This is a simulated, rather than real, execution, since no binary code has to run in this phase of analysis. A token preserves values of the corresponding local process variables in its special token memory. At any moment of a simulated execution any variable may be inspected and its value modified. When a desired sequence of states is selected (a test scenario is designed) its corresponding script is generated automatically and the program may start its real execution.

16.5.1   Interactive simulation of token movements

Development of test scenarios specified in Figure 16.9 strongly relies on interactive simulation of individual token movements (steps) within a test window. Each single step of a token involves determining its new state based on its current state. A current state of a token can either be a *symbolic* (simulated) state, or a *dynamic* (real) state. A symbolic state is obtained from the previous state by symbolic interpretation of the related step. A dynamic state is the one that has been physically reached by the corresponding process upon trapping it. In such a case **STEPS** opens a test window dynamically and indicates initial token positions in it, according to the current log content.

Determining of a new symbolic state based on the current state that is "dynamic" will normally occur when exercising the first step of a token into a dynamically opened test window. Any further step of any token within the window will involve then only symbolic states. In consequence, a symbolic state of any token reaching the window bottom will involve a combination of symbolic expressions as well as real values of program variables. Because of this property we consider symbolic interpretation of paths inside a test window to be a sort of *dynamic symbolic interpretation*. Dynamic symbolic interpretation enables overriding recorded values of selected variables as well as modifying the order of originally

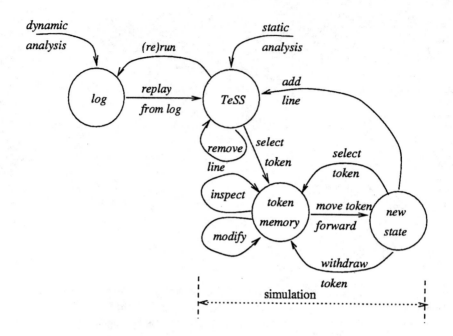

Figure 16.9: Operations on tokens in **STEPS**.

recorded events.

This is a new testing technique, which enables interactive design and prototyping of test scenarios based on three kinds of information: real *values* of data, actual *timing* relations of individual processes, and *states* that have been demonstrated to be reachable. Owing to the test window "dynamic opening" facility, generation of test scripts based on dynamic symbolic interpretation of token movements within a window can automatically generate test scripts for reproducible re-execution of the parallel program from any of its initial states to some explicitly determined target states. This information can be retrieved even when buried deeply in a program structure, since the program log provides all the necessary data values.

16.5.2   Parallel simulation of token movements

Skeletal simulation performed by **EDPEPPS** (see Chapter 18 and Chapter 19) exercises paths through the parallel program without taking into account any processing or decision nodes. Moreover, each time a token visits a decision node, a selection of *true/false* alternative is random. This technique of simulation enables integration of **STEPS** with the **EDPEPPS** tool. As far as the multi-thread model used by **STEPS** is concerned, it corresponds to skipping predicates in the respective decision statements and token memory variables [5].

Of course, many of the paths selected by **EDPEPPS** on the basis of its skeletal simulation of token movements may be irrelevant, as there may be no input data that can satisfy specific conditions obtained as a sequence of randomly executed control statements. Nevertheless, any path going through the skeletal program representation implies at least one scenario; its feasibility can be checked by means of symbolic interpretation supported by **STEPS**. Only feasible scenarios would then produce valid test scripts to be run next with a real system code to provide a basis for a more detailed investigation of other possible scenarios, as shown already in Figure 16.9.

16.6   Conclusions and future work

Further development of STEPS has been concentrating on two tasks: integration with SEPP tools to build up a framework for quality testing, and collecting data to assess applicability of structural testing methods to the application software used in parallel programming.

The first task involves: the distributed debugger tool DDGB [1] (see Chapter 13), the graphical development environment GRADE (see Chapter 10 and Chapter 17), and tools of the EDPEPPS environment (see Chapter 18 and Chapter 19):

- STEPS and DDBG were successfully integrated within the SEPP project. DDGB can accept TeSS files generated by STEPS. Owing to this, errors detected with scenarios developed by STEPS can be localized with inspection and control mechanisms provided by DDGB. The *Deterministic re-Execution and Interactive Program Analysis (DEIPA)* tool was developed to act as an intermediary between STEPS and DDGB, capable of recognizing and processing TeSS files and converting them into sets of commands for the distributed debugger [6].

- STEPS will accept logs produced for Grapnel to generate TeSS scripts. This feature is under input, as it requires extension of Grapnel programs to generate logs with the information concerning execution of communication statements. Since the replay of token movements by STEPS requires also information on the static program structure, identification of communication events requires either extension of the static analyzer shown in Figure 16.4 from the PVM+C syntax to the GRP files syntax (quite complex and less desired solution), or a simple (and more desired) addend to the GRADE environment which can generate the C code stubs for the static analyzer in STEPS.

- STEPS will analyze feasibility of test scenarios exercised by EDPEPPS. This feature is also under development, and is aimed at implementing parallel simulation of token movements described before. It just requires developing a tool for converting log formats from EDPEPPS to STEPS.

The second task requires development of a special database for collecting historic data from real software projects. Such a framework, comprising a database of *Quality Evaluation Documents (QED)* and a QESA tool for their acquisition, processing, and visualization [4]. The QESA tool covers all phases of software development, and collection of relevant data has just been started for several industrial projects. Initial indications are, however, that systematic structural testing of software applications used in parallel programming is not cost-effective. This is because of the relatively high costs of preparing experiments. With this regard, random testing requires much less effort [2]. On the other hand structural testing can exercise tested programs more thoroughly, and with enough resources can detect more errors. Therefore it is recommended to explore with it only those cases of program behaviour that already have been qualified as anomalous. One example of this philosophy is the parallel simulation of token movements by combining EDPEPPS and STEPS, as mentioned before.

References

[1] J.C. Cunha, J. Lourenço, and V. Duarte. Using DDBG to support testing and high-level debugging interfaces. *Computers and Artificial Inteligence*, 17(5):429–439, 1998.

[2] H. Krawczyk, B. Krysztop, and J. Proficz. Suitability of the time controlled environment for race detection in distributed applications. *Future Generation Computer Systems*, 1999. (to appear).

[3] H. Krawczyk, M. Kuzora, P.and Neyman, J. Proficz, and B. Wiszniewski. STEPS - a tool for testing PVM programs. In *Proc. SEIHPC-3 Workshop*, Madrid, Spain, 1998.

[4] H. Krawczyk, Sikorski, S. M., Szejko, and B. Wiszniewski. A tool for quality evaluation of parallel and distributed software applications. In *Proc. 3rd Int. Conf. Parallel Processing and Applied Mathematics PPAM'99*, pages 413–426, Kazimierz Dolny, Poland, 1999.

[5] H. Krawczyk and B. Wiszniewski. *Interactive Testing Tool for Parallel Programs*, chapter Software Engineering for Parallel and Distributed Systems, pages 98–109. Chapman & Hall, London, 1996.

[6] J. Lourenço, J.C. Cunha, H. Krawczyk, P. Kuzora, M. Neyman, and B. Wiszniewski. An integrated testing and debugging environment for parallel and distributed programs. In *Proceedings of the 23rd EUROMICRO Conference (EUROMICRO'97)*, pages 291–298, Budapeste, Hungary, September 1997. IEEE Computer Society Press.

Chapter 17

Program Development with **GRADE**: A Case Study

Tomàs Margalef, Ferenc Szalai and Norbert Podhorszki

Abstract

This chapter shows the complete programming life-cycle using the integrated environment. The GRAPNEL environment includes tools for designing and coding parallel/distributes applications, but also tools for program monitoring, debugging and performance analyzing. The N-body application is designed and developed following all the steps of parallel/distributed programming.

17.1 Introduction

In the previous chapters a complete parallel/distributed programming environment for development and analysis of parallel/distributed applications that can be executed in a cluster computing environment was introduced. The chapters of Part I. describe the general theoretical concepts related to the different phases of cluster computing development. The second part of the book focuses on the description of the set of tools developed in the SEPP and HPCTI projects funded by the European Commission. Now, the objective of this chapter is to show the use of the tools described in the previous chapters to develop a complete application. Therefore, we now must describe the complete programming life-cycle using the integrated environment. In some sense this chapter tries to be a summary of the previous chapters. On one side it tries to provide a general overview of the integrated programming environment and could be read as a self-contained chapter. The reading of this chapter should offer to the user a wide (but not deep) knowledge of the possibilities of the environment. On the other side, there are continuous references to the previous chapters of the book where the user can find a more detailed information related to each particular subject and tool.

However, there are several aspects that must be considered before starting the programming phase itself. It means that when the programmer is planning to develop a parallel/distributed application with this integrated environment there are several features that must be carefully analyzed before starting the coding phase of the application.

17.2   The Programming Life-Cycle using the **GRADE** environment

In Chapter 1 of this book a general view of parallel program development has been described. However, the analysis done in that chapter does not consider any particular tools or integrated environment. The objective of this section is to describe the whole program development cycle considering the programming model and tools included in the **GRADE** environment.

When the user wants to develop a parallel/distributed application using the **GRADE** environment, the first point that he/she must consider is the programming model supported by the environment because the programming model has strong implications in the application design. In this environment the model supported is based on message-passing with static process structure and fixed communication patterns among the processes.

This static characteristic of the programming model implies that the user/ programmer must design the application carefully before starting the coding phase of the application. He/she must decide which processes will be involved in the application, which will be the role of each process and how these processes will communicate. Although this design phase has a strong theoretical analysis component, the graphical programming tool of the **GRADE** environment (see Chapter 10) offers a direct support to this design phase due to the top-down approach imposed by the **GRAPNEL** graphical programming language. Within this language the user must start with the high level structure of the application. It implies that he/she must start by the definition of the processes involved in the application and how they communicate. In this high level specification the user can design the application in an abstract way where he/she identifies the main processes and the general structure used to communicate, without considering the specific aspects and the internal details of each process or the complete communication actions involved.

When this general structure is defined the user must go into the internal design and coding of each process including the required levels of abstraction. It means that the user can complete the application coding by defining the processes in a top-down approach. In this way, he/she is able to design and code the complete application (processes and communications) avoiding the classical problems related to unclear program structure.

This top-down approach imposed by the **GRAPNEL** language has another clear advantage. Since the user starts by defining the higher level of abstraction of the application and later on he/she enters in the actual coding of the application internals, it is possible to re-use existing code to codify the internals. It is possible that the user has a sequential version of the application that was coded with a huge effort some time ago. If now the user wants to develop a parallel/distributed version of the same application probably it is not necessary to start from scratch but he/she could reuse many functions. Therefore, it would be possible to use the **GRADE** environment to parallelize an existing sequential application with a relatively low effort.

The design and coding phases are very important but there are some new phases that should be considered in program development. These phases are related to program correctness, performance analysis and scalability studies:

1. *Graphical program pre-compilation*: Once the program has been designed and coded it must be pre-compiled to a classical programming language including a message passing library (e.g., C and PVM). Usually the graphical programs include graphical information which is not useful for a classical compiler but it is only useful for the graphical programming environment. Therefore, all this graphical information must

be converted into message passing primitives or C structures (see Chapter 11). In this pre-compilation process the coherence of the program structure must be tested. It means, for example, if the communication actions are correctly connected and the same data types are sent and received.

2. *Program correctness testing*: When the program has been compiled and can be executed on a parallel/distributed system it is necessary to ensure that the program really works properly and the desired operations and calculations are done in such a way that the results generated by the program are the expected and correct ones. However, as it is well known and also happens in classical sequential programming in many cases programs do not produce the desired results and they must be debugged using some debugging facility. However, as it has been shown in Chapter 5 and Chapter 13, the debugging of parallel/distributed programs offers much more complex features than sequential debugging.

3. *Performance analysis*: Another feature that must be considered in parallel /distributed programming is the performance analysis. The user that decides to use a parallel/distributed system is actually interested in the program performance. It means that he/she wants that his/her program executes in the shortest possible time or provides the best throughput or in general minimize some performance index. Therefore, the programming environments must provide the tools required to allow the user to know about the actual behaviour of the parallel/distributed application.

4. *Scalability studies*: Besides all the features mentioned above, in many cases the user would be interested in studying the behaviour of the application in different conditions (e.g., system with more CPUs) and in many cases these conditions are not available. This implies the use of some simulation tools that must be integrated into the environment.

These are not the only features that appear related to the parallel/distributed programming. There are other features that also involved and can modify the behaviour of the application in a significant way.

All these points show that the parallel/distributed programming activity involves a diversity of tools that must be included in the parallel programming environment. The use of graphical programming tools, like GRAPNEL and GRED, is only the first step in the parallel programming life-cycle, and there are many other tools involved during the program design and development.

Following the programming cycle, the next tool that is used after the graphical program creation is the GRP2C pre-compiler (see Chapter 11). This tool takes the file containing all the information related to the program (including the graphical information) and creates a C program with the required PVM message passing primitives.

Before executing the program, it is necessary to distribute its processes among the workstation cluster or the processors of the parallel computer. This step can be done manually in the GRADE environment or by some automatic mapping tool included in the environment (see Chapter 12).

Once the program processes have been mapped onto the system processors, the program is ready to be executed. In this situation the user can follow two complementary tasks:

1. Execution on a real system: In this case the user decides to execute the program on a real system and then there are two important tools to be used: the debugger

to test the correctness of the program and fix all the bugs found in the program (see Chapter 13), and the monitoring tool to determine the actual behaviour of the program (see Chapter 14).

2. Simulation of the execution: In this case the user is interested in getting some information about the program behaviour in different conditions and in this case it is necessary to use the simulation tool included in the environment (see Chapter 15).

No matter whether the user has chosen the real execution or the simulation, in many cases he/she is interested in the performance analysis of program behaviour by analyzing the trace file that is generated by the monitoring tool or by the simulator. The usual way of analyzing such trace file is by using a visualisation tool, like PROVE, that offers to the user a set of views about the program behaviour (see Chapter 14).

In the following sections of this chapter the use of each tool will be shown on a complete example. In this way the complete example will be analyzed in the different phases and steps of program development.

17.3   An application example: the N-body Problem

The N-body problem is a very important problem of computational physics. The main objective is to determine the trajectories of "many" bodies (some millions) in a potential field. For different applications different potential fields are used:

1. Gravitational in Astrophysics.

2. Lennard-Jones in Molecular physics.

3. Electrodynamical in Plasma physics.

The general idea of the problem is quite simple since the objective is to calculate the trajectory of each body along the time-line. From the initial position and speed of each body, the interaction is calculated in order to determine the next position and speed for each body. The new positions and speeds are used to calculate the new interactions and so on.

Since there are many bodies involved and the calculation of interactions is quite time consuming, the problem requires high computing capabilities [1–3].

The direct algorithm, that calculates the interactions among all possible body pairs, is the algorithm that produces the most precise solution, but it is also the most expensive in terms of computational time. Therefore, several algorithms have been developed to provide approximate solutions with a lower computational time. One of such algorithms is the fast oct-tree algorithm. In this algorithm, it is assumed that when a body is separated from a subset of the rest of the bodies, the interaction of all this subset can be approximated by a single body with a weight equivalent to the total weight of the subset located in the center of mass of the subset. The simulation space is divided into smaller cells which are in turn divided into smaller cells, and so forth. The tree is adaptive in the sense that the cells are more finely resolved where the density of bodies is higher.

The data partitioning for a 2D example is shown in Figure 17.1. In this figure the root level represents the complete plane with all the bodies. This plane is divided in four sub-planes (first-level) and the bodies are distributed among the sub-planes. Those sub-planes with a higher body density are divided again and so on.

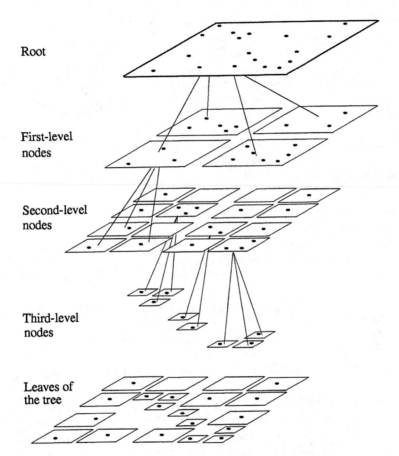

Root

First-level
nodes

Second-level
nodes

Third-level
nodes

Leaves of
the tree

Figure 17.1: The N-body problem cell partitioning

17.4   Programming the N-body problem with GRADE

In Section 17.3 the N-body problem has been presented and a short description of a parallel algorithm has been provided. Now the user is ready to design the application to solve the problem. At the highest level of abstraction, the programmer must define the main processes involved in the computation and the corresponding interprocess communication structure among these processes (as it has been described in Section 17.2).

In the implementation of the N-body problem we introduce a simplification of the algorithm. Instead of using the adaptive division of the space into cells, we simply divided the space into 8 equal size cells. With this assumption the GRAPNEL code of the program is shown in Figure 17.2, Figure 17.3 and Figure 17.4.

The general structure of the program is based on a master process which distributes the data to multiple worker processes. These worker processes compute the interactions among the bodies that were assigned to them and return the results to the master process. In Figure 17.2 this general structure for a configuration of four workers is shown. The process in the center is the master that communicates with the workers (in this case called slave0, slave1, slave2 and slave3).

It must be pointed out that the number of workers is fixed during the design phase and usually it is much lower than the bodies. Moreover, it is clear that depending on the density in the different sub regions some workers will spend more time than others doing the required calculations. Therefore, in order to avoid some workers becoming idle because the master is waiting for the results of the busiest worker, it is necessary to distribute the data in a dynamic way. This means that the master must distribute small pieces of work among the workers. Each package sent by the master contains the data related to some bodies, as well as the information concerning the center of mass of other subregions. When a worker finishes its previously assigned work it asks the master for more. The master sends some new data to that idle worker. When all the data has been distributed the master must wait for the results. As soon as each worker is providing its results, the master sends a message indicating them that all the data corresponding to this time iteration has already been distributed and they must wait for the last worker to finish to start the distribution of the new data corresponding to the new time iteration.

The internal structure of the master process is shown in Figure 17.3 as it is defined using GRAPNEL. The outer loop represents the time iteration. Each cycle of this loop represents a time interval. On the other hand, the inner loop represents the data distribution to idle workers and the conditional branch indicates if there are some additional data to be processed or there are no more data and the message indicating the end of the time iteration must be sent. In the case of the worker (see Figure 17.4) the structure is almost the same, but from the opposite site. The outer loop represents time iteration, the inner loop represents the subregion data distribution and the conditional detects the end of iteration message from the master.

17.5   Executing an application in the GRADE environment

In the previous section the programming phase of the N-body application has been briefly described. It would be possible to enter in exact details related to all the internal code of each process. However, this deep analysis is out of the scope of this book. The complete

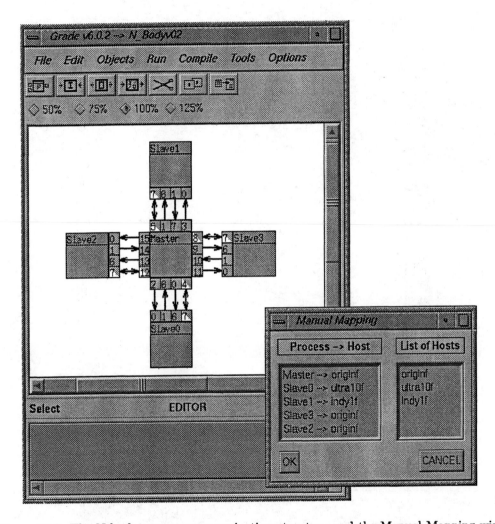

Figure 17.2: The N-body process communication structure and the Manual Mapping window

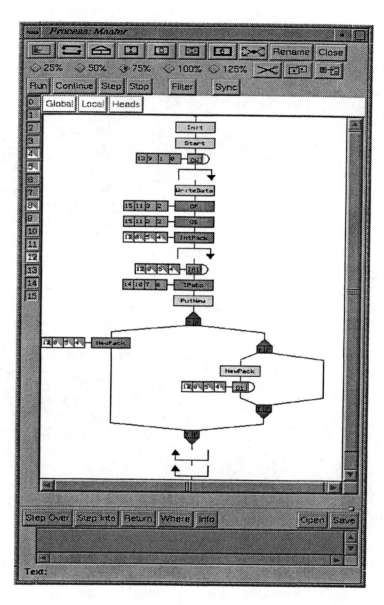

Figure 17.3: The Master process

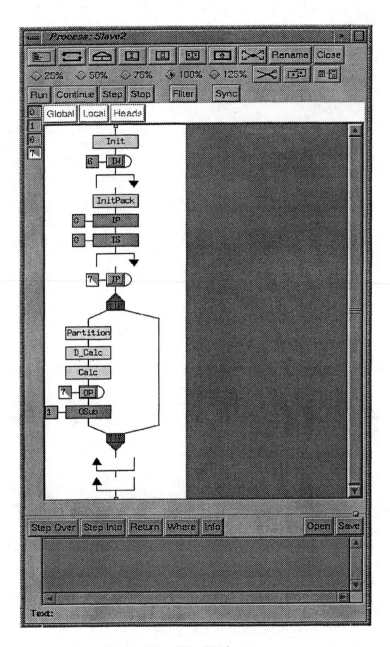

Figure 17.4: The Worker process

GRAPNEL code of the program can be found in the following web site www.lpds.sztaki.hu.

Assuming that the programmer has completed the application coding he must face the execution of the application. In order to be able to run the application there are several tools that must be used.

17.5.1 Mapping the application processes

Once the application has been coded, it is necessary to assign the processes involved to the workstations and/or the processors of the system. In this particular example, the application includes one master process and four worker processes (however, this number could be increased quite easily just by doing some copy and paste operation with the GRED editor). The environment offers the possibility of doing this mapping manually or automatically. These options are available in the Tools Menu.

1. *Manual mapping*: In this case, the environment offers a window where the processes of the application and the machines available are shown. In this window the user can select the processes and assign them to the machines just using the mouse buttons (see Figure 17.2).

2. *Automatic mapping*: In this case, the user can select a mapping algorithm (see Chapter 12) and the processes are assigned as a result of the mapping algorithm. It is possible to modify the automatic mapping by using the manual mapping tool afterwards.

In any case, the main goal of the mapping phase is to provide the assignment of processes to processors that provides the best execution time for the application. Therefore, this is a critical point that strongly depends on the application and on the specific system features (the application processes, their communication structure, the number of machines in the system and their capabilities).

17.5.2 Compiling the application

In the GRADE environment there is a pull-down menu for the compilation of the application. The objective is to pre-compile the graphically designed application to generate the C/C++ code including the message passing primitives and then compile this C/C++ program to create the executable files (see Chapter 11). However, this compilation step presents the particularity that in an heterogeneous system there are different possible target machines, and, moreover, the target machine for each process can vary from one execution to another by just modifying the mapping assignment. Therefore, if the user compiles the application just for one mapping assignment, then when the mapping is modified it is necessary to recompile the application, because executable files are not in the corresponding target machine.

In order to avoid this re-compilation for each re-mapping of the application, the compile pull-down menu offers a "Build All" option that compile all the processes in all the machines available in the system. In this way, the mapping assignment can be modified without recompiling the application.

When the "Build All" option is selected, the environment starts a window for each machine in the system where the compilation messages are displayed.

17.5.3 Running the application

The final goal of developing a parallel/distributed application is actually running the application. After developing and compiling the application it is possible to run it. From the GRADE environment there is a pull-down menu to run the application. From this menu the user can control the program execution, by running all the processes, stopping, continuing or killing them.

When the application is started the running processes become green and the application console is started. In Figure 17.5 the processes corresponding to the N-body application (Master and four workers) are shown in green during the execution of the application. The printouts generated by all the processes are displayed in this console window. In the lower part of Figure 17.5 the application console is also displayed. When the application is stopped, the processes become red and when the application is killed the processes become orange again.

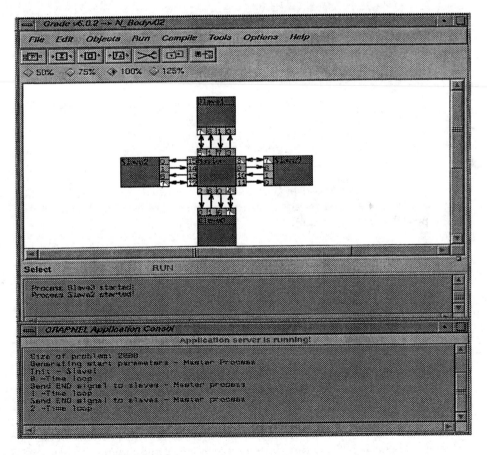

Figure 17.5: The N-body application running

When the processes finish their execution normally they become orange, but if they finish the execution abnormally, they become yellow.

17.5.4   Debugging the application

As it has been mentioned in Section 17.2, it is necessary to check the correctness of the application in order to ensure that it performs the expected operations and provides the right results. As it is well known it is quite common that programs do not provide the expected results because there is some bug due to some design problem or some coding detail. This fact is much more likely in parallel or distributed programming than in sequential programming because the communications among the application processes introduce a critical source of problems. It is really important to control all the communications in order to avoid behaviors that produce wrong results. For these reasons it is very important to use debugging tools that help the user to fix the bugs in the program and facilitate these tedious task.

The **GRADE** environment offers a debugger tool that offers the classical facilities of sequential debuggers (breakpoints, step execution, stop process, and so) but extended to a parallel/distributed environment.

Debugging in **GRADE** is based on three types of windows as illustrated by Figure 17.6:

- the **GRADE** Application window

- the Process window

- the Debug Information window

The joint use of this three types of windows makes the debugging extremely simple and fast comparing to other parallel systems. The debugging information can be observed at four levels. The **GRADE** Application window represents the top level where the color of processes informs the user about the state of the processes:

- Light-blue means that the debugger is already attached to the processes but the processes have not started yet their run (this is the state where the initial breakpoints can be placed at the processes).

- Green means that the process is running.

- Red means that the process is suspended either on breakpoint or on a communication.

- Yellow means that the process is killed.

- Orange (the original color of processes) means that the process finished its work.

The second level is the process window level where program execution can be graphically animated at the process graph. It means that the execution of a process can be observed node by node: the node which is currently executed is highlighted by a red frame (see the node Partition in Figure 17.6). This node by node execution is similar to the step by step execution of textual programs but in a higher abstraction level, i.e., at the graph level. Of course, breakpoints can be placed at any node and the execution of a process can be allowed until such a breakpoint is hit. At this time the execution of the process stops at the first C/C++ instruction of the graph node.

The third level is the textual code level (currently C/C++). At this level the usual breakpoint and step by step execution techniques can be used. For example, in Figure 17.6, a breakpoint is shown in the textual part of the Process window which shows the textual code of the highlighted graph node Partition.

Finally, stack information and the values of variables can be watched in the Debug information window. The higher part shows the called functions and their stack levels, while the lower part can give information on the value of any data structure including records and higher dimension arrays.

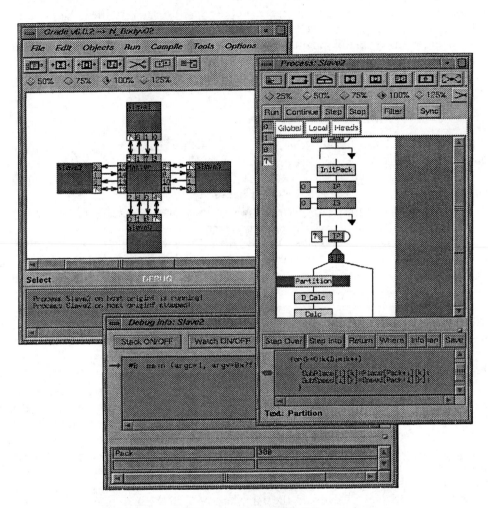

Figure 17.6: Debugging in the GRADE environment

17.6 Performance analysis in the GRADE environment

The final part of the life-cycle is related to performance analysis of the developed application. This performance analysis can be based on real execution or simulation. In this section this performance analysis will be carried out.

17.6.1   Monitoring the application

When the user wants to measure the performance of the application the first step is to monitor its execution by using a monitoring tool. The monitoring tool included in the GRADE environment is the Tape/PVM monitor (see Chapter 14). With this tool the user can generate a trace file that can be analyzed later on. To activate the generation of the trace file it is only necessary to select the "Monitoring" option in the "Tools" pull-down menu. Actually, these kind of monitoring tool does not offer any direct information to the user. It just creates a trace file to be analyzed by using other kind of tools, such as a visualisation tool.

17.6.2   Performance visualisation

The information included in the trace file is very hard to analyse by hand. Visualisation tools usually provide some views that present the information included in the trace file in a way much easier to understand and analyse by the user. The visualisation tool included in the GRADE environment is the PROVE (see Chapter 14).

The main window of the PROVE visualisation tool shows a space-time diagram where the information concerning the activity of each process on each time interval is displayed. In the X axis the time line is represented, meanwhile in the Y axis the different processes are displayed by horizontal bars. In these bars each time interval is represented by a different color depending on the status of each process (computing, waiting for a message, sending a message,...). This display is completed with some arrows among the bars representing the communication actions among the processes.

A very important and novel facility offered by PROVE is the click-back facility, i.e., it is able to relate each event in the trace file with the code line that has generated such event. It means that for example if you click an arrow indicating a message sent, the code line that generated that message will be high-lightened.

The key point of these visualisation tools is that they must provide to the user with the required information to be able to analyse the performance of the application, detect if there is any performance problem and determine how the application should be modified to avoid the performance bottlenecks and improve the performance. In the N-body example, there is one master and four workers. The space-time diagram of the N-body program running on a heterogeneous cluster consisting of two machines: originf (an SGI computer) and ultra10f (a Sun computer) is depicted in Figure 17.7.a. The figure shows the execution of one time iteration of the algorithm. (Recall that the outer loop of both the master and slave processes correspond to the time iteration.) Examining the space-time diagram of other time iterations we can observe that they are very similar and hence it is enough to study only one of them. Looking at the figure it looks obvious that there is a strong performance bottleneck in the program execution. The master process allocates 8 work packages to the slaves in every iteration. First it sends out one package to each slave, then waits the results. When a slaves sends back a result package, the master immediately sends to a new work package to the same slave as long as work packages are still available in the iteration. When the last work package is allocated, the master should wait for the last result package before it can start the next iteration with another 8 work packages.

It is clearly shown in Figure 17.7 that the master process should wait for the last package from Slave1 nearly as long as the other packages were processed in parallel by the four slaves. (Black color represents real computation, dark-grey represents waiting for an input message

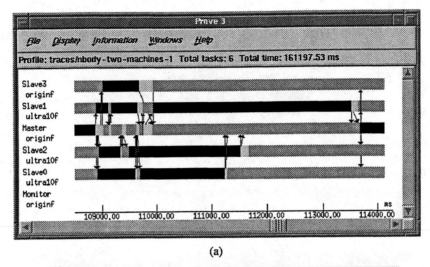

(a)

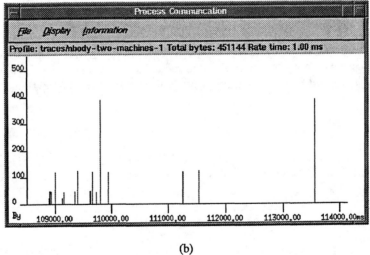

(b)

Figure 17.7: The space-time diagram (a) and the process communication window (b) of
PROVE

and light-grey represents waiting for the completion of an output action in the space-time diagram of Figure 17.7.a.) Meanwhile the last package is waited for by the **Master** only one slave works, the others are idle. If we look at the Process Communication window of PROVE (Figure 17.7.b) we can see the reason of this behavior. Each vertical bar represents a message sent among the processes. The height of a vertical bar is proportional with the size of the message. (In the real system the bars have different colors representing different pairs of communicating processes. Unfortunately, the book does not contain any colored figure.) It can be seen in Figure 17.7.b that the size of messages are significantly differ having nearly an order of magnitude difference between the smallest and largest ones. As it was mentioned in Chapter 14 the time intervals of the windows of PROVE are always synchronized just like in Figure 17.7 the two windows show the same time range. Comparing the two windows it becomes clear that the last work package of the time iteration is much larger than the other work packages and hence obviously its processing takes much more time.

The size of a work package is proportional with the number of particles inside the simulated cell. Just looking at the windows of PROVE we can conclude that the number of particles in the cells vary in a large extent and this leads to unbalanced program execution. It means that the simplifying assumption that we applied in implementing the original algorithm was not correct and hence it is necessary to realize the adaptive cell division in order to get really high performance which is proportional with the number of processors.

17.6.3 Simulation

As it has been widely described in Chapter 7 and Chapter 15 simulation represents a very useful approach for rapid prototyping and performance prediction in different conditions. For example, it would be possible to simulate the application with a different number of machines, but it also would be possible to simulate the execution with higher number of workers. This test could be very useful to study the scalability of the application.

17.7 Conclusions

The GRADE environment offers a complete and integrated environment with a set of tools that offers to the user the possibility of designing and developing parallel/distributed applications and follow the complete life-cycle in a quite friendly and simple way. In this chapter, the complete life-cycle has been done for an example application: the N-body problem.

Acknowledgements

This work has been supported by the CICYT under contracts TIC 95-0868 and TIC 98-0433.

References

[1] J.E. Barens and P. Hut. A hierarchical o(nlogn) force-computation algorithm. *Nature*, 324:446–449, 1986.

[2] W.T. Rankin and J.A. Board. A portable distibuted implementation of parallel multipole tree algorithm. In *IEEE Symposium on High Performance Distributed Computing*, 1995.

[3] J.K. Salamon, M.S. Warren, and G.S. Winckelmans. Fast parallel treecodes for gravitational and fluid dynamical n-body problems. *Journal on Supercomputer Applications*, 8:129–142. 1994.

Chapter 18

Tools of EDPEPPS

Thierry Delaitre, Mohamed-Jamal Zemerly, George R. Ribeiro-Justo,
Olivier Audo and Stephen C. Winter

Abstract

This chapter decribes the tools of the EDPEPPS environment which is based on
a performance-oriented parallel program design method. The EDPEPPS environment
supports graphical design, performance prediction through modelling and simulation,
CPU characterization, debugging and visualization of predicted program behaviour.

18.1 Introduction

A portable message-passing environment such as Parallel Virtual Machine (PVM) [7] permits a heterogeneous collection of networked computers to be viewed by an application as a single distributed-memory parallel machine. The issue of portability can be of great importance to programmers but optimality of performance is not guaranteed following a port to another platform with different characteristics. In essence, the application might be re-engineered for every platform [11]. Traditionally, parallel program development methods start with parallelizing and porting a sequential code on the target machine and running it to measure and analyze its performance. Re-designing the parallelization strategy is required when the reached performance is not satisfactory. This is a time-consuming process and usually entails long hours of debugging before reaching an acceptable performance from the parallel program. The EDPEPPS environment described in this chapter is based on a rapid prototyping philosophy such that complete parallel algorithms, outline designs, or even rough schemes can be evaluated at a relatively early stage in the program development life-cycle, with respect to possible platform configurations, and mapping strategies. Modifying the platform configurations and mappings will permit the prototype design to be refined, and this process may continue in an evolutionary fashion throughout the life-cycle before any parallel coding takes place.

The EDPEPPS environment comprises five main tools:

- A graphical design tool (PVMGraph) [8] for the design of parallel applications, based on PVM.

- A simulation utility (PVMPredict) implemented on top of SES/Workbench simulation engine [13] which is based on discrete-event simulation.

- A visualization tool (PVMVis) for animation of program execution using traces generated by the simulator and visualization of platform and network performance measures and statistics.

- A CPU characterizer (Chronos) for computational code based on basic operations in C to allow the simulator to predict the execution time of each block depending on which machine the code is executed.

- A debugging tool (PVMDebug) based on the distributed debugging tool DDBG [3, 4] which provides debugging functionalities for distributed C/PVM programs.

Other tools used in the environment for integration purposes are:

- A trace instrumentation utility (Tape/PVM) [10].

- A translator (SimPVM) [6] from C/PVM code to queueing network graphical representation.

- A reverse engineering tool (C2Graph) to translate from existing C/PVM parallel applications into PVMGraph graphical representation based on the SAGE++ toolkit [2].

The advantage of the EDPEPPS environment is that the cyclic process of design-simulate-visualize is executed within the same environment. Also the EDPEPPS environment allows generation of code for both simulation and real execution to run on the target platform if required. EDPEPPS is also modular and extensible to allow modifications and change of platforms and design as and when required.

The various tools within the EDPEPPS environment will be described in the next section.

18.2   Description of the Integrated EDPEPPS Environment

Figure 18.1 shows the components of the EDPEPPS environment. The design process within the EDPEPPS environment starts with the graphical design tool (PVMGraph) by building a graph representing a parallel program design based on the PVM programming model. The graph is composed of computational tasks and communications. The tool provides graphical representation for PVM calls which the user can select to build the required design.

The software designer can then generate (by the click of a button) C/PVM code (.c files) for both simulation and real execution. The environment also provides a tool to translate existing parallel C/PVM code into graphical representation suitable for PVMGraph. The software designer can then experiment with the environment by changing the parallelization model or other parameters, such as the number of processors or processors types, to optimize the code.

In the simulation path each C/PVM source code file obtained from the PVMGraph is instrumented using a slightly modified version of the Tape/PVM trace pre-processor [10]. The output is then parsed using the CPU Time Analyser (CTA) to characterize the code and insert *cputime* calls at the end of each computational block. The instrumented

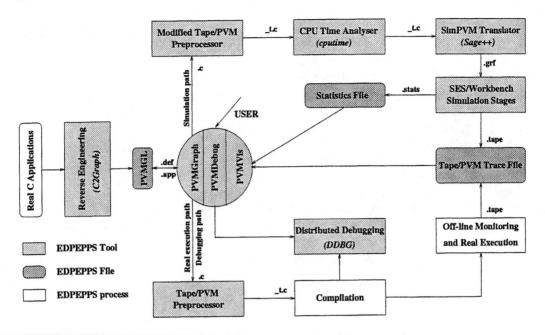

Figure 18.1: The EDPEPPS Integrated Environment.

C source files are translated using the SimPVM Translator [6] into a queueing network representation suitable for Workbench graph (.grf file). SES/Workbench translates the graph file into the Workbench object oriented simulation language called SES/*sim* [14] using an SES utility (*sestran*). The *sim* file is then used to generate an executable model using some SES/Workbench utilities, libraries, declarations and the PVM platform model. The simulation is based on discrete-event modelling. SES/Workbench has been used both to develop, and simulate platform models. Thus the SES/Workbench simulation engine is an intrinsic part of the environment. All these actions are hidden from the user and are executed from the PVMGraph window by a click on the simulation button and hence shown in Figure 18.1 in one box under "Simulation Stages". The simulation is based on discrete-event modelling. SES/Workbench has been used both to develop, and simulate platform models. The simulation executable code is run using three input files containing parameters concerning the target virtual environment (e.g., number of hosts, host names, architecture, the UDP communication characteristics and the timing costs for the set of instructions used by the CTA [5]). The UDP model and the instruction costs are obtained by benchmarking (benchmarks are provided off-line) the host machines in the network.

The simulation outputs are the execution time, a Tape/PVM trace file and a statistics file about the virtual machine. These files are then used by the visualization tool (PVMVis) in conjunction with the current loaded application to animate the design and visualize the performance of the system. The design can be modified and the same cycle can be repeated until a satisfactory performance is achieved.

In the real execution path the Tape/PVM pre-processor is used to instrument the C source files and these are then compiled and executed to produce the Tape/PVM trace file required for the visualization/animation process. This step can be used for validation of simulation results but only when the target machine is accessible. The visualization tool (PVMVis) offers the designer graphical views (animation) representing the execution of the designed parallel application as well as the visualization of its performance. The performance visualization presents graphical plots, bar charts, a space-time chart, and histograms for performance measures concerning the platform at three levels (the message passing layer, the operating system layer and the hardware layer).

In the debugging mode, the user will be able to debug the loaded C/PVM application. The distributed debugging of the application is handled by controlling the execution of all the tasks using a textual window representing the code for each task. The textual window in the debugging mode is slightly different from that of the design and offers the user basic features of a debugging tool, which are "continue", "run", "break", "next", "interrupt" and also the display of signs for breakpoints and execution step. The breakpoints can be set using the graphical as well as the textual representations of the code. The PVMGraph, PVMVis and PVMDebug are incorporated within the same Graphical User Interface where the designer can switch between these possible modes. The following sections describe in more detail the main tools within EDPEPPS.

18.2.1   PVMGraph

PVMGraph is a graphical programming environment to support the design and implementation of parallel applications. PVMGraph offers a simple yet expressive graphical representation and manipulation for the components of a parallel application. The main function of PVMGraph is to allow the parallel software designer or programmer to develop PVM applications using a combination of graphical objects and text. Graphical objects are composed of boxes which represent tasks (which may include computation) and arrows which represent communications. The communication actions are divided into two groups: input and output. The PVM actions (calls) are numbered to represent the link between the graph and text in the parallel program. Also different types and shapes of arrows are used to represent different types of PVM communication calls. Parallel programs (PVM/C) can be automatically generated after the completion of the design. Additionally, the designer may enter PVM/C code directly into the objects.

The graphical objects and textual files are stored separately to enable the designer to re-use parts of existing applications [8].

18.2.2   PVMVis

The main objective of this tool is to offer the designer graphical views and animation representing the execution and performance of the designed parallel application from the point of view of the hardware, the design and the network.

The animation is an event-based process and is used to locate an undesirable behaviour such as deadlocks or bottlenecks. The animation view in PVMVis is similar to the design view in PVMGraph except that the pallet is not shown and two extra components for performance analysis are added: barchart view and platform view. The barchart view shows historical states for the simulation and the platform view shows some statistics for selected performance measures at the message passing layer, the operating system layer and the hardware layer.

18.2.3   PVMDebug

PVMDdebug is based on a Distributed Debugging tool (DDBG) [3, 4] which provides a set of debugging functionalities for distributed programs written in C/PVM.

In order to debug a distributed application and to control the execution of the distributed tasks, the debugger needs to know all PVM task identifiers (tids). During the execution, the graphical task objects in PVMGraph do not have their tids because their values change at each run. Therefore, a debugging interface in the form of a wrapper program and a mapping table was developed to manage the link between the graphical objects and the PVM execution tasks. The wrapper program uses the on-line monitoring facility in PVM and collects the PVM events from the application and routes them to PVMDebug which manages the mapping list [1].

PVMDebug is fully integrated within the EDPEPPS environment and provides a subset of the DDBG functionalities.

The major differences between the PVMGraph window and that of PVMDebug (see Figure 18.2 for a snapshot of PVMDebug window, note that only one window for the family of spawned tasks, *slave2*, is opened) are:

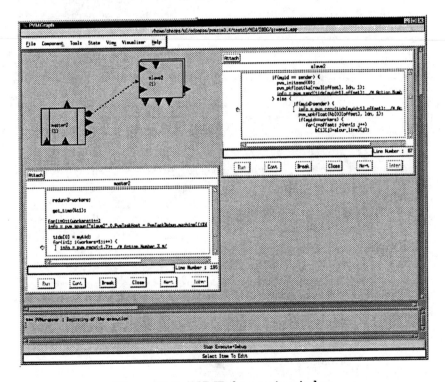

Figure 18.2: PVMDebug main window.

- the textual windows in PVMDebug, buttons are added to provide debugging capabilities and as well as a display area window for visualizing breakpoints and the execution pointer. Breakpoints can also be set on the graphical objects directly.

- an additional textual window to display the steps of the execution and to collect the messages from the application.

- a run-time graphical animation (highlighting) to indicate the states of the tasks.

18.2.4   Chronos: The CPU Time Analyzer

The CPU Time Analyzer (Chronos) is called only in the simulation path to estimate the time taken by computational blocks within a parallel algorithm. Chronos characterizes a workload by a number of high-level language instructions (e.g., float addition) [5] taking into account the instruction and data caches effect. Assumptions have been made to reduce the number of possible machine instructions to 43 (see [5] for more details on these assumptions). The costs associated with the various instructions are kept in a file in the hardware layer accessible by the SES utilities. These costs are obtained by benchmarking the instructions on different machines.

Chronos first parses an instrumented C/PVM program using the SAGE++ toolkit. In the second stage, Chronos traverses the parse tree using the SAGE++ library and inserts *cputime* calls with the number of machine instructions within each sequential C code fragment. A *cputime* call is a simple function with a fixed number of parameters (a total of 31). This is different from the number of machine instructions because the instruction cache duplicates some of the instructions (hit or miss). Each parameter of the *cputime* function represents the number of times each instruction is executed within the sequential C code fragment. The only exception is the last parameter, which determines whether the instruction cache is hit or miss for the code fragment in question (see [5] for more details).

18.2.5   C2Graph

This tool is provided to allow existing C/PVM parallel code to be directly used within the EDPEPPS environment rather than building the design from scratch. The C/PVM application files are first parsed using SAGE++ to get the .dep files (generated by SAGE++). These files are then traversed by the C2Graph translator which also uses the SAGE++ library routines. The translator also takes into account the PVM calls in the original code and generates their corresponding graphical representation in the PVMGraph files. The translator then determines the master process, positions it with the other tasks by calculating appropriate coordinates for them in the PVMGraph screen, and writes the PVMGraph definition files (.def) for each task. The translator finally writes the application file (.app) required for PVMGraph. Currently SPMD programs cannot be handled by PVMGraph and hence the translator splits SPMD programs into master and slave programs if provided with one (see [12] for more details).

18.2.6   SimPVM Translator

From PVMGraph graphical and textual objects, executable and "simulatable" PVM programs can be generated. The "simulatable" code generated by PVMGraph is written in a special intermediary language called SimPVM, which defines an interface between PVM-Graph and SES/Workbench [6].

To simulate the application, a model of the intended platform must also be available. Thus, the simulation model is partitioned into two sub-models: a dynamic model described in SimPVM, which consists of the application software description and some aspects of the platform (e.g., number of hardware nodes) and a static model which represents the underlying parallel platform.

The SimPVM language contains C instructions, PVM and PVM group functions, and constructs such as computation delay and probabilistic functions.

18.2.7 PVMPredict: The EDPEPPS Simulation Model

The EDPEPPS simulation model, PVMPredict, consists of the PVM platform model library and the PVM programs for simulation. The PVM platform model is partitioned into four layers (see Figure 18.3): the *message passing layer*, the *PVM group layer* which sits on top of the message passing layer, the *operating system layer* and the *hardware layer*. Modularity and extensibility are two key criteria in simulation modelling, therefore layers are decomposed into modules which permit a re-configuration of the entire PVM platform model. The modelled configuration consists of a PVM environment which uses the TCP/IP protocol, and a cluster of heterogeneous workstations connected to a 10 Mbit/s Ethernet network.

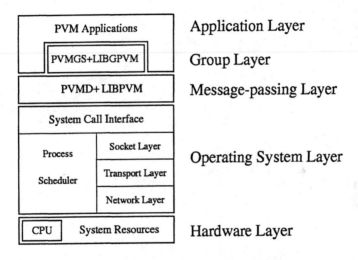

Figure 18.3: Simulation model architecture.

A PVM program generated by the PVMGraph tool is translated into the SES/Workbench simulation language and passed to its simulation engine, where it is integrated with the platform model for simulation. The message-passing layer models a single (parallel) virtual machine dedicated to a user. It is composed of a daemon which resides on each host making up the virtual machine, a group server and the libraries (PVM and PVMG) which provide an interface to PVM services. The daemon and the group server act primarily as message routers. They are modelled as automatons or state machines which is a common construct for handling events.

The LIBPVM library allows a task to interact with the daemon and other tasks. The PVM library is structured into two layers. The top level layer includes most PVM programming interface functions and the bottom level is the communication interface with the local daemon and other tasks.

The major components in the operating system layer are the System Call Interface, the Process Scheduler and the Communication Module (see Figure 18.3). The Communication Module is structured into 3 sub-layers: the Socket Layer, the Transport Layer and the Network Layer. The Socket Layer provides a communications endpoint within a domain. The Transport Layer defines the communication protocol (either TCP or UDP). The Network Layer implements the Internet Protocol (IP).

The Hardware Layer is comprised of hosts, each with a CPU layer, and the communications subnet (Ethernet). Each host is modelled as a single server queue with a time-sliced round-robin scheduling policy. The communications subnet is Ethernet, whose performance depends on the number of active hosts and the packet characteristics. Resource contention is modelled using the CSMA/CD (Carrier Sense Multiple Access with Collision Detection) protocol. The basic notion behind this protocol is that a broadcast has two phases: propagation and transmission. During propagation, packet collisions can occur. During transmission, the carrier sense mechanism causes the other hosts to hold their packets.

18.3   Conclusion

This chapter has described the tools of the EDPEPPS environment which is based on a performance-oriented parallel program design method. The environment supports graphical design, performance prediction through modelling and simulation, CPU characterization, debugging, and visualization of predicted program behaviour. Existing parallel applications can also use the environment which provides a tool (C2Graph) to transform the code into graphical design suitable for PVMGraph. The designer is not required to leave the graphical design environment to view the program's behaviour, since the visualization is an animation of the graphical program description.

Future work on EDPEPPS includes integrating the SEPP testing tool (STEPS) [9] and a performance-based intelligent design assistant tool. It is also planned to generalize the simulation model and extend it to support other platforms such as MPI.

Acknowledgments

This project is funded by an EPSRC PSTPA programme, Grant No.: GR/K40468 and also by EC Contract Numbers: C193-0251 and CP-93-5383.

References

[1] A. Audo. Integration of the DDBG Distributed Debugger within the EDPEPPS Toolset. Technical report, Centre for Parallel Computing, University of Westminster, London, June 1998. Final Year BEng Project Technical Report.

[2] F. Bodin, P. Beckman, D. Gannon, J. Gotwals, S. Narayana, S. Srinivas, and B. Winnicka. Sage++: An object-oriented toolkit and class library for building fortran and C++ restructuring tools. In *Proc. 2nd Annual Object-Oriented Numerics Conference*, 1994.

[3] J.C. Cunha, J. Lourenço, and V. Duarte. Using DDBG to support testing and high-level debugging interfaces. *Computers and Artificial Inteligence*, 17(5):429–439, 1998.

[4] José C. Cunha, J. Lourenço, and T. Antão. An Experiment in Tool Integration: the DDBG Parallel and Distributed Debugger. *Journal of Systems Architecture*, 45(11):897–907, 1999. Elsevier Science.

[5] T. Delaitre, M.J. Zemerly, J. Bourgeois, G.R. Justo, and S.C. Winter. Final Model Definition. Technical report, Centre for Parallel Computing, University of Westminster, London, April 1997. EDPEPPS EPSRC Project (GR/K40468) D3.1.4, EDPEPPS/23.

[6] T. Delaitre, M.J. Zemerly, J. Bourgeois, G.R. Justo, and S.C. Winter. Final Syntax Specification of SimPVM. Technical report, Centre for Parallel Computing, University of Westminster, London, March 1997. EDPEPPS EPSRC Project (GR/K40468) D2.1.4, EDPEPPS/22.

[7] A. Geist, A. Beguelin, J. Dongarra, W. Jiang, R. Manchek, and V. S. Sunderam. *PVM: Parallel Virtual Machine – A Users' Guide and Tutorial for Networked Parallel Computing*. MIT Press, 1994.

[8] G.R. Justo. PVMGraph: A graphical editor for the design of PVM programs. Technical report, Centre for Parallel Computing, University of Westminster, London, February 1996. EDPEPPS EPSRC Project (GR/K40468) D2.3.3, EDPEPPS/5.

[9] H. Krawczyk and B. Wiszniewski. *Analysis and Testing of Distributed Software Applications*. Research Studies Press Ltd., UK, 1998.

[10] E. Maillet. Issues in performance tracing with Tape-PVM. In J. Dongarra et al., editors, *Proc. Second European PVM User's Group Meeting, Lyon*, pages 143–148. Hermes, 1995.

[11] A. Reinefeld and V. Schnecke. Portability vs efficiency? parallel applications on PVM and Parix. In P. Fritzson and L. Finmo, editors, *Parallel Programming and Applications*, pages 35–49. IOS Press, 1995.

[12] F. Schinckmann. Reverse engineering tools for converting PVM-C applications into PVMGraph format. Technical report, Centre for Parallel Computing, University of Westminster, London, July 1997. EDPEPPS EPSRC Project (GR/K40468) D2.2.2, EDPEPPS/36.

[13] Scientific and Engineering Software Inc. *SES/workbench Reference Manual, Release 3.1*. 4301 Westbank Drive, Austin TX 78746, 1996.

[14] K. Sheehan and M. Esslinger. The SES/*sim* Modeling Language. In *Proceedings of The Society for Computer Simulation*, pages 25–32, San Diego, CA, July 1989.

Chapter 19

Parallel Software Development with EDPEPPS

Mohamed-Jamal Zemerly, George R. Ribeiro-Justo, Thierry Delaitre and Stephen C. Winter

Abstract

This chapter describes the EDPEPPS environment by presenting the various steps involved in the parallel software development process. The chapter describes the design, prototyping, and performance analysis of a case study. The chapter shows how the environment allows the user to design a paralel algorithm, build and execute the prototypes, evaluate the design, and finally debug the intermediate and final codes.

19.1 Introduction

Rapid "evolutionary" prototyping is a useful approach to the design of (*high-performance*) parallel software in that complete algorithms, outline designs, or even rough schemes can be evaluated at a relatively early stage in the program development life-cycle, with respect to possible platform configurations, and mapping strategies. Modifying the platform configurations and mappings will permit the prototype design to be refined, and this process may continue in an evolutionary fashion throughout the life-cycle before any parallel coding takes place.

The advantage of the EDPEPPS environment is that the cyclic process of design-simulate-visualize is executed within the same environment. EDPEPPS is also modular and extensible to allow modifications and change of platforms and design as and when required.

The EDPEPPS environment described in the previous chapter comprises five main tools: PVMGraph, PVMVis, PVMPredict, Chronos, PVMDebug. Other tools used in the environment for integration purposes are: Tape/PVM, SimPVM, and RET (reverse engineering tool). The reader is referred to the previous chapter for more details about each of the EDPEPPS tools.

This chapter presents the various steps involved in the parallel software development with EDPEPPS. In particular, the design, prototyping and performance analysis of a case study

(Parallel Givens Linear Solver). The following section presents the EDPEPPS development stages. Section 4 presents the results obtained for the case study to validate the models used. Finally, in section 5 we present conclusions and future work.

19.2   EDPEPPS Development

The EDPEPPS development does not prescribe any parallel design method but we usually apply a general method such as PCAM (Partitioning, Communication, Agglomeration and Mapping) introduced by Foster [4]. Using PCAM tasks (processes) are identified and the inter-task communications defined and later refined, by amalgamating some tasks which are finally mapped to the hardware (processors).

The section illustrates the use of the EDPEPPS environment by showing how a user can: design a parallel algorithm (the pipeline Givens algorithm, [5], shown later is selected here), build and execute the prototypes, evaluate the design and finally debug the intermediate and final code. For legacy parallel applications the process can start by using the reverse engineering tool which can produce a graphical representation in PVMGraph, the EDPEPPS design tool, rather than starting the design from scratch.

19.2.1   Designing a Parallel Algorithm

As in PCAM [4], this phase starts with the identification of the main tasks. The EDPEPPS graphical design tool (PVMGraph) assists the designer in creating a graphical representation of the tasks. At the same time, PVM skeletons are automatically created. The designer can also reuse existing tasks. When a task is named, PVMGraph automatically imports a task with that name if it already exists. EDPEPPS does not prescribe any partitioning strategy, the designer is free to use the most suitable one [4]. The outcome generated by this step is a collection of task nodes, represented graphically, together with their PVM description.

The next step is the definition of each task (general) behaviour. The behavioral description consists of defining how the processes react to events (messages) they receive and which events they generate. More specifically, this is done by selecting PVM primitives. In PVMGraph, each primitive is represented by a graphical symbol, so the behaviour can be described graphically. Again, for each graphical symbol added, PVMGraph automatically inserts the textual representation (code) in the task skeleton. Later, the designer can refine the textual representation. The resulting artifact is also a collection of tasks but some of them with their behaviour only partially defined. This means that the tasks nodes contain symbols representing part of their behaviour.

The following step in the design is the definition of the communication structure as in PCAM. This corresponds to the description of the relationships between the tasks. PVM allows the communication structure to be defined or modified arbitrarily during execution. Therefore, during the design the communication structure can be only partially defined. Another important aspect of PVM is the need to explicitly specify the configuration of tasks in terms of creation and destruction. This means to specify which tasks are spawned or killed by peer tasks.

Grouping is possible but not as in PCAM. Tasks are grouped only to simplify communication. The graph can be enhanced by the concept of sub-graphs which represent collections of nodes. In EDPEPPS, it is also possible to create a collection of instances of the same task as group or family. This representation is useful for reducing the complexity of the graphical representation (see later for an example).

Finally, the mapping can also be defined graphically by indicating in which virtual machines the tasks will be executed. However, the mapping does not have to be defined explicitly in PVM. In fact, it can even be left to PVM which uses a heuristic method to distribute the tasks across the virtual machine. This concept is graphically similar to that of a group except that a task can be member of more than one group but can only be allocated to a single virtual machine. Notice that EDPEPPS combines the software description and hardware description (see later for more details).

What follows is a description of the user actions needed to build a design prototype (figures showing the Givens algorithm used later in the case study Section 19.3, will be used for illustration).

The first action the user should take is to start PVMGraph. The user starts a **new** design from the **File** menu and gives it a name. Then the user should select the tasks required for the design from a palette which contains graphical objects (icons) on the left, as can be seen in Figure 19.1. A single task in PVMGraph represents a single program (represented by the first **Task** icon from the palette). A *family of spawned tasks* object (3rd item of palette) can be selected, if the same instance of the program is executed in parallel many times as in the case of master-slave parallel design paradigm (see "slave2" object). The user will then have to decide on the communication calls he needs to build a skeleton of the application. The communication calls of PVM are each represented by an object in the same palette, which can be scrolled down to get the other calls. By selecting an object from the palette and clicking in the main area of the design, the user can select, in a step by step fashion the number of tasks as well as the communication structure required for the design. The parameters for the communication call must be filled in by the user by selecting the *edit* option from the **component** menu in the Menu bar and clicking on the objects of the call. The parameters window for the call in question will appear and once this is completed, the window should be closed by clicking on the **Done** button at the bottom of the window (see Figure 19.1 for an example of the *pvm_spawn* and *pvm_send* parameters' windows). This requires some basic understanding for PVM calls.

Once the skeleton is built, the user can start writing the tasks (programs) by selecting the **edit** button and clicking on the task to be edited. A textual window such as the one shown in the Figure 19.1 will appear and the user can enter C code in the usual way (copy and paste features can be used). Note that in the textual window the lines of code representing the graphical objects are protected (shown underlined) and these cannot be edited in the textual window by editing the parameters of the calls as described before. Note that most PVM calls can be selected including group functions such gather, scatter, reduce, bcast, etc. The graphical object can only be moved using the **Move Protected Code** button provided in case more calls need to be introduced (which in this case will be appended to the end of the program and not where the user intends them to be). The number given for each call represents the link between the graph and text in the task. The textual window in Figure 19.1 shows a part of the C code inserted for the task "slave2" for the Givens algorithm. It is worth noting here that the number of the "slave2" tasks that can be spawned can be changed from the master and this can be passed as an argument to the master when executed as will be seen later in Section 19.2.2.

The ability to **delete**, **edit** or **move** objects can be achieved by selecting the corresponding options from the *Component* options from the main menu.

The hardware mapping may be selected using the *pvm_spawn* call by spawning every task on a different machine as shown in its parameter window or a graphical mapping can be selected using the *Virtual Node* object from the palette and circling the task with a

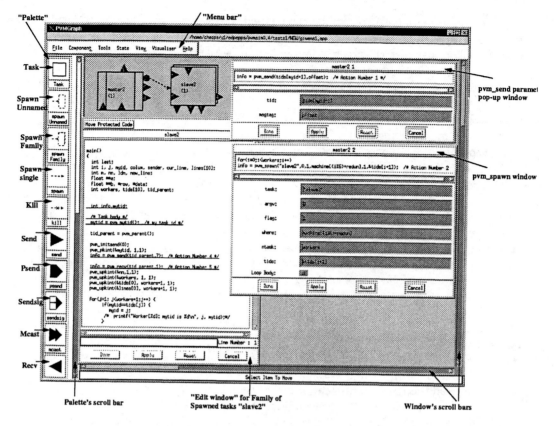

Figure 19.1: The PVMGraph tool.

rectangle and by filling a machine name in the box provided. Membership of a group is also circled in the same way using the *Task Group* option instead but the color of the group rectangle will be green rather than black for the virtual node.

Once the application is designed the user should **save** and *Generate Code* by selecting the corresponding buttons from the File option from the main menu. This step will save the programs and the application file needed for the following steps. This should also be done after any change made to the design to take effect. If the real execution of the algorithm is required then the user should select the **Generate Makefile** from the same menu and compile and run the algorithm on the actual hardware. This process should be done outside the PVMGraph window. It is still not integrated yet although the selections from the main menu, **Tools**, to build/compile and execute the real algorithm are already provided.

19.2.2   Deploying the Prototypes

The EDPEPPS prototypes for each application can be created at any stage of the development as soon as a (incomplete) task graph is produced. An important issue is what minimum information is required to provide precise performance prediction [3]. In EDPEPPS, the user should provide a specification of the program distribution or mapping and some information about each task's functional behaviour or sequential algorithm. However, this information is not mandatory as a default mapping can be used, and no sequential algorithm is required.

The sequential part of a task can also be defined as *sequential blocks* which are usually specified in an abstract way as an approximation of the execution time or workload [3]. EDPEPPS provides several other functions which allow the designer to specify abstract algorithms (e.g. *cputime*, *cpudelay*, or *delay*).

Even program skeletons can exhibit complex performance behaviour. So, the issue of what information is necessary and how to detect performance bottlenecks has to be an essential part of the methodology. Performance tools must support this activity as the mere use of analytical models may not help very much.

The following describes the steps required in EDPEPPS to generate a prototype at any step of the design process.

Once a "version" of the design is completed the user can enter the configuration parameters by selecting **ConfigureSim** from the **Tools** main menu option (see Figure 19.2). Note that the highlighted parameters in the last row are run-time arguments passed to the "master2" program and signify the number of processors to spawn, 7, the size of the data array, 256 × 256 and the data filename, *data*. The first two parameters are requesting to generate a trace file and a statistics file so that the performance can later be visualized using the PVMVis tool. The user should not change the other filenames as these are configured at setup time.

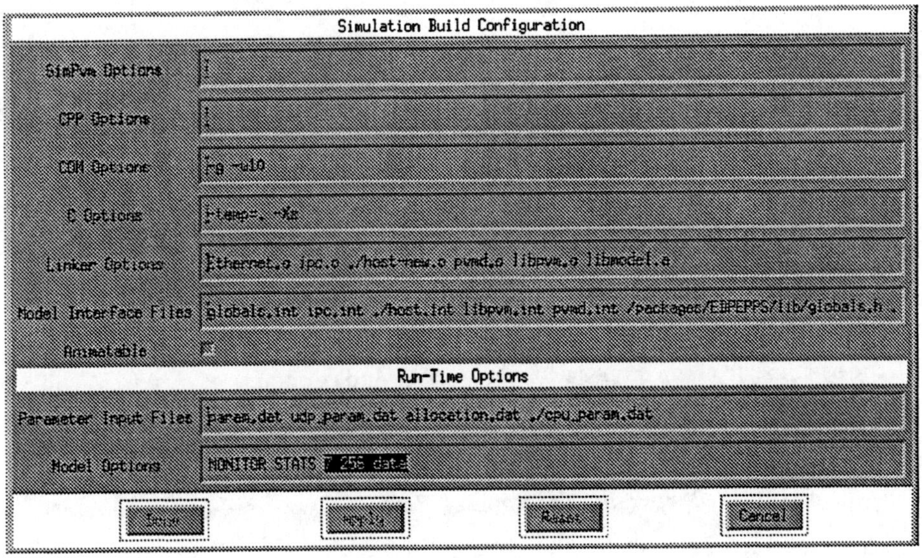

Figure 19.2: The simulation configuration window.

The next step is to select the **BuildSim** option from the **Tools** main menu to generate the simulation code. This step will instrument the code by inserting the Tape/PVM parameters in the code to generate a trace file (if requested), estimate the number of the instructions within each C computational block in the code using the CPU characterizer tool (which inserts the *cputime* calls into the code, which will be used by the simulator for prediction) and then translate the code into graphical representation suitable for the simulation tool using the SimPVM tool. The UDP packet parameters and CPU parameters (for selected high-level language instructions such as float add, store int, etc.) for each of the available machines are obtained by benchmarking. Suitable programs are run, preferably with no or little load if possible to maintain accuracy, on each machine to obtained the required parameters. When the **BuildSim** option is selected another window (see Figure 19.3) will appear showing the progress of the above operations. If any error was found it will be flagged and the whole operation will stop giving the type of error and a line number where the error might be located. If no errors were found then the summary message of "0 errors, 0 warnings" should appear followed by the last message in the window which will show that the executable model is finished to build. The user can then click on the bottom row **Return to Design** to return to the design window.

The next step is to select the **ExecuteSim** from the **Tools** main menu to execute the simulation. Figure 19.4 shows the progress of the simulation execution when selected. Although this is not shown here, the user will be asked about the following information:

- The period between reportings of the current simulation time in seconds.

- The hardware mapping of the master process, thus overwriting any previous mapping.

- The number of lines between which a CPU utilization update is written to the statistics file. The default is to write one update every 100 lines, thus reducing the size of the trace file significantly and hence the time of processing of the file at visualisation time).

At the end of the simulation the total time and the names of the trace file and statistics file will be given, provided that the simulation runs without any errors (deadlocks) which requires that a debugging session (using PVMDebug) should be started to fix the problem. As in the previous step the user can then click on the bottom row **Return to Design** to return to the design window.

19.2.3   Evaluating the Design

In EDPEPPS, the visualization tool (PVMVis) provides two main types of support. A step-by-step animation of the design together with statistical information about the various layers of the systems, from the application level (tasks and communications) to the operating systems (scheduling and communication protocols) hardware (processor and network) level. The important aspect is that at any time the designer can have a snapshot of the whole system performance. However, the task of finding what is the cause and the exact location of bottlenecks is still the designer's responsibility. Typical steps needed to evaluate a design are given next.

PVMVis can be invoked from PVMGraph by selecting the **Visualise** option from the **State** main menu option. The window here is similar to the design window but here no palette is shown but instead a bar-chart window (showing space-time chart) and a platform view, which shows graphs for selected performance measures such as mean CPU utilization and network load, on the right (see Figure 19.6). Also extra buttons to **Begin, Start/Stop** and **Next** step are provided as well as an animation speed selection scale (1-10 events per seconds) and Current time and event counters. Figure 19.5 shows the progress of the animation of the simulation execution of the Givens algorithm with 7 "slave2"s in PVMVis. The figure shows a snapshot of the animation in progress. The lines between processors in the main window signify communication between 2 processors (the call issued first will be displayed and the other one will be connected to it once executed). On the line a number

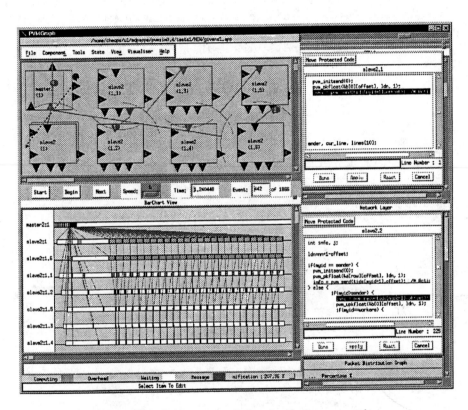

Figure 19.5: Animation of the simulation execution.

is shown signifying the number of messages in the queue between the same processors (a higher number is caused by a bottleneck and most probably will trigger packets collisions).

The bar chart (space-time chart) is also shown giving information to the user about the use of the resources from the various tasks in various colors (as used in most visualization tools). The textual windows for all the processes can be opened (here only 2 were opened and displayed on top of the platform view which can be seen in Figure 19.6) and the text of the PVM call responsible for the event can be seen highlighted when executed. The figure shows a send and a receive for the two tasks opened highlighted in the textual window. The user also can zoom in or out on the space-time chart. By clicking on any line or object (line or box) the user triggers the display of information (data size, time and processors involved) about the call causing the object to happen and, if the textual window of the task is opened, the line responsible for the object is also highlighted.

Figure 19.6 shows a snapshot of PVMVis after the animation of the simulation execution is completed. The platform view shows the mean CPU utilization for one of the processors (last one number 6, most busy) and the network (Ethernet) load graph. Other graphs such as the other CPU utilization for the other processors, Packet Distribution in volume and size and the number of packet collisions can be shown by scrolling the bar at the side.

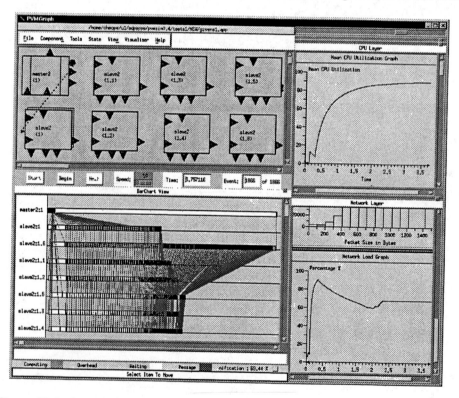

Figure 19.6: Animation of the simulation execution (barchart and platform view).

After analyzing the performance measures (including the execution time obtained from the simulation) and comparing to other runs, the user can choose to go back to the design tool and change the configuration by adding or removing tasks or changing the mapping of the processors. The user may also change the whole design if he/she wishes but this will require more drastic measures and may require starting from the beginning. The user can keep changing parameters, mappings or designs until satisfied that the final version is the optimal version.

The case study shown later in Section 19.3 will illustrate how the EDPEPPS environment was used to select between two different design strategies each with different parameters and mappings. The study will show how one was able to identify the optimal design with the best number of processors to use.

19.2.4 Debugging the Code

A distributed debugger (PVMDebug) based on DDBG (see Chapter 13) [1, 2] is also integrated in EDPEPPS to provide basic debugging facilities.

In order to invoke the debugger the **Debug** state is selected from the Menu bar **State** option. A new window similar to PVMGraph will appear except that the left Palette, as in the case of PVMVis, is not provided. The difference here is in the textual windows of the tasks and in the new debugging pink window appearing at the bottom giving information about the status of the debugging,

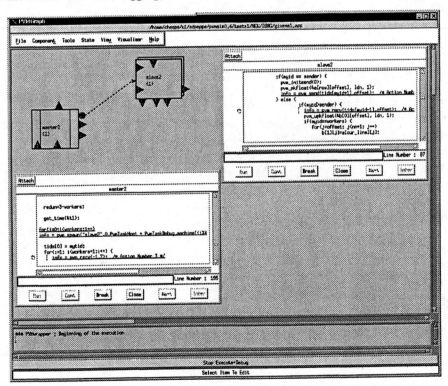

Figure 19.7: PVMDebug main window.

Figure 19.7 shows a snapshot of the PVMDebug window for the Givens application with the textual windows for the processes opened (only one window for the family of spawned tasks, *slave2*, is opened).

As will be explained in the pevious chapter the user is provided with debugging buttons in the textual window to "continue", "run", "break", "next", "interrupt" and also the display of signs for breakpoints and execution step. The breakpoints can be set using the graphical as well as the textual representations by clicking on the object on which the break is wanted, in the case of graphical, or by clicking in the textual window on a line and clicking on break. The undoing of the breaking point can be done by repeating the same breaking actions. Once the error is found the user can correct it and go back to the design stage by selection of the *design* state from the Menu bar option **State**.

19.3   A Case Study

A case study is presented here to illustrate the use of the EDPEPPS environment. The selected case study is a communication intensive application based on two parallel Givens Linear Solver method developed in [5]. The EDPEPPS environment can help the designer to choose the best algorithm and predict the results for a larger network, which in most cases is not available, if required to help sizing the application by choosing the best number of processors. In this case study we also assess the accuracy of the EDPEPPS CPU characterization toolset using the sequential Givens code.

19.3.1   Description of the Sequential Givens Linear Solver

The Givens linear solver can be represented in the form: $Ax = b$, where A is a non-singular square matrix, b is the right hand side vector and x is a vector of unknowns. The Givens rotation method selected here is particularly interesting since it does not require *pivoting*, a difficult problem to parallelize, is numerically stable and inherently more accurate than other methods [5]. The Givens transformation is defined by a 2×2 rotation matrix:

$$G = \begin{pmatrix} c & s \\ -s & c \end{pmatrix} \tag{19.1}$$

where $c^2 + s^2 = 1$.

A Givens rotation is used to eliminate the elements of a vector or a matrix as follows:

$$\begin{pmatrix} c & s \\ -s & c \end{pmatrix} \times \begin{pmatrix} a \\ b \end{pmatrix} = \begin{pmatrix} r \\ 0 \end{pmatrix} \tag{19.2}$$

where $c = \frac{a}{\sqrt{a^2+b^2}}$ and $s = \frac{b}{\sqrt{a^2+b^2}}$

The Givens algorithm for solving a linear system with N equations can be decomposed into two computational stages. The first one is the triangulation of the initial matrix, this stage is represented by the execution of the elimination block N times. The second stage is the substitution block which solves the triangular matrix.

19.3.2   Description of the two Parallel Givens Algorithms

The triangulation stage, which is the most time consuming part (with complexity of $O(N^3)$ as opposed to $O(N^2)$ for the back-substitution stage) is parallelized with two different techniques: collective and pipeline. The back-substitution stage is also programmed differently in the two algorithms as will be discussed later.

Initially, block-row data decomposition, which divides the matrix horizontally and assigns adjacent blocks of rows to neighbor processors is used in both methods. At the first step (A) in the collective method, all processors eliminate the required columns for their rows (except the first row for each processor) in parallel. Then to eliminate the columns of the first rows (step B), collective communication is used to collect the first rows from processors (rows are collected by the processor which is holding the corresponding row of the current eliminated column, say *sender*) and distribute the rows back. The back-substitution stage is started by the last processor and its results are broadcasted to other processors and then in a similar way all the processors solve their triangulated matrices in a back-pipeline way.

In the second pipeline method the same first step A (as in method 1) is used but instead of using collective communications to eliminate the columns of the first rows (step B in method 1), the row in question is passed from the sender to its neighbor to eliminate its column and then passed in a pipeline fashion through other neighbors until all the columns are eliminated. The last processor keeps the lines in a full matrix to be used in the back-substitution stage later on its own.

19.3.3   Results and Discussion

The two methods were designed using the EDPEPPS environment and results for both simulation and real execution (on a real network) were obtained. The network used for this algorithm consists of 3 Ultra-Sparc 10 machines with 300MHz, 1 Pentium II with 233 MHz, 1 Pentium 150MHz, 1 Super-Sparc 20 with 75 MHz, 1 Super-Sparc 5 with with 60 MHz. The mapping of tasks onto machines was done differently in the two algorithms based on few simulation tests and the final optimal mapping only is used for the results shown here. The mapping for the machines was done in increasing power order (but giving priority to the fastest machines if the number of processor is less than the total 7) for the pipeline method and in decreasing power order for the collective method.

The tests were done for problem sizes of 256 and 512 equations but for the 256 size we did not get any significant speedup relative to the fastest machine in the network as the algorithm is communication intensive and this affects the performance for small problem sizes.

Figure 19.8 shows the results for the simulation and real execution measurements (averages of 10 times taken at night) for both the collective and the pipeline (b) methods.

The figure shows clearly that the measurements and predictions for both methods are in good harmony with maximum error well below 10% (except for one case for the collective algorithm with 7 processors, 12%). All the measurements including the benchmarks have been performed at night at low ambient network load and the standard deviation for all the measurements did not exceed 5% on any of the runs. As expected, the figure also shows the superiority of the pipeline algorithm over the collective algorithm even for small number of processors. Note that the machines are heterogeneous and adding more processors sometimes will result in increasing the execution time rather than improving it. For the 512 problem size we obtained a speedup of 2 and 2.25 for 4 and 5 processors respectively for the pipeline algorithm. As expected, increasing the number of processors above 5 (4 for the collective) in both cases increases the execution time as the other processors (other than the UltraSparc and Pentium II - 233 MHz) are considerably slower than the fastest four. However, in heterogeneous networks of workstations the CPU utilization is another important factor which should be considered when analyzing the figures for the speedup or

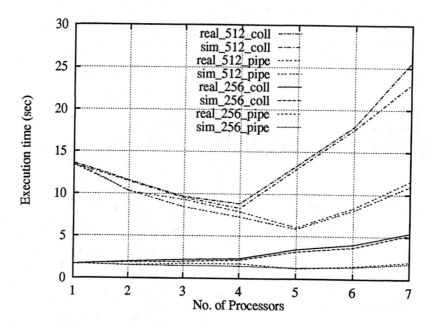

Figure 19.8: Comparison between predictions and measurements for Parallel Givens: collective and pipeline (the sequential results for one processor are for the UltraSparc 10 as it is one of the fastest machine with error of 1.5% only.)

the execution time. This is because a network is a multi-tasking environment and reducing the load on one fast machine, even at the expense of larger execution time, will give a chance for other tasks queueing on that machine to be executed faster. Knowing that the pipeline algorithm is superior to the collective one, the user can then experiment with adding more powerful processors than available to see if better speedups can be obtained. For example, by substituting the Pentium I and less powerful machines by UltraSparc 10 or Pentium II machines. However, we were unable to validate this experiment with real execution due to the unavailability of more powerful machines.

19.4   Conclusion

This chapter has described the EDPEPPS environment which is based on a performance-oriented parallel program design method. The environment supports graphical design, performance prediction through modelling and simulation, and visualisation of predicted program behaviour. The designer is not required to leave the context of the graphical design environment to view the program's behaviour, since the visualisation is an animation of the graphical program description. It is intended that this environment will encourage a philosophy of program design, based on a rapid synthesis-evaluation design cycle, in the emerging breed of parallel program designers.

The success of the environment depends critically on the accuracy of the underlying simulation system. Preliminary validation experiments showed average errors between the simulation and the real execution of less than 10%.

Important directions of our work are to generalize the simulation model and extend it to support other platforms, such as MPI, and to develop a "design assistant" component based on intelligent performance analysis.

Acknowledgments

This project is funded by an EPSRC PSTPA programme, Grant No.: GRK40468 and also by EC Contract Numbers: C193-0251 and CP-93-5383.

References

[1] J.C. Cunha, J. Lourenço, and V. Duarte. Using DDBG to support testing and high-level debugging interfaces. *Computers and Artificial Inteligence*, 17(5):429–439, 1998.

[2] José C. Cunha, J. Lourenço, and T. Antão. An Experiment in Tool Integration: the DDBG Parallel and Distributed Debugger. *Journal of Systems Architecture*, 45(11):897–907, 1999. Elsevier Science.

[3] A. Ferscha and J. Johnson. Performance Prototyping of Parallel Applications in N-MAP. In *2nd International Conference on Algorithms & architectures for Parallel Processing*, pages 84–91. IEEE CS Press, June 1996.

[4] I. Foster. *Designing and Building Parallel Programs*. Addison-Wesley, 1995.

[5] J. Papay, M.J. Zemerly, and G.R. Nudd. Pipelining the givens linear solver on distributed memory machines. *Supercomputer Journal*, XII(3):37–43, 1996.

Index

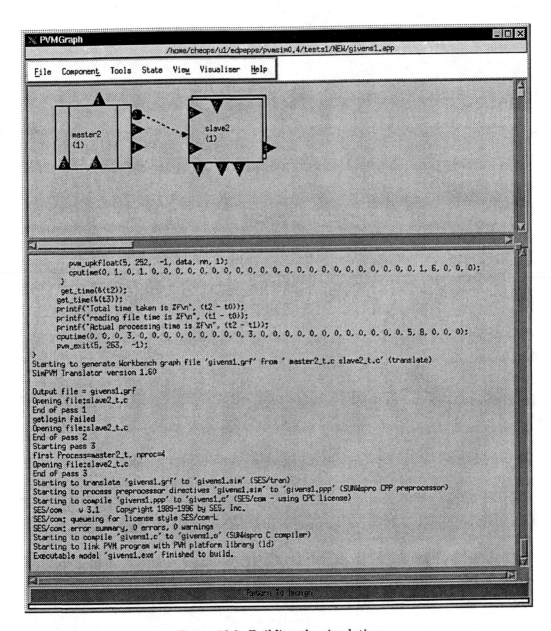

Figure 19.3: Building the simulation.

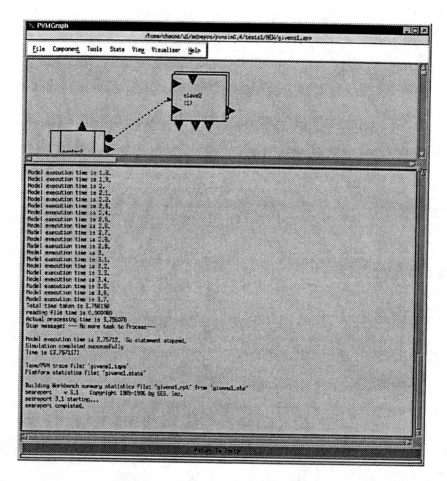

Figure 19.4: Executing the simulation.